Environmental Economics

The Addison-Wesley Series in Economics

Environmental Economics:
Theory, Application, and Policy

DUANE CHAPMAN
Cornell University

▲ **ADDISON-WESLEY**

An imprint of Addison Wesley Longman, Inc.

Reading, Massachusetts • Menlo Park, California • Harlow, England
Don Mills, Ontario • Sydney • Mexico City • Madrid • Amsterdam

Senior Sponsoring Editor: Andrea Shaw
Associate Development Editor: Rebecca Ferris
Senior Production Supervisor: Juliet Silveri
Marketing Manager: Amy Cronin
Marketing Coordinator: Jennifer Thalmann
Cover Design: Dick Hannus
Senior Cover Design Supervisor: Regina Hagen
Composition, Illustration, and Packaging Services: Pre-Press Co., Inc.
Manufacturing Coordinator: Tim McDonald

Cover image © 1999 PhotoDisc, Inc.

Library of Congress Cataloging-in-Publication Data

Chapman, Duane.
    Environmental economics: theory, application, and policy / Duane
Chapman.
      p.   cm.
    ISBN 0-321-01435-9 (alk. paper)
    1. Environmental economics.   2. Sustainable development.
    3. Environmental policy.   I. Title.
    HC79.E5C463 1999
    333.7—dc21   99-39382
                                                        CIP

1 2 3 4 5 6 7 8 9 10—CRW—0302010099

CONTENTS

Environmental Economics: Theory, Application, and Policy is written for the broad diversity of students interested in environmental economics who major in economics, business, natural resources, environment, engineering and science, liberal arts, and agriculture. The goal of this text is to provide an introduction to environmental issues as well as environmental economics by analyzing not only the hypothetical approach to world oil use or air pollution but also by introducing the students and readers to the actual data and methods used by experts working in each field. In order to do this, it is necessary to give greater emphasis to science and multidisciplinary background than is usually the case with economics texts. Biodiversity, climate change, air pollution, forestry: all require some modest understanding of the subject matter as well as the methods of economic analysis.

The text is crafted to reflect the diversity and challenge of the nature of the subject, from biodiversity to air pollution, from commercial forestry in the United States to protected areas in Africa, from oil resources to environmental justice. Throughout, the objective is to introduce the methods used to analyze issues. It is a preparation for understanding the different perspectives in making effective environmental policy. It is an introduction to the use of economic tools to make a contribution to environmental policy.

A unique feature of the book is the way in which chapters interact. Cross-references between theory and application foster overall integration of subject matter. In addition to the extensive review of the basics on air and water pollution control, forestry, agriculture, environmental accounting, benefit-cost analysis, and the literature in the valuation of externalities, there is considerable material on emerging major subjects in the field. These new subjects include macroeconomics and trade, agriculture, ecological economics, sustainability, issues in equity, and the relationship between legislation and environmental economics.

The text is also intended to reflect the healthy tension between environmental economics and ecological economics. Each of the two professional groups—the

Association of Environmental and Resource Economists (AERE) and the International Society for Ecological Economics (ISEE)—has its own professional association and its own professional journal. In my view, AERE has a somewhat greater focus on quantitative methods of analysis and on economic concepts and theory. In contrast, ISEE gives a degree of emphasis to policies for environmental protection, the role of values in economics, and transdisciplinary work. Their divergence of emphasis and interests is legitimate and important, but they share a common commitment to the use of objective methods of analysis in pursuit of environmental protection and economic efficiency. Richard Bishop, past president of AERE, has co-authored Chapter 20 on sustainability. Richard Norgaard, president of ISEE, has contributed the foreword to the text.

Finally, I want to note that I have attempted to prepare a text that is essentially positive in its outlook, assuming that past gains in environmental protection will be maintained and that future progress is both desirable and possible. It is pro-environment but also pro-business.

Organization

Our first goal in studying environmental and resource economics is to show that economics matters in actual application. The second goal is to describe the tools that economists use in moving from theory to application.

The book is organized into six sections and an appendix. Part 1 on economic theory, concepts, and methods includes six chapters. Chapter 1 covers the basic concepts of competition, monopoly, externalities, and economic welfare and shows the basic consequences of each type of economic organization or theory in terms of its relationship both to economics and to the environment. Other chapters in this section introduce environmental accounting (Chapter 2), methods of valuing the non-market aspects of environmental protection (Chapter 3), benefit-cost analysis and discounting (Chapter 4), equity and environmental justice (Chapter 5). The last chapter in the section (Chapter 6) provides a more mathematical introduction to the basic theory in renewable resources such as fisheries and forests and to the theory of resource depletion as applied to finite resources such as oil, coal, iron and steel, and so on.

Part 2 focuses on two chapters particularly related to individual consumer decisions. One (Chapter 7) is on personal and household energy as it relates to both the economic and the environmental impact arising from different approaches in heating and lighting and the gains that have been made in this area. The second chapter, Chapter 8 (written with Matt Schwartz), deals with renewable energy as it relates to the economic environment for solar energy and to alternative vehicles and the pollution impact of each.

Part 3 takes up the issue of global resource limitations. The theory of depletion is applied to actual data on world oil resources, both proven and undiscovered (Chapter 9). The limits to growth question is discussed as it relates to broad industrial resource availability (Chapter 10). The Meadows literature on global limits is critically evaluated. Recycling, world population, and income growth are each addressed as it relates to this issue.

Part 4 addresses four important areas in which environmental policy in the United States has had major successes in the sustainable use of renewable environmental resources. Air pollution control (Chapter 11), water quality (Chapter 12), agriculture (Chapter 13, written with Brent Sohngen), and forestry (Chapter 14) are each considered, and the major policy issues in each are taken up.

Part 5 looks at the global environment, in particular biodiversity and endangered species (Chapter 15), the Kruger National Park in South Africa (Chapter 16), the broad global issue of macroeconomics, trade, and the environment (Chapter 17), and climate change (Chapter 18). Whether the subject is the spotted owl program, the ban on ivory trade, the Environmental Kuznets Curve, or the Kyoto Protocol, the focus is on the nature of using economics to understand the making of environmental policy.

Finally, Part 6 consists of two contributed chapters. The first, Chapter 19, on ecological economics by Jon Erickson, is a critique of mainstream environmental economics and an advocacy of a different perspective on the use of economics. This chapter may be viewed as, in part, a criticism of the mainstream assumptions of the text itself. The last chapter, Chapter 20, on sustainability by Richard Bishop and Richard Woodward, takes on the difficult challenge of translating sustainability into workable concepts. They apply their ideas to global warming and biodiversity as well as providing a discussion of the safe minimum standard.

The book concludes with an appendix (written by Andrea Kreiner) on the evolution of environmental policy and legislation, an important influence on the modern growth in environmental economics and environmental resource management.

Pedagogy

Chapter 1 (Competition, Monopoly, and Social Welfare) has been developed to work both as an introduction to economics for students without prior economics courses and as a review for students with some knowledge of economics. Twenty-seven terms (externality, marginal revenue, etc.) are highlighted in italics as they are introduced and are summarized in a chapter glossary that repeats the definitions.

Each chapter ends with a series of questions for discussion and analysis that offer opportunities to apply the chapter's material through class discussion or individual analysis of economic concepts, environmental issues, and through the use of quantitative problems.

Flexibility

For class organization, in general I would not recommend the use of all 20 chapters in a semester introductory course. (It would be possible, perhaps, for a junior-senior course in which all of the students had prerequisites in intermediate microeconomics.) Different emphases are appropriate to reflect the academic interests of students and instructors. For example, an economics department will desire a different chapter organization than does a business management department. An environmental studies department might want a third approach. In addition, different geographic areas—for example, Western United States versus urban Eastern United States—will each lead to different chapter organization. (For the instructor, different examples of organization of the material for these different objectives are included in the Instructor's Manual.)

The book is designed to be used without requiring calculus and advanced mathematics. However, for classes and instructors with the capability and interest in doing so, calculus can be used to enhance understanding, in particular the appendix to

Chapter 1 on microeconomic theory and Chapter 17 on macroeconomics, trade, and the environment. Notably, Chapter 6 on economic theory and environmental resources makes use of basic calculus to introduce the subjects of the bioeconomics of renewable resources and the theory of exhaustible resource depletion.

Supplements

The Instructor's Manual provides several resources to assist the instructor in using the text. A summary distills each chapter's important concepts and highlights connections to other chapters. In addition, there are tips for sparking discussions, answers to the in-text questions for analysis and discussion, representative homework assignments, and sample tests. The manual offers illustrative syllabus schedules oriented toward different academic interests: a one-quarter course in an economics department and a semester course in an environmental studies program. There is discussion of areas where intermediate economics and the use of calculus can be productive and suggestions for instructors teaching environmental economics as the first economics course for most students. In addition, the manual provides transparency masters of each figure in the text, a very practical feature. The manual is available to qualified U.S. instructors that adopt the text, but in some cases it may not be available to international adopters.

A Web site located at **www.awlonline.com** encourages interaction between instructors, students, and the author. The primary purpose is to discuss aspects of courses and their subject matter and also to communicate and discuss new developments in environmental economics and environmental policy. To this end, the Web site has numerous links to Internet resources in environmental economics. It will be possible to exchange e-mail communications with the author; a message board will also allow students and professors to exchange ideas. Finally, the Web site offers information about three types of material that can be of assistance to instructors and students. First, there are suggestions for video segments that demonstrate the nature of environmental problems and methods of analysis used in environmental economics. Second, the Web site carries suggestions about field trips that can be undertaken in association with courses in environmental economics. Finally, there are suggestions about guest lecturers from business, government, and citizens' groups and some tips on securing their enthusiastic participation in a course.

Acknowledgments

In closing, please note my strong "thank you" to individuals whose support was essential in developing this text. In particular, I'd like to thank Jean Agras, Roger Beck, Amy Chapman, Natalie deCombray, Neha Khanna, Una Moneypenny, Andrew Novakovic, William Tomek, and Susan Weitz. In addition, special thanks to the individual contributors to the text, Richard Norgaard, Matt Schwartz, Brent Sohngen, Jon Erickson, Richard Bishop, Richard Woodward, and Andrea Kreiner. (A brief professional biography of these contributors follows the foreword.) Finally, I would like to acknowledge the careful and constructive work of many environmental economists who worked with Addison Wesley Longman in providing constructive and valuable criticism in previous drafts of this text, and especially Brent Sohngen, who tested the final manuscript in his class prior to publication.

Special acknowledgment and thanks to:

Richard Bryant
University of Missouri, Rolla

Wayne Carroll
University of Wisconsin, Eau Claire

Mark T. Dickie
University of Southern Mississippi

Trellis Green
University of Southern Mississippi

Darwin Hall
California State University, Long Beach

Jane Hall
California State University, Fullerton

Donn M. Johnson
Quinnipiac College

Arik Levinson
University of Wisconsin, Madison

Peter Meyer
University of Louisville

John R. Moroney
Texas A & M University

Richard Norgaard
University of California, Berkeley

Adam Rose
Pennsylvania State University

Jonathan Rubin
University of Tennessee, Knoxville

Anne Sholtz
California Institute of Technology

Brent Sohngen
The Ohio State University

Stephen Swallow
University of Rhode Island

Robert Turner
Colgate University

John C. Whitehead
East Carolina University

Nancy A. Williams
Loyola College

Andrea Shaw and Rebecca Ferris at Addison Wesley Longman (and previously John Greenman) were uniformly positive and encouraging in their approach to bringing this text to publication. A thank-you to everyone.

WHY ENVIRONMENTAL ECONOMICS?

BY RICHARD B. NORGAARD

Duane Chapman has produced an environmental economics text that looks outward rather than inward. He realizes, for example, the critical difference between environmental economics as rationalization of the status quo and environmental economics as a way of exploring the problems of our economy and seeking better solutions. He has prepared an especially eye-opening textbook by breaking and expanding the mold in many important dimensions.

Chapman starts out with central economic concepts developed in the context of petroleum markets. The discussion takes us right into the real-world issues of competition and monopoly power, profits, and rent, followed shortly after by pollution costs imposed on others and national defense as a public good. Nothing is minced to make reality more palatable here.

Subsequent chapters develop criteria for making economic decisions from both public and private perspectives, providing readers with sufficient historical context so that we can see the conditions under which economic concepts were initiated and developed over time and hence how they may need to change again. Importantly, economic problems are also addressed early in the text as equity problems as well as problems of efficiency. The big questions of sustainability are addressed early and elsewhere in this text, and they are considered in depth in the concluding chapters. In addition, and in a way that is unlike other mainstream texts, alternative approaches to economics are explored to give us new ideas with which to work. Chapman takes us directly into the complex world of economic thinking applied to our real economy. Plan on going through some of this material several times. Fortunately, it is worth it.

Chapman breaks the mold in additional ways. Acknowledging that the Industrial Revolution was an energy transition that coevolved into complex linkages between fossil fuels, economic and political power, environmental pollution, and global warming, he elaborates on energy economics and the possibilities for switching to renewable energy and increasing the efficiency with which we use energy. Acknowledging that we are in another major round of macroeconomic restructuring and globalization, Chapman directs specific attention to what we think we know and what we do not know about these issues. The hammers and saws of economics, particularly methods of environmental valuation, come with instructions for their safe use.

Most importantly, Chapman rarely discusses economics in the abstract. He provides environmental and technical production data on their own terms and supplements the data with sound case studies. The data and examples continually validate that there is a world out there, beyond economic reasoning and language, that needs to be addressed by economics—addressed on its own terms. Occasionally, Chapman goes one step farther by providing intriguing personal narratives, in effect insisting that economics also must be true to our personal experiences and values.

Chapman's goal was to bring good science into an environmental economics text, to author a book that combines scientific and economic interpretations of our worldly problems so that students become knowledgeable about both. At the same time, he included other economists as authors with perspectives more "ecological" than his own (Bishop and Woodward, Erickson, Sohngen, Schwartz, and even me).

These are not minor recarvings of the dominant environmental textbook mold. Chapman's new, bigger mold establishes a new direction, setting at least one strand of environmental economics texts on a solid, new course. Like economics itself, however, the text is a construction in process in which we can all join. Today's students have the opportunity—no, the obligation—to assure that they learn and apply environmental economics, as well as questioning and participating in its continued advance, in a manner that supports environmental sustainability and a future with human dignity.

Richard B. Norgaard is Professor of Energy and Resources and of Agricultural and Resource Economics at the University of California at Berkeley. He is President of the International Society for Ecological Economics.

ABOUT THE AUTHOR

Duane Chapman worked as an economist for the National Park Service and the Atomic Energy Commission before joining the faculty at Cornell University in 1971, where he is now Professor of Environmental Economics.

He earned a Ph.D. from the University of California at Berkeley and a B.A. from Michigan State University. He has worked as a consultant to banks and citizen groups, energy companies, and international organizations. In the early 1970s, he (with colleagues Tim Mount and Tim Tyrrell) did pioneering work on energy-demand forecasting and conservation. In the late 1970s, he led a research effort for the U.S. Senate on the structure and performance of the petroleum industry.

In the 1980s, Chapman, working for the EPA, organized a computer simulation of the economic response of electric utilities to federal policies to reduce acid rain emissions.

During both decades, he continued studying the economics of nuclear power, including work with the Pennsylvania Senate (on economic aspects of the Three Mile Island accident), the State of New York (on the nuclear waste problem at West Valley), and on the nuclear problems at the Washington Public Power Supply System.

He has worked for the World Bank and USAID in the 1990s, and at the Universities of Zimbabwe (in Harare), and of Natal (in Durban, South Africa). His research is reflected in 150 publications in these fields, in journals, books, monographs, and congressional testimony.

Chapman's lifelong interest in the environment led him, in late October of 1976, to backpack alone across the High Sierra and the High Peaks–Mount Whitney region from Lone Pine to Mineral King. As an amateur mountaineer, he climbed the 14,000-foot Mount Sill. With Richard Norgaard, who wrote the foreword to this text, he challenged the rapids of Tuolomne, a Class 4 river on the western slope of the Sierra Nevada range. He has twice canoed the full 130 miles of the undammed part of the Missouri River on the famous Lewis and Clark route. He has traveled from the Congo's copper belt, through Zambia and Zimbabwe, to Johannesburg and Durban. Currently, he enjoys subzero winter camping and wrestles with the preservation and management issues related to his 165-acre stand of old-growth woods. The woods are rich in commercial timber value, but are home to hermit thrushes, shrikes, jumping mice, flying squirrels, wild turkeys, great horned owls, bobcats, bears, and coyotes.

▲ **Richard C. Bishop** recently completed a two-year term as president of the Association of Environmental and Resource Economists. He has worked on economic issues associated with the California condor and the bald eagle as well as the Exxon Valdez oil spill and ground and surface water pollution. He has been particularly interested in the economic dimensions of sustainability and safe minimum standards. Bishop is a professor and the chair of the Department of Agricultural and Applied Economics, University of Wisconsin, Madison.

▲ **Jon Erickson** is an assistant professor in Economics at the Rensselaer Polytechnic Institute, which began the first Ph.D. program in ecological economics. He has played a leading role in the Adirondack Research Consortium, an interdisciplinary organization focused on the sustainable development and preservation of the Adirondack Park. His other research includes community quality of life and climate change.

▲ **Andrea Kreiner** is past chair of the Board of Directors of the National Pollution Prevention Roundtable. Kreiner is currently managing the Office of Business and Permitting Services for the Delaware Department of Natural Resources and Environmental Control, encompassing environmental justice, permitting assistance, and pollution prevention programs.

▲ **Richard B. Norgaard** is president of the International Society for Ecological Economics. Among the few to know the Glen Canyon of the Colorado River before Lake Powell, he also was the first to raft the Tatshenshini River in Canada and Alaska. Norgaard's work on coevolution and sustainability as intergenerational equity has had a major impact on the growth of ecological economics. He is a professor of Energy and Resources and of Agricultural and Resource Economics at the University of California at Berkeley.

▲ **Matthew Schwartz** has worked with the United States Department of Energy in the Office of Alternative Fuels. Formerly with Industrial Economics, Inc., an environmental consulting firm, Schwartz was enrolled in the M.B.A. program at M.I.T. as this book went to press. He is particularly interested in environmental management.

▲ **Brent Sohngen** is an assistant professor at Ohio State University. Sohngen is a member of a governor's commission on water quality in Ohio. He has been a leading contributor to research on U.S. and global forest management, conservation, and climate change, in the *American Economic Review* and elsewhere.

▲ **Richard T. Woodward** is an assistant professor at Texas A & M University. His research focuses on issues of economic sustainability, environmental amenities, uncertainty, and the quantitative methods used to study these issues.

PART I

ECONOMIC THEORY, CONCEPTS, AND METHODS

COMPETITION, MONOPOLY, AND SOCIAL WELFARE

Introduction: Why Study Economics?

It is apparent that Environmental Economics and Ecological Economics are moving toward a redefinition of "resource." Increasingly, we need to think of "environmental resources" as exhibiting two economic characteristics: they are closely linked to natural resources, and they have significant external value related to environmental protection.[1]

Considered in this way, acid rain's impact on forests, the health impact of water pollution, and biodiversity protection in parks all have related aspects, and they are all subject to similar methods of economic analysis and public policy. Typically, an innovation in one area becomes the basis for new policy in another area. The best recent example of this interrelationship is marketable permits, which were first used on a broad scale in reducing acid rain emissions from power plants in the United States (see Chapter 11) and are now a major part of the international debate on climate change (see Chapter 18).

This textbook summarizes the broad types of economic policies used to manage the use or protection of environmental resources. It is in this area that economics is particularly important; economics and economic analysis affect environmental policy, and policy often sets the framework for environmental impact. Whether the focus is business, government, or the individual, environmental economics and policy are important.

The appendix to this book outlines the evolution of the legislative framework for environmental protection, from air and water quality to national forests and endangered species. This chapter introduces environmental economics as having real-world value, a tool that can encourage efficient and effective environmental protection.

The focus in this text is on the U.S. experience in an international and global context. In part, this focus is appropriate because of the extensive successes in the United States in the latter part of the 20th Century. Arguably, the United States was the world leader in the actual practice of pollution control and in National Park protection.

The 21st Century will be dominated by new problems such as climate change, biodiversity, park protection in developing countries, and the need for pollution prevention in newly industrialized countries. This type of new agenda of major problems may reduce U.S. leadership. Nevertheless, the policies developed and the lessons learned in the United States and other high-income countries in the 20th Century may be redesigned for global use in the 21st Century.

But why study environmental economics? Why should economic theory be part of environmental economics? Many environmentalists are uncomfortable (or bored!) with economics, and they think an introductory chapter should begin with environmental problems, bringing in economics only as necessary. An opposing viewpoint, held by some in economics or business, is that environment is simply one of many standard categories within economics, and that economic theory need not be reviewed specifically for environmental subjects.

My perspective is that the basic economic concepts are very valuable in understanding how national and world economies work. With increased understanding of economics, we can make better decisions in business, in consumer affairs, and in public policy—in all of the dimensions of economic life that affect the environment.

Consider that two decades ago it was widely anticipated that crude oil resources would be depleted and that oil and gasoline prices would increase for many years. In fact, oil and gasoline prices are now at historically low levels. Why was the period of very high prices followed by low prices in the 1990s?

Or consider the example of residential solar electricity. The "oil shocks" and nuclear problems of the 1970s caused an explosion of new interest in small technologies, especially solar energy. It was hoped that affordable, renewable, pollution-free solar power would displace conventional energy. At the time, residential solar electricity was a more-developed technology than were personal computers. Today, personal computers are widely used, and residential solar electricity is still struggling. Why?

Economic theory helps us understand each of these cases. Nine types of issues in environmental economics illustrate how theory increases our understanding of the real world:

▲ *Resource use.* How much of a natural resource will be used? This question applies equally to the use of forests for lumber or wilderness, and to the amount of gasoline that is produced and sold.

▲ *Resource depletion.* How long will natural resources last? Will we exhaust our endowments of metal, energy, and forest, or does economics provide a different perspective?

▲ *Technological innovation.* Commercial feasibility is a major factor affecting many new technologies that have environmental significance. Whether renewable energy or other new technologies (biodiversity mapping, mining metals with recycled sulfur), economic analysis assists in understanding market feasibility for these emerging technologies.

▲ *Environmental impact.* The scale of economic activity has a major effect on environmental impact. For some types of pollutants, such as acid rain emissions from a copper smelter or greenhouse gas emissions, the releases are proportional to production. Does environmental quality decline or increase as a nation's income level rises?

▲ *Pollution prevention and control.* The level of pollution depends on technology in pollution prevention, so, at a cost, both copper production and electricity generation can be increased while pollution is reduced.

▲ *Macroeconomics.* How are the national and global levels of production and living standards affected by environmental policy?

▲ *Trade-offs and allocation.* Economic theory can be used to define and illustrate the best trade-offs between production, consumption, and environmental policy.

▲ *Efficiency.* How large should protected areas be? Is there a "best" level of pollution control? The economic concepts arising from optimization and benefit-cost analysis help us understand the trade-offs involved in efficient policies.

▲ *Incentives versus regulation.* The effectiveness of environmental policy is improved when business and consumers can see that market incentives are working. Is direct regulation (often called command-and-control) usually bad for business? Are there problems where regulation and market incentives can work together?

Many of us would offer a different list of issues where economics helps solve the problem. A businessman's list would be framed differently, as would that of an environmentalist or another environmental economist. This group of subjects is broadly representative. In each area, economic theory helps define the problem and illuminate the solution.

For some students, this material will be a brief introduction. For others, it will be a review of aspects of economics they have studied in other courses. In the next section, the theory of competitive markets introduces the ideas of competition, monopoly, levels of consumption, and environment.

The Theory of Competitive Markets

Competition* in economics has a rather precise definition. It means that no single buyer, seller, company, or consumer can control the prices at which products are bought and sold. It implies that there are so many buyers and sellers that no one of them can influence industry prices. These two assumptions imply a third: entry into the market is unrestricted, and any person or firm may become a producer, or buyer, or conceivably both.

Economic competition is not the same as advertising. As F. M. Scherer notes, business firms compete in advertising in order to create *product differentiation* for their brands in terms of consumer acceptance.[2] A product that is standard and uniform, such as gasoline, may nonetheless be viewed by consumers as having distinct properties. My favorite discussion on this point was held by Stanley Learned, President of the Phillips Petroleum Company, and Rand Dixon, Chairman of the Federal Trade Commission:

> FEDERAL TRADE COMMISSION: *Do you exchange any gasoline [with other major oil companies] in the East?*
>
> PHILLIPS PETROLEUM: *We have some exchange, yes.*
>
> FEDERAL TRADE COMMISSION: *That makes it hard for you to call yours Phillips, doesn't it?*

---

*Each of the terms and concepts printed in italics is included with a definition in Appendix A to this chapter.

PHILLIPS PETROLEUM: As long as they meet our specifications.

FEDERAL TRADE COMMISSION: You put a little pinch of something in it that makes it a little different?

PHILLIPS PETROLEUM: Yes; we have an additive which allows us to advertise. I don't know if it does anything for the gasoline.[3]

If the president of Phillips Petroleum didn't know whether additives matter, how can the rest of us? Gasoline additives serve primarily as a device for encouraging consumer loyalty. This is not wholly without economic reason, for brand loyalty in marketing gives stability to production and refining, and this in turn may lower costs. Since buyers perceive a difference between brands, companies can raise or lower prices by small amounts without having much influence on total consumption or market share.

Electricity is also uniform and homogeneous as received by households. The large majority of customers perceive no difference between Pacific Gas and Electric's electricity and New York State Electric & Gas's electricity. It might be argued that the existence of external social cost from air pollution or nuclear power affects the customer's view of the quality of electricity. Most buyers, however, see electricity itself as a homogeneous product.

The world petroleum market can serve to introduce the economic theory of competition.[4] At the same time, since petroleum is so basic to the modern industrial economy and many global environmental problems, the illustration of theory can also introduce a major subject area. However, the concepts that are introduced are generally relevant to environmental and resource questions. In the discussion that follows, we are assuming a long-range perspective of several years. With respect to costs, for example, we assume that businesses plan and control equipment, buildings, labor, marketing, and other components of production and sales.

A short-range perspective can be very different: this week the cost of driving is essentially the cost of gasoline. In the long run, the cost of several years' driving includes the cost of the automobile, as well as the cost of gasoline. The summary in this chapter is simultaneously an introduction and a review: these concepts are of course developed more completely in other textbooks and courses.[5]

Figure 1.1 shows the basic elements of a competitive market. The *demand curve* P shows how price and sales interact: a higher price means lower sales, and a lower price leads to increased sales. The demand curve is a straight line here; it could be any shape that is downward sloping.

Elasticity is an important economic concept related to the demand curve. It is the percentage change in sales caused by a percent change in price.[6]

In the mid 1990s, $16 per barrel was a typical price for crude oil. In the figure, that price on the vertical axis intersects the demand curve to define a world demand of 22 billion barrels. (A barrel of oil contains exactly 42 gallons.)

Marginal cost is the minimal additional cost of producing more barrels of oil. For an industry, it is the sum of the producers' individual marginal cost curves.[7] In Figure 1.1, marginal cost increases slightly as production rises. This would reflect the use of higher-cost oil fields at higher production levels.

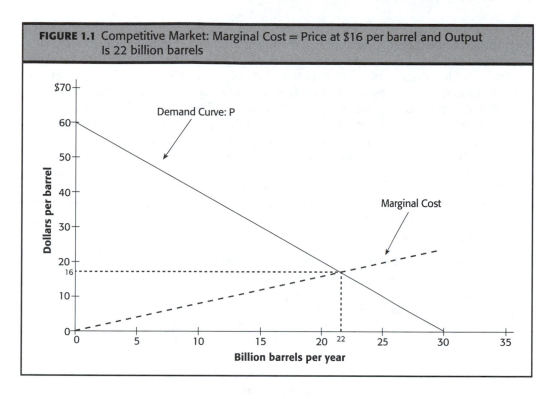

FIGURE 1.1 Competitive Market: Marginal Cost = Price at $16 per barrel and Output Is 22 billion barrels

In the figure, it is evident that at a world production level of 10 billion barrels annually, marginal cost would be about $7.30 per barrel. At the 22 billion barrel production level, marginal cost has risen to $16 per barrel.

Since marginal cost reflects the cost of additional production, the competitive industry would always increase production to the level where price and marginal cost were equal. Suppose this didn't happen. Suppose production was at 10 billion barrels. The price would be $40 per barrel. Since the price from additional sales is $33 greater than the cost of more output, some producers would increase production until the total rose to the 22 billion barrel level. Of course, the profitable increased output also might come from new producers entering the market.

Suppose production was above the competitive level, say at 25 billion barrels. Now marginal cost at $18 is above price at $10. Obviously, with cost exceeding price, some part of this production is not paying for itself. The industry would reduce production until it sliced off this loss; 22 billion barrels is the production level at which further reduction in production would be unnecessary and unprofitable.

In summary, profit motive leads individual producers to maximize their profit, avoid losses, and adapt their production levels to market outcomes where marginal cost and price are equal. In economic theory, this is a competitive equilibrium, which is socially desirable. This competitive equilibrium, as you will see in the last section of this chapter, gives the greatest total value above cost to consumers and producers.

There are obviously certain difficulties with this concept that competition in markets creates the greatest total value. Up to this point we have studiously ignored respiratory ailments caused by air pollution, acid rain, and climate change, as well as radioactive hazards, monopoly, government regulation, consumer ignorance, subsidies, and other economic goals besides money. However, economic theory holds that, in the absence of these problems, this competitive solution is efficient and therefore serves the public welfare. It is *Pareto Optimal*: no one can be made better off without someone else being made worse off. (The concept is attributed to Vilfredo Pareto, a European economist.) As a consequence, production is done in the most efficient manner possible, consumers maximize their utility, and this is more or less the best of all possible worlds. In other words, if competition exists, Pareto Optimality follows, and each consumer and producer pursuing their own consumption and profit create the most welfare for society.[8]

Economists who study these issues have concluded that there are several logical requirements that must be met in order for a competitive industry to be optimally efficient. These conditions are:

1. Every other industry must also be competitive.
2. Economic knowledge must exist everywhere. Consumers must have a general knowledge of how long a car will last, what the annual fuel and maintenance bill will be, and so forth. They must understand the difference in annual heating costs when they choose between gas and electric heating. In other words, producers and consumers must have access to information about the costs and benefits of their choices.
3. Everyone—business and consumers alike—must act as if they are guided by the pursuit of maximum financial or personal gain. For economic society, it doesn't matter whether a dollar is spent on a student's air fare to Europe or for the heating bill of a retired couple. However, fairness can be part of the personal economic calculus: altruism, bequests to future generations, and other external values are increasingly accepted in the definition of personal gain.
4. Consumers must be insatiable, always desiring higher levels of consumption. (This is implied by the preceding point.)
5. *Economies of scale* must not be pervasive; if they are, monopoly becomes efficient. (Economies of scale mean that the cost of production declines as production levels grow.)
6. There must be no external social costs, such as damage to public or employee health or general environmental degradation. If there are, then competitive industry develops a level of production and consumption that is above the desirable level.

This discussion has been straightforward in its introduction of economic concepts. However, the picture is too simple to represent the economic workings of the world petroleum industry. There are five important qualifications. First, environmental aspects have not yet been included in this summary of theory. Second, the major consumer markets for petroleum are in refined products such as gasoline rather than in crude oil. Third, there is always a time lag in consumer response to price changes as consumers adjust. Fourth, there has been no representation of resource depletion, an important subject to be taken up in Chapters 6 and 9. Fifth, the demand curve is not constant, but is actually shifting upward over time as world population and income rise. The point is that the competitive theory can be introduced with real-world data as illustration, but it is no more than an introduction. Environmental costs will be incorporated into this basic outline of economic theory. Environmental economics is particularly useful in combining an emphasis on efficiency in competitive markets with a focus on economic policies that encourage efficient environmental protection.

Monopoly Pricing and Economic Rent

The theoretical concept most commonly used to supplement competitive theory is profit monopoly. Profit monopoly theory and the competitive theory share an assumption that profitability is the guiding light of economic behavior. It usually supposes that competition is desirable and possible. But *monopoly* postulates the absence of competition and the existence, for one reason or another, of conscious control over production and price levels.

Basically, monopoly power means the active ability to use market power to control price and output. A monopolistic industry can increase its revenue while it raises prices to customers. This increase occurs even if customers reduce the amount of purchases.

At this point, it is useful to write out the arithmetic equations for the demand curve and for marginal cost, and to add four others: *revenue, total cost, profit,* and *marginal revenue.*

$$P = 60 - 2 * Q \qquad \text{(demand)} \qquad (1\text{-}1)$$

$$MC = 72.8¢ * Q \qquad \text{(marginal cost)} \qquad (1\text{-}2)$$

$$REV = P * Q = 60 * Q - 2 * Q^2 \qquad \text{(revenue)} \qquad (1\text{-}3)$$

$$TC = .364 * Q^2 \qquad \text{(total cost)} \qquad (1\text{-}4)$$

$$AC = TC/Q = .364 * Q \qquad \text{(average cost)} \qquad (1\text{-}5)$$

$$\Pi = REV - TC = 60 * Q - 2.364 * Q^2 \quad \text{(profit)} \qquad (1\text{-}6)$$

$$MR = 60 - 4 * Q \qquad \text{(marginal revenue)} \qquad (1\text{-}7)$$

Bringing all of the definitions together,

P = price of crude oil, $/bl

Q = annual world production and use of crude oil, billion barrels per year

MC = marginal cost, additional cost of production at a given output level, $/bl

REV = total annual revenue, equal to price times quantity sold, billion dollars per year

TC = total cost of production, including a fair return on investment, billion dollars per year

AC = average cost of production of a barrel of crude oil, equal to total cost divided by production, $/bl

Π = profit, annual excess of revenue over total cost, billion dollars

MR = marginal revenue, additional revenue at a given sales level, $/bl

Under this theory, world oil producers can control global production levels to get the maximum possible profit. Figure 1.2 shows profit. It indicates that, hypothetically, the highest yearly profit would be nearly $400 billion at an output level of 12.69 billion barrels. Raising production to, say, 15 billion barrels, would lower profit. Reducing production from 12.69 billion barrels would lower profit. This production level of 12.69 billion barrels is the hypothetical profit maximizing production for a monopoly that can control both production and price. The profit level is significantly higher than would be possible for a competitive oil industry.

While Figure 1.2 makes the maximum profit appear obvious, it is actually the result of three different factors. First, as the quantity is increasing, the elasticity response means that price has to be lowered to increase sales. Second, the most obvious factor is that the rising sales quantity increases total revenue, so the producer is balancing the revenue loss from the price elasticity effect against the revenue gain from the increasing quantity sold. The final factor is the small continuous cost increase as production grows. So, the monopolist takes all three factors into account and finds maximum profit from Equation (1-6) is at 12.69 billion barrels,[9] as in Figure 1.2.

Profit maximization could also be shown with a graph with price on the horizontal axis, and profit on the vertical axis. This figure if drawn would indicate that the best price for a world monopoly would be nearly $35 per barrel. This is the price (as in Equation 1-1) where buyers would purchase the monopoly goal of 12.69 billion barrels.

It is more conventional to use marginal cost and marginal revenue to show the profit maximization for a monopoly. *Marginal revenue* is the additional revenue going to a firm for selling another unit of its output. The intersection of marginal revenue and marginal cost in Figure 1.3 defines the monopoly's optimal production of 12.69 billion barrels on the horizontal axis, and the associated optimal price of al-

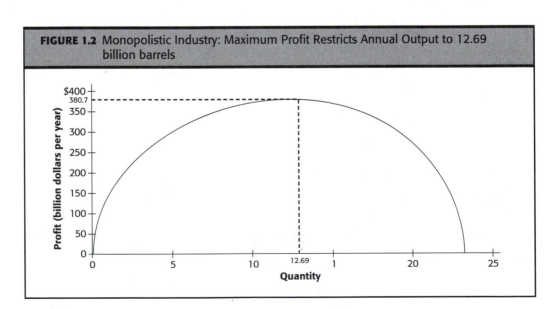

FIGURE 1.2 Monopolistic Industry: Maximum Profit Restricts Annual Output to 12.69 billion barrels

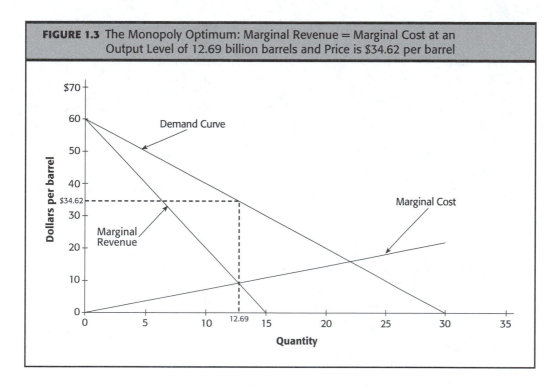

FIGURE 1.3 The Monopoly Optimum: Marginal Revenue = Marginal Cost at an Output Level of 12.69 billion barrels and Price is $34.62 per barrel

most $35 on the vertical axis. In the figure, marginal revenue declines more sharply than the demand curve as sales increase. This is because of the nature of demand curves and elasticity: to increase sales levels, price must be lowered. So, for each additional unit sold, revenue increases from that sale, but revenue is offset by the negative impact of the lower price on other sales.

When marginal revenue falls to zero and becomes negative after Q = 15, total revenue is reduced. The lower prices needed to increase sales are reducing total revenue.

In Figure 1.3, marginal revenue and marginal cost intersect at Q = 12.69 billion barrels. The intersection value for MR and MC is $9.24. To the left, marginal revenue is greater than marginal cost, indicating that profit can increase by raising production. To the right of their optimal production level, marginal cost has passed above marginal revenue, which indicates that producers have lost profit by moving above 12.69 billion barrels. So, just as P = MC defined the competitive market, MR = MC defines the monopolistic market.[10]

The term *economic rent* is used by economists to measure the magnitude of an advantage held by a group of producers. In its broadest sense, it is simply the difference between a producer's average cost and the market price of a commodity. It can originate in several ways: it can be locational, the lower cost for a farmer with good soil or access to transportation to markets. It might be related to scarcity, as impending depletion raises the price and demand for a resource. It can also arise from new technology and patents.

Here, in this context, economic rent arises from monopoly. Since the total cost (from Equation 1-4) is $58.62 billion at the production level of 12.69 billion barrels, the average cost is $4.62. With the price near $35 per barrel in this theoretical example, the economic rent is $30 per barrel. In total, the annual revenue would be $381 billion above cost. *Producer surplus* is closely related to economic rent, and applies to both competitive and monopolistic theories. It is the difference between revenue and total producer cost, the "surplus" above cost.[11]

(Note: A mathematical illustration in the Appendix to this chapter shows the calculations for price, profit, sales, and other variables. Especially, see Table B.1 in Appendix B.)

An important distinction exists between economic profit and accounting profit as it is generally used. In normal usage, "profit" is similar to net income, the income a business has earned after paying its expenses and taxes, and accounting for depreciation of its buildings and equipment.

In contrast, in economic terminology, business owners receive a normal return of, say, 15 percent to 20 percent per year on their financial investment in the business. Owners and investors are paid for the *opportunity cost* of their investment: what they could have earned in an alternative investment opportunity.[12]

Consequently, cost of doing business is considered in economics to include a normal return on capital investment, and producer surplus is the excess of revenue above costs, including the opportunity cost of capital.

Is the world oil market controlled by a monopoly? Most independent observers such as Maury Adelman think not.[13] I agree that it is not now monopolistic as that has been defined in this chapter. In fact, the term "monopoly" used here clearly does not apply to world oil. Strictly speaking, the type of monopoly just discussed is often referred to as "pure monopoly," because it describes how a single all-powerful firm controlling all of a market might operate.

In considering the global oil industry, economists have emphasized two other concepts, each of which is related to monopoly. A cartel involves joint decision-making on both prices and production. An oligopoly is somewhat weaker, meaning only that each producer considers the plans of other producers when a company or government makes its plans for output and pricing. In theory, both cartels and oligopolies can seek monopoly profit through their production and pricing decisions.[14]

OPEC (the Organization of Petroleum Exporting Countries) is actually a group of governments of oil-producing nations. From 1973 to the early 1980s, it was a cartel (a committee working as a monopoly and sharing the profit). Figure 1.4 shows more than four decades of average crude oil prices, adjusted for inflation. It is evident, however, that OPEC could not lead the industry to maintain the high price levels reached in the early 1980s. In fact, in real inflation-adjusted dollars,[15] the late 1990s crude oil price actually fell to the lowest level in the last half of the 20th Century. In Chapter 9, this question will be revisited in the context of the issue of potential depletion of conventional crude oil and the economic concepts of game theory.

At this point, it is interesting to recall an observation made by Robert M. Solow and William Nordhaus:

> *Monopolies are the conservationists' best friends: higher prices lead to lower consumption, a stretching out of finite resources, and possibly even lower prices in the future.*[16]

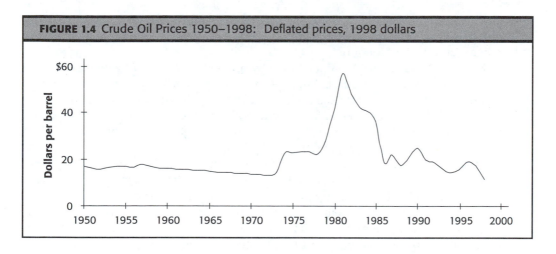

FIGURE 1.4 Crude Oil Prices 1950–1998: Deflated prices, 1998 dollars

In other words, since profit maximizing for a monopoly leads to lower sales and production than would occur in a competitive industry, limited reserves would last longer.

Environmental Externalities, Public Goods, and Economic Welfare

The concepts of *social value* and social cost form the basis for the economist's view of the social optimum. When efficiency is considered from a national perspective, *social cost* is defined as the cost to society of producing and consuming a good. Therefore it includes not only the market costs of production already discussed but *external social cost* as well. Frequently, externality is a shorter term used to mean either negative or positive external effects.

The growth in importance in externality concepts has accompanied a growing interest by economists in the nature of *public goods*. In economics, a public good is a commodity or service whose essential nature is that every individual may use as much as they desire without affecting its availability to others. Each person's use is independent of payment level.

Traditionally, use of air and water were portrayed as public goods.[17] However, if we acknowledge that our individual or business use of air and water may add to pollution of that resource, the traditional definition of a public good is too narrow.

In this text, we will consider a public good somewhat differently. We will define a public good in an environmental context as an environmental resource with wide access to many users, and with significant positive and negative external value associated with the use and management of that resource. As we shall see in later chapters, the need to manage environmental public goods and externalities gives rise to the role of government in coordinating or managing environmental policies.

These nonmarket concepts are particularly relevant for energy because the magnitude of external environmental impact is probably greater for energy than for any other sector of the economy.

External social costs are unintentional by-products of economic activity with negative impact on human welfare. Damage to health, property, and the environment is the major dimension of external social cost. There is no acceptable method of measuring such damage in monetary terms, notwithstanding the considerable research that has been done on the subject. (Valuation is taken up again in Chapters 3 and 4.)

One review has been prepared by the California Public Utilities Commission, as summarized by the U.S. General Accounting Office. Table 1.1 reports dollar-value external social cost damage estimates per ton of some major air pollutants. Note that for four of the five pollutants, the damage estimates per ton are higher in heavily polluted areas than in clean areas. The purpose of this table in this chapter[18] is to introduce the concept of external social cost. While Table 1.1 focuses attention on pollutants from energy use, Table 1.2 focuses on the energy source rather than the pollutant. Selected aspects of external cost for petroleum are shown in Table 1.2. As an approximation, $15 per barrel is a representative value of external social cost implied by the table. These authors believe that total external costs of oil use are in the same range as current market cost.

If we consider the available information, it is clear that the social cost of oil is considerably higher than its market cost alone. Figure 1.5 illustrates marginal social cost (MSC). It includes the private sector's costs of production and the external social cost of energy use. Economists frequently assume that the demand curve is equivalent to the marginal social value. Therefore, the intersection of marginal social cost and marginal social value define the optimum level of sales at 16.5 billion barrels annually. Social cost pricing would have a price of $27 per barrel.

The assertion that the demand curve was equivalent to marginal social value follows from the economists' view that the value of consumption is reflected by the area under a demand curve. Suppose we have three persons who might buy a car.

TABLE 1.1 External Social Cost Damage Estimates for Air Pollutants (dollars per ton)

	Polluted Areas in Southern California	Clean Areas in California
Sulfur oxides	$30,000	$2,000
Nitrogen oxides	40,500	9,500
Particulate matter	9,000	6,000
Reactive organic gas	29,000	1,500
Carbon in the atmosphere	40	40

Source: US-GAO, "Considering Externalities in Selecting Fuel Sources," GAO/RCED–95–187, May 1995. The geographic regions are formally defined as "nonattainment area" or "attainment area." These numbers represent the authors' estimates of the average monetary value of damage caused by each type of air pollution.

TABLE 1.2 External Social Cost (ESC), Petroleum Use

	Author			
	Hall	*Hall*	*Viscusi*	*Fankhauser*
Type of externality	Ozone and particulate damage	National security	Gasoline and air pollution	Greenhouse gas
ESC as reported	$11.59/bl	$10.04/bl	15¢ per gal	$20.30 per tonne carbon
ESC, $/bl nearest dollar	$12	$10	$6	$2

Note: Viscusi's figure is partially contained in Hall's $12 number. Hall intends that his total is appropriate: $22/bl. Fankhauser's figure is conceptually additive to Hall or Viscusi. $15 is used in the text here as representative. (For sources, see Endnote 19.)

Mr. Ackley will pay $25,000 if he needs to. Ms. Brown will pay less, $20,000. Professor Cardiff is the least willing to pay: he feels he can only afford $15,000 at the very most. Figure 1.6 indicates this three-person demand curve. If the price is $25,000, only one person will buy: Ackley. The value to him is block A, $25,000. If the price is $20,000, Brown will buy also, and the value to her is block B. Finally, if the price is $15,000, Cardiff will buy, adding block C. At the $15,000 price, the value to all three persons is A + B + C: $60,000. The value to all three consumers is considerably higher than the price because most consumers—if they had to—would be willing to pay more.

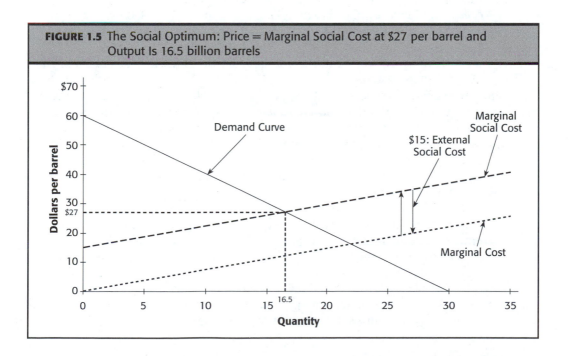

FIGURE 1.5 The Social Optimum: Price = Marginal Social Cost at $27 per barrel and Output Is 16.5 billion barrels

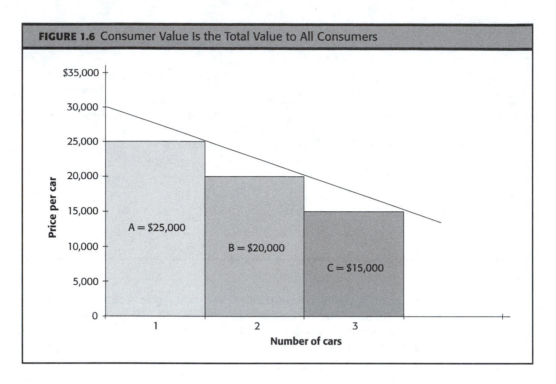

FIGURE 1.6 Consumer Value Is the Total Value to All Consumers

Notice that the shaded area A + B + C almost fills the area under the demand curve. With more customers, the value to consumers becomes very close to being the area under the demand curve. In Figure 1.7, 26 potential customers are shown, A−Z. Just as in Figure 1.6, A is willing to pay the most, then B, then C, and so on. Buying a car is worth P^A to A, P^B to B, P^C to C, and so on. At an actual price of P^*, all consumers A−U will buy, leaving V−Z out of the market.

As in Figure 1.6, the total value to consumers is the value to each person buying: A + B + C + D and so on through Q + R + S + T + U. The important thing to see is that the sum of these shaded blocks A−U is very close to the area under the demand curve. When the demand curve is based upon millions of consumers, the shaded area is almost exactly equal to the area under the demand curve. This kind of reasoning has led economists to conclude that consumer value is the sum of the value to all consumers of every unit of consumption. It is equivalent to the area under the demand curve. *Consumer surplus* is the excess of consumer value above the cost paid for the product.

Economists have concluded that consumer value can often serve as a measure of social value.[20] In Chapters 3 and 4, we take up the problem of measuring value. For simplification here, we will temporarily use the customary assumption that social value measures the value to society of using a commodity, and it is measured by consumer value.

Earlier in the chapter, we noted that a competitive equilibrium defines the maximum total value to consumers and producers. Now this can be illustrated. A competitive industry maximizes the excess of consumer value above production cost. In

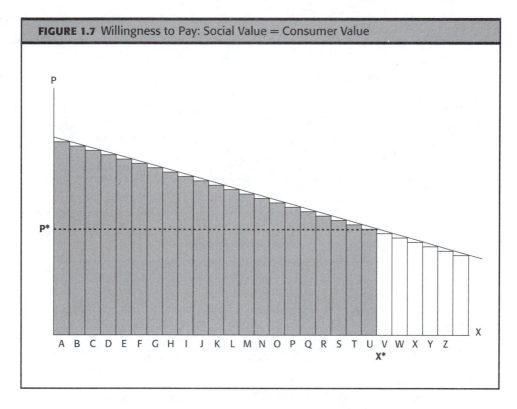

FIGURE 1.7 Willingness to Pay: Social Value = Consumer Value

other words, as shown in Figure 1.8, competition gives the highest possible sum for producers and consumers surplus.

There is no widely accepted term for this sum, but it can reasonably be defined as *net economic surplus*, and it is included in the following equations. Consequently, since net economic surplus is represented by the shaded area in Figure 1.8, competition—where price equals marginal cost—maximizes this amount. In the Appendix Table B.1, the "Competition" case has the highest amount of net economic surplus for the three theories shown there.

However, this concept of net economic surplus has not recognized environmental impact as it is reflected in external social cost. If net economic surplus alone is maximized, it can in some circumstances be associated with significant environmental externalities.

How do perfect competition and monopoly compare in terms of social welfare? One method is to define *net social value* as the difference between social value and social cost for each level of production. Net social value is the total gain to society from production and consumption by all consumers, and is reduced by external cost.

This definition of net social value (NSV) completes the last equations:

$$CV = 60 * Q - Q^2 \qquad \text{(consumer value)} \qquad \text{(1-8a)}$$

$$CS = CV - REV \qquad \text{(consumer surplus)} \qquad \text{(1-8b)}$$

$$PS = REV - TC \qquad \text{(producer surplus)} \qquad \text{(1-8c)}$$

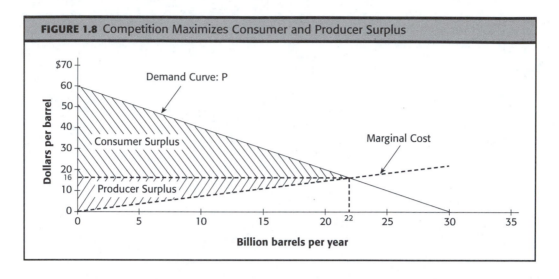

FIGURE 1.8 Competition Maximizes Consumer and Producer Surplus

$$NES = CS + PS \qquad \text{(net economic surplus)} \qquad \text{(1-8d)}$$

$$NSV = CV - SC \qquad \text{(net social value)} \qquad \text{(1-8e)}$$

$$SC = TC + ESC \qquad \text{(social cost)} \qquad \text{(1-8f)}$$

$$ESC = 15 * Q \qquad \text{(external social cost)} \qquad \text{(1-8g)}$$

$$NSV = 45 * Q - 1.364 * Q^2 \qquad \text{(net social value)} \qquad \text{(1-8h)}$$

In the external social cost (ESC) equation, $15 reflects the representative value per barrel of oil discussed in the text. The net social value (NSV) equation is simply consumer value less social cost

When net social value is the highest possible, the *social optimum* is attained. With the optimal oil use of 16.5 billion barrels from Figure 1.5, the maximum possible net social value is $371 billion.

How do the three theories compare? Note a surprise: the monopoly output level is much closer to the social optimum than it is to the competitive production level. Similarly, the socially optimal price ($27) is closer to the monopoly price than it is to the theoretical competitive price. So the numerical illustration seems to echo the Solow-Nordhaus point of view.

We should not suppose that a general policy of acceptance of monopoly is superior to competition. In the context of the highest possible net social value to society, that follows from a combination of environmental pricing in the market, in business and industry, and in competition.

Questions for Discussion and Analysis

1. Growth in population and income shifts demand curves upward and to the right. If the marginal cost curve is the same in Year 1 and Year 10, show how the equilibrium prices and quantities change.

2. Suppose hypothetically that external social cost from climate change and air pollution damage grows significantly in the coming decades. Assume it reaches $30/barrel. With graphs, show the impact that it will have on the net social value case.

3. In this chapter, externalities are negative. However, positive external values also exist, arising from the beneficial unintended by-products of economic activity. How many can you describe? (Suggestion: consider reading now the discussion of horse and hog farms in Chapter 13.)

4. How many environmental public goods can you suggest? Explain why each qualifies.

5. Suppose you were an economist working for an international oil company and OPEC. What strategies would you plan for maximum profit? Consider how other oil producers would react to your strategies. Is there a feasible monopoly strategy today?

6. What do you think about Pareto Optimality as a basis for making environmental policy? Illustrate your perspective with a hypothetical case involving animal waste from a large livestock operation.

7. Consider Questions 1 and 2 again. Assume the demand curve for Year 10 becomes $P = 100 - 2Q$. External social cost is $30/barrel. Work out the new numerical results for the competitive industry case in Table B.1.

8. Following Question 7, work out the new results for the monopolistic case.

9. Following Questions 7 and 8, what are the results now for maximum social welfare?

10. For each of these cases, what are the pricing rules that determine quantities and prices?

Appendix A: Glossary of Economic Concepts

Average cost: The average cost of production for one unit, calculated by dividing total cost by total production.

Competition: No single producer or consumer can influence the price at which a product is bought or sold.

Consumer surplus: The excess of consumer value above the cost paid by consumers for a product.

Consumer value: The value to consumers of using a product. In economic terms it is frequently supposed that consumer value is measured by the area under a demand curve, which shows the value to all consumers of every unit of consumption.

Demand curve: Graphic representation of the demand function, which is a relationship showing the amount of a good that buyers will wish to purchase at different prices. It is affected by population, prices of competing goods, income, and advertising. It can be linear as well as curved.

Demand function: The quantitative relationship between the amount of a product consumed and the economic factors that affect that consumption: price, personal and national income, population, and the availability and prices of alternatives.

Economic rent: In its broadest sense, simply the difference between average cost and price, in $/barrel, for example. Or the difference between total cost and total revenue, in dollars per year. It can arise from advantage in location, scarcity, or monopoly.

Economies of scale: Average and marginal cost of production are both declining as production levels increase. As a firm's output rises, it can produce all units at a lower average cost.

Elasticity: The percentage change in the amount of a product which is purchased, divided by the percentage change in price. An "income elasticity" is similarly defined: percentage change in demand divided by percentage change in income.

External social cost: An unintended by-product of economic activity with negative impact on human welfare, such as health damage to the public and employees, property loss, and environmental degradation.

Externality: External social cost or external social benefit.

Marginal cost: The incremental cost to the firm of producing an additional unit.

Marginal revenue: The additional revenue to the firm from selling another unit. In a monopolistic industry where the firm or group of firms controls production and price levels, marginal revenue will always be less than price. In a competitive industry, marginal revenue for a firm is always identical to price.

Monopoly: One producer or a group of producers can increase profit by withholding production and raising prices.

Net economic surplus: The sum of consumer and producer surplus, excluding environmental externalities. This is identical to consumer value less total producer cost.

Net social value: The total gain to society from production and consumption of a commodity. It includes all the positive value of consumption from all consumers, and is reduced by external social cost and the company's total production cost. Maximum net social value is the social optimum.

Opportunity cost: For an investment, the value of lost opportunities. A common example is defense expenditures: these investments require that a nation forego an equivalent expenditure on education, or personal consumption. The opportunity cost concept is also applied to natural resource use, and labor.

Pareto Optimal: No one can be made better off without someone else being worse off. Economic theory shows that a competitive economy with proper economic incentives to manage environmental externalities can be Pareto Optimal.

Producer surplus: The excess of revenue to producers above total production cost. Sometimes used as equivalent to economic rent.

Product differentiation: The process of individualizing essentially identical products of different firms, irrespective of price differences, to create brand loyalty. Buyer preference for one product over another may result from advertising, durability, service, tradition, or customer idealism. The degree or type of external social cost associated with a particular company may be a legitimate type of product differentiation for some customers; e.g., electricity from nuclear power compared to electricity from a windmill.

Profit: In general, equals revenue less operating costs, interest expenses, depreciation and depletion charges, and allocated tax expenses.

Public good: Traditionally, a commodity or service that each individual may use as much as they desire without affecting its availability to others. Air and water have been considered to be public goods. In this textbook, a public environmental good is a resource that has wide access to many users, with significant positive and negative external value associated with its management and use.

Revenue: The receipts from sales received by a company or industry; usually dollars per year. By definition, equal to price times quantity sold.

Social cost: The cost incurred by a society in using a product. It includes the cost of production by the company and external social cost.

Social optimum: The level of production and consumption for an industry with maximum gain in social value less social cost. This will be the production level where marginal social cost and marginal social value—measured by price—are equal.

Social value: In general, social value is equal to consumer value for a product, and market price measures marginal social value. However, social value can be defined to include positive externality value as well as consumer value.

Total cost: The cost incurred by a producer in making and marketing a product. Does not include environmental externalities. (See **Social cost**.) Depending on the context, it may include a fair return on invested capital, say 15 percent.

Appendix B: Mathematical Illustration

Only basic algebra is necessary for the first eleven equations and the table. The calculations illustrate the world petroleum discussion in this chapter and should be read in association with the definitions and equations in the text. (For the last four appendix equations only, basic calculus is helpful.) The *demand function* is:

$$P = 60 - 2Q \tag{A1}$$

Since revenue is price times quantity,

$$REV = 60Q - 2Q^2 \tag{A2}$$

Marginal revenue (the rate of change of revenue with respect to output) is

$$MR = 60 - 4Q \tag{A3}$$

Marginal cost (the rate of change in total cost with respect to output) is

$$MC = .728Q \tag{A4}$$

The competitive solution requires price to equal marginal cost:

$$P = MC, \text{ or } 60 - 2Q = .728Q \text{ at } Q = 22 \tag{A5}$$

In contrast, the monopoly solution requires marginal revenue to equal marginal cost:

$$MR = MC, \text{ or } 60 - 4Q = .728Q \text{ at } Q = 12.69 \tag{A6}$$

Economic rent can be found by subtracting total cost (defined to include a normal return on investment) from total revenue. The numerical answers for both the competitive and monopoly solutions are shown in the Table B.1.

TABLE B.1 Solutions for Competition, Monopoly, and Environment

	Competition	Monopoly	Maximum Net Social Value
Oil production, use	22 Bbl	12.69 Bbl	16.5 Bbl
Price, $/bl	*$16/bl*	$34.62/bl	*$27/bl*
Total revenue, $bill	$352	$439.3	$445.5
Total producer cost, $bill	$176.2	$ 58.6	$ 99.1
Producer surplus, $bill	$175.8	**$380.7**	$346.5
Consumer value, $bill	$836	$600.4	$717.8
Consumer surplus, $bill	$484	$161.1	$272.3
Net economic surplus, $bill	**$659.8**	$541.8	$618.7
External social cost, $bill	$330	$190.4	$247.5
Social cost, $bill	$506.2	$249	$346.6
Net social value, $bill	$329.8	$351.4	**$371.2**
Marginal cost, $/bl	*$ 16*	*$ 9.24*	*$ 12.01*
Marginal revenue, $/bl	*–$ 4*	*$ 9.24*	*–$ 6*
Marginal social cost, $/bl	*$ 31.02*	*$ 24.24*	*$ 27*

Note: **Bold** type shows the amounts that are the highest possible maximum values for each case. *Italics* show the marginal values that help find the maximum for each case. Economic rent is also defined as producer surplus in this table. In the Table, bl means barrels, and Bbl means billion barrels.

$$\Pi = REV - TC = 60 * Q - 2.364 * Q^2 \tag{A7}$$

The social optimum is based upon the incorporation of external environmental cost into social cost. So, as defined earlier in the chapter,

$$SC = TC + ESC = .364Q^2 + 15Q \tag{A8}$$

Marginal social cost reflects the rate of change in social cost as output changes, and

$$MSC = .728Q + 15 \tag{A9}$$

Net social value is the difference between consumer value and social cost, as defined earlier in the chapter,

$$NSV = 45Q - 1.364Q^2 \tag{A10}$$

Net social value is maximized when price equals marginal social cost:

$$P = MSC, \text{ or } 60 - 2Q = .728Q + 15, \text{ at } Q = 16.5 \tag{A11}$$

Table B.1 shows comparative solution values for the competitive industry, the monopoly, and the social optimum. Note that the Solow-Nordhaus paradox is reflected in the table: the monopoly output level is closer to the social optimum than is the competitive solution.

The following four equations require elementary calculus. First, note that each marginal equation is the derivative of its associated total equation.

$$MR = \frac{dREV}{dQ} \tag{B1}$$

$$MC = \frac{dTC}{dQ} \tag{B2}$$

$$P = \frac{dCV}{dQ} \tag{B3}$$

Second, observe that the maximum net social value can be found by differentiating net social value, Equation (A10), and setting this derivative equal to zero to find the maximum:

$$\frac{dNSV}{dQ} = 45 - 2.728Q = 0, Q = 16.5 \tag{B4}$$

To be complete, note that the second derivative of (B4) is negative, indicating that $Q = 16.5$ is maximum net social value rather than a minimum.

Notes to Chapter 1

1. Hanley, Shogren, and White seem to imply a similar meaning by defining natural resources as originating in the biosphere, atmosphere, and geosphere. See N. Hanley, J. F. Shogren, and B. White, *Environmental Economics in Theory and Practice* (New York: Oxford University Press, 1997). The authors define environment as including "life forms, energy, material resources, and the atmosphere" (page 1).
2. F. M. Scherer, *Industrial Market Structure and Economic Performance*, 2d ed. (Boston: Houghton Mifflin, 1980), page 10. The concept of product differentiation originated with Edward Chamberlin in 1933 in *The Theory of Monopolistic Competition*.
3. U.S. Senate, Committee on the Judiciary, *Petroleum Industry Competition Act of 1976*, Report to accompany S.2387, June 28, 1976, page 15.
4. The illustrative material on world petroleum in this chapter is partially adapted from my discussion of introductory theory and the electric utility industry in D. Chapman, *Energy Resources and Energy Corporations* (Ithaca: Cornell University Press, 1983).
5. For example, two readable texts that offer a full introduction to these concepts are Ralph T. Byrns and Gerald W. Stone, *Economics* (New York: HarperCollins, 1995) and Robert Frank, *Microeconomics and Behavior* (New York: McGraw-Hill, 1994).
6. For example, in the figure, raising the price from $16 to $17 would reduce sales from 22 billion barrels to 21.5 billion barrels. In other words, a 6.25 percent price increase would reduce sales by 2.27 percent, so the elasticity is -0.36 (i.e., -2.27 percent $\div$ 6.25 percent). This can be calculated by the equation for the demand curve in the next section.
7. For a truly competitive market, an industry supply curve is also the sum of the marginal cost curves of individual firms.
8. The linkage between competition, Pareto Optimality, and producer profit and consumer satisfaction is often referred to as the "First Theorem of Welfare Economics." It reflects the "Invisible Hand" argument of Adam Smith, writing in 1776: "Every individual . . .

intends only his own gain, and he is . . . led by an invisible hand to promote an end which was no part of his intention. . . . By pursuing his own interest he frequently promotes that of the society more effectually." From his *An Inquiry into the Nature and Causes of the Wealth of Nations*, Edwin Cannan, ed. (New Rochelle, NY: Arlington House, 1966), volume 2, pages 29, 30.

9. Of course, the advanced student knows that differentiating the profit function in Equation (1-6) is a common, useful method to find the profit maximum.

10. The student with a previous course in economics knows that, in a competitive market, price is the marginal revenue for an individual producer.

11. Economists use the concepts of long run and short run to reflect different assumptions about fixed investment. Pindyck and Rubinfield use these concepts to define short run and long run producer surplus. R. S. Pindyck and D. L. Rubinfield, *Microeconomics* (New York: Macmillan, 1989), Chapter 8.

12. Byrns and Stone, op cit (pages 500–501) cover accounting profit and economic profit in some detail.

13. M. A. Adelman, "The World Oil Market: Past and Future," 1994 *Energy Journal* Special Issue (15): pages 3–11. Many economists might prefer oligopoly as the best term; see Chapter 9.

14. Frank, and Byrns and Stone, (see Note 5) explain cartels, oligopolies, and monopolies in detail.

15. "Real, inflation-adjusted dollars" enable us to compare prices and incomes in different years by factoring in inflation. The method is explained in Chapter 4.

16. William D. Nordhaus, "Resources as a Constraint to Growth," May 1974 *American Economic Review*, 64:2, page 25. Nordhaus was discussing Robert Solow's comments in his "The Economics of Resources or the Resources of Economics," May 1974 *American Economic Review* 64(2): pages 1–14.

17. For example, W. Nicholson, *Microeconomic Theory* (Chicago: Dryden, 1985), page 708 uses this traditional meaning of a public good. Also, see R. H. Frank, *Microeconomics and Behavior* (New York: McGraw-Hill, 1994), Chapter 19; and R. T. Byrns and G. W. Stone, *Economics* (New York: HarperCollins, 1995), Chapter 32.

18. In Chapter 11 the status of air pollution policy and economics will be examined more intensively. Estimates of environmental damage are reviewed more substantially in Chapters 4 and 5.

19. The sources for Table 1.2 are Darwin Hall, "Social Cost of CO_2 Abatement from Energy Efficiency and Solar Power in the United States," 1992 *Environmental and Resource Economics* (2): pages 491–512; and, "Oil and National Security," November 1992 *Energy Policy*, pages 1089–1096. Also, W. K. Viscusi, et al, "Environmentally Responsible Energy Pricing," 1994 *Energy Journal* 15(2): pages 23–42; and Table 1, External Social Cost Estimates of Petroleum, in D. Chapman and J. Erickson, "Residential Solar Electricity in Developing Countries," April 1995 *Contemporary Economic Policy* 13(2): pages 98–108. Also, S. Fankhauser, "The Social Cost of Greenhouse Gas Emissions," 1994 *Energy Journal* 15(2): pages 23–42. Another summary is U.S. Energy Information Administration, *Electricity Generation and Environmental Externalities*, DOE/EIA-0598 (Washington, DC, September 1995).

20. There are some logical problems with this. Even if negative environmental externalities have been considered in the concept of social cost, there is sometimes a need to consider positive externality. For example, a farm may provide positive scenic and wildlife habitat value for urban and suburban neighbors. Although this is an unintended by-product of the farm's economic activity, it is sufficiently real so that non-farmers have supported legislation for property tax shelters for farms in many states. This subject is discussed in later chapters, especially 13 (Agriculture), 15 (Biodiversity and Endangered Species), and 16 (Kruger National Park).

CHAPTER 2

MEASURING ECONOMIC WELFARE AND ENVIRONMENTAL QUALITY

Is world income increasing? Is environmental quality advanced or reduced by economic growth? In economics, these two questions are the subject of considerable controversy. In this chapter, we analyze the basic perspectives developed by the major schools of thought and discuss some of the empirical data. We will use the concept of environmental externality introduced in the last chapter to explore the meaning of environmental quality. It will be evident that there is material enough to support opposing views.

GDP, GNP, and IPP: Is World Income Increasing?

If we are to examine the relationship between income and environment, we first need to define income. Gross Domestic Product (GDP) and Gross National Product (GNP) are the two best known definitions of a nation's income. GDP is the total production of goods, services, and investment in a country; production is valued at market prices. The major categories for GDP expenditure for 1997 are in Table 2.1.

Gross National Product is similar to GDP but has an important distinction. GDP includes only goods and services produced within a country, but GNP also consid-

TABLE 2.1 U.S. Gross Domestic Product, 1997 (billions of dollars)	
Personal consumption expenditures (food, personal computers, appliances, etc.)	$5,489
Housing construction	327
Business investment (factory machines, buildings, inventory)	845
Government national defense purchases	416
State, local, and federal civilian expenses	1,103
Trade balance (net imports)	−97
Total GDP, $billion	$8,083

Source: Economic Report of the President, February 1998, page 280.

ers ownership of production. GNP includes in a nation's product the value of production that its citizens own in other countries, and it excludes the value of production within the country that is owned by business and individuals in other countries. For some countries, such as the United States, the two definitions give similar estimates.[1]

However, where there is significant foreign ownership, the GDP and GNP numbers will be noticeably different. In 1992, Hong Kong had a higher GNP than GDP. This is probably because Hong Kong business owned and operated factories in China and throughout the world. In contrast, for Puerto Rico, GDP was the higher. This is because much of Puerto Rican business is owned by U. S. and other corporations.[2]

For large economies such as the United States and Japan, the difference between GNP and GDP is negligible, and GDP has become the primary focus for national income data. However, for developing countries, GNP is probably somewhat more closely linked to available national income after netting out the impact of foreign ownership. The World Bank continues to rank the world's economies by GNP per capita, as in the first column in Table 2.2.

In that first column, if GNP per capita measures economic welfare, then Japan is considerably ahead of the United States by more than $10,000 per person.

TABLE 2.2 GNP per Capita Adjusted for Price Differences 1996 and Human Development Index 1995

Economy (selected)	GNP per Capita (original)	Purchasing Power Factor	Corrected GNP per Capita	Ranking of Selected Economies	Human Development Index
Japan	$40,940	.572	$23,420	3	2
Germany	28,870	.731	21,110	4	4
U.S.	28,020	1.000	28,020	1	1
Hong Kong	24,290	.999	24,260	2	7
Italy	19,880	1.001	19,890	6	5
U.K.	19,600	1.018	19,960	5	3
Israel	15,670	1.027	16,100	7	6
South Korea	10,610	1.233	13,080	8	8
Brazil	4,400	1.441	6,340	10	10
Mexico	3,670	2.088	7,660	9	9
Russia	2,410	1.739	4,190	11	11
China	750	4.440	3,330	12	12
India	380	4.158	1,580	13	13
Malawi	180	4.944	890	14	14
World Average	**$5,130**	**1.011**	**6,330**		

Source: World Development Report 1998/99, Table 1. U.K. is United Kingdom. World average covers 133 countries. The "Purchasing Power Factor" column is calculated from the per capita values. The Human Development Index is from United Nations's Development Program, *Human Development Report 1998* (New York and Oxford: Oxford University Press, 1998).

However, international comparisons use the dollar because the U.S. economy is the major world economy, producing 25 percent of total world GNP. This introduces a problem. There are significant price differences between Japan and the United States. Food products and imported products are generally much more costly in Japan than in the United States. The final step in GNP per capita estimates is to factor in international price differences. With this price level correction, the United States becomes the world leader in GNP per capita for 1995. This is shown in Table 2.2 for several countries.

While the Japanese and German values for GNP per capita are adjusted downward by this process, the developing country estimates all increase. Notice that the purchasing power correction raises the China and India figures for GNP per capita above $1,500.

The Human Development Index includes GDP per capita with purchasing power factor adjustment and also includes statistics on literacy and life expectancy. As shown in the table, its rankings are similar. This index is significant because it has included non-monetary factors in a definition of living standards and is generally accepted by economists.

Inflation, Real Income, and the Environmental Kuznets Curve

Economists have been successful in calculating comparative income levels in different countries. Another important analytical success is the concept of a "real dollar." It uses an inflation index to show how income levels and prices compare in different time periods.

For example, we know that the average worker in private industry earned an average of $137 weekly in 1972,[3] and this rose to $424 in 1997. But how do we factor in inflation? The consumer price index rose more than 300 percent over the period. The actual method is simple:

$$\text{1972 Real Wages, in 1997\$} = \frac{\text{1972 Wages}}{\text{CPI}_{1972} \div \text{CPI}_{1997}} \tag{2-1}$$

The calculation is executed in Table 2.3. The result is that real weekly earnings, adjusted for inflation, declined from $526 in 1972 to $424 in 1997.

TABLE 2.3. Inflation and Real Dollars		
Weekly Earnings	*CPI 1982–1984 = 100*	*Weekly Earnings in 1997 dollars*
1972 $137	.418	$526 for 1972
1997 $424	1.605	$424 for 1997

$$\$526 \text{ (1972 real wages in 1997 dollars)} = \frac{\$137}{.418 \div 1.605}$$

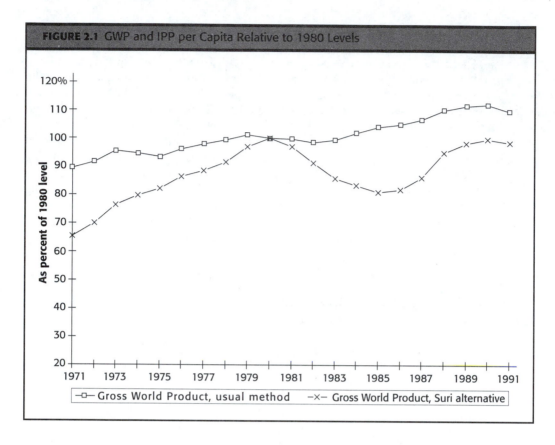

FIGURE 2.1 GWP and IPP per Capita Relative to 1980 Levels

─□─ Gross World Product, usual method   ─×─ Gross World Product, Suri alternative

An interesting problem arises because DPI (disposable personal income) per capita increased from 1972 to 1997 while wages were falling. The interpretation that reconciles both trends is that production workers' earnings have declined since 1972, but income for other wage earners and for property owners has risen. In his review in the *Journal of Economic Literature*, Gary Burtless attributes much of the decline in U.S. production workers' real wages to growing international competition. He also finds that income differentials within the United States are affected by educational levels.[4]

One interesting question that follows from these calculations relates to world income. Has the average worldwide per capita income risen or fallen? Most international economists believe that GNP per capita on a worldwide basis has increased, after adjusting for inflation as well as changing exchange rates between countries. The generally increasing trend is captured by the upper curve in Figure 2.1. It is termed "GWP," or Gross World Product, because it measures Gross National Product on a worldwide basis.

The IPP (International Purchasing Power) curve has been estimated by Vivek Suri.[5] It shows no increase from 1980 to 1991. Most economists think the optimistic curve for per capita world income is correct.

While interpreting economic and environmental statistics is controversial, economic forecasting is open to all. The British magazine *The Economist* asked former OECD finance ministers, London garbage men, Oxford University students, and chairmen of multinational firms to make 10-year predictions about the global economy. At the end of ten years, yes, the garbage men were in first place, tied with company chairmen. The students were in third place, the finance ministers last.[6]

One reason these results matter is because economists believe that the public demand for environmental quality is related to income. There are two distinct versions of this theory. The first version is linear, and I have labeled it the "Ruttan Theory," after Vernon Ruttan.[7] In Figure 2.2, the Ruttan curve shows environmental degradation beginning at a high level, but declining as income increases. In contrast, the "Environmental Kuznets Curve" shows environmental degradation to be rising in an initial stage, up to a turning point, which may be in the $4,000 to $5,000 range. During this phase of economic development, pollution levels and forest degradation increase as incomes grow. However, beyond the turning point, demand for environmental protection reduces both pollution and forest loss.[8] It is important to see that in both theories income levels and living standards strongly influence the desire for environmental quality.

Some economists think that the interaction of trade and rising incomes contribute to rising global pollution. Michael Porter, in contrast, holds that competitive

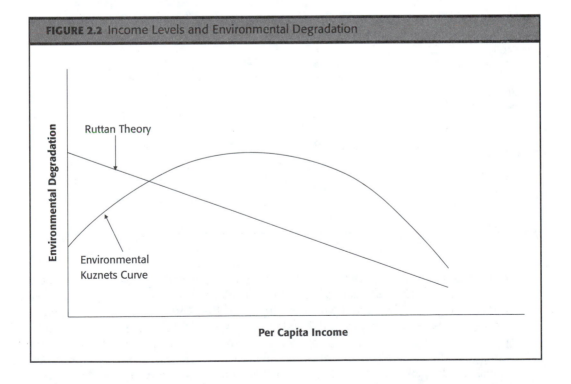

FIGURE 2.2 Income Levels and Environmental Degradation

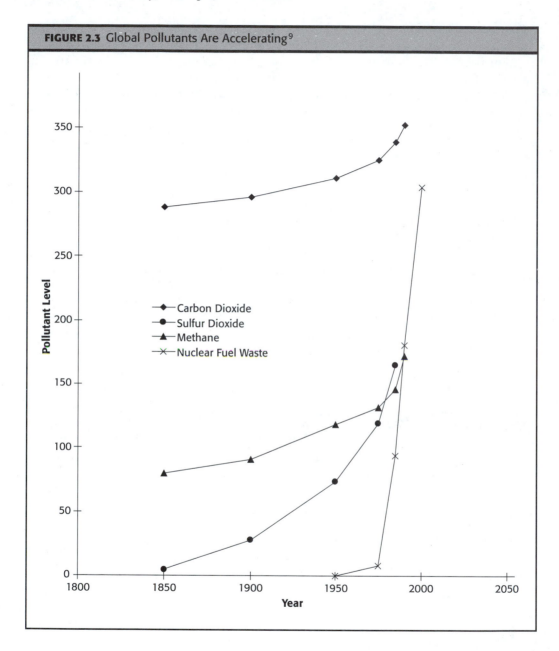

FIGURE 2.3 Global Pollutants Are Accelerating[9]

trade enhances both incomes and environmental quality. This important subject is part of Chapter 17, Macroeconomic Growth, Trade, and the Environment.[10]

   While the Environmental Kuznets Curve and the Ruttan Theory are probably reasonable when applied to individual countries, the global picture does not support either concept. Figure 2.3 reports recent data on total pollutants for carbon dioxide and methane concentration in the air, total weight of sulfur dioxide emissions, and the amount of accumulated nuclear fuel waste. Each of these global pollutants is growing exponentially. If good data were available for the world volume of sewage and other major pollutants, these statistics would probably have similar curves. Figure 2.1 showed that global average income is probably growing (the general belief), but may not be (the Suri curve). Figure 2.3 shows rising global pollution. There is certain to be more research and more controversy on this contentious question of the interaction between income and preferences for environmental protection.

Environmental Accounting and the Index of Sustainable Welfare

In the late 1980s, several innovative economists began working on the concept of environmental accounting. Early leaders in this movement have been Robert Repetto, Ernst Lutz, and Salah El Serafy. They were joined in the 1990s by the U.S. Department of Commerce.[11]

Environmental accounting recognizes that external social cost (the Chapter 1 concept) should be incorporated into the definitions of national and world income. If an individual country is rapidly exhausting its soil, forests, and oil, then normal GDP accounting is overstating that country's income. Environmental accounting has arisen through the interest in sustainability: gain or loss in environmental resources should be considered as equivalent to gain or loss in building construction or depreciation.

This concept is illustrated in Table 2.4 as a hypothetical partial accounting for the world economy in 1996. It should be emphasized that the entries are illustrative. Presently there is no generally accepted factual basis for estimating these global values.

While Table 2.4 is intended only to be illustrative, some economists and scientists have attempted an environmental accounting of all the earth's ecosystem benefits

---

TABLE 2.4 Hypothetical Environmental Accounting, World Basis Air and Water Quality, Oil Depletion, Soil Erosion, and Timber   (trillion U.S. dollars, 1995)

Gross World Product, sum of all GNPs	$28.0 trillion
Less: Loss of air and water quality	.8 trillion
Depletion of world resources	.3 trillion
Soil erosion for agriculture	.6 trillion
Harvesting and loss of world's forests	.5 trillion
Total environmental depletion	$2.2 trillion
Depreciation of factories, business, homes	$3.5 trillion
Equals: Real Net World Product, adjusted for depletion of environmental resources and normal economic depreciation, illustration	$22.3 trillion

Note: All entries except Gross World Product are illustrative.

to human society. The Costanza group's best estimate is $33 trillion on an annual basis, while Pimentel's group finds a much lower $3 trillion per year.[12]

This work is innovative and controversial, focused on problems of unquestionable importance, but with numerical values of uncertain confidence. The accuracy and acceptance of future work on both the global and national levels will determine the importance of the role that environmental accounting will play in both economic and environmental policy.

Repetto's pioneering work in Indonesia[13] provided an example of the potential for empirical environmental accounting for individual countries. Repetto's team calculated estimates for soil erosion and the depletion of petroleum resources. Their work was thorough. For their analysis of forestry accounts, they estimated new growth as well as the larger reductions from harvesting and deforestation. Figure 2.4 shows that environmental accounting was significant. Without it, conventional GDP grew 7 percent annually over the period. With environment in the accounts, growth in revised net domestic product (RNDP) was smaller, at 4 percent.

It turned out that annual loss in soil fertility was about equal to the annual gain in crop production. Repetto's group notes "These estimates suggest that current increases in farm output in Indonesia's uplands are being achieved almost wholly at the expense of future output. . . . The process of soil erosion represents a transfer of wealth from the future to the present."

Efforts at environmental accounting in the United States have had unexpected results. The Commerce Department's work in 1994 focused on the year 1987 for a comprehensive empirical study of the United States. The results: both timber and oil resource values were higher at the end of the year than at the beginning. Contrast this empirical result with the hypothetical negative depletion effects for the world values in Table 2.4 and the Indonesian work in Figure 2.4.

The problem encountered in the U.S. work is that prices for both oil and timber increased significantly during the year. This represents an important methodological challenge for economists: forest timber is being harvested, and oil is being produced, but if prices fluctuate, how should the remaining resources be valued? Future research needs to resolve this problem if adoption of environmental accounting is to be facilitated.

Herman Daly, John Cobb, and Clifford Cobb expanded environmental accounting significantly with their development of the ISW, the Index of Sustainable Welfare.[14] The subject is a redefinition of GNP per capita in the United States over the period 1950–1986. It is partially related to the Human Development Index (Table 2.2), but the ISW includes analysis of environmental externalities as well as variables related to education and health.

The positive externalities are significant, summing to more than one-third of GNP. The most important item is housework. Daly and the Cobbs reviewed empirical studies of unpaid work by housewives for child care, cleaning, and cooking. They conclude that this unpaid work averages 50 hours per week, and they assign it an hourly value equal to the average paid wage of domestic workers. It equals 7 percent of GNP.

The negative external social costs sum to 50 percent of the GNP in the United States. The most important category is long-term environmental damage at 15 percent of GNP. The authors believe it is directly linked to energy use, and they assess the damage as equivalent to 50¢ per barrel of oil, in 1972 dollars. We can use the

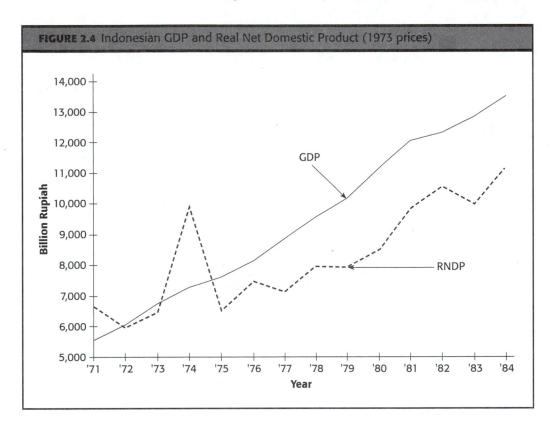

FIGURE 2.4 Indonesian GDP and Real Net Domestic Product (1973 prices)

economic method discussed above for correcting for inflation. Therefore, in 1994 dollars, the Daly group assesses long-term environmental damage of energy use as equivalent to $1.75 per barrel of oil. Since each barrel holds 42 gallons of oil, this is a low externality figure of 4¢ per gallon. (Compare this Daly-Cobb value to the $15 per barrel external social cost range in Table 1.2 in the first chapter. Obviously, Daly and Cobb are much lower in their estimate.)

The Daly group assigns dollar values to seven other external environmental costs. All together, the 23 positive and negative externalities are about 80 percent of GNP. The end result of this accounting is a picture where the per capita index of sustainable welfare in dollars peaked between 1969 and 1979, while conventional real GNP per capita is still rising. Part of their work is reproduced in Figure 2.5. Clifford Cobb continued this approach in the 1990s with the Genuine Progress Indicator.[15]

In another popular context, the Institute for Southern Studies has taken a different approach to environmental accounting and indexing. They have developed 20 environmental indicators for each state and have repeated the process for 20 economic indicators. The indicators in each category are summed to arrive at a final "Environmental Health Score" and an "Economic Health Score." The results are summarized in Figure 2.6.[16]

Notwithstanding the nonacademic aspects of this work, the correlation between economic value and environmental value is evident. The figure raises again the question of the "Environmental Kuznets Curve." Is the high correlation because

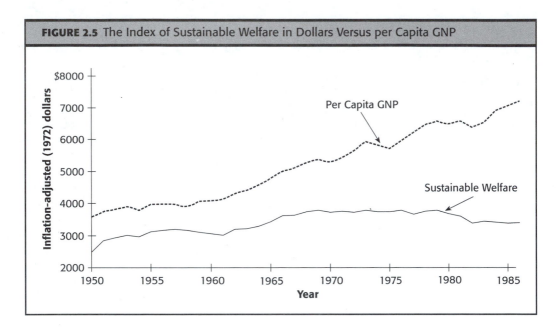

FIGURE 2.5 The Index of Sustainable Welfare in Dollars Versus per Capita GNP

economic growth leads to environmental protection, or does the correlation arise because high environmental quality encourages economic growth?

Finally, as an example of the cultural and social differences that affect our meaning of environmental quality, I want to summarize the most surprising results of a survey of industrial and professional leaders in the Russian industrial city of Novokuznetsk. Located in southern Siberia, this city is a major world producer of steel, coal, aluminum, and chemicals. The most important environmental problem was identified as crime. It came ahead of major health hazards from air and water pollution. Obviously, the definition of environment depends on the country.[17]

The Gallup International Institute reports some provocative findings that economists need to reconcile with other work.[18] The Gallup Institute used a survey sample of 30,000 individuals in 24 countries, on every continent but Australia. Low, middle, and high income countries were appropriately represented. The conclusion is surprising: "Public concern over environmental problems was more likely to decline rather than increase with the level of national affluence."

In summary, world incomes appear to be rising, as is global pollution. The United States follows Japan on GNP per capita incomes, but when purchasing power differences are considered, the United States is the world leader in average income per capita. In general, the process of adjusting national incomes for prices raises the apparent income levels of low income countries.

The adjustment for inflation in prices over time allows the comparison of incomes in different years, and the general conclusion is that global and U.S. incomes have risen, but not for all groups.

The Environmental Kuznets Curve holds that environmental degradation increases as countries develop, but that as incomes pass the $4,000–$5,000 per capita

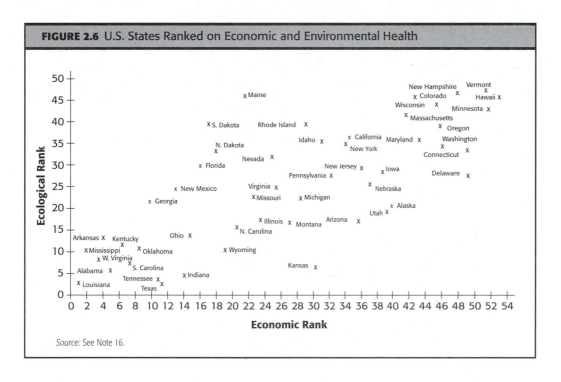

FIGURE 2.6 U.S. States Ranked on Economic and Environmental Health

Source: See Note 16.

mark, pollution levels fall as higher incomes allow greater levels of environmental protection. In Chapter 12 (Water Quality Economics), this concept is explored in the context of income and expenditures on sanitation and clean water supply.

Environmental accounting raises important issues about sustainability and the measurement of externality values and national income. Chapters 19 and 20 (Ecological Economics and Sustainability) address the broad question of sustainable economic welfare. Chapter 3 examines innovative thinking in environmental economics that is beginning to measure the value of positive and negative externalities.

Questions for Discussion and Analysis

1. Do you think the distinction between GNP and GDP is important? Explain your conclusion.

2. In 1972, the price of gasoline averaged 36¢ per gallon in the United States. Use Equation (2-1) to find the inflation-adjusted price today for that price. How does it compare to current prices?

3. It is widely believed that Native Americans lived in harmony with their environment. How might this belief contradict the Ruttan Theory and the Environmental Kuznets Curve (EKC)?

4. Russia and Mexico experienced reduced incomes over the 1990s. What does the EKC predict for the environment?

5. Most economists believe that global incomes are rising. If this is true, what does the EKC predict?

6. The growing interest of environmental economists in sustainability has led to significant interest in environmental accounting and measures of sustainable welfare. Summarize both: do you believe they are useful economic concepts? What are some of the problems in their use?

7. The Institute for Southern Studies, an advocacy group, prepared the study used for Figure 2.6. Should this affect our interpretation of the figure's validity?

Notes to Chapter 2

1. The expenditure or cost definition of GDP is used in Table 2.1. There is also a standard income-based definition of GDP and GNP. It includes wages and salaries, business income, and depreciation. Both the income definition and the expenditures definition will have the same total for each year. This will be well known to the student with macroeconomics courses using such texts as Robert J. Gordon, *Macroeconomics* (1993), and Ralph T. Byrns and Gerald W. Stone, *Economics* (New York: HarperCollins, 1995).

2. The discussion of the differences between GDP and GNP for Hong Kong and Puerto Rico are from *World Development Report 1994.*

3. *Economic Report of the President*, February 1998, Statistical Tables. This is also the source of the data on disposable personal income per capita.

4. Volume 13(2):800–816, June 1995.

5. The basic difference in method between The World Bank and Suri-Chapman is the use of deflation indexes. The World Bank relies upon inflation data reported by each country for each year, then adjusts the whole series with a single exchange rate. The Suri method uses only the U.S. GNP deflation index for all countries, after adjusting for exchange rates for each year. International Purchasing Power (IPP) is not identical to the Purchasing Power Factor in Table 2.3. IPP calculations assume that dynamic change in international purchasing power of national currencies is reflected by changing exchange rates between those currencies and the U.S. dollar. For details, see "Are World Living Standards Rising?" Chapter 4 in V. Suri, *Environment, Trade, and Economic Growth*, Ph.D. Dissertation, Cornell University, 1997.

6. From *The Economist*, June 3, 1995, page 70.

7. Writing in 1971, Vernon W. Ruttan argued that the demand for environmental quality not only increases with income, but grows more rapidly than the increase in income. In economic terminology, the elasticity of demand for environmental quality increases as income grows. From Ruttan's Presidential Address "Technology and the Environment," *American Journal of Agricultural Economics*, December 1971, 53(5):707–717. Ruttan also suggested that the capacity to solve problems of living standards and environment is negatively affected by population density and the rate of population growth. Figure 2.2 shows the Ruttan Theory as predicting that the decline of environmental degradation is derived from the demand for environmental protection.

8. Peter J. G. Pearson used the phrase "Environmental Kuznets Curve" in 1994. The concept was used by Selden and Song, Grossman and Krueger, and others. It is linked to the work of Simon Kuznets 40 years earlier because of the similar U-shape of the relationship between income inequality and rising income. See *References* for complete references for Selden and Song, Grossman and Krueger, and Antle and Heidebrink.

9. The source for Figure 2.3 is D. Chapman, J. Agras, and V. Suri, "International Law, Industrial Location, and Pollution," Fall 1995 *Indiana Journal of Global Legal Studies* 3(1):5–33.

10. The Porter Theory and literature is an important part of Chapter 17.
11. See publications by Repetto, Lutz, El Serafy, and U.S. Department of Commerce, Bureau of Economic Analysis entries in *References* below.
12. Both the Costanza and Pimentel groups' work are summarized in "Putting a Price Tag on Nature," 16 May 1997 *Science* 276:1029.
13. See Repetto et al. in *References* below.
14. The Index is based upon the calculations of Clifford Cobb and is presented in detail in the appendix of *For The Common Good* by Herman E. Daly and John B. Cobb, Jr. (Boston, MA: Beacon 1989, 1994). The mention in the text of percent of GNP for externalities relates to the GNP value for 1986.
15. C. Cobb, T. Halstead, and J. Rowe, "If the GDP Is Up, Why Is America Down?" October 1995 *The Atlantic Monthly*, pages 59–78.
16. Institute for Southern Studies, "Gold and Green," Durham, NC, 1994.
17. The survey was undertaken by Rob Robinson and me in 1995 as part of the Novokuznetsk 2010 Project. The Project was headed by Ray Reaves, then Planning Director of Allegheny County, and was sponsored by US-AID. Robinson is a planner with Urban Design Associates in Pittsburgh.
18. R. E. Dunlap, G. H. Gallup, Jr., and A. M. Gallup, *Health of the Planet*, Gallup International Institute, Princeton, 1993. The conclusion was made by Dunlap in a letter to 26 May 1995 *Science* 268:1115.

References (for Notes 8, 11, 13)

Agras, J., and D. Chapman, "A Dynamic Approach to the Environmental Kuznets Curve," *Ecological Economics*, in press.

Antle, John M., and Gregg Heidebrink, "Environment and Development," *Economic Development and Cultural Change*, April 1995 43(3):603–625.

Suri, V. and D. Chapman, "Economic Growth, Trade and Energy: Implications for the Environmental Kuznets Curve," May 1998 *Ecological Economics*, 25(2): 195–208.

El Serafy, Salah, "The Proper Calculation of Income from Depletable Natural Resources," in *Environmental and Resource Accounting and Their Relevance to the Measurement of Sustainable Income*, (Ernst Lutz and Salah El Serafy, eds.), World Bank, Washington, DC, 1988.

Grossman, G. M., and A. B. Krueger, "Environmental Impacts of a North American Free Trade Agreement," in *The U.S.-Mexico Free Trade Agreement*, (P. Garber, ed.), MIT Press, Cambridge, MA, 1993, pages 165–177.

Lutz, Ernst, ed., *Toward Improved Accounting for the Environment*, World Bank, Washington, DC, 1993.

Pearson, Peter J. G., *Energy, Externalities, and Environmental Quality: Will Development Cure the Ills It Creates?* Surrey Energy Economics Centre, University of Surrey, Guildford, UK, 1994.

Repetto, Robert, William Magrath, Michael Wells, Christine Beer, and Fabrizio Rossini, *Wasting Assets: Natural Resources in the National Income Accounts*, World Resources Institute, Washington, DC, 1989.

Selden, Thomas M., and Daqing Song, "Environmental Quality and Development: Is There a Kuznets Curve for Air Pollution Emissions?" *Journal of Environmental Economics and Management*, September 1994 27(2):147–162.

U.S. Department of Commerce, Bureau of Economic Analysis, "Integrated Economic and Environmental Satellite Accounts," and "Accounting for Mineral Resources: Issues and BEA's Initial Estimates," in *Survey of Current Business*, April 1994 74(4).

CHAPTER 3

VALUING THE ENVIRONMENT AND BENEFIT-COST ANALYSIS

Preface: One Historical Perspective

The quantitative analysis of environmental benefits has made considerable progress in the last quarter of the 20th Century. If today's techniques had been available earlier, public policies may have taken different paths. In particular, the notorious Snail Darter–Tellico Dam controversy in Tennessee would probably have had a different outcome.

My introduction to this Little Tennessee River area arose on several canoe trips with friends, one in particular being an enthusiastic trout angler. This was before construction of the dam. I can still recall the wonder of putting ashore for a wilderness camp under the silhouette of The Great Smokies. To my amazement, everywhere we stepped we saw Native American and Pioneer artifacts. Pipes, awls, shot, nails, arrowheads, all there to remind us of another era.

I later learned that we had been at the site of the main city of the Cherokee Nation prior to the 1800s. This was Echota, a Cherokee capital until the infamous "Trail of Tears" moved most of the Cherokee to Oklahoma. Nearby were the remains of Fort Loudon, the first English settlement west of the Southern Appalachian mountains.

The Tellico Dam was built by the Tennessee Valley Authority, with recreation and power being its primary benefits. The recreation was to be based upon the dam's reservoir: water-skiing, boating, reservoir fishing. One of the incidental benefits was recreational property development. Farmland around the reservoir was first condemned by the TVA, and then resold to new buyers for real estate development. In this process, families that had farmed along the Little Tennessee River for a century were removed.

The controversy over the dam is widely known because a local fish, the snail darter, was endangered by the project. Consequently, the project was temporarily halted. Finally, Congress exempted the Reservoir Project from the requirements of the Endangered Species Act, and the dam was completed.

Allan Randall[1] argues that benefit-cost analysis gave contradictory results on the narrow margin of net benefits for the project. If modern methods of analysis

Acknowledgment: To William Schulze, John Whitehead, and Gregory Poe on valuation, and to Jon Erickson on historical perspective here.

(particularly contingent valuation) had been available in the early 1970s, before the reservoir flooded the river basin, a logical approach would have considered the valuation of the loss of Cherokee and Pioneer history. With contingent valuation of the historical significance of the site included, there seems to me little doubt that the project would have been rejected.

In economic theory, each individual seeks maximum satisfaction by finding the right balance between income or utility, material consumption and nonmonetary values, and risk or safety. The objective of valuation is to determine methods for the empirical estimation of the values placed upon environmental goods, resources, and policies. It is the general question of environmental valuation which is the subject of this chapter.

Measuring Environmental Benefits: Prospect Theory and Relative Gain

Is our perception of environmental value strongly affected by the direction of the change?

The pioneering work of Kahneman and Tversky[2] has been adopted by many environmental economists because of its helpfulness in clarifying the issue of environmental benefit valuation. As explained in recent work, their theory of relative change predicts that environmental loss is relatively more important than is environmental gain.

The problem of African elephant protection helps illustrate the theory. The current population of elephants throughout Africa is about 600,000. Suppose a worldwide study concludes that there is a global willingness to contribute to a fund to protect more elephants. The survey shows that about $15 billion might be contributed to add a 20 percent increase of 100,000 elephants to the current population level. But it also shows that if, instead, 500,000 more elephants were to be protected, doubling the population, the fund would raise only $5 billion more, a total of $20 billion. The value of elephants to the global public is not increasing as rapidly as the growth in the elephant population level. This is represented in the upper-right section of Figure 3.1; that curve shows diminishing willingness to pay as the number of additional elephants declines.

Now suppose that, instead of considering a relative increase in the protected population, there is a proposal to reduce the level by 500,000 elephants down to 100,000, an 83 percent reduction. This might arise because at some future date all of the current protected areas cannot be continued, or because with increased human population, elephant-human conflict accelerates.

According to the figure, the global community would be willing to pay $100 billion to avert the proposed reduction in elephants.

In its basic form, the Kahneman-Tversky theory asserts that the actual current number of elephants is not important: we value change, and we especially wish to avoid negative change. If the status quo were to be 2 million elephants rather than the actual 600,000, the theory predicts a small willingness to pay for an increase, and a large willingness to pay to prevent loss. Logically, the authors consider both relative change and absolute numbers to be important.

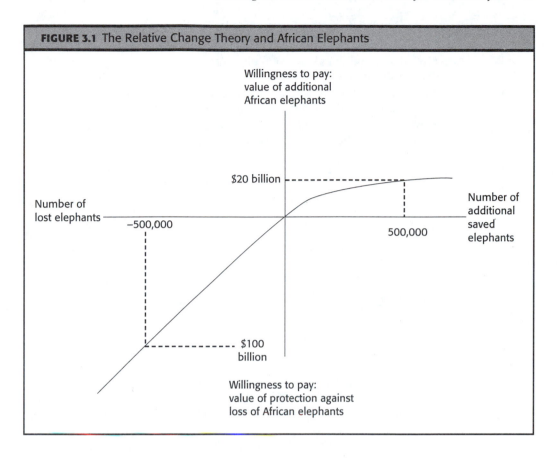

FIGURE 3.1 The Relative Change Theory and African Elephants

The authors of the theory called it 'prospect theory,' to reflect the importance of the prospect of change. The theory has been illustrated with reference to African wildlife, a subject explored in greater detail in Chapter 16. This brief introduction to African wildlife can illustrate several concepts which are frequently used in the discussion of external environmental cost and value. They are defined in Table 3.1. Of course, these definitions are widely used in considering other subjects. For example, the original meaning of bequest is defined as a gift left by a will from one relative to another. The concept has expanded to include bequests to colleges, as well as to organizations which promote the protection of African wildlife. In environmental economics, the bequest concept plays a small but growing role in climate change economics; it is taken up in Chapter 18.

These concepts can reflect both positive and negative impact. For example, positive existence value for African elephants is widely shared, although the range of values is likely to be very great. However, households in African villages that have experienced serious crop damage or personal injury may hold negative existence values for nearby elephants.

The conceptual problems become very real when empirical efforts are undertaken to measure these values, particularly with contingent valuation.

TABLE 3.1 Economic Concepts of External Nonmarket Environmental Value

Altruism: An individual or group places positive value on the welfare of other individuals or groups.

Bequest: The welfare of future generations of a family or of society is considered in making decisions now.

Existence: Value is derived from knowing that some aspect of the environment exists, apart from the individual directly seeing or experiencing the value.

Option: A chance or probability of a future visit or use creates a positive value.

Comment: In Chapter 15, "Biodiversity and Endangered Species," externality concepts are explored in greater detail, especially Table 15.6 and the discussion of it. The first discussion of external nonmarket environmental values is due to John Krutilla in 1967.[3]

Contingent Valuation: The Economic Value of Environmental Benefits

The use of survey methods to determine values for environmental protection has grown rapidly in the 1990s. The number of publications probably exceeds 2,000.[4] This survey or experimental method has come to be called 'contingent valuation,' or CV. It implies that valuation is made contingent on the circumstances described in the survey. Estimated value is dependent upon the actual experiment or survey. In the survey, CV researchers describe the environmental good or resource, describe the change in the resource to be valued, present descriptions of policies and payments, and then ask valuation questions. Questions #2 and #3 in the Exxon Valdez survey in Table 3.2 show how respondents are asked about the value of nonmarket externalities.

An excerpt of a detailed questionnaire related to the Exxon Valdez oil spill is represented in the table; it is abstracted from work by several leaders in the contingent valuation field.[5] One result from the study: the mean willingness to pay for a program to reduce the risk of similar damage was a one-time tax payment of $31 per household.

The contingent valuation survey has also been applied to air pollution control benefit estimation. As coal-burning power plants began to be developed in the Southwestern United States, the problem arose of valuing the benefits of clean air. Rowe, d'Arge, and Brookshire[6] surveyed both residents and tourists near Farmington, New Mexico. They showed photographs to survey participants, with each photograph representing different pollution and visibility levels. They reported an average willingness to pay (WTP) of $7 per month for residents to avoid pollution-reduced visibility falling from 75 miles to 25 miles. The residents would assume this cost through higher electric rates or a payroll deduction.

In contrast, if the electric utilities were to pay residents for the right to increase pollution, compensation demanded as the average willingness to accept (WTA)

TABLE 3.2 Excerpt Adapted from a Contingent Valuation Questionnaire, Valdez Alaska Oil Spill, by Mitchell and Carson for the Alaska Attorney General

#1. We are faced with many problems in this country, none of which can be solved easily or inexpensively. I am going to name some of the problems, and for each one I'd like you to tell me whether you think we should spend more, the same, or less money than we are spending now.

	Great Deal More	Some- what More	Same Amount	Some- what Less	Great Deal Less	Not Sure
Giving foreign aid to poor countries	1	2	3	4	5	6
Making sure we have enough energy for homes, cars, and business	1	2	3	4	5	6
Fighting crime	1	2	3	4	5	6
Making highways safer	1	2	3	4	5	6
Improving public education	1	2	3	4	5	6
Protecting the environment	1	2	3	4	5	6

CARD 4, read to respondents by interviewers with indicated instructions

During the period of the spill there were about one and a half million seabirds and sea ducks of various species in the spill area inside and outside Prince William Sound. (POINT)

   As you can see from this card, 22,600 dead birds were found. (POINT)

   The actual number of birds killed by the oil was larger because not all the bodies were recovered. Scientists estimate that the total number of birds killed by the spill was between 75,000 and 150,000.

   About three-fourths of the dead birds found were murres, the black and white bird I showed you earlier. This is shown in the first line of the card. (POINT) Because an estimated 350,000 murres live in the spill area, this death toll, though high, does not threaten the species.

   One hundred of the area's approximately 5,000 bald eagles were also found dead from the oil. The spill did not threaten any of the Alaskan bird species, including the eagles, with extinction. (PAUSE)

   Bird populations occasionally suffer large losses from disease or other natural causes. Based on this experience, scientists expect the populations of all these Alaskan birds to recover within 3 to 5 years after the spill. (PAUSE)

(Continued)

TABLE 3.2 *(Continued)*

CARD 5

The only mammals killed by the spill were sea otters and harbor seals. This card shows information about what happened to Prince William Sound. According to scientific studies, about 580 otters and 100 seals in the Sound were killed by the spill. Scientists expect the population size of these two species will return to normal within a couple of years after the spill.

Many species of fish live in these waters. Because most of the oil floated on the surface of the water, the spill harmed few fish. Scientific studies indicate there will be no long-term harm to any of the fish populations.

#2. Of course, whether people would vote for or against the escort ship program depends on how much it will cost their household.

At present, government officials estimate the program will cost your household a total of $_____. You would pay this in a special one-time charge in addition to your regular federal taxes. This money would only be used for the program to prevent damage from another large oil spill in Prince William Sound. (PAUSE)

If the program cost your household a total of $_____ would you vote for the program or against it?

#3. What if the final cost estimates showed that the program would cost your household a total of $_____. Would you vote for or against the program?

#4. What is it about the program that made you willing to pay something for it?

#5. Before the survey, did you think the damage caused by the Valdez oil spill was more serious than was described to you, less serious, or about the same as described?

#6. Is anyone in your household an angler, birdwatcher, backpacker, or environmentalist?

#7. This card shows amounts of yearly incomes. Which category best describes the total income from all members of your family before taxes? Please include all sources.

Notes: Parenthetical statements such as "PAUSE" and "POINT" are instructions for the interviewers. In questions #2 and #3, various amounts were used according to a preset pattern. The amounts were in six stages from $5 to $250. Another question repeated #3 with a different amount used by the interviewer. The questionnaire included 51 questions, but no respondent answered all of them.

Respondents were told that oil companies would also contribute through a special tax to the oil spill prevention program. However, respondents were not asked their willingness to pay for the program if oil companies were required to finance it completely through higher gasoline or heating oil prices.

The authors estimate lost passive use value from the oil spill at $2.8 billion. This is the result of their survey estimate of $31 per household, multiplied by 91 million households.

greater pollution was a much higher $71 per month. This strong difference between WTP and WTA is analogous to the prediction of the Kahneman and Tversky theory of relative gain and relative loss. Here, the implication may be that moral liability is attached to the agent that creates the problem, even if the product—electricity—is widely used by all the residents. In fact, survey participants always state a higher value for accepting a loss (WTA) than they will indicate through willingness to pay (WTP) to prevent the loss.[7]

There are many acknowledged problems with the contingent valuation survey method.[8] *Embedding* means that important values not directly related to the immediate question may influence the actual response. Suppose I ask the question "What are you willing to pay to reduce power plant pollution in the Grand Canyon?" The respondent may be considering the reduction of power plant pollution in all of the Western National Parks. In this case, the Grand Canyon pollution problem is embedded within the Western Parks pollution problem. Consequently, the responses about the Grand Canyon may overstate actual values relevant to that location itself.

Hypothetical bias may arise if the respondents know that in fact they will make no payment. This may lead some of the respondents to give a higher willingness to pay in the survey than they otherwise would. Some recent research has actually collected payments from persons in the survey and compared the actual payments to stated willingness to pay. As expected, actual payments turn out to be less than survey WTP.

Strategic bias can be used if the respondent seeks a 'free ride,' believing that other participants will financially support the environmental policy. This is particularly a problem for public goods as defined in Chapter 1. However, the 'free ride' problem may be reduced by the hypothetical nature of CV questions.

Survey technique bias can influence responses in many ways. As discussed, WTP is always less than WTA. Mail surveys will generally have fewer respondents than personal interviews, but interviews may influence the direction of responses.

These issues and others are reviewed in the report of a respected panel of economists for the National Oceanic and Atmospheric Administration (NOAA). It was chaired by two Nobel prize economists, Kenneth Arrow and Robert Solow, and issued its findings in the *Report of the NOAA Panel on Contingent Valuation*. To summarize, "The Panel concludes that under [a number of stringent guidelines] CV studies convey helpful information. . . . There will always be controversy where intangible losses have to be evaluated in monetary terms."[9]

The Travel Cost Method

The contingent valuation method has dominated recent work in environmental valuation. The travel cost method (TCM) originated in the 1960s through efforts to value outdoor recreation at multipurpose reservoir projects.

Both methods have the same objective: estimating the value of environmental resources. Each seeks to estimate the WTP for using or protecting a resource. In Chapter 1, consumer value was defined as the value to consumers of using a product (see Figures 1.7 and 1.8). For nonmarket environmental resources, valuation

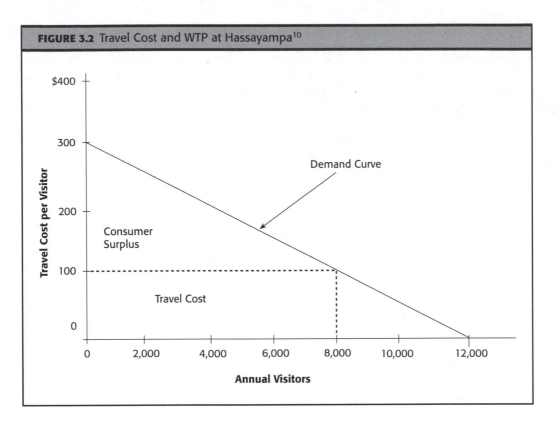

FIGURE 3.2 Travel Cost and WTP at Hassayampa[10]

seeks to measure a similar willingness to pay for environmental objectives. As we noted at the end of that chapter, environmental public goods and related externalities are important components of environmental valuation.

The TCM, however, focuses on use values rather than Table 3.1's nonmarket values. Figure 3.2 represents a study of visitors to the Hassayampa River Preserve in Arizona, operated by the Nature Conservancy.[11] It is a protected wooded area, an undisturbed river ecosystem of cottonwoods and willow, with surrounding mesquite chaparral.

The figure is a simplified representation of the Crandall, Colby, and Rait study of Hassayampa visitors. It shows a demand curve where the number of visitors to this natural area is related to the travel cost per visitor. The 8,000 visitors averaged $100 cost per person to visit the preserve.

The valuation concept of willingness to pay to visit a site is very similar to the logic in Chapter 1 that relates the demand curve to consumer value, cost, and consumer surplus. The consumer surplus of visitors to Hassayampa is the area above travel cost and below the WTP demand curve.

This TCM lends itself to empirical work, but, as with the contingent valuation method, results must be carefully interpreted. Embedding can be a problem here also. For example, a family may have been on their way to the Grand Canyon, and the value of their stop at the Hassayampa may not accurately be reflected in their travel cost. The TCM is often used in conjunction with contingent valuation, so that the two methods provide comparative benchmarks for value estimation.[12]

Valuing Environmental Quality's Impact on Real Estate: The Hedonic Approach

A third technique for measuring the empirical significance of environmental externality is the housing value method. The basic assumption[13] is that measuring the interaction of pollution with housing values shows a behavioral willingness to pay as acted upon in actual markets. It is formally defined as 'HPV,' hedonic property value. The word 'hedonic' in the phrase emphasizes the idea that economists are seeking observable monetary aspects of satisfaction with housing.

A property value study will typically use statistical analysis to relate housing values to pollution levels, or nearness to a polluted site. The study will also consider the household's number of children, income, and education. In this respect it is similar to a CV study: the investigation seeks to identify all the major factors affecting value and then isolate the measure of external environmental social cost.

The Schulze group focused on home property values affected by the formal designation of nearby hazardous waste sites. Because cleanup is financed by a national trust fund, the hazardous sites are popularly known as "Superfund Sites." Their review of 13 studies led them to offer the generalized relationship that property value losses are significant near Superfund Sites, and have disappeared before a distance of 7 miles from sites. Figure 3.3 is adapted from their work[14] and shows the results of two studies.

Just as real estate value is affected by a home's location with respect to hazardous waste sites, economic research has found that air pollution levels affect residential property values. At high levels, particulate soot, ozone, carbon monoxide, and sulfur gas affect breathing and illness for healthy individuals. At low levels, visibility is reduced without significant health impact except for sensitive individuals with asthma and other respiratory illnesses. Consequently, there is an observable relationship between home values and air pollution. In addition, there is corrosion of building surfaces, vehicles, historical structures, and other physical and natural objects as a result of air pollution damage.

Barry Field's review of studies of seven North American cities finds a clear but modest relationship. A $200,000 home would lose $5,000–$6,000 in sale value if air pollution is increased 20 percent, according to this relationship.[15]

With a different type of air pollution, a study of hog manure odor found that a 1 percent increase in manure per acre resulted in a nine-tenths of 1 percent reduction in real estate value for houses within one–half mile of the manure. The loss in value declined as distance from the manure increased. Perhaps 'hedonic analysis' does not capture the full meaning of the problem.[16]

The survey by V. Kerry Smith and Ju-Chin Huang is more comprehensive as well as more cautious. They review 37 empirical studies and conclude that the HPV method shows a significant but small relationship between housing values and air pollution. They also emphasize the importance of income in defining the housing

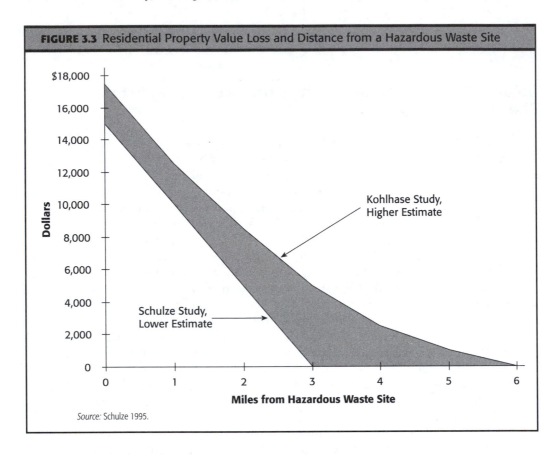

FIGURE 3.3 Residential Property Value Loss and Distance from a Hazardous Waste Site

Source: Schulze 1995.

value–pollution relationship. A consensus viewpoint of the extensive research on HPV is put well by Smith and Huang: "Based on the evidence available for air pollution, the [hedonic property value] model has proved successful in detecting the direction of air quality's influence on residential property values."[17]

The Value of Life, Health, Risk, and Safety

Contingent valuation and property value techniques were reviewed in the context of pollution problems such as hazardous waste sites and air pollution levels. Both methods are considered to be 'hedonic' techniques: they seek to measure and quantify satisfaction with the human and natural environment. A third approach, health and risk analysis, employs economics to quantify the relationship between environmental protection and improved human health and safety. In evaluating the economic benefits of reduced risk of death, economists are again exploring a subject that is simultaneously important and controversial. Some aspects of the subject are reasonably empirical. Table 3.3 was prepared by Kip Viscusi.[18] Of the personal hazards shown there, heavy cigarette smoking is the most serious, and accidental death by fire is the least likely.

TABLE 3.3 Fatality Risk in the United States

Source of Risk	Annual Fatality Risk
A. General	
Cigarette smoking (1.5 packs per day)	1 in 150
Cancer	1 in 300
Motor vehicle accident	1 in 5,000
Home accident	1 in 11,000
Poisoning	1 in 37,000
Fire	1 in 50,000
B. Occupational	
Mining	1 in 3,200
Construction	1 in 4,300
Manufacturing	1 in 2,400
Retail sales	1 in 56,000
Finance, insurance, real estate	1 in 77,000

Source: Viscusi, pages 1913 and 1929.

Many factors, however, enter into our personal subjective valuation of objective risk. Some of these factors include personal preference for or aversion to particular risky activities, health and genetic history, age, the perception of family obligations, and the individual's trade-off between risk and income.

Before reviewing the advances that have been made in this field, it is helpful to outline some of the difficulties in measuring value. Suppose that we have perfect knowledge about an individual's subjective trade-off between risk and compensation. Figure 3.4B shows it sharply increasing as risk grows toward a 50-50 probability of death. In contrast, at the very lowest levels of risk in Figure 3.4A, it is fairly constant. But there is an indication in Figure 3.4A that this hypothetical individual requires a minimum value of $500 to accept any risk of death.[19]

Another individual might have very different preferences. For example, a person who is not risk averse may accept some risk with no consideration of compensation, and require lesser compensation at every level of risk.

There is an unpleasant ethical and logical problem implicit in Figure 3.4. The compensation curve is accelerating as fatality risk increases. Consider that an average annual fatality risk of .01 (one in one hundred) over a 70-year life implies a lifetime average chance of .49 of a death from an accident or environmental hazard.[20] So the rapid increase in the curve reflects the subject's awareness that the subject's own mortality is increasingly the focus of attention.

Consider this dilemma: in a group of 50, one person can accept a near-certain death that saves the other 49, or all 50 can accept a .02 (one in fifty) mortality risk.

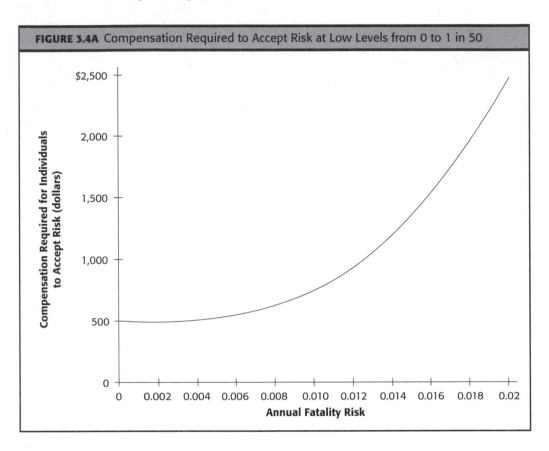

FIGURE 3.4A Compensation Required to Accept Risk at Low Levels from 0 to 1 in 50

In statistics, the expected outcome is similar for each alternative: the most likely statistical result is one death from the group of 50. But we cannot know which alternative is superior. It is a question of ethics and philosophy.

We can, however, use the figure to see that the hypothetical individual would demand $2,500 to accept a risk of .02 (one in fifty) per year. Fifty similar individuals would demand a total of $125,000. In contrast, any one of these hypothetical persons would require $4 million to accept a .25 (one in four) annual risk.

Consequently, regardless of the true numerical values, if the shape of the figure is correct, economic theory leads us to suggest spreading risk over as many individuals as possible. Many economists prefer the term 'value of a statistical life' rather than 'value of life' because they wish to emphasize the nature of assessing risk with (usually) low annual probabilities of death.

This has been abstract. In reality, individuals and households face decisions which reflect the Figure 3.4 trade-offs. Law enforcement and career military service have significantly nonzero probabilities of service-related death and disability, as does such civilian work as farming and ranching, construction, and mining.

A general problem in empirical work is the distinction between expert opinion, public opinion, and actuality. A Schulze survey finds that only about 25 percent of the public trusts scientists to be reasonably accurate in their estimates of Superfund

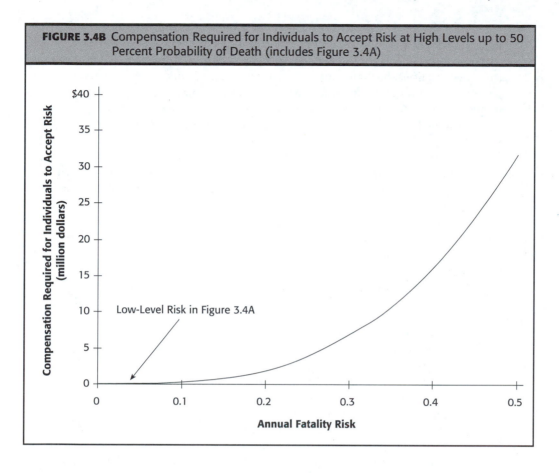

FIGURE 3.4B Compensation Required for Individuals to Accept Risk at High Levels up to 50 Percent Probability of Death (includes Figure 3.4A)

Site hazard, and the perception is common that scientists underestimate risk. Viscusi believes that individuals generally overestimate low probabilities, and underestimate high probabilities.[21]

I must admit some sensitivity to this issue. In an earlier book,[22] I concluded that expected fatalities from coal mining and coal burning far exceeded expected fatalities from nuclear power when both were calculated on an equivalent energy basis. After the Chernobyl nuclear reactor accident caused many fatalities directly and premature deaths for others, I realized that my own calculations were erroneous, particularly for nuclear plants in the former Soviet Union.

In terms of actual implementation of nonmarket valuation of life, risk, and safety, economists have used several empirical methodologies. *Human capital* estimation was an early approach. It treats the economic value of an individual in a manner parallel to the treatment of investment capital. One simple approach would be to use GDP per capita as an indicator of the average annual value each person adds to a national economy. In the United States in mid-1998, this was $30,000.

But this simple approach does not recognize the difference between employed persons and retired and other nonworking persons. If value is defined as GDP per employed person, the result is $130,000 per working person. Two seemingly logical measures of each person's economic contributions differ by a factor of 4.

There are other problems with the human capital approach. Should persons (housewives, househusbands, etc.) providing unpaid family care and services be included or excluded? Do retired persons without earned income have formal economic value? What about income differences between regions and occupations?

A final obstacle with the human capital technique arises from the significance of time. Does $50,000 worth of GDP in 2000 have the same meaning as $50,000 in 2050? This of course involves inflation adjustment, but it also raises the question of time preferences and discounting, which are taken up in the following chapter.

Because of these and other problems with the human capital method of estimating the value of lives saved, economists have instead turned their attention to contingent valuation surveys and empirical risk analysis. Currently economists are concentrating on these two general approaches as being the most powerful in valuing the benefits of environmental protection, for human lives as well as for the natural components of ecosystems.

In his comprehensive survey of economic estimates of the value of life, Viscusi used Table 3.4 to summarize contingent valuation survey results. As predicted by the Kahneman-Tversky theory earlier in this chapter, respondents in the Gerking study wanted more compensation to accept higher risk ($8.8 million) than they were willing to pay to reduce risk ($3.4 million). Also, note in the Viscusi study that the mean value ($9.7 million) is much higher than the median value ($2.7 million). This implies that some individuals are very concerned about risk, in the sense that their values are very high.

Although contingent valuation has been assuming a growing importance in value of life calculations, most of the work has been in the analysis of data on risk, income, and occupation. As noted elsewhere in this chapter, we assume that individuals are making trade-offs between risk and income.[23] Table 3.4 includes some occupational risk data. Analyzing these kinds of data with respect to work, income, and other factors typically results in a finding of $3 million to $7 million[24] as the economic value of life. Table 3.5 is a summary of Viscusi's review. In terms of a representative figure, $5 million per life (in 1998 dollars) is a median value for the 40 studies that Viscusi reviewed.

However, these values and the $5 million typical value arise from Viscusi's review of studies in high income countries. Another review finds that economists working in the Intergovernmental Panel on Climate Change have very different estimates. A Bangladeshi life is typically valued at $150,000. In contrast, a representative value in this study for a U.S. life is $1.5 million.[25]

Summary/Conclusion

The valuation of external environmental benefits and costs has made progress in the last two decades. Contingent valuation (the survey or experimental approach), the travel cost methodology, hedonic property valuation, and the methodologies for valuing life and safety were introduced here. These methods will be applied in suc-

TABLE 3.4 Summary of Value of Life Estimates Based on Survey Evidence

Author	*Nature of Risk*	*Survey Methodology*	*Implicit Value of Life, 1990 $*
Acton	Improved ambulance service, post–heart attack lives	Willingness to pay question, door-to-door Boston sample	$100,000
Jones-Lee	Airline safety and locational life expectancy risks	Mail survey willingness to accept increased risk, U.K. sample	$15.6 million
Gerking, deHaan, and Schulze	Job fatality risk	Willingness to pay, willingness to accept change in job risk in mail survey	$3.4 million WTP, $8.8 million WTA
Jones-Lee	Motor vehicle accidents	Willingness to pay for risk reduction, U.K. survey	$3.8 million
Viscusi, Magat, and Huber	Automobile accident risks	Interactive computer program with risk–cost tradeoffs	$2.7 (median) $9.7 (mean) (in million dollars)
Miller and Guria	Traffic safety	Series of contingent valuation questions, New Zealand survey	$1.2 million

Source: Viscusi, "The Value of Risks to Life and Health," *Journal of Economic Literature*, Vol XXXI, December 1993 page 1940.

ceeding chapters, particularly in the analysis of the spotted owl program (see Chapter 15) and visibility protection in the Grand Canyon (see Chapter 4).

Can the new valuation methods be used in developing countries? The answer is a qualified "yes." In one comparison of air pollution reduction benefits, the Alberini and Cropper group analyzed the WTP in Taiwan to avoid colds and respiratory disease.[26] They found that after adjusting for the income difference between Taiwan and the United States, WTP for better health is comparable but not necessarily equal. As new research is undertaken, we will learn more about transferring benefit estimates for environmental protection from high income countries into a context for developing nations.

TABLE 3.5 The Economic Value of Saved Lives: A Summary of the Viscusi Review		
Type of Study	*Number of Studies Reviewed*	*Median Estimate*
Occupational risk and income	27 studies	$6 million
Consumer market preferences	7 studies	$1 million
Contingent valuation surveys	6 studies	$5 million

Note: In 1998 dollars.

We have had a brief look at some of the limitations of valuation. The problems discussed here include embedding, strategic bias, survey technique bias, expert versus public opinion, and the WTP-WTA difference.[27] The evaluation of nonmarket benefits and costs in environmental economics is charged with controversy, and competent economists can come to different conclusions. Nevertheless, this new work is focused on exciting questions. In the next chapter, we will use a contingent valuation survey of willingness to pay for air pollution cleanup in the Grand Canyon to introduce benefit-cost analysis.

Questions for Discussion and Analysis

1. Income elasticity is similar to price elasticity. It is the percentage change in a value associated with a 1 percent change in a per capita income. Suppose income elasticity is +1.25 for environmental contingent values. If per capita U. S. incomes increase 50 percent, what would be the new WTP for improved Grand Canyon visibility?

2. You are going to visit the Gettysburg National Military Park, the Blue Ridge Parkway, and the Great Smoky Mountains National Park. Discuss how you might use the TCM and the CV methods to estimate the value to you of these protected areas.

3. Table 3.1 focuses on the protection of positive externalities. Do those definitions apply to the value of a statistical life?

4. In determining environmental policy, should income levels of affected persons be considered positively or negatively?

5. Develop specific illustrations of embedded values that apply to the CV, TCM, HPV, and VOSL methods.

6. What additional compensation would you require to accept a product with a .002 probability of causing a fatality? A 0.3 probability?

7. Survey your class or your friends about willingness to pay to contribute to the protection of African elephants. What explains the differences in individual values? Could you structure your survey so that you could construct a WTP curve? Do you think hypothetical bias affects your survey results?

Notes to Chapter 3

1. Allan Randall reviews the economics of the project in Chapter 22 of his *Resource Economics: An Economic Approach to Natural Resource and Environmental Policy*, 2nd ed., Wiley, New York, 1987.
2. Although their theory was originally formulated in the context of financial investment and risk, it has been adopted by some environmental economists because of its power to explain empirical data. The original source is D. Kahneman and A. Tversky, "Prospect Theory: An Analysis of Decision under Risk," March 1979 *Econometrica*, 47(2):263–292.
3. John Krutilla, "Conservation Reconsidered," June 1967 *American Economic Review*, 54(4):777–786.
4. My academic advisor advocated this approach in 1947 and 1952 (e.g., S. V. Ciriacy-Wantrip, *Resource Conservation*, University of California Press, 1952, pages 240–244.) Robert Davis first used the method in 1963 in his "Recreation Planning as an Economic Problem," *Natural Resources Journal* 3(2):239–249. Paul Portney reports a 1994 bibliography by Richard Carson and others that lists 1,674 contingent valuation studies. (Paul Portney, "The Contingent Valuation Debate: Why Economists Should Care," Fall 1994 *Journal of Economic Perspectives*, 8(4):3–18.
5. From Richard T. Carson, Robert C. Mitchell, W. Michael Hanemann, Raymond J. Kopp, Stanley Presser, and Paul A. Ruud, *A Contingent Valuation Study of Lost Passive Use Values Resulting from the Exxon Valdez Oil Spill*, A Report to the Attorney General of the State of Alaska, November 10, 1992.
6. Robert Rowe, Ralph C. d'Arge, and David Brookshire, "An Experiment on the Economic Value of Visibility," March 1980 *Journal of Environmental Economics and Management*, 7(1):1–19. This early use of contingent valuation examined strategic bias and survey instrument bias.
7. Theoretically, the problem of WTP-WTA divergence arises from the consideration of compensating and equivalent variations. Discussion of this latter topic is typically in more technical literature such as Freeman *op. cit.*, Chapter 3, and Richard E. Just, Darrell L. Hueth, and Andrew Schmitz, *Applied Welfare Economics and Public Policy*, Prentice-Hall, Englewood Cliffs, NJ, 1982. The WTP-WTA question in contingent valuation is reviewed in Ronald G. Cummings, David S. Brookshire, and William D. Schulze, *Valuing Environmental Goods: An Assessment of the Contingent Valuation Method*, Rowman and Allenheld, Totowa, NJ, 1986, especially pages 217–221. Goodstein (pages 88–89) has a good introductory summary of the WTP-WTA divergence.
8. There is extensive literature evaluating contingent valuation. Two of these sources are (1) Kenneth Arrow, Robert Solow, Edward Leamer, Paul Portney, Roy Radner, and Howard Schuman, "Report of the NOAA Panel on Contingent Valuation," January 1993 *Federal Register* 58(10):4602–4614; and (2) Paul Portney, W. Michael Hanemann, Peter Diamond, and Jerry A. Hausman, their separate contributions to the Symposium on Contingent Valuation, Fall 1994 *Journal of Economic Perspectives* 8(4):3–64.
9. Discussed in Arrow pages 4603–4604.
10. Figure 3.2 is suggested by the work of Crandall et al. Their site visitation was positively associated with age and negatively with income. In this figure, consumer surplus in aggregate is $800,000 and aggregate WTP of visitors would be $1.6 million. The travel cost method was first proposed by Harold Hotelling in a letter to the National Park Service in 1947.
11. K. B. Crandall, B. G. Colby, and K. A. Rait, "Valuing Riparian Areas: A Southwestern Case Study," April 1992 *Rivers* 3(2):88–98.

12. See J. C. Huang, T. C. Haab, and J. C. Whitehead, "Willingness to Pay for Quality Improvements: Should Revealed and Stated Preference Data Be Combined?" November 1997 *Journal of Environmental Economics and Management* 34(3):240–255. Crandall et al. did this kind of comparison in their Hassayampa study. A. M. Freeman III reviews the TCM in his *The Measurement of Environmental and Resource Values: Theory and Methods* (Washington, DC: Resources for the Future, 1993).

13. There is considerable debate among economists on this point: under different plausible circumstances, housing values could overstate WTP or understate it. As Schulze et al. (1995, pages 15–17) discuss, the existence of several industrial sites may lead to apparent overestimates for any one site. This is analogous to the embedding problem in contingent valuation. Alternatively, high real estate transfer costs could result in housing values which understate WTP. See William Schulze et al. "An Evaluation of Public Preferences for Superfund Site Cleanup," presented at the Annual Meeting of the American Economic Association, Washington, DC, January 7, 1995, 36 pages.

14. Schulze, *op. cit.*

15. Field, page 144. The percentage reduction in the value of a house is an average of .14 of 1 percent for a 1 percent increase in air pollution. Field reports ranges; the figure .14 of 1 percent is an average of midpoints.

16. Raymond Palmquist, Fritz Roka, and Tomislav Vukina, "Hog Operations, Environmental Effects, and Residential Property Values," February 1997 *Land Economics* 73(1): 114–124.

17. V. Kerry Smith and Ju-Chin Huang, "Hedonic Models and Air Pollution: Twenty-five Years and Counting," 1993 *Environmental and Resource Economics* (3), page 389. Also see "Can Markets Value Air Quality? A Meta-Analysis of Hedonic Property Value Models," by Smith and Huang in 1995 *Journal of Political Economy* (103)1:209–227.

18. W. Kip Viscusi, "The Value of Risks to Life and Health," December 1993 *Journal of Economic Literature* (13):1912–1946.

19. The figures reflect an indifference to risk and compensation of A = \$500 + $p^3 \times$ \$250 million; p is the annual fatality risk.

20. The calculation is probability of accidental death over lifetime = (1 − probability of annual fatality) * * 70 year life.

21. Schulze 1995, pages 9–13. Viscusi, page 1919.

22. D. Chapman, *Energy Resources and Energy Corporations, op. cit.,* page 269.

23. See Freeman *op. cit.,* pages 423–425, and Viscusi (pages 1913–1916) for their summaries of the economic theory of risk and income.

24. Viscusi, page 1930. In 1990 dollars.

25. Neha Khanna and Duane Chapman, "Time Preference, Abatement Costs, and International Climate Change Policy: An Appraisal of IPCC 1995," April 1996 *Contemporary Economic Policy* 13(2):56–66.

26. A. Alberini, M. Cropper, *et al,* "Valuing Health Effects of Air Pollution in Developing Countries: the Case of Taiwan," October 1997 *Journal of Environmental Economics and Management* 34(2):107–126. One example: a WTP estimate of \$20 to avoid a one-day cold in Taiwan compares to income-adjusted projections of \$18 and \$35.

27. See the references in Note 8 above for their review of these and other issues in valuation.

CHAPTER 4

BENEFIT-COST ANALYSIS AND DISCOUNTING

Benefit-Cost Analysis: History and Applicability

Although the technique of benefit-cost analysis has become widely used internationally and at the World Bank, its origins lie in Western Europe, and its major development as an environmental policy tool was in the United States.

There are two distinct but related European sources. One important early concept is 'consumers surplus,' introduced in Chapter 1. In 1844, Jules Dupuit argued that the French government's development of roads and bridges creates value to users above and in excess of the tolls they pay for use.[1]

In a separate but related concept, A. C. Pigou in England in the 1920s argued that there is a divergence between private economic product and social economic product. Of particular interest is his illustration of this idea with references to child labor, maternity leave for working mothers, alcohol, war, and factory pollution.[2] In these cases, he argued, private markets oriented around profit produce too much of the product, as well as the consequent negative byproducts. Through taxation or regulation, government could influence markets to increase social welfare.

It is clear from the context and detail that Pigou was developing the now widely used concept of externality: an unintended byproduct of economic activity that raises or lowers the economic welfare of other consumers or businesses. Pigou also discussed positive externalities, including parks, lighthouses, and afforestation as needed government activities. In modern economics, taxes on products that produce externalities, and taxes on negative externalities themselves, are both referred to as 'Pigouvian taxes.'

Historical development of benefit-cost analysis then shifted to the United States. During the economic depression of the 1930s, federal public works agencies in the United States undertook major water construction projects to develop irrigation water, electricity, municipal water, and to provide flood control. In 1936, Congress required these agencies to identify economic benefits "to whomsoever they may accrue." After 1950, benefit-cost analysis was implemented through federal guidelines in the "Green Book," *Proposed Practices for Economic Analysis of River Basin Projects*.[3] Many agencies implemented estimates of both Dupuit's consumer surplus and Pigou's positive externality in valuing the nonmarket economic benefits of federal construction of water projects.

With the growing concern about water and air quality in the 1960s, economists began to apply benefit-cost analysis to environmental problems. To the best of my knowledge, the now-standard graph representing marginal benefits and costs of pollution control was first used by Allen V. Kneese in 1964 in his study of water pollution control.[4] (These concepts were introduced in Chapter 1 and are illustrated in Figure 4.2 later in this chapter.) In air pollution control, Ronald Ridker was apparently the first economist to apply benefit-cost techniques.[5]

Notwithstanding the growing interest in environmental economics, respected figures in benefit-cost analysis and the economic theory of public policy were slow to recognize the importance of the field. The American Economic Association's 1969 reader by Kenneth Arrow and Tibor Scitovsky contained no reference to environment or to environmental economics. Similarly, Mishan's influential *Cost-Benefit Analysis* (1971) made only brief passing reference to environmental economics. In England, an influential 1965 review article on benefit-cost analysis failed to mention either environment or pollution.[6] Nevertheless, by the 1980s the use of benefit-cost analysis was becoming firmly established in environmental applications.[7]

One well-known application of the technique was the estimation of the economic benefits and costs of complete lead removal from U.S. gasoline. The Environmental Protection Agency calculated the financial losses from health damage and mortality from continued lead use. The Agency calculated a benefit estimate for improved health arising from lead prohibition and compared it with the increased refinery cost of meeting octane levels without lead. The result was a clear net benefit for lead removal.[8]

Discounting and Interest Rates

In the 1980s, the U.S. National Park Service (NPS) believed that air pollution was significantly reducing visibility in the Grand Canyon National Park in the winter. On clear days, visibility in the Park can exceed 150 miles. Pollution by itself can reduce visibility by more than 50 percent. An Arizona power plant contributed most of the pollution through coal burning.

If 70 percent of the sulfur pollution were removed, the NPS said, then visibility would be significantly closer to its natural clarity. NPS used the contingent value method to estimate the willingness to pay for reducing pollution in the Grand Canyon. A representative result was an estimated WTP (willingness to pay) benefit of $210 million annually.[9]

On the cost side, sulfur scrubbing equipment at a power plant would cost about $330 million to install and $75 million each year to operate. These estimates are summarized in Table 4.1.

There are many substantial questions about these assumptions. For example: do Mexican copper smelters cause the problem rather than the Arizona power plant? Do visitors or others actually care about pollution in the Grand Canyon? Did the NPS underestimate the cost of reducing sulfur pollution? Would 90 percent pollution control be better than 70 percent? How important is uncertainty?

TABLE 4.1 Grand Canyon Estimates of Benefits and Costs for Sulfur Control at Arizona Power Plant (inflation-adjusted dollars)

1. Contingent valuation estimate of willingness to pay for better visibility	$210 million annually
2. Construction cost for sulfur removal equipment	$330 million investment
3. Operation and maintenance cost	$75 million annually
4. Sulfur pollution reduction at 70 percent effectiveness	25,000 tons annually

Source: USEPA[10].

In this chapter, the objectives are limited. We want to show how the best level of pollution control can be determined by using the methods for comparing benefits and costs occurring in different years. This comparison is of interest because the original investment cost of construction for the sulfur scrubbers is a one-time investment for equipment that is expected to work for 30 years. In contrast, the expected benefits from better visibility occur in each of these 30 years. How do we compare a one-time capital investment with 30 years of benefits? In benefit-cost analysis, economists use the technique of discounting to evaluate benefits and costs that occur in different years.

First consider the construction of the sulfur pollution control system. It can be represented as having a 'turnkey' cost of $330 million. The word 'turnkey' means the contractor finishes construction at a fixed date, and expects payment for the work. The owner of the power plant arranges payment on this date, and begins operating the scrubbers. It is as if the new owner on a single day wrote a check to the contractor, "turned a key," and began using the equipment.

In contrast, the benefits and the operating costs are both counted on an annual basis over 30 years. The economic concept necessary to compare costs and benefits is the *levelized annual cost*. It is calculated by determining the annual payment that would be required to pay off a loan. It is the amount that, if paid regularly throughout the period, would exactly pay off a loan in the amount of the initial investment. From an opportunity cost perspective, the levelized annual cost represents the yearly value of foregone opportunities which would have existed if funds had not been committed to the plant. The first step in the calculation is the *levelized cost factor*, which is then used to calculate levelized annual cost.

$$\text{lcf} = \frac{r(1 + r)^n}{(1 + r)^n - 1} \tag{4-1a}$$

$$\text{LAC} = \text{lcf} * \text{construction cost} \tag{4-1b}$$

TABLE 4.2 Benefit-Cost Analysis Illustration for the Grand Canyon National Park (levelized annual cost)

A. Basic reduction in sulfur pollution from plant: 70 percent

B. Costs

Levelized annual cost, construction	$35 million, annually
Annual operation and maintenance	$75 million, annually
Total annual costs, construction and operation	$110 million, annually

C. Benefits, WTP for visibility cleanup $210 million, annually

D. Net benefits $100 million, per year

E. Benefit-cost ratio: 1:9

The lcf is the levelized cost factor, and the LAC is levelized annual cost, expressed in dollars per year. The NPS used 10 percent to represent market interest rates, so, for a 30-year expected life for the sulfur pollution control equipment,

$$\text{lcf} = \frac{.1(1 + .1)^{30}}{(1 + .1)^{30} - 1} = .106, \text{per year}$$

$$\text{LAC} = .106 * \$330 \text{ million} = \$35 \text{ million, per year}$$

The levelized annual cost of $35 million annually would exactly pay off a mortgage-type loan on a mortgage of $330 million, at 10 percent interest, over a 30-year period.

Incidentally, the concept of the levelized cost in Equation (4-1) is similar to several other terms which have the same arithmetic definitions. Some economists will use terms such as mortgage, annual equivalent amount, annuity, or levelized capital cost instead of lcf or LAC.

In Table 4.2, we see the results of introducing discounting into benefit-cost analysis. Annual benefits at $210 million exceed total annual costs by a significant amount, and net benefits are $100 million annually. The benefit-cost ratio shows that benefits are almost twice the costs.

Present Value or Annual Discounting?

Some economists prefer to use present value concepts in discounting. For example,

$$\text{PVB} = \sum_{t=1}^{n} \frac{\$210 \text{ million annually}}{(1 + r)^t} \tag{4-2}$$

TABLE 4.3 Present Value Method of Benefit-Cost Analysis	
I. Present value of	
Initial construction cost for sulfur removal equipment	$330 million
Present value of annual operation and maintenance cost	$707 million
Present value of all costs	$1,037 million
II. Present value of annual WTP for visibility cleanup benefits	$1,980 million
III. Net benefits present value	$943 million
IV. Benefit-cost ratio: 1.9	

Present value represents, for today, the value of a future schedule or stream of payments. So, Equation (4-2) would give the present value of $210 million annually in benefits. When the annual amount is constant, the result is simpler:

$$PVB = \frac{1 - (1 + r)^{-n}}{r} * \text{annual amount} \qquad (4\text{-}3a)$$

$$PVB = pvf * \text{annual amount} \qquad (4\text{-}3b)$$

For our Grand Canyon illustration, the present value of benefits is $1,980 million. Similarly, the present value of operation and maintenance cost is $707 million.

Interest rate discounting for present value and for levelized annual cost have an exact relationship. In fact, the *present value factor* is simply the inverse of the levelized cost factor, as in Equation (4-4):

$$pvf = \frac{(1 + r)^{n} - 1}{r(1 + r)^{n}} \qquad (4\text{-}4a)$$

$$pvf = \frac{1}{lcf} \qquad (4\text{-}4b)$$

Therefore, the present value factor for the Grand Canyon case is 9.43.[11] With this, the present values of costs and benefits are calculated for Table 4.3. Note an important point of comparison between this table and Table 4.2: the benefit-cost ratios are identical. This will always be the case: present value and levelized annual cost discounting always have the same benefit-cost ratios.

The real value of discounting concepts is that they allow economists and policy makers to partially overcome the problem of benefits and costs occurring in different time periods. We will be able to expand their usefulness and draw upon discounting to analyze many major environmental problems where time is a significant factor.

The "Best" Efficient Level of Pollution Control

In this analysis of the benefits and costs of cleaning up visible sulfur pollution in the Grand Canyon, we have assumed that 70 percent of the sulfur in the coal should be controlled and thereby kept from entering the atmosphere. In fact, the National Park Service recommended 90 percent control, while the power plant managers recommended no control or 70 percent control.

The NPS recommendation of 90 percent control is related to efficiency analysis. To understand this idea, it is helpful to return to the concepts of competition and optimum economic welfare that were introduced in Chapter 1. If the benefits of pollution control were to be revenues to a private firm, it would find the pollution reduction level where net benefits (benefits exceeding costs) were at the highest possible level. This highest possible level of net benefits may not be at 100 percent pollution control because costs at this 100 percent control level might be very high.

In Chapter 1, the maximum net social value is at the production level where marginal social value meets marginal social cost. In benefit-cost analysis, maximum net benefits are gained where marginal benefit meets marginal cost. In the field of pollution control, the efficient level of control is at the point where the marginal cost of pollution abatement has become equal to the marginal benefit of that abatement.

These relationships are represented in a general way in Figures 4.1 and 4.2. The actual application of these concepts to the Grand Canyon study is more complex than this, and is explained in greater detail elsewhere.[12] Nevertheless, the figures do represent an outcome where net benefits are maximized with 90 percent sulfur control at the power plant, and the meeting of marginal benefits and marginal costs at this level of control.

Social Versus Private Discounting

A difficult problem in environmental economics can arise when the expenses for environmental protection must be paid now and the benefits are received far into the future. If a market-based interest rate such as 10 percent per year is used, the calculation of net benefits and a benefit-cost ratio may be incorrect in some cases.

Suppose that a private or federal program to extinguish long-term fires in abandoned underground coal mines would reduce coal-burning gases released into the atmosphere. This would mean less pollution from oxides of sulfur and carbon. The benefits would be $50 million annually for 50 years, and the cost would be $750 million spent now (remember, this is an illustration, not an actual study as with the Grand Canyon case). In the first column in Table 4.4, levelized cost is calculated for a 10 percent interest rate. The result is $76 million annually, and net benefits are negative. This result says reject the project.

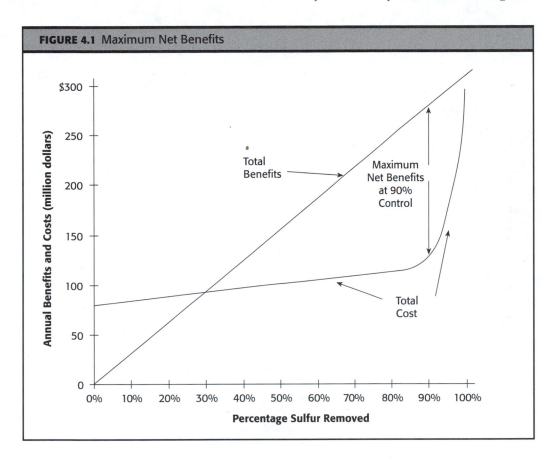

FIGURE 4.1 Maximum Net Benefits

Now consider a 3 percent rate instead of a 10 percent rate. The levelized cost factor in the table is much lower, and consequently net benefits become significantly positive. This result says support the project.

Another obvious example of the importance of discounting arises with climate change. Assume a significant hypothetical catastrophe 50 years from now, with damage of $500 billion. This future event could be avoided by expending $10 billion now. If the discount rate is 10 percent, net benefits are negative. With a 3 percent discount rate, the present value of net benefits is a positive $104 billion.[13]

Which rate is correct? The NPS study of the Grand Canyon used both discount rates, 3 percent and 10 percent. Fortunately for the NPS, net benefits are positive in both cases, unlike the situation in Table 4.3.

Current thinking in economics is moving toward the idea of using a 3 percent discount rate to evaluate environmental policy. For example, in William Nordhaus' pioneering work in climate change, all of his analyses use a 3 percent rate,[14] which declines in future years. The reasoning is complex, but in a simple format the idea can be expressed this way: first, we believe that per capita income continues to grow into the future, so that future generations will have higher living standards than do

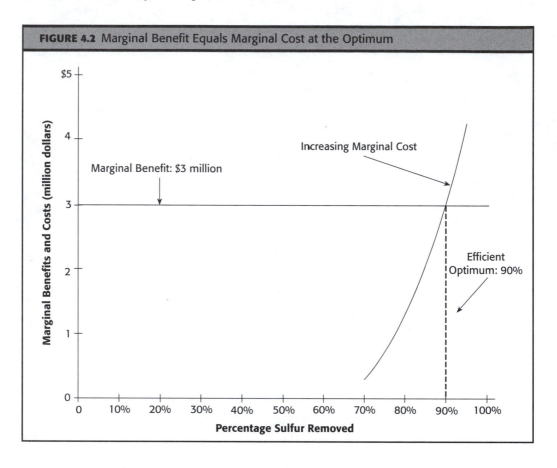

FIGURE 4.2 Marginal Benefit Equals Marginal Cost at the Optimum

current generations. Second, we assume that higher living standards are always preferable, but our level of satisfaction may not increase as rapidly as our income.

These two assumptions are important to the conclusion. The social interest rate is related to the difference between the market interest rate and the rate of growth in living standards. As an example, let's assume the inflation-adjusted interest rate for commerce is 5 percent, and the rate of growth of per capita world income is 2 percent. The social interest rate could be as high as 3 percent.[15]

Is global per capita income rising? In Chapter 2 we saw that the large majority of economists believe the empirical answer is "yes." However, we also noted a small possibility that the global picture of per capita income may be flat over the recent decades. For much of Africa and the former Soviet Union, living standards have been declining. In these areas, the social discount rate may actually be higher than the market rate. The implication is that significant decline in living standards in these regions is reflected in heavy social discounting of environmental values, and greater value is attached to consumption and production.

In a growing body of theoretical economic literature, Richard Howarth and Richard Norgaard have argued that income transfers between present and future generations can resolve part of the problem.[16] Perhaps this line of thinking will produce a solution.

TABLE 4.4 The Importance of Social or Private Discount Rates: Illustration		
	Case I: Discount Rate is 10%/yr	*Case II: Discount Rate is 3%/yr*
A. Assumed benefit, 50 years	$50 million/yr	$50 million/yr
B. Cost of fire suppression	$750 million now	$750 million now
C. Levelized cost factor (lcf) for 50 years	.101	.039
D. Levelized annual cost	$76 million/yr	$29 million/yr
E. Net benefits	−$26 million/yr	+$21 million/yr
F. Benefit-cost ratio	0.66	1.72

Just as our expectations about the future influence our approach to environmental discounting, so does our perception of the role of income differences between countries and between groups. Some economists argue that lower income causes a much higher emphasis on the present.[17] If this is true, then developing countries will use higher interest rates, and discount their future and the planet's future more severely.

For economists, an extreme position advocates no discounting for severe global problems. This position argues that, for basic questions related to humanity's future, each generation is of equivalent importance, and permanent environmental damage in the next century is as important as damage or cost that might be incurred today. Although the 'no discounting' position is extreme, one supporter is well known, the pioneer in economic philosophy E. J. Mishan. A similar view was held by the philosopher John Rawls.[18]

A well-known empirical study by Cropper, Aydede, and Portnoy addressed this problem.[19] They used the contingent valuation approach to survey 3,000 U.S. households. The questions in the survey were focused on possible government policies now and in the future that would save lives through pollution reduction. Their three main conclusions are (1) social discount rates are much lower than commercial market rates, (2) a long-term environmental problem of 100 years has a lower discount rate than a 5-year problem, and (3) in the context of saving lives through pollution reduction, the long-term real social discount rate may be about 4 percent for a 100-year future.[20]

However, this study offers empirical support for "zero discounting" as well as for the 4 percent social discount rate. A 4 percent figure is justified by the survey because it is the actual empirical number for saving lives a century into the future. If the study's results are extended to 500 years, zero discounting for the future environment is also supported. The apparent social discount rate falls to one-sixth of 1 percent and continues to decline.[21]

On the income level question, the authors find a possible small preference of lower income persons for higher market discount rates. In contrast, there is no difference between income groups regarding their preferences for saving lives.

Eternity Discounting: Inflation and Real Interest Rates

In the preceding discussion about discounting and valuing the future environment, we noted a possible time horizon of 500 years. In the context of the global environment, problems such as nuclear fuel waste storage, climate change, and endangered species protection have a time scale of this magnitude.

We can calculate levelized cost factors where we are looking at a nearly infinite time horizon to consider environmental policies. Turning to Equation (4-1a) earlier in the chapter, if n equals infinity,

$$\text{lcf} = r, \text{if } n = \infty \qquad (4\text{-}5)$$

So, for very long time periods, the levelized cost factor equals the interest rate. This is true both for a social discount rate as well as a market interest rate.

A valuable near-term technique is the adjustment of interest rates for inflation. This is analogous to the process for adjusting prices for inflation (see Chapter 2). The real interest rate approximately equals the market interest rate less the inflation rate.[22] Therefore, if commercial private sector interest rates are 9 percent, and inflation is 3 percent, then the real market interest rate is 6 percent. In fact, for high-grade corporate bonds, 6 percent is a 10-year inflation-adjusted real interest rate.[23] The relationship is

$$\text{real interest rate} = \text{market interest rate} - \text{inflation rate} \qquad (4\text{-}6a)$$

$$6 \text{ percent} = 9 \text{ percent} - 3 \text{ percent} \qquad (4\text{-}6b)$$

Both techniques have important applications in benefit-cost analysis and environmental economics. A real interest rate adjusted for inflation is lower than the current market interest rate. Consequently, using the real interest rate gives greater weighting to the future. (Remember Table 4.4 above.) And as we shall see in a later chapter on climate change, the incorporation of a very long time perspective in discounting has major implications for current policy affecting future generations.

Summary

Benefit-cost analysis must compare values and costs that occur at different times. Discounting is the basic tool that economists use to handle this problem. One-time costs can be converted to annual payments, and net benefits as well as a benefit-cost ratio can be calculated. The methods of calculation are similar to those used in calculating mortgage or other loan payments.

Many economists prefer to work with present value discounting rather than with levelized annual cost. Since the discounting factors in the two methods are always inverses, benefit-cost ratios are always identical, regardless of which discounting method is utilized.

With these discounting methods, the environmental economist can bring positive and negative externality into a common analytical framework of ordinary market costs and values. A case relating to the cleanup of air pollution in the Grand Canyon illustrates the method; the positive external benefits were based upon use of the contingent valuation method.

The optimal or best level of pollution control depends upon the ability to find the level that gives the greatest net benefits. Maximum net benefits will be at the level of pollution control where the marginal benefit of pollution reduction equals the marginal cost of abatement. Usually this will be at a level with less than 100 percent pollution control. In the Grand Canyon case, the apparent optimum level is at 90 percent pollution reduction.

A major problem arises over the question as to whether the appropriate discount rate for environmental work is similar to commercial interest rates. This is especially important where today's choices have consequences for future generations in succeeding centuries. For policy related to global climate change, nuclear waste storage, or biodiversity, this problem of social discounting has become important. Economists are typically using a 3 percent social discount rate for very long term environmental analysis. However, a minority favors lower or zero social discount rates.

Increasingly, U.S. policy requires benefit-cost analysis of environmental, safety, and health regulations. At the same time, valuation of nonmarket externalities is of growing importance in benefit-cost analysis.[24] Chapters 3 and 4 have been a highly simplified introduction to methods of analysis with origins in the 19th Century, and with applications to the national and global problems of the 21st Century.

Questions for Discussion and Analysis

1. Why do you think environmental economics developed in the 1970s and not previously?

2. Suppose you are working for a local government that is considering a plan to purchase an old-growth woods and create a protected area. You are going to issue bonds to finance the $1 million purchase. At 6 percent interest for 20 years, what would be the annual payment?

3. Consider your answer to Question 2 and assume you have valued the nonmarket benefits at $70,000 per year. What is the benefit-cost ratio? If the interest rate were to be 2 percent, what would be the benefit-cost ratio? What would the net benefits be at each of the two interest rates?

4. An environmentalist might believe that the optimal policy is no pollution. A businessperson may think that optimality means the lowest average cost for removed pollution. An economist would advocate finding the levels of pollution reduction that maximize net benefits. Which point of view do you have? Discuss your reasoning.

5. In Questions 2 and 3, benefits and costs are expressed in levelized annual amounts. Do the same analysis in present value benefits and costs.

6. Do you think social and private discount rates differ significantly? Which case in Table 4.4 do you prefer? Explain your preference.

7. What interest rate would you use to evaluate possible climate change damage two centuries from now?

Appendix: Discounting and Interest Rate Relationships

Assume each amount C_t is paid in at the end of the indicated year. PV means present value at the end of "Period 0," which of course is also the beginning of Year 1. F_n means a future value at the end of Year n.

1) Future Value of a Current Value, at Compound Interest: $F_n = (1 + r)^n C_0$

2) Future Value of a Variable Income Stream: $F_n = \sum_{t=1}^{n} (1 + r)^{n-t} C_t$

3) Future Value of a Constant Annual Income Stream: $F_n = \dfrac{(1 + r)^{n-1}}{r} * C$

4) Present Value of a Future Amount: $PV = \dfrac{F_n}{(1 + r)^n}$

5) Present Value of a Variable Income Stream: $PV_0 = \sum_{t=1}^{n} \dfrac{C_t}{(1 + r)^t}$

6) Present Value of Constant Income Stream: $PV_0 = \dfrac{1 - (1 + r)^{-n}}{r} * C$

7) Levelized Annual Cost of Present Value: $LAC = \dfrac{r(1 + r)^n}{(1 + r)^n - 1} * PV$

8) Levelized Annual Amount of Future Amount: $LAA = \dfrac{r}{(1 + r)^n - 1} * F_n$

The 'factors' are always derived from the part of the equation on the right side of the equal sign. For example, the levelized cost factor for Equation 7 is $r(1 + r)^n / [(1 + r)^n - 1]$.

Notes to Chapter 4

1. Jules Dupuit, "On Measurement of the Utility of Public Works," 1844, reprinted in Kenneth J. Arrow and Tibor Scitovsky, eds., *Readings in Welfare Economics*, by The American Economic Association (Homewood, IL: Irwin, 1969):255–283.
2. A. C. Pigou, *The Economics of Welfare*, 4 editions, 1920–1932. In the third edition (London: Macmillan, 1952), see pages 183–192. In Pigou's terminology, environmental externality is a Type II divergence.
3. The quotation is from the Flood Control Act of 1936, as discussed in Robert Dorfman, "Forty Years of Cost-Benefit Analysis," (Cambridge, MA: Harvard University, August 1976), 28 pages. The "Green Book" was issued in 1950 by the Federal Inter-Agency River Basin Committee, Subcommittee on Benefits and Costs. Also, see discussion beginning page 2 in Eckstein, Otto, *Water Resource Development* (Cambridge, MA: Harvard University Press, 1958). The major agencies were the Army Corps of Engineers, the Bureau of Reclamation, and the Tennessee Valley Authority. Incidentally, benefit-cost analysis is the term used in the United States, while "cost-benefit analysis" is preferred in the U.K.
4. Allen V. Kneese, *The Economics of Regional Water Quality Management* (Baltimore, MD: Johns-Hopkins Press, 1964), especially page 45. A thank-you to Olli Tahvonen for reminding me of this pioneering work.

5. Ronald G. Ridker, *Economic Costs of Air Pollution* (New York: Praeger, 1967), especially page 5.

6. Kenneth J. Arrow and Tibor Scitovsky, eds., *Readings in Welfare Economics op. cit.*, pages 255–283; E. J. Mishan, *Cost-Benefit Analysis: An Introduction* (New York: Praeger, 1971); and A. R. Prest and R. Turvey, "Cost-Benefit Analysis: A Survey," December 1965 *The Economic Journal* 125:68–735.

7. One major example: V. Kerry Smith, *Environmental Policy under Reagan's Executive Order: The Role of Cost-Benefit Analysis* (Chapel Hill, NC: University of North Carolina Press, 1984). This period saw the arrival of several significant texts including William J. Baumol and Wallace E. Oates, *The Theory of Environmental Policy*, 2nd ed. (Cambridge, England: Cambridge University Press, 1988); Jon M. Conrad and Colin W. Clark, *Natural Resource Economics: Notes and Problems* (Cambridge, England: Cambridge University Press, 1987); Anthony C. Fisher, *Resource and Environmental Economics* (Cambridge, England: Cambridge University Press, 1981); Myrick A. Freeman, III, *Air and Water Pollution Control: A Benefit Cost Assessment* (New York: Wiley, 1982); John M. Hartwick and Nancy D. Olewiler, *The Economics of Natural Resource Use* (New York: Harper and Row, 1986); Charles W. Howe, *Natural Resource Economics: Issues, Analysis, and Policy* (New York: Wiley, 1979); John V. Krutilla and Otto Eckstein, *Multiple Purpose River Development: Studies in Applied Economic Analysis* (Baltimore, MD: Resources for the Future and Johns Hopkins Press, 1958); and David W. Pearce and R. Kerry Turner, *Economics of Natural Resources and the Environment* (Baltimore, MD: Johns Hopkins Press, 1990). Of course, the list includes the previously cited text by Randall. These books generally addressed the application of benefit-cost analysis to environmental policy in one or more chapters. Widely used texts by Field, Goodstein, and Tietenberg (all cited in earlier chapters) generally make extensive use of benefit-cost analysis.

8. There were two groups with major health effects. One group was middle-aged commuters who suffered increased heart attacks and strokes from breathing airborne lead from car exhaust. The second affected group was urban youth who experienced loss of intellectual capacity from lead poisoning. Source is U.S. Environmental Protection Agency, *Costs and Benefits of Reducing Lead in Gasoline, Final Regulatory Impact Analysis* (Washington, DC: February 1985).

9. This material is adapted from the NPS regulatory review: U.S. Environmental Protection Agency, *Regulatory Impact Analysis of a Revision of the Federal Implementation Plan for the State of Arizona to Include SO_2 Controls for the Navajo Generating Station* (February 5, 1990 (draft)). The NPS has prepared a valuable video showing the sources of SO_2 in Mexico and the United States and the impact on visibility in the Grand Canyon. National Park Service Air Quality Division, "Diminishing View," video (Denver, CO: 1990).

10. *Ibid.*

11. Since the present value factor (pvf) is the inverse of the levelized cost factor (lcf), pvf = 1/.106, or 9.43. Many economists use the concept of "present value" to compare values that fall in different years. The definitions relevant to the present value concept are in the Appendix to this chapter, as are the definitions for levelized cost. Both present value and levelized cost techniques are utilized in this text in forest economics (Chapter 14), climate change analysis (Chapter 18), world oil resources (Chapter 9), as well as in this Grand Canyon case and in other chapters.

12. USEPA: see Note 9. In Figures 4.1 and 4.2, total benefits and marginal benefits are both linear. The actual NPS studies do not address this point; some of the basic issues in damage function analysis are introduced in the air pollution chapter.

13. The present value of that hypothetical future damage is $4 billion at a 10 percent discount rate, and a very different $114 billion at a 3 percent discount rate. This is calculated

with Equation (4) in the Appendix. So the present value net benefits are negative $6 billion at 10 percent, and positive $104 billion at 3 percent.

14. W. G. Nordhaus, *Managing The Global Commons: The Economics of Climate Change* (Cambridge, MA: MIT Press, 1994); and "An Optimal Transition Path for Controlling Greenhouse Gases," November 1992 *Science.*

15. Nordhaus *op. cit.* Intergovernmental Panel on Climate Change, 1995, *Second Assessment Report, Working Group III on Economic Implications*, Draft; and N. Khanna and D. Chapman, "Time Preference, Abatement Costs, and International Climate Policy: An Appraisal of IPCC 1995," 1996 *Contemporary Economic Policy*, in press. There are many variants of the same concept. It arises from the work of Frank Ramsey, John Maynard Keynes, and Otto Eckstein. One version related to the text here is: $p = i + \Theta * g$. The social interest rate is p, the market interest rate is i, the rate of growth in future per capita consumption and income is g, and Θ is a conceptual term which relates per capita income or consumption to personal satisfaction. In economic theory, Θ is the elasticity of the marginal utility of consumption.

16. R. B. Howarth and R. B. Norgaard, "Intergenerational Choices under Global Environmental Change," in *Handbook of Environmental Economics*, D. W. Bromley, ed. (Cambridge, MA: Blackwell, 1995):111–138.

17. References on this point include: C. W. Clark, "Economic Biases Against Sustainable Development," in *Ecological Economics: The Science and Management of Sustainability*, R. Costanza, ed. (New York: Columbia University Press, 1991):319–330; C. Perrings, "An Optimal Path to Extinction? Poverty and Resource Degradation in the Open Agrarian Economy," 1989 *Journal of Development Economics* 30:1–24; and S. V. Ciriacy-Wantrup, *Resource Conservation: Economics and Policy* (Berkeley: University of California Press, 1963):104–106. Also D. W. Adams and D. A. Fitchett, *Informal Finance in Low Income Countries* (Boulder, CO: Westview, 1992):342; and D. Chapman, "Environment, Income, and Development in Southern Africa: An Analysis of the Interaction of Environmental and Macroeconomics," Occasional Paper No. 23 (Durban, South Africa: University of Natal Economic Research Unit, 1992).

18. J. Rawls, *A Theory of Justice* (Cambridge, MA: Harvard University Press, 1971):293–298. E. J. Mishan, *Cost-Benefit Analysis: An Informal Introduction* (London: Allen & Unwin, 1975):209. A contingent valuation study also concluded that the social discount rate may be zero: J. C. Case, *Contributions to the Economics of Time Preferences*, Ph.D. dissertation (Laramie, WY: University of Wyoming, 1986).

19. M. L. Cropper and P. R. Portnoy, "Discounting Human Lives," Summer 1992 *Resources* 108:1–4, and M. L. Cropper, S. K. Aydede, and P. R. Portnoy, "Public Preferences for Life Saving," Discussion Paper CRM 92-01 (Washington, DC: Resources for the Future Center for Risk Management, 1992). Also see their "Rates of Time Preference for Saving Lives," May 1992 *American Economic Review*, 80(2):469–472.

20. Suggested by r declining to .038 for T = 100 in Cropper and Portnoy, page 3.

21. For this relationship, r asymptotically approaches zero as T becomes large: $r = 0.7965/T$. In a linear relationship, the social discount rate falls to zero by 122 years. This latter function is $r = 0.0866 - 7.12 \times T/10{,}000$. Cropper, Aydede, and Portnoy, pages 30, 31.

22. Actually, to be precise for discrete discounting, $RIR = [(1 + MIR)/(1 + IR)] - 1$. The precise value for the example in the text would be 6.8 percent. For exponential discounting using e^{at}, the Equations (4-3a) and (4-3b) are exactly correct.

23. For 1985–94, Aaa corporate bonds averaged a 9.1 percent annual yield. Inflation as measured by the GDP deflator grew at 3.3 percent annually. Rounded off, the real interest rate was 6 percent. Source is *Economic Report of the President*, 1995, pages 278 and 358.

24. Kip Viscusi provides a review of these developments in the Summer 1996 *Journal of Economic Perspectives* 10(3):119–134.

CHAPTER 5

EQUITY, ENVIRONMENT, AND ECONOMICS

What Is, or What Ought to Be?

If an individual can be said to represent an era, A. C. Pigou and his *Economics of Welfare* moved the study of economics away from its predilection for moral judgment.[1] He favored an objective view, defining economics as a science throughout the early and mid-1900s. His position is that economics "is a positive science of what is and tends to be, not a normative science of what ought to be."[2]

In the post–World War II era, Paul Samuelson was a leader in developing a strong empirical emphasis in economics, arguing that mathematical theory and observation made the old thinking irrelevant.[3]

Positivism (our economic terminology for "describing what is" in an empirically testable way) carried the field completely. Neoclassical economics, as we call it, is so firmly not moralistic that the debate is confined to one or two pages in introductory economics texts.

Surprisingly, 1996 saw the debate taken up in a new context: climate change impact and policy. In Chapter 18, we will see that if we use high discount rates or low values of human life for very poor countries, then economics applied in a mechanistic way seems to tell us that the fate of India and Bangladesh may be unimportant. Yet this position is so unappealing that leading economists began to debate this serious problem. In this discussion they have initiated a new terminology. *Prescriptive* means a mild advocacy, an "ought to be" concept. *Descriptive* means "the world as it is." So, at the end of the 20th Century, economists returned in a small way to a much older problem.[4]

Notwithstanding this climate change debate, the question of ethics and equity remains on the margins of economic thought, a mere distant rumbling removed from day-to-day mainstream economics.

Economic Philosophy: Pareto and Compensation, Benefit-Cost Analysis, Rawls, and the Polluter Pays Principle

As introduced in Chapter 1, the concept of Pareto Optimality is closely identified with the competitive theory of economic organization. It holds that the sum of consumers value (less producers cost) is maximized by competition.[5] This ideal economic organization is Pareto Optimal: all individuals have attained a level of economic welfare and efficiency such that no change can improve one person's welfare without reducing that of another.

This, in turn, led to the concept of Pareto Improvement, a policy or change that improves welfare for one or many people, without reducing anyone's welfare. Unfortunately this criterion is very strict. Since most environmental programs and policies impose some cost, however small, on some individuals who do not benefit, the Pareto Improvement criterion would reject most environmental policies.[6]

One way out of this dilemma would be to consider only those programs and policies where individuals who gain would compensate individuals who lose, however small that loss might be. The main point here is that a good policy, technology, or program with major net gains would enable beneficiaries to compensate losers, and so total welfare is enhanced. This idea is given the name 'Kaldor-Hicks criteria' to recognize the role played by John R. Hicks and Nicholas Kaldor in developing the concept.[7]

Benefit-cost analysis reflects the ideas of Pareto Improvement and the Kaldor-Hicks criteria. As we saw in Chapter 4, benefit-cost analysis placed a strong emphasis on increasing net social value regardless of distribution or compensation. The basic legislation emphasized this lack of concern with differential impact, asserting that benefits are calculated "to whomsoever they may accrue."[8]

The 'Polluter Pays Principle' combines an ethical perspective with a practical objective. Basically, this Principle holds that the individuals or businesses that cause pollution are responsible for the costs of pollution control, or the payment of compensation to pollution victims.[9] It implies an absence of subsidies to the polluters. For example, tax credits and cash incentives for polluters are prohibited by a strict interpretation of the Principle.

One practical goal of this Principle is in the field of trade. European Union countries favor this criterion because it eliminates a comparative advantage in trade for countries with lower environmental standards. It prevents a member country from subsidizing an exporting industry to gain a comparative advantage. Similar industries in different countries with comparable pollution potential will have similar costs, thereby eliminating potential competition in terms of cost savings from pollution control avoidance.

Table 5.1 defines the Polluter Pays Principle and other ethical concepts introduced here in a very basic way. Of course, the original sources provide a full explanation of each idea, and Kneese and Schulze[10] are very helpful.

The Natural Rights criterion has developed in the context of biodiversity, as noted in Chapter 15. Proponents of this view believe that human society should protect all species regardless of possible value to humans.

The philosophy of John Rawls and his Theory of Justice has been of considerable interest to environmental economists concerned about ethical values. The Rawls approach is complex; its environmental significance can be described as a process, summarized in three parts.

First and foremost, according to Rawls, equal economic opportunity and civil liberties should be available to everyone.[11] Second, this equal access to opportunity would

TABLE 5.1 Basic Summaries of Ethical Criteria in an Environmental Context[12]

1. **Benefit-Cost Analysis**: changes in resource use and environment are desirable if the net gain is positive, regardless of the differential impact on groups and individuals.

2. **Coase Theorem**: environmental protection can be efficient regardless of the agent assuming costs; corrective action by the 'victims,' or payments by them to polluters may be appropriate, as well as the assumption of costs of prevention or compensation by polluters.

3. **Compensation Test**: a new environmental policy, technology, or product is desirable if the gain to beneficiaries is so large that they could compensate losers.

4. **Egalitarian Criterion**: the well-being of society in terms of income and environmental quality is measured by the well-being of the worst-off person in that society.

5. **Natural Rights**: other species and ecosystems have the right to existence regardless of their valuation by humans.

6. **Pareto Criterion**: some persons should be made better off by a change in resource use, and no one should be worse off.

7. **Polluter Pays Principle**: individuals or businesses causing pollution are responsible for the costs of control and of compensation to victims.

8. **Rawls' Theory of Justice**: equal access to economic opportunity and civil liberties may result in greater equality in wealth, income, and influence, reducing the imposition of environmental damage on an unfair basis.

Please note the alphabetical ordering; no other ranking is intended.

increase the relative equality of income, wealth, and political influence. Third, as a consequence, it would be more difficult for any group to impose the acceptance of severe environmental externalities on any other income, ethnic, or geographic group.

Sometimes Rawls' theory (#8 in the table) is simplified as the egalitarian criterion, the fourth entry in Table 5.1.

Rawls' concern about fairness is logically related to the concept of 'Environmental Justice,' the subject of a later section in this chapter. However, before addressing this concept, the Coase Theorem gives a very different perspective. It places efficiency in the paramount position and is less concerned about fairness.

The Coase Theorem: Who Pays for Safe Water?

In 1960, R. H. Coase developed an original approach to the question of responsibility for correcting pollution and environmental degradation. In his view, economists had failed to understand that efficient outcomes could follow if the individuals experiencing damage would pay the individuals causing the damage to modify their behavior.[13] This is a "Beneficiaries Pay" concept.

Depending upon perspective, this may be seen positively as an argument for incentives to polluters, or negatively as bribes to polluters. Coase used several examples; his cattle ranch and grain farm case illustrate the logic. In the absence of a fence, cattle trample the farm's grain, causing economic damage. Of course, the rancher could voluntarily build a fence, and the net economic output for society as a whole (profit from cattle and grain, less fence cost) is increased. But, Coase argues, the farmer can build a fence, or pay the rancher to build a fence, and net economic output for society as a whole is just as high.

If the cost to the farmer of building the fence is less than the value of output that he is losing, there is an economic incentive for the farmer to build the fence, thereby maximizing social welfare, even though he might be the "victim" of unfair grazing practices being followed by the rancher. On the other hand, if the cost of the fence is greater than the loss in value of grain output, social welfare is maximized by not building the fence at all. (This example shows that the pursuit of economic efficiency may lead to an outcome that some will see as unfair.)

The Coase farm and ranch example is still relevant in range country in the western United States. In one Oregon incident in 1996, a landowner shot 11 of a neighbor's cows that were grazing along his creek. But according to local law, the property owner (not the adjacent rancher) is required to build and maintain fencing. Consequently, the landowner was arrested and charged with criminal mischief.[14]

Although the rancher-farmer conflict may seem dated, the problem of neighbors with conflicting values is very relevant to current environmental policy. Consider the general issue when new development brings residential housing into areas traditionally associated with agriculture or industry. The esthetic values and economic interests of the newcomers may differ significantly from those held by long-time residents. If newcomers want higher standards of environmental protection, should they contribute to the costs of pollution prevention?[15]

In general, economists believe that the Coase Theorem is a strong argument for assigning property rights to various types of environmental quality. With clearly established property rights, individuals and businesses can work out efficient solutions privately or in court, without requiring government regulation.

The New York City–Catskill water project illustrates the proposition. The New York City water system serves 9 million people in the City and in surrounding cities and suburbs. Historically, the water has been very clean, and used without filtration. The source for 90 percent of the water is the Catskill Mountain region between the Hudson and Delaware Rivers.

However, growing development in the Catskills has raised concerns that the water may become contaminated with bacteria and viruses from human sewage and farm animal waste. The types of gastrointestinal illness include infections from Giardia, E. coli, Salmonella, and Cryptosporidium. This latter parasite became very well known in the 1990s, causing one-half million illnesses and 50 deaths in Milwaukee and Las Vegas. (Chapter 12 on Water Quality Economics introduces the basic health aspects of water supply.)

New York wanted to continue to meet EPA criteria for preventing illness from these disease agents. In broad terms, there are three options: (1) the City could build a filtration plant at a cost of $5 billion; (2) the City could provide economic incentives to Catskill communities for sewage and animal waste treatment; or (3) federal and state agencies could require the Catskill communities and farms to undertake the necessary measures.

With coordination by the federal EPA and the New York State government, 34 watershed towns reached an agreement with New York City. The City will pay about $700 million to Catskill communities and farms to follow practices that will protect the water quality.[16] In one sense this agreement implements the Coase Theorem because the "victim" (the City) is paying the polluter. The beneficiaries are assuming the cost.

In terms of real-world accomplishment, both are better off. New York City continues to protect the health of its residents, and at a much lower cost than would be needed with a filtration plant. The Catskill communities benefit because they are formally excused from the full cost of water quality protection, and receive sizable payments from the City. They also receive an additional benefit in terms of reduction of local health damage because of better water quality.

Figure 5.1 is a hypothetical situation which shows how a general urban-rural water program is influenced by the concepts in the Coase Theorem. It is generally patterned after the New York City–Catskills Agreement. But, because there are many complex substantive components in the actual agreement, we will generalize to a broad hypothetical case involving Metropolis City and its nearby rural region, Lakeland.

Health damage in Metropolis does not begin until waste discharge passes beyond the threshold of 4 billion gallons annually. Then it climbs rapidly, reaching $3 billion in damage if waste is at the 8 billion gallon level.

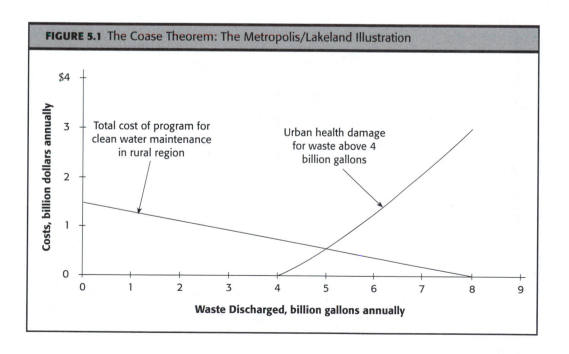

FIGURE 5.1 The Coase Theorem: The Metropolis/Lakeland Illustration

There are no program costs if all 8 billion gallons are discharged as waste in Lakeland. Conversely, each billion gallons costs $200 million to control, and if there is no waste discharge because of full control, there is a program cost of $1.6 billion.

As is the case in the real New York City–Catskills Agreement, our hypothetical city of Metropolis could build and operate its own filtration plant. At an annual cost of $2 billion per year, the optimal solution would be to prevent health damage by keeping untreated discharge water at the 4 billion gallon level.

In this illustration, we should define total social cost as the sum of all three categories: health damage, program cost, or filtration cost for each level of waste discharge. As Figure 5.2 indicates, the most efficient level of discharge is 4 billion gallons. This is because the damage curve is zero initially, but then rises sharply as waste passes the 4 billion gallon figure.[17]

There are many possible water discharge outcomes involving the Lakeland prevention program, filtration, health damage, and cost sharing between Metropolis City and Lakeland. Table 5.2 shows five of the possibilities. They are ordered #1 through #5 on the basis of total cost to the "victim," the City.

Obviously, this defines a ranking for Lakeland as well. In Case #1, for example, there is no prevention program. But this Case has unacceptably high health damage to the City. In the total social cost row, this case is the highest, and therefore least desirable on an efficiency basis.

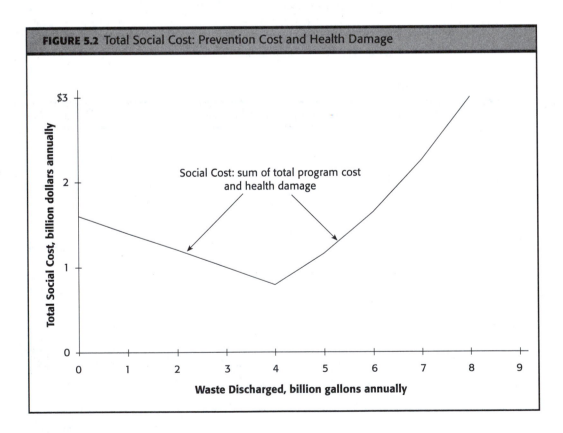

FIGURE 5.2 Total Social Cost: Prevention Cost and Health Damage

Social Cost: sum of total program cost and health damage

TABLE 5.2 Metropolis, Lakeland, and the Coase Theorem
(dollar values in billion dollars per year)

	#1 *No Program, No Filtration*	#2 *Filtration but No Program*	#3 *City Pays Full Program Cost*	#4 *City, Lakeland Divide Cost*	#5 *Lakeland Pays Full Cost*
A. Cost to City					
Payments to Lakeland	$0	$0	$.8	$.4	$0
Filtration plant	$0	$2	0	0	$0
Health damage	$3	$0	0	0	$0
Total Cost to City	$3	$2	$.8	$.4	$0
B. Cost to Lakeland					
Payments from City	$0	$0	($.8)	($.4)	$0
Program cost	$0	$0	$.8	$.8	$.8
Total Cost to Lakeland	$0	$0	$0	$.4	$.8
C. Total social cost to City and Lakeland	$3	$2	$.8	$.8	$.8
D. Water summary:					
Waste discharge	8	4	0	0	0
Clean water (billion gallons)	0	4	8	8	8

Note: remember that this is a hypothetical illustration of the Coase Theorem and the Polluter Pays Principle. It is suggested by the real New York City–Catskills Agreement.

Filtration without a prevention program (#2) eliminates the health damage, but at a high financial and social cost.

The last three cases are each optimal: four billion gallons are cleaned by the program, leaving four billion gallons discharged. These three cases differ according to the source of payments for the program. In Case #5, the Polluter Pays Principle requires full Lakeland payment of the $.8 billion annual program cost. In Case #4, the City pays 50 percent, and in Case #3 it pays 100 percent.

In actual political situations involving a wealthy city and a poorer rural area, Cases #3 and #4 are more likely to be feasible. And these cases reflect the interaction of the Coase Theorem and the Polluter Pays Principle with efficiency. If the hypothetical polluting region of Lakeland pays full cost, we have an efficient outcome. But also, if the "victim" here, Metropolis, assumes some or all of the pollution prevention cost in Lakeland, that is efficient as well. Both principles are compatible with efficient results in pollution control and environmental protection.

TABLE 5.3 Conditions for Effective Coase-Type Environmental Programs

1. Ability to organize.
2. Income of "victims" high enough to pay polluters.
3. In bargaining, both sides can offer something.
4. Transaction cost is low.
5. Damage source clearly identified.
6. Damage is reversible.

Coase-type agreements offer the opportunity to maintain environmental protection without a regulatory organization managing detailed standards. Table 5.3 identifies six conditions which indicate when a Coase-type agreement might be effective.

Both sides must be able to organize in such a way that leadership can represent the parties and make a real commitment to implementation. This is the first condition. The second condition requires the sufferers of pollution to have sufficient income to contribute significantly to pollution control costs for the polluter.

The third requirement is related to the prior condition; each side must be able to trade something of value to other sides. Typically, the polluter can offer pollution reduction, while the affected side offers financial help.

Fourth, the mechanics of negotiation and implementation must be low enough in cost so that the agreement is feasible. This would ordinarily mean the costs of legal and technical personnel: economists term this 'transaction cost.'

Fifth, the damage source must be clearly identified as well as the physical means of pollution reduction. Finally, the damage should be reversible or preventable. Water pollution illness is usually reversible, but large-scale fatal damage is not.

Of course, the Metropolis City–Lakeland illustration was designed to reflect these conditions. But, much more significantly, the real case for New York City and the Catskills appears to meet the requirements. As the agreement is implemented, it will be of considerable interest to see if its potential is realized.

But, what of those cases where these conditions are not met? Do ethics and efficiency always mesh so smoothly? In some respects, the cases where both polluter-pays regulation and Coase-type agreements fail in practice are situations which do not meet these requirements. There seems to be a tendency for this group of problems to involve ethnic minorities, and this latter kind of circumstance has come to be identified as the 'Environmental Justice' issue.

Environmental Justice and Economics

Environmental justice is a movement promoting the fair treatment of people of all races, income, and culture with respect to the development, implementation, and enforcement of environmental laws, regulations, and policies. Fair treatment implies that no person or group of people should shoulder a disproportionate share of the negative environmental impacts resulting from the execution of this country's domestic and foreign policy programs.[18]

This definition of environmental justice is philosophically related to Rawls' Theory of Justice. No group, whether delineated by race, class, gender, or age, should incur a disproportionate share of negative environmental externality.

Environmental justice assumes that a disadvantaged group would oppose the imposition of unusual environmental damage, and this describes the context of the City of Chester problem. The Chester case focuses on the allegations of discriminatory practice in the location and operation of waste treatment facilities. Chester is 14 miles southwest of Philadelphia. Between 1987 and 1996, five waste management facilities were approved for location in the predominantly Black community of Chester. As a result of industrial pollution, as well as the effect of waste operations, the EPA believes, pollution-linked health damage is unacceptably high.[19] The major findings are summarized in Table 5.4.

A *New York Times* reporter described the impact this way: "A walk results in a nearly constant assault on the senses. The air is thick with acrid smells and, often, smoke. Dump trucks rumble through throughout the day. Conditions often force residents to flee inside and seal their windows."[20]

On a positive note, the concern about potential discrimination has led several local industries and Pennsylvania's governor to work with Chester to improve both its economic and environmental standing.[21]

If we apply the ethical criteria from Table 5.1 to the Chester case, we have mixed results. Rawls' Theory of Justice, the Polluter Pays Principle, and the Egalitarian Criterion all suggest that Chester's unusual accumulation of waste and pollution is unethical. On the other hand, Benefit-Cost Analysis and the Coase Theorem seem to say that the result is acceptable because it is efficient.

By examining the written record pertaining to Chester, it does seem that the racial composition or poverty of the Chester community is a factor in the siting of waste and polluting facilities.[22] Is this unique, or part of a wider problem?

An important study by Brooks and Sethi provides empirical support for the hypothesis that Black communities experience greater pollution. They studied toxic emissions and exposure for each zip code area in the United States. They found that the elasticity of exposure is 2.8, that is, increasing the Black percentage of the population by 1 percent increases toxic exposure by 2.8 percent.[23] Another result: the elasticity of exposure with respect to voter participation is

---

TABLE 5.4 Findings in EPA Technical Study for Chester Environmental Justice Case[24]

▲ Lead in the blood of children is unacceptably high.
▲ Cancer risk from pollution in Chester exceeds acceptable levels.
▲ Kidney, liver, and respiratory disease from pollution in Chester exceeds acceptable levels.
▲ Health risk from eating contaminated fish is unacceptably high.

negative, −3.8. Here, the implication is that communities that vote heavily, whether White or Black, reduce the probability of their communities' exposure to toxic emissions.

But what ethical principle applies in the case where a disadvantaged group seeks a program with environmental hazards in exchange for financial compensation? This second case centers on the storage of high level nuclear fuel waste on Native American Indian tribal land. It is complex, and its solution does not adapt easily to the existing ethical principles in environmental economics.

In this case, tribal leadership has sought to secure the right to nuclear waste storage because of the associated financial incentives. This is understandable, because the per capita income for Native Americans is about 55 percent of the level of White Americans.[25]

The problem has arisen because of the federal policy of planning centralized storage for spent nuclear fuel waste from nuclear power plants. The storage problem, in turn, is very difficult because of the need to provide secure storage on the order of one million years.[26] A federal facility in Nevada at Yucca Mountain near Death Valley is planned on a long-term basis but may not open.

However, seeking short-term storage locations, the government began to offer cash incentives to tribal governments. This program operated from 1990 to 1995.[27] Following the program's termination and its last cash awards, private consortia of nuclear utilities continued to negotiate with the tribes. The two leading tribal governments in the federal program each reached agreements. The Mescalero Apache program, however, has terminated, and only the Skull Valley Goshute agreement continued in the late 1990s.[28]

In the context of environmental justice as defined above in the Presidential Executive Order, the Skull Valley Goshute present a challenge. Unlike the Chester case, here an ethnic minority *seeks* a disproportionate share of negative environmental impact in exchange for financial reward.

Another perspective on this case is that safety and efficiency provide the best criteria for evaluating nuclear fuel waste storage programs. The criteria should be independent of race or income, emphasizing minimal waste transport and the technical competence necessary to reduce the risks of radioactive exposure, nuclear accidents, and terrorist actions.[29]

Environmental justice is perhaps marginal to our normal concept of ethical issues in environmental economics. Yet it is clear that it raises parallel questions with respect to the ethical criteria discussed in this chapter.

Summary

The challenging ethical problem of this generation's responsibility for the future environment and economy is taken up in the final chapters on Ecological Economics and Sustainability, and in Chapter 18 on Climate Change Economics and Policy.

This chapter has surveyed some of the leading ethical issues in environmental economics. Most of the criteria are grounded in economics. However, two of these concepts are noneconomic in origin. The Natural Rights principle and Rawls' Theory of Justice originated outside of the field of economics, but both concepts have become of interest to economists.

The Coase Theorem has been of particular importance to environmental economists. It assumes that efficiency and environmental protection can both be served if "victims" pay polluters to control pollution. This is in direct opposition to the Polluter Pays Principle favored in Europe.

With a hypothetical watershed illustration suggested by the New York City–Catskills Agreement, the interaction between upstream sewage/animal waste treatment and city water quality becomes important. Although several criteria suggest efficient policies, their political and equity impacts differ.

The possibility of discrimination in environmental protection has led to the development of environmental justice as an active field of inquiry. In the City of Chester case, citizens are opposed to the apparent disproportionate siting of waste treatment facilities in their town.

However, the Goshute Skull Valley–nuclear waste case is in sharp contrast. Here, the Goshute Indians seek nuclear fuel waste storage on their property in order to obtain substantial financial payments. This Goshute effort follows a federal program which sought to locate nuclear fuel waste on Native American tribal lands.

Questions for Discussion and Analysis

1. In 1972, Justice William O. Douglas supported "the conferral of standing upon environmental objects to sue for their own preservation." In contrast, Stephen Swallow asserts that humans determine value and that natural objects cannot have value apart from that determined by humans. Can you reconcile these two points of view?

2. Apply the Coase Theorem to these assumptions: (a) Damage from a ranch's cattle to a farm's wheat is $15,000 per year. (b) It would cost the farm $10,000 annually for a contract to build and maintain a fence to prevent the damage. (c) With its experienced cowhands, the ranch could build and maintain the fence for $4,000 per year. What are three possibilities? Are they all efficient? Fair?

3. Analyze the argument that the Polluter Pays Principle reduces competition derived from the avoidance of environmental protection costs by producers.

4. Suggest two examples of environmental policies that would be supported by the application of the Pareto Criterion.

5. In the New York City–Catskills program, a high-income "victim" is compensating a lower-income region for reducing their pollution. Do you think this is a necessary characteristic of Coase-type solutions that work in the real world?

6. Consider a hypothetical case in which vehicular pollution by high-income commuters causes significant environmental damage to a low-income residential

neighborhood. Analyze the environmental policies that would be supported by (a) Rawls' egalitarian approach, (b) the Coase Theorem, and (c) the Polluter Pays Principle.

7. Why isn't the Chester problem related to environmental justice being resolved in a manner similar to the New York City–Catskills program? Would the Coase Theorem apply here?

Notes to Chapter 5

1. In Chapter 19, Jon Erickson notes the historical linkage between the interest in moral judgment by the early social utilitarians (such as Mill and Bentham), and the modern focus on ecological economics.

2. A. C. Pigou, *The Economics of Welfare* (London: MacMillan, 1920), page 5 in the fourth edition, 1952.

3. In Samuelson's "Introduction" to J. de V. Graff's *Theoretical Welfare Economics* (Cambridge, UK: Cambridge University Press, 1971), Samuelson is uncomfortable with ethics playing a role in economics, and strongly endorses the Pareto Criterion discussed below.

4. Intergovernmental Panel on Climate Change, Volume III, *Climate Change 1995: Economic and Social Dimensions* (Cambridge, UK: Cambridge University Press, 1996), Chapter 4.

5. The usual formulation of this statement holds that competition maximizes the sum of consumers and producers surplus. This, as defined in Chapter 1, is identical to consumers value less producers cost.

6. A good introduction to the Pareto Improvement and the Kaldor-Hicks criteria is in J. A. Lesser, D. E. Dodds, and R. O. Zerbe, Jr., *Environmental Economics and Policy* (Reading, MA: Addison Wesley Longman, 1997), pages 58–63.

7. Of course, the original controversy was more complex than this summary: see N. Kaldor, "Welfare Propositions of Economics and Interpersonal Comparisons of Utility," 1939 *Economic Journal* 49:549–552; J. R. Hicks, "Foundations of Welfare Economics," 1939 *Economic Journal* 49:696–712; T. Scitovsky, "A Note on Welfare Propositions in Economics," 1941 *Review of Economic Studies* 9:77–88; E. J. Mishan, *Cost-Benefit Analysis* (New York: Praeger, 1971), pages 316–321. A broad technical review is in R. E. Just, D. L. Hueth, and A. Schmitz, *Applied Welfare Economics and Public Policy* (Englewood Cliffs, NJ: Prentice-Hall, 1982), Chapters 1–3.

8. See the first section in Chapter 4, the discussion of Congressional legislation defining the application of benefit-cost analysis.

9. The best discussions of this Principle are in European and Canadian publications. In particular: B. C. Field and N. D. Olewiler, *Environmental Economics: First Canadian Edition* (Toronto, Montreal: McGraw-Hill Ryerson, 1995), pages 416-417; World Commission on Environment and Development, *Our Common Future* (Oxford: Oxford University Press, 1987), pages 220–222; and J. B. Opschoor and H. B. Vos, *Economic Instruments for Environmental Protection* (Paris: OECD, 1989), pages 27–30. Seligman notes that liability funding for Superfund hazardous sites is one form of the Polluter Pays Principle; H. Seligman, "Liability Funding and Superfund Clean-up Remedies," May 1998 *Journal of Environmental Economics and Management* 35(3):205–224. Her empirical work finds that, where responsible parties are active in both management and finance, the result is lower costs for clean-up remedies.

10. A. V. Kneese and W. D. Schulze, "Ethics and Environmental Economics," Chapter 5 in A. V. Kneese and J. L. Sweeney, eds., *Handbook of Natural Resource and Energy Economics* (Amsterdam: North Holland, 1985).

11. The first point here is a simplified summary of Rawls' "two principles of justice," and his "general conception of justice," pages 60–62 in J. Rawls, *A Theory of Justice* (Cambridge, MA: Harvard University Press, 1971). The second and third points in the text here were developed in discussion with Jon Erickson and Neha Khanna, March 1997. Kneese and Schulze take a somewhat different approach to Rawls, emphasizing the distributive aspects of Rawls' work as well as its complexity.

12. The Egalitarian Criterion in Table 5.1 is from Kneese and Schulze, *op. cit.* The Pareto and Benefit-Cost criteria are also discussed by them, and in Chapters 1 and 4 of this text. The other criteria are discussed in the text here. The Natural Rights criterion is related to nonhuman value, a concept which appears in Chapter 19 on Ecological Economics and in the Biodiversity Chapter 15.

13. R. H. Coase, "The Problem of Social Cost," October 1960 *Journal of Law and Economics*: 1–44. Coase was awarded a Nobel Prize in 1991 for his work.

14. *High Country News*, November 29, 1996, page 3.

15. A point suggested by Stephen Swallow. Also see *High Country News*, August 3, 1998, page 5.

16. The basic reference is *New York City Watershed Memorandum of Agreement, Final Draft*, September 10, 1996. The *New York Times* periodically addresses the subject.

17. The usual marginal analysis with MB = MC is awkward here, because this illustration has what economists call a "corner solution"; the optimal minimum social cost is at the point with zero health damage and 4 billion gallons annual waste discharge, without the filtration plant. The plant is always more costly than the Catskills prevention program, so the plant is not represented in the figures.

18. U.S. Departments of Defense and Energy, and U.S. EPA, Strategic Environmental Research and Development Program, Envirosense Home Page, "Presidential Executive Order 12898-Environmental Justice," February 27, 1997.

19. U.S. EPA, Region III, "Environmental Risk Study for the City of Chester, Pennsylvania," in conjunction with the Pennsylvania Department of Environmental Resources, June 1995.

20. *New York Times*, "Suit Says Racial Bias Led to Clustering of Solid-Waste Sites," May 29, 1996, page A15.

21. Personal communication, Una Moneypenny (Cornell University) and Patrick Anderson, U.S. EPA, Southeast Pennsylvania Section Chief, March 7, 1997.

22. See references in Notes 19 and 20.

23. Their study analyzed toxic exposure and its relationship to each zip code area's characteristics with respect to race, voter participation, income, education, and other socioeconomic variables. N. Brooks and R. Sethi, "The Distribution of Pollution: Community Characteristics and Exposure to Air Toxics," February 1997 *Journal of Environmental Economics and Management* 32(2):233–250.

24. "Risk Study," *op. cit.,* Note 19 above.

25. U.S. Bureau of the Census, *Statistical Abstract of the United States* (Washington, DC: U.S. GPO), pages 50, 471.

26. See D. Chapman, *Energy Resources and Energy Corporations* (Ithaca, NY: Cornell University Press, 1983), pages 261–264.

27. J. D. Erickson, D. Chapman, and R. E. Johnny, "Monitored Retrievable Storage of Spent Nuclear Fuel in Indian Country: Liability, Sovereignty, and Socioeconomics," 1994 *American Indian Law Review* 19(1):73–103. Also, see the articles by Noah Sachs, Grace Thorpe, and four others on "Monitored Retrievable Storage," Fall 1996 *Natural Resources Journal* 36(4):641–724.

28. *Nuclear Fuel*, "Tired of Waiting, 11 Utilities Sign Lease with Goshutes for Storage Facility," January 27, 1997. Most Goshutes live in nearby Salt Lake City; seven Goshute

households live on their land. The Skull Valley land has previously been leased for rocket testing. Tooele County is also the location of facilities for chemical weapons testing, a nerve gas incinerator, and two hazardous waste incinerators.

29. Ben Rusche, Director, U.S. Office of Civilian Radioactive Waste Management, statement before the U.S. Senate Committee on Environment and Public Works, Subcommittee on Nuclear Regulation, June 18, 1987, especially page 12. Other siting criteria include a location without nearby hazardous material facilities, and federal ownership.

CHAPTER 6

ECONOMIC THEORY AND ENVIRONMENTAL RESOURCES: AN INTRODUCTION

In the first chapter, the concept of environmental resources included both economic and natural ecosystem activities. This chapter introduces economic theory related to the use of renewable biological and exhaustible mineral resources. It concludes with the conceptual approach to efficient environmental policy. Theoretically, optimizing methods can be applied to both pollution prevention and species protection.

While the first chapter served both as an introduction or as a simplified review of basic economic theory, this chapter is more complex. Calculus is helpful here, while it is not necessary to understand Chapter 1. Even so, there is sufficient numerical and graphic presentation for the ambitious student to understand most of the relevant economic concepts without calculus.

Renewable Biological Resources: A Question of Sustainability

Sustainability in use is of growing concern for our renewable resources. Fisheries, forests, and pasture all share biological characteristics that have economic significance. Consider a hypothetical forest growing from a cleared area. (The area may have been cleared by fire, timber harvesting, storm damage, or other causes.) Initially, the growth rate is very rapid if the forest is undisturbed. However, as the forest grows, crowding reduces access to sunlight and perhaps water and nutrients. The growth rate peaks, and then growth declines.

Of course, the stock of biomass continues to accumulate as long as the growth rate is positive. But, as the rate of growth slows, the stock approaches the maximum carrying capacity of the area. In theory, once attaining this maximum carrying capacity, the stock is stable at this level on an indefinite basis. Chapter 14 uses these concepts to explain forestry economics.

In reality, all of the possible causes of clearing a forest may occur at any time, moving growth and stock off of the idealized path just described. When this happens, when harvesting or unexpected damage reduces the biomass stock, growth is renewed at earlier rates.

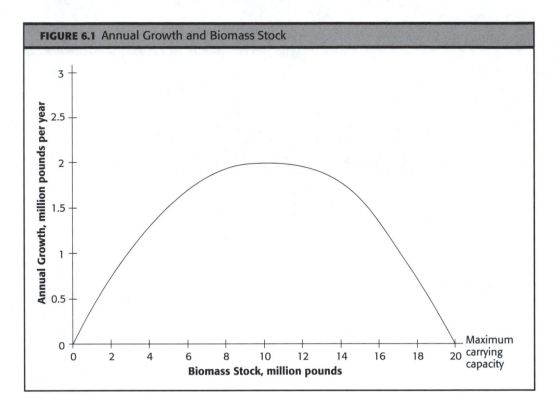

FIGURE 6.1 Annual Growth and Biomass Stock

But these concepts can be introduced in the context of illustrating elementary fishery economics. Figure 6.1 shows the relationship of growth rate and biomass for ecofins, an imaginary species, perhaps a fish, or a shellfish, or an aquatic whalelike mammal. The figure and associated Table 6.1 apply to one of many localized areas where ecofins are found.

In this illustration, when there is no existing biomass, growth is zero because there is no reproduction. If the local ecofin fishery is actually extinct, there can be no growth without reintroduction of reproducing stock from some other area.

When the biomass stock is above zero, say at 2 million pounds, the annual growth is 0.72 million pounds, or 36% at that point. At a higher stock level, say 8 million pounds, the growth is a higher 1.92 million pounds, but at a lower rate of 24%.

The highest volume of growth is with a biomass level of 10 million pounds, where the natural growth is 2 million pounds annually. (All weight values in this illustration are in million pounds.) But, although this is the greatest amount of stock, the growth rate has declined to 20%.

The natural carrying capacity of this small ecofin fishery is 20 million pounds. At this biomass stock level, crowding has eliminated net increase. Of course, individuals in the population continue to reproduce, but the net growth in biomass has ceased. The death rate matches the birth rate, and net change is zero. The population has reached its carrying capacity.

TABLE 6.1 Annual Growth and the Stock of Biomass for Ecofins (million pounds)

Biomass Stock Level	Annual Growth	Growth Rate Annual Percent
0	0	0%
2	0.72	36%
4	1.28	32%
6	1.68	28%
8	1.92	24%
10	2.00	20%
12	1.92	16%
14	1.68	12%
16	1.28	8%
18	0.72	4%
20	0	0%

The biomass stock level is growing each year, but, since the growth rate declines, it slowly approaches the maximum carrying capacity, as represented in Figure 6.2.

It may be apparent that the figures and Table 6.1 are based upon a mathematical representation of population growth. The relationship is

$$AG = rX * \left(1 - \frac{X}{K}\right) \tag{6-1}$$

$$AGR = \frac{AG}{X} = r * \left(1 - \frac{X}{K}\right) \tag{6-2}$$

AG represents the annual growth in million pounds per year. K is the maximum natural carrying capacity, and X is the current stock of biomass. The final term, 'r,' is basic to the concept: it represents the intrinsic or natural growth rate. When the existing biomass level X is only a small fraction of carry capacity K, the annual growth rate (AGR) is very high. As the existing stock approaches carrying capacity, the growth rate becomes very small.

Equation (6-1) is logistic, and is often referred to as a Schaefer model after one of the pioneers of its use, M. B. Schaefer.

Other functions can also have the symmetrical growth curve in Figure 6.1 with the S-shaped biomass curve in Figure 6.2. A simple quadratic equation[1] would have similar characteristics, and is often used in forestry economics as it is in the forestry chapter here.

The intrinsic natural growth rate has been estimated for several fisheries. Some of these values are shown in Table 6.2, as well as the estimates of maximum carrying capacity. The table also shows the maximum sustainable yield harvest.

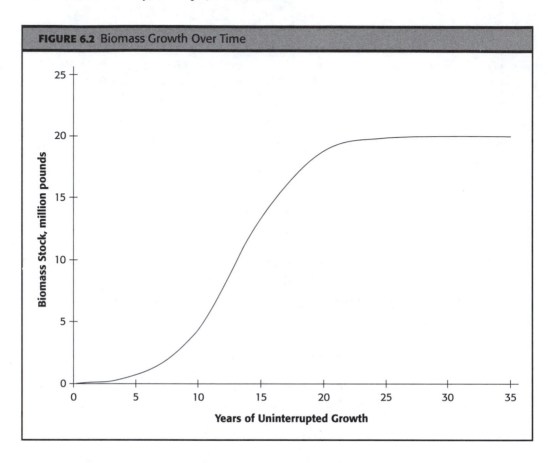

FIGURE 6.2 Biomass Growth Over Time

Sustainability, in this context, means choosing the annual harvest rate so that each year the growth in biomass equals the amount harvested. Table 6.2 includes the yearly maximum sustainable yield values for the whales, halibut, and lobsters shown there. The table (and Figure 6.1) also give the same sustainable yield values for ecofins.

In fact, any harvest level in the Figure 6.1 curve is sustainable. How is the maximum sustainable yield found? By maximizing Equation (6-1), the value for the annual maximum sustainable yield harvest is found.[2] With this Schaefer logistic curve, the results are very simple:

$$H_{msy} = \text{maximum AG} \tag{6-3}$$

$$H_{msy} = \frac{rK}{4} \tag{6-4}$$

$$X_{msy} = \frac{K}{2} \tag{6-5}$$

H_{msy} is the maximum sustainable yield harvest. X_{msy} represents the biomass stock level where maximum sustainable yield harvest is at its highest possible level. For

TABLE 6.2 Representative Estimates of Intrinsic Natural Growth Rates and[3]
Carrying Capacity

Maximum Carrying Capacity (K)	Intrinsic Natural Growth Rate (r)	Maximum Sustainable Yield MSY-H	Species
400,000 whales	.08	200,000 whales	Fin whale, Antarctic
136,000 whales	.29	68,000 whales	Blue whales
20 million pounds	.40	10 million pounds	Ecofins, fictional
80.5 million tonnes	.71	40.25 million tonnes	Pacific halibut, area 2
3.26 million pounds	1.29	1.63 million pounds	Miminegash lobsters
3.50 million pounds	1.80	1.75 million pounds	Port Maitland lobsters

Note: 'Tonne' is a metric ton, equal to 1.1 U.S. tons. The 'ecofins' are the fictional species used in the text to illustrate economic theory. The two lobster fisheries are in maritime Canada provinces.

ecofins, the H_{msy} is 2 million pounds each year, and the biomass stock level to support this amount of harvesting is a population at 10 million pounds.

To this point, the emphasis has been on the biological characteristics of a fishery. The next step is to see how prices, fishing costs, organization, and external values affect fishing levels and possible extinction.

Suppose that ecofins sell at boatside at $1.50 per pound, and the local ecofinnery is too small for its catch to influence market prices.

Also, assume that running an ecofin boat costs $80,000 per year. This figure includes fuel, hired labor, supplies, and loan, lease, and other boat charges.

Finally, assume each boat catches one percent of the existing biomass stock on an annual basis. This relationship develops the overall link between boats on the water, biomass stock, and harvest:

$$H = aEX \qquad (6\text{-}6)$$

$$\frac{H}{E} = aX \qquad (6\text{-}7)$$

E is the number of boats, often defined by economists as reflecting effort. The ratio H/E, of course, represents harvest catch per boat.

The coefficient 'a' is usually termed the catch coefficient. It shows the percentage of ecofins that each boat can expect to catch in a year. So, with 'a' defined as one percent per boat, if the biomass stock level X is at 6 million pounds and 83 boats start the year fishing, the total catch will be 5 million pounds. This translates into about 60,000 pounds per boat. Since the price is $1.50 per pound, each boat makes $90,000 in sales, which more than covers its cost.

However, there is a serious problem here. Turning to Table 6.1, if the biomass stock is at 6 million pounds, the annual growth is only 1.68 million pounds, far below the year's catch of 5 million. Clearly this level of harvest is not sustainable. In fact, Figure 6.1 indicates the maximum sustainable yield is only 2 million pounds. With this current harvesting level at 5 million pounds, stocks will be reduced.

This discussion is about an 'open access fishery,' meaning that each individual boat can catch as many ecofins as possible each year. With the data already at hand, the equilibrium situation for sustainable harvest, number of boats, and biomass stock can be determined. The logic is simple: if boats are losing money, some will drop out, reducing the number on the water next year. If they are making a profit, new boats will start fishing. The theory here is building on the competitive market described in the first chapter.

Since equilibrium in a competitive open access fishery will stabilize when total revenue and total cost are in balance, then

$$TR_{syoa} = TC_{syoa} \tag{6-8a}$$

$$p * H_{syoa} = c * E_{syoa} \tag{6-8b}$$

$$\$1.50 * H_{syoa} = \$80,000 * E_{syoa} \tag{6-8c}$$

The subscript for harvest and for boats means 'sustained yield open access,' the competitive solution. With Equations (6-1) through (6-8), both total revenue and total cost for the fishery can be reformulated so that each can be shown as they change with the number of boats.[4] This is Figure 6.3, which is placed on a sustainable yield basis. In the figure, the open access sustainable yield level for fishing boats is E_{oa}, where total rev-

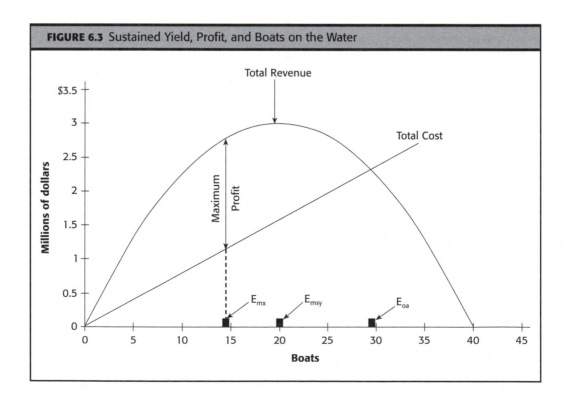

FIGURE 6.3 Sustained Yield, Profit, and Boats on the Water

TABLE 6.3 Basic Assumptions for Ecofin Fishery Cases		
Variable	*Definition*	*Amount*
K	maximum carrying capacity	20 million pounds
r	intrinsic natural growth rate	.4
p	price	$1.50 per pound
a	catch rate	1% of X, existing biomass
c	boat cost	$80,000 per boat annually

enue and total cost are equal. The open access equilibrium is with 29.33 boats, and the complete solution for the open access fishery is in Tables 6.3 and 6.4.

In Table 6.4, the competitive open access fishery harvests 1.56 million pounds annually on a sustainable basis. This is fairly close to the maximum sustainable yield of 2 million pounds, but the stock level X_{syoa} is much lower than X_{msy}.

Note, however, that cost per pound is much higher and the harvest per boat is much lower.

In this example, there is no consumer surplus calculated because there is no change in price. Producer surplus has the same meaning as in the first chapter: the difference between total revenue from sales and total cost. For open access, there is no producer surplus. In contrast, maximum sustainable yield results in producer surplus of $1.4 million annually.

The greatest producer surplus arises when the ecofin fishery is managed to maximize profit. In other words, number of boats and sustainable harvest level should be found where marginal revenue equals marginal cost. For competitive open access, the comparable rule is to find the solution where price equals marginal cost. This maximum profit boat and harvest level is also shown in Table 6.4 and Figure 6.3. Producer surplus is at the highest possible level, $1.62 million annually.

The number of boats and the cost per pound of catch are at their lowest for this case, and catch per boat as well as producer surplus are at their highest levels.[5]

This controlled fishery could be managed in two ways. It could be managed as a monopoly by an owner, in the manner suggested in Chapter 1. Alternatively, a government agency could fix boat and harvest levels. (Fishery management policies are discussed in somewhat greater detail at the end of this chapter.)

To this point, nonmarket environmental values have not affected market decisions. But suppose ecofins have considerable existence value, in a manner comparable to the external social value possessed by dolphins, whales and elephants. For example:

$$NSV = TR - TC + v * X \qquad (6\text{-}9)$$

NSV is net social value again, as it was in Chapter 1. TR and TC still are total revenue and total cost. Now the term 'vX' represents the existence value of unharvested stock X, and v is this external value per pound of uncaught ecofin. In this case, then, net social value is total profit from the annual harvest plus the positive

TABLE 6.4 Sustainability, Open Access, and Optimal Control for the Ecofin Fishery

Variable	Policy Cases		
	Maximum Sustainable Yield	*Open Access Competition*	*Maximum Profit Producer Surplus*
X, existing biomass stock, million pounds	10	5.331	12.67
E, boats in fishery number per year	20	29.33	14.67
H, harvest per year million pounds	2	1.56	1.86
H/E, harvest per boat pounds	100,000	53,333	126,667
TC/H, cost per pound	80¢	$1.50	63¢
TC, total cost in fishery per year	$1.6M	$2.35M	$1.17M
TR, total revenue per year	$3M	$2.35M	$2.79M
PS, producer surplus $ per year	$1.4M	0	$1.62M

externality value of surviving ecofins. With the simple ecofin illustration in use here, the solution for optimal number of boats is not too difficult.[6] It is

$$E^*_{nsv} = \frac{r}{2a}\left(1 - \frac{c}{pak}\right) - \frac{v}{2pa} \qquad (6\text{-}10)$$

In fact, the solutions for the open access and maximum profit cases can each be related to the optimal net social value E^*_{nsv} level. They are

$$E^*_{nsv} = E^*_{\pi} - \frac{v}{2pa} \qquad (6\text{-}11a)$$

$$E^*_{oa} = 2E^*_{\pi} \qquad (6\text{-}11b)$$

Suppose the 'v' existence value is 20¢ for each harvested pound of ecofins. The result is to define the optimal harvest at 1.28 million pounds annually, with a stock level X approaching the maximum carrying capacity. This is summarized in Table 6.5.

If existence value is high enough, then no fishing leads to the highest net social value. In this illustration, 44¢ is the switch-over value. When v is less than 44¢ per pound, net social value is increased by harvesting ecofins. When v is 44¢ and higher, no fishing is the best policy.[7]

Although this is just an introduction to the theory of fishery resources and their environmental value, it does provide the basis for fundamental conclusions. Open ac-

TABLE 6.5 The Case Where the Existence Value of the Population Level Affects Social Value: The Results

Variable	Optimal Results
v	20¢ per pound unharvested stock of ecofins (assumed)
X	16 million pounds stock level
E	8 boats
H	1.28 million pounds yearly
H/E	160,000 pounds catch per boat
TC/H	50¢ cost per pound
TC	$640,000 total cost of boats in fishery
TR	$1.92 million total revenue yearly
PS	$1.28 million annual producers surplus
EV	$3.2 million annual existence value of uncaught ecofins
NSV_{nsv}	$4.4 million, optimal net social value for existence value and producers surplus
NSV_{ps}	$4.15 million, maximum profit net social value
NSV_{msy}	$3.4 million, maximum sustained yield net social value
NSV_{oa}	$1.07 million, open access net social value

Note: Compare Table 6.4 to these values.

cess fishing reduces fish populations below levels that would be maintained by other management policies. One environmental group argues that, on a global basis,

> . . . *too many fishermen are competing for a limited resource and that the incentive for increasing capacity and effort remains unchanged. To bring fishing fleet capacity into line with sustainable fishing, the world's fishing states will have to reduce the world fleet by two thirds.*[8]

This economist, working with the World Wildlife Fund, may have overstated his case. But his interest is clearly focused on the topics just reviewed.

This discussion of sustainable management of biological resources has concentrated upon fisheries. However, Chapter 14 on forestry economics applies these concepts as well. Economic incentives leading to extinction are also relevant to both fish and forests; this topic is taken up later in this chapter as well as in the forestry chapter.

Finite Resources: Use and Depletion

Economists have been concerned with potential exhaustion of limited economic resources for much of this century, and economic theory has developed a rigorous perspective which gives them clear answers within its own framework. In two later chapters, on the "Limits to Growth" issue and "World Oil: A Strategic Limited Resource?" potential depletion is considered in greater depth for actual resources. The last chapter on sustainability returns to the subject.

These concepts are intended to apply to any economically useful environmental resource whose rate of natural formation is so slow as to be essentially zero. This is the case for a broad array of industrial and consumer commodities: metals such as iron, aluminum, and copper; fossil energy (petroleum, natural gas, coal); gold, platinum, etc. Usually it is clear whether something is finite or renewable: sunlight and most forests are renewable, while diamonds and conventional crude oil are finite.

There are, however, some resources where the classification is awkward. Is a thousand-year-old forest a limited or renewable resource? Water is considered a renewable resource, but how about underground aquifers of geologic water that were deposited millions of years ago? Commonplace, everyday sand and gravel might be finite, but each is so easily obtainable that the classification is irrelevant. Nevertheless, notwithstanding the borderline cases, the classification is usually clear, and is of interest with respect to basic industrial metals and fossil energy.

The approach here is to first describe the problem of dividing a limited resource between two periods, to maximize profit, or alternatively to maximize social welfare. Suppose, as an illustration, that there are 8 grams of kryptonite to divide between this year and next. There is a demand curve for kryptonite which is

$$P = 20 - 2 * Y \qquad (6\text{-}12)$$

From this initial two-period decision, the next step is finding the number of years to exhaustion. For both cases (the two-period case and the optimal period to exhaustion case), we want to look for general patterns and rules in sales and pricing.

Finally, we see how technological innovation and new commodities can have a powerful influence on the economics of finite resources.

This basic problem seems simple, very similar to the economics of crude oil in the introductory illustration of economic theory in the first chapter. In fact, it may seem even simpler because kryptonite is costless to its current owner, so initially cost relations are not a problem.

Suppose the owner does not care about society's welfare, seeking simply to maximize the accumulated profit from selling kryptonite:

$$\text{maximize PS} = P_1 * Y_1 * (1 + r) + P_2 * Y_2 \qquad (6\text{-}13)$$

PS is producer surplus again. Sales are made at the end of each period. The profit from the first period is immediately invested and earns an interest rate 'r.' Consequently, the owner wants to choose the values for Y_1 and Y_2 so that, given the demand function and the finite supply of 10 grams, producer surplus takes the highest possible value.

(Important note: this problem is often expressed as present value, a concept in discounting and time preferences which is explained in greater depth in Chapter 4. The results are identical, regardless of the discounting method that is used.)

Assume that the kryptonite owner lends out the first year's revenue at 20% interest, perhaps developing a credit card business for students.

One obvious solution to the problem is to divide the 8 grams equally, so 4 are sold in each period, at a price of $12 per gram. (This price is found from the demand curve.) So revenue is $48 at the end of each period, and the first period's profit earns an additional $9.60 from reinvestment at 20% interest. Result: $105.60 in producer surplus.

Now look at a very different possibility: all 8 grams are sold in the first period, and the revenue is reinvested. In the demand curve, the price must be lowered to $4 to sell the 8 grams. Reinvesting the $32 earns an additional $6.40 in interest, so PS is a much lower $38.40 in this case.

Without using calculus, we could undertake a series of similar calculations dividing the 8 grams between the two periods in several different ways. The result would look like Figure 6.4. This can be done with a series of tables like Table 6.6, which shows the kinds of results to be expected for different amounts sold in each of the periods.

The figure shows that the absolute maximum producer surplus can be found when 51.1 percent is sold in the first period. In other words, 4.091 grams in Year One, and 3.909 grams in Year Two. The profit is $105.63 at the end of the period.

Table 6.6 with these values illustrates an important principle in economic theory. Note that

$$MR_1 = \frac{MR_2}{1 + r}, \text{ or} \tag{6-14a}$$

$$MR_2 = (1 + r) * MR_1 \tag{6-14b}$$

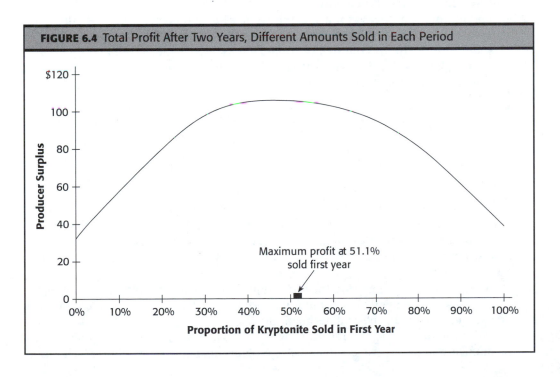

FIGURE 6.4 Total Profit After Two Years, Different Amounts Sold in Each Period

TABLE 6.6 A Monopolist Squeezes the Maximum Profit from Kryptonite over Two Years

	Year 1	Year 2
Grams of kryptonite sold	4.091	3.909
Price of kryptonite	$11.82/g	$12.18/g
Revenue	$48.34	$47.62
Marginal revenue	$3.636/g	$4.364/g
Total contribution to earnings, including interest on first year profit	$58.01	$47.62

Comment: Remember that profit is maximized as of the end of the second year, with the first year's profit invested at 20% interest. The resulting producer surplus is $105.63. Marginal revenue (as defined in Chapter 1) is $20 - 4 * Y$.

This is a general rule for solving a limited resource problem: the amounts are divided between periods so that discounted marginal profits (marginal revenues in this case) are equalized between periods.

This is an important rule. It gives us insight into how producers will organize production, profit, and prices for a limited resource. Note that Table 6.7 reflects this rule: each year's marginal profit is 20 percent higher than the value for the preceding year. Marginal profit increases at the rate of interest.

In the very simple case for a competitive market and no producer cost, the price increases at the rate of interest. What about the best number of years? Is it 2, or something else? It turns out that the optimal number of years to sell kryptonite is 5. But, in order to solve this problem, it is necessary to restate the profit goal for the kryptonite monopoly. It is

$$\text{maximize NPV(PS)} = \sum_{t=0}^{T-1} \frac{P_t(Y_t) * Y_t}{(1 + r)^t}, \tag{6-15}$$

$$\text{and} \sum_{t=0}^{T-1} Y_t \leq S.$$

S represents the original supply of kryptonite, 8 grams. So, the goal is to maximize the net present value of producer surplus by finding the length of time T and the values for each year for output and sales Y_t. The solution has to accommodate a constraint: all the production over all of the years in the period cannot exceed the original stock S.

One approach is to expand the method in Table 6.6, and simply use an optimization program on a personal computer. Another approach is to use mathematical techniques to find the best values for T and Y.[9]

With either method, the results show T = 5 to be best. For this kryptonite problem, each year's sales are less than the year before, and appear in Table 6.7. This time

TABLE 6.7 The Greatest Profit for Selling Kryptonite Is with a Five-Year Period

Year	Amount Sold	Price	Marginal Profit	Profit	Discounted Profit
0	2.72	$14.57	$9.14	$39.56	$39.56
1	2.26	$15.48	$10.96	$34.97	$29.14
2	1.71	$16.58	$13.16	$28.36	$19.69
3	1.05	$17.90	$15.79	$18.83	$10.90
4	0.26	$19.47	$18.95	$5.12	$2.47
Total	8.00			$126.84	$101.76

Comment: Payments are received at the beginning of each year. The discount factor for determining discounted profit is $1/(1 + r)^t$. Amounts in the table are rounded. The present value of the two-year amounts in Table 6.6 is $105.63/(1 + r)$, or $88.03. Remember that the present values of discounted marginal profit are equal for each of the years.

path forms the lower curve in Figure 6.5. Economic theory says this generally declining curve will appear whenever costs are constant and the demand curve is fixed.

However, if the demand curve is itself rising because of growing population and income, the time path for production can grow in the near term, as in the upper curve in the figure. Ultimately, it peaks and then declines to exhaustion. This is important, because it is in contrast to the usual perspective that a scarce resource

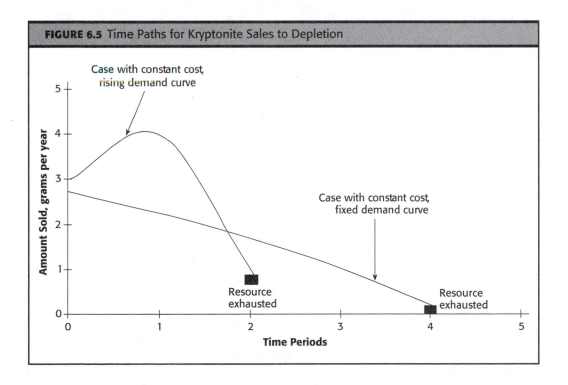

FIGURE 6.5 Time Paths for Kryptonite Sales to Depletion

should always be declining in use. World oil markets may fit these circumstances of rising global demand curves, and the theory is applied to actual data in Chapter 9.

'Backstop technology' is a concept used by economists to indicate a feasible but more costly substitute for a finite resource. For example, solar electricity is a potential backstop substitute for electricity generated from fossil fuels. Similarly, ethanol from corn or sugar is a backstop for gasoline for vehicles. (Both are analyzed in Chapter 8.)

For cases with backstop technology, theory predicts that use of the finite resource will continue, and the amounts used of both the conventional resource and the substitute will be influenced by their relative prices.

In general, the path of price growth will reflect the conditions first noted with Equation (6-14) for the two-period case. The general 'marginal profit' rule is

$$M\pi_0 = \frac{M\pi_1}{1 + r} = \frac{M\pi_t}{(1 + r)^t} = \frac{M\pi_T}{(1 + r)^T} \qquad (6\text{-}16)$$

The new variable is $M\pi_t$, marginal profit in period t. In other words, when the optimal time path for sales has been found, discounted marginal profit has been equalized in all time periods and increases at the rate of interest.

Two of the possible price paths are represented in Figure 6.6. In the first, increasing price shows the response when the demand curve is fixed, and the prices in this figure are the same as in Table 6.7.

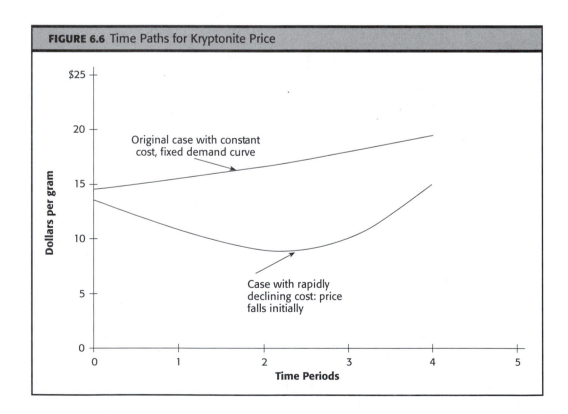

FIGURE 6.6 Time Paths for Kryptonite Price

But the lower price curve in Figure 6.6 reflects a complex and realistic change in assumption. The cost of producing each gram of kryptonite is declining. Consequently, equalizing discounted marginal profit in Equation (6-16) would lead to the shape of the lower curve in the figure. Price declines in the near term and then increases.

In fact, depletion theory will predict many types of future price paths, depending upon the specific assumptions about shifts in demand curves and production costs. We cannot logically conclude that a declining price is evidence of an unlimited resource.

Considering the effort to reach this point, it is only a small additional step to write down the equation that gives the exact values for the maximum present value profit. It is

$$Y^*_t = Y_m - \frac{(T * Y_m - S)}{F} * (1 + r)^t \tag{6-17}$$

This equation will provide the exact values in Table 6.7. No other possible production schedule will yield as high a producer surplus. (Equation [6-17] is used to analyze world oil in Chapter 9.)

Y_m is the amount that would be sold each year by the monopolist if kryptonite was unlimited. In this case, Y_m would be 5 grams every year. Since the resource is limited, the actual sales are reduced each year by the second term. In that second term, S still represents original stock, 8 grams of kryptonite. Multiplying T by Y_m gives the sales over the five periods if 5 grams could have been sold each year. So, the term in parentheses $(T * Y_m - S)$ is reflecting scarcity, the difference between potential profit maximizing sales and the available stock. For the kryptonite problem, this scarcity term has a value of 17.

In the denominator, F represents a discounting term, and is $((1 + r)^T - 1)/r$. Finally, the term $(1 + r)^t$ shows the accelerating impact of scarcity over time.

This is a valuable result, because if we know or can assume the numerical values for original stock and the interest rate on the right-hand side of Equation (6-17), we can write and plot the optimal values for any appropriate resource.

To this point, we've used a monopolist selling kryptonite. Suppose instead the owner was intending to promote maximum social welfare by simulating a competitive market. He would use a similar but distinct equation:

$$Y^*_t = Y_c - \frac{(T * Y_c - S) * (1 + r)^t}{F} \tag{6-18}$$

Given the demand curve for kryptonite, the unconstrained competitive sales level would be $Y_c = 10$, twice the monopoly level. This curve starts at a higher level, and declines more quickly to exhaustion.

Perhaps it is useful to conclude the introduction to the theory of depletion by turning away from kryptonite and considering an important real-world issue. Figure 6.7 is taken from the analysis of world oil in a later chapter; it shows one possible set of competitive and monopolistic paths to exhaustion of conventional crude oil. In both cases, theory is predicting near-term growth in use, which in fact occurred throughout the 1990s. Notice that an effective monopoly would stretch out the period of use of conventional oil, a point first observed in Chapter 1.

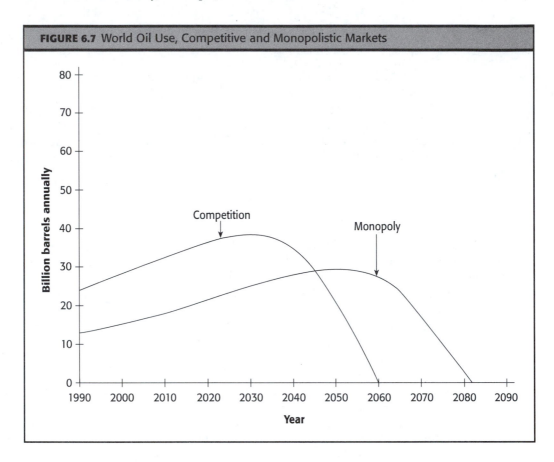

FIGURE 6.7 World Oil Use, Competitive and Monopolistic Markets

Optimizing the Balance: Environmental Protection and Degradation

Many people have difficulty with the economist's ability and willingness to analyze the efficiency aspect of environmental protection: the economist may find that some level of pollution, or old forest loss, or local species extinctions is acceptable.[10]

Economic logic is illustrated in both panels in Figure 6.8. In the upper panel, the middle curve SV represents the social value for protecting the population of a species, from zero percent to a maximum population level of 100 percent of carrying capacity K. (This percent is equivalent to X as a proportion of K.) In the upper curve, the social cost of protection SC_A is so high that it is always higher than SV: extinction is efficient. In the lower social cost curve, SC_B is less than SV for a considerable range. The maximum net social value is at about 44% protection. It is this level of protection that leads to the maximum gain of social value above social cost.

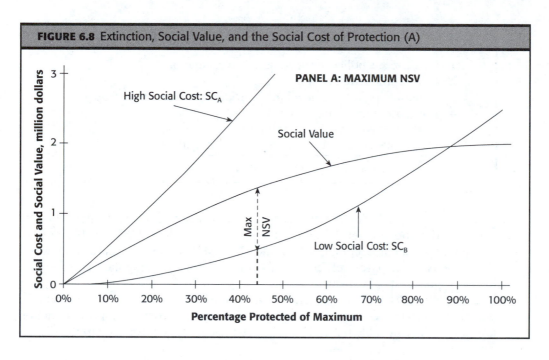

FIGURE 6.8 Extinction, Social Value, and the Social Cost of Protection (A)

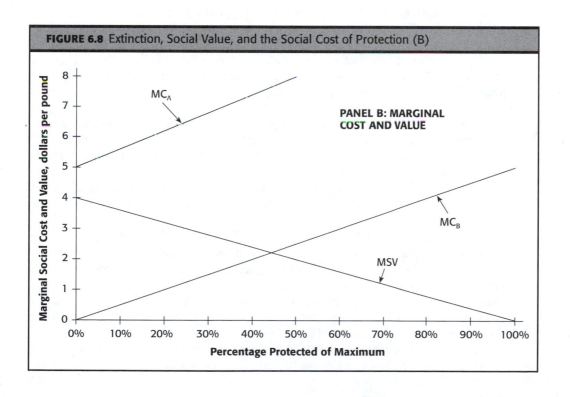

FIGURE 6.8 Extinction, Social Value, and the Social Cost of Protection (B)

TABLE 6.8 Biological and Economic Factors That Seem to Encourage Extinction

1. Open access policy for harvesting; no regulation
2. Low reproduction (low r)
3. Minimum population level for reproduction (see Figure 6.9)
4. Low cost of harvesting (low c)
5. High effectiveness of effort (high a)
6. Low or negative external value (low or negative v)

Note: The variables r, c, a, and v are used in the discussion of ecofins.

The lower Panel B simply represents the marginal social cost and value from the curves in the upper panel. Of course, the intersection where $MSV = MC_B$ defines the same optimal protection at 44%. And, since MC_A is always greater than MSV, this reflects the apparent efficiency of extinction for this imaginary species with high marginal cost of protection.

Hypothetically, this logic applies to any form of life: forests, fish, wildlife, and so on. The underlying economic and biological factors that seem to support extinction are summarized in Table 6.8 as they relate to the concepts introduced in the discussion of ecofins.

In the real world, this logic explains why many species with negative externality value were extinguished locally, such as wolves, panthers, and grizzlies. The passenger pigeon case is different. These once-common U.S. birds numbered in the billions. They were hunted to extinction for meat, and because farmers considered them pests. 'Martha,' the last survivor, died in a zoo in Cincinnati in 1914.[11] This case might be explained by the high success rate of hunters and the low cost of hunting, interacting with no significant positive externality at that time, and a minimum population threshold for continuing reproduction.

Hartwick and Olewiler believe that open access is perhaps the major factor in local fishery extinction. They note, "We can think of no cases in which a commercially valued species was exhausted in a fishery managed by a sole owner or regulated by governments."[12]

Given an open access policy, the other factors in Table 6.8 come into play. A low reproduction rate for whales (see Table 6.2) is a problem in preventing extinction for some harvested species.

Many species follow the minimum threshold curve outlined in Figure 6.9. For them, when population falls below a minimum threshold level because of harvesting or disease, the population moves to extinction. This may be a problem for small bighorn sheep populations in the Western United States.

Low cost for harvesting and high catch rates can interact to make harvesting of the last members of a local species inevitable. This has probably been a factor in species as diverse as lobsters and black bear in many localities.

Finally, of considerable and growing importance, externality value is significant in determining whether open or controlled access policies prevail. Increasingly, the

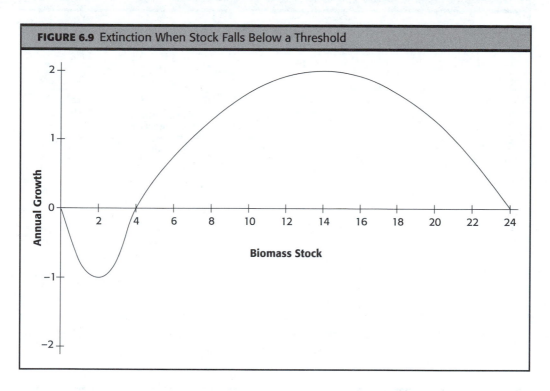

FIGURE 6.9 Extinction When Stock Falls Below a Threshold

'v' value has changed from negative to positive for North American predators. Wolves, panthers, and coyotes are expanding their ranges and populations in regions in which they had previously been hunted to extinction.

The economic approach to pollution control is identical in its logic to the approach to species protection. Compare Figure 6.10 on pollution control to Figure 6.8. The horizontal axis showing percentage pollution removal in Figure 6.10[13] is comparable to the horizontal axis in Figure 6.8, which represents, for the endangered species, the proportion of maximum carrying capacity that is protected.

In pollution control technologies, marginal cost frequently rises sharply as control approaches 100 percent. Marginal benefits in a locality are frequently either constant or declining slowly. As a result, as both panels in Figure 6.10 imply, optimal net benefits usually occur at less than 100 percent pollution control. In other words, efficiency usually means some level of pollution is appropriate, even after extensive prevention efforts.

There are exceptions, of course. No high level radiation nuclear fuel waste is allowed outside secure areas, for example. Figure 6.10 applied to this case would mean that, when marginal benefit and marginal cost are at 100 percent control, marginal benefit is still much greater than marginal cost.

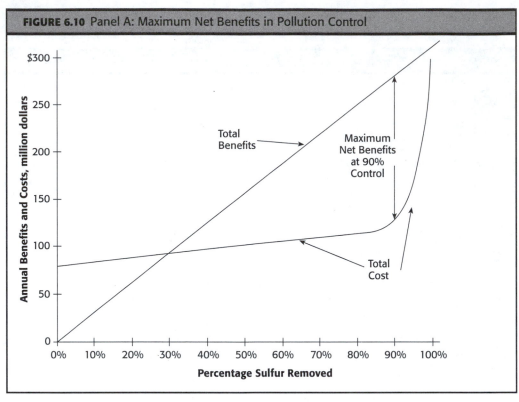

FIGURE 6.10 Panel A: Maximum Net Benefits in Pollution Control

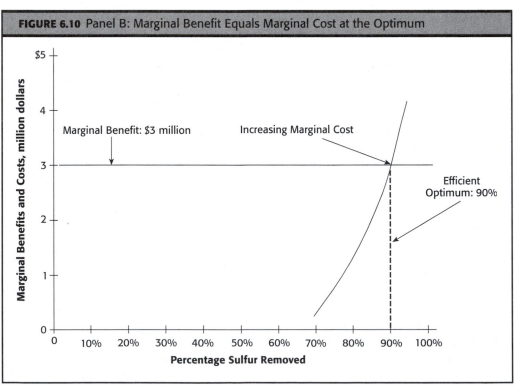

FIGURE 6.10 Panel B: Marginal Benefit Equals Marginal Cost at the Optimum

Summary

This chapter introduces three of the major contributions of economic theory to the protection and use of environmental resources. In the area of renewable biological resources such as forests and fisheries, the fictional ecofin helps us understand the economics of sustainable use. Managing a fishery (or a forest) at maximum biomass carrying capacity results in the highest sustainable stock, but essentially no harvesting.

Four types of markets and policies were reviewed: competitive open access, maximum physical sustained yield, regulated harvesting, and regulated harvesting with the inclusion of environmental values in management. Each approach leads to different levels of sustained biomass stock, harvesting, profit, and social value.

Extinction occurs when economic and biological factors interact and public policy is absent, or the social cost of protection exceeds the benefit of protection.

In the second major area in the chapter, depletion theory is applied to exhaustible resources. Depletion theory helps us understand how prices may either rise or fall (in the near term) for limited resources. As a conventional resource moves toward exhaustion (in the theoretical absence of substitutes), market prices and quantities increasingly depart from those that would occur with unlimited amounts of the resource.

If economic substitutes are available, they strongly influence prices and rates of use for the exhaustible resource.

The chapter concludes with a review of optimization and marginal analysis. Whether the subject is pollution prevention or endangered species, the insights from economic theory help us understand how markets work for environmental resources, and why different economic incentives and policies have different results.

The fourteen chapters that follow help explain the interaction of economics and environment; the theory introduced in this chapter[14] enhances our understanding of how things work, and how economics can be employed in pursuit of environmental protection and resource use.

Questions for Discussion and Analysis

1. Define maximum sustainable yield. Would a profit-maximizing single owner of a fishery harvest more or fewer fish than maximum sustainable yield? Why? If the fishery were instead in open access with more than one user, would more or fewer fish be harvested than with maximum sustained yield?

2. Suppose that the marginal benefits of saving a local population of red-speckled toads are (where A is the number of toads saved)

$$MB = 400 - A$$

and the marginal costs are

$$MC = 250 + A$$

How many toads should be saved now? Explain why.

3. Table 6.7 shows that the optimal number of years to sell kryptonite with a 20 percent interest rate is five years. Would the number of years increase or decrease if the interest rate decreased to 8 percent? Can you explain why?

4. If the stock of copper is fixed, and we already have found all the deposits on earth, what would explain a declining price for copper?

5. Monopolists are often called conservationists when it comes to nonrenewable resources. Can you explain why?

6. If you were a regulator, describe the methods you could use to eliminate open access in the ecofin fishery. For each method you choose, describe how it would affect the number of boats, annual catch, fish stock, and profits.

Notes to Chapter 6

1. For example, $AG = a + bX - cX^2$. For this expression to be identical to Equation (6-1), then $a = 0$.
2. For students of calculus, take the first derivative of AG in Equation (6.1) with respect to X. AG and H will be at their highest at this point. Set the first derivative equal to zero, and solve for X as a function of K. $H_{msy} = AG$ at its maximum, and the result is Equations (6-4) and (6-5) in the text.
3. The sources for Table 6.2 are Colin Clark, *Mathematical Bioeconomics* (New York: Wiley, 1976), pages 48, 49; Tom Tietenberg, *Environmental and Natural Resource Economics* (New York: HarperCollins, 1996), page 288; John M. Hartwick and Nancy Olewiler, *The Economics of Natural Resource Use* (Reading, MA: Addison Wesley Longman, 1998), page 132. The fictional ecofins are used here to introduce the economic theory of biological resource use.
4. Total revenue TR is $paKE - (pa^2KE^2)/r$. As usual, $TR = pH$. Marginal revenue per boat on a sustainable basis is $paK - (2pa^2KE)/r$. The solution is $E_{syoa} = r/a - rc/pa^2K$.
5. The maximum sustainable producer surplus solution where marginal revenue per boat equals marginal cost per boat is $E^* = (r/2a) * (1 - c/pak)$.
6. To optimize net social value, differentiate NSV with respect to E. With this derivative equal to zero at maximum NSV, solve for E. The result is Equation (6-10).
7. In this case, when $v \geq pr(1 - c/pak)$, then $E^*_{nsv} \leq 0$.
8. Gareth Porter, "Too Much Fishing Fleet, Too Few Fish: A Proposal for Eliminating Global Fishing Overcapacity," World Wildlife Fund, August 28, 1998, page 3, and Executive Summary, page 2. Also see *New York Times*, "Reduce Surplus in Fishing Fleet," August 23, 1998.
9. The introductory presentation here uses discrete values. The theory is usually expressed with continuous functions in an optimal control format. The content of the results, of course, are identical. Also see Note 14 below.
10. The argument for efficiency in species protection is given in depth in John M. Hartwick and Nancy D. Olewiler, *The Economics of Natural Resource Use* (Reading, MA: Addison Wesley, 1998), pages 126–133.
11. American Museum of Natural History, *Fact Sheet*, October 22, 1996.
12. Hartwick and Olewiler, *op. cit.*

13. Figure 6.10 is taken from Chapter 4.
14. Clark, Tietenberg, and Hartwick and Olewiler (see references, Note 2) all address the subjects of this chapter in greater detail. Clark is accessible with advanced mathematics. Tietenberg, and Hartwick and Olewiler, can be read by students with intermediate economics. The mathematics and theory in Equations (6-16) to (6-18) are in D. Chapman, "World Oil: Hotelling Depletion or Accelerating Use?" Winter 1993 *Nonrenewable Resources*, Journal of the International Association for Mathematical Geology, 2(4): 331–339, and the appendix in D. Chapman and N. Khanna, "World Oil: The Growing Case for International Policy," January 2000, *Contemporary Economic Policy*, in press.

PART II

RENEWABLE ENERGY ECONOMICS AND CONSERVATION

CHAPTER 7

PERSONAL AND HOUSEHOLD ENERGY: ECONOMICS AND ENVIRONMENT

The preceding six chapters explored some of the major areas of theory, philosophy, and methods in environmental economics. The next four chapters are focused on particular subjects related to the economic aspects of possible physical limitations to economic growth. Later chapters take up the current state of affairs of the major environmental resources: air and water quality, agriculture, and forestry. (The final chapters address more global issues of biodiversity and endangered species protection, macroeconomic growth, climate change, and sustainability.)

But why begin this next step by studying such a low-key topic, household and personal energy use? It is because individual personal decisions about consumption can have national and global consequences. Home heating and lighting affect the magnitude of acid rain damage and global climate change. Economics helps us understand why we make the choices we do, and why some presumably positive policies have been unsuccessful in practice. At the same time, market forces have helped shape some decisions that considerably reduced personal energy use and environmental impact.

Introduction: Economics Has Promoted Conservation

The next chapter on renewable energy ends with a cautionary note: the new technologies work, but for most purposes they are not economically competitive now.

The implication for the environment is clear. Conventional energy accounts for 80 percent of major air pollutants and an even higher percentage of greenhouse gas emissions. Renewable energy has not increased its share of U.S. energy in nearly two decades. With conventional energy prices at historically low levels, the growth of energy-derived pollution may resume.

The overall economic picture for conservation technologies in homes is more positive. In spite of the low energy prices of the 1990s, conventional energy use by households declined by 16 percent from the early 1980s. This decline was primarily because of less energy used in home heating, which fell by 33 percent.[1] On average, each 10 percent reduction in home energy use is almost matched by a comparable reduction in air pollution, and perhaps nuclear waste accumulation.

But in order to understand how economics interacts with energy conservation and use, we need to outline the basic processes by which energy is used.

Keeping Warm

In the 1990s, the average household had two people in their 40s, and a family income of about $35,000.[2] They owned their home of five or six rooms, which was built in the 1960s in a suburb. The size of this average house was about 2,000 square feet, the family believed it was adequately insulated, and it may have had trees shading the house in the afternoon. The family cooked one hot meal, took 15 baths a week, did seven loads of washing, and set the thermostat at 70 degrees when the heat was on and they were at home.

Heating is the largest single form of energy use in the home. In Table 7.1, the average home uses 55 MBtu for heating, more than one-half of the total. (For the average household, vehicle energy use exceeds in-the-home energy. Table 7.2 shows the major categories of consumer energy use.)

TABLE 7.1 Energy Use in the Home, Average Million Btu per Year for Each Residence[3]

Heating	55 MBtu
Hot water	19 MBtu
All appliances	17 MBtu
Refrigerator	5 MBtu
Air conditioning	5 MBtu
Lighting	3 MBtu
Total all uses	104 MBtu

Note: This does not include energy lost in generating and transporting electricity, which is shown in Table 7.2.

TABLE 7.2 Residential Energy Use: Vehicles and Homes, Average Million Btu per Household[4]

A. Gasoline for personal household vehicles	132 MBtu
B. Energy use in the home	104 MBtu
C. Additional energy at power plants to generate residential electricity	68 MBtu
D. Total household energy: vehicles, home, power plant generation for home	304 MBtu

Note: For 96.6 million households, the total annual energy use is 30 quadrillion Btu. The average U.S. household uses 9 percent * 10^{-8} of total world energy. The average annual cost per household in the United States is about $3,000. Typically, this is equally divided between gasoline purchases and home energy expenditures.

Obviously there is considerable variation around these statistical averages, in type of housing as well as the people in the household. But the relationships between housing, heating, climate, and individual households are constant and applicable everywhere on the planet. The basic economics of home heating energy can be summarized in four simplified equations. These basic relationships can be used in a personal benefit-cost analysis to determine the most cost-effective heating system. They also serve well to explain whether insulation and conservation in the home save energy.

The first equation defines the relationship between the individual home, the normal outdoor climate, and heating energy needed in the home.

$$EH = HDD * HL * 24 \qquad (7\text{-}1a)$$

'EH' means energy for heating the home, measured in MBtu per year. It is measured in the United States in MBtu, millions of British thermal units.[5] If, for example, an electrically heated home in the Northern United States needed 120 MBtu each year, and electricity cost $35 per MBtu, then the annual heating cost would be $4,200 in an average year.

The term 'HDD' is heating degree days, on an annual basis. It is calculated separately for each day of the year. Suppose that for a particular fall day in Paradise Valley, California, the day's high is 70 degrees Fahrenheit and the low is 40 degrees. The midpoint between the high and the low is 55 degrees. The midpoint of 55 degrees is subtracted from the benchmark of 65 degrees, resulting in 10 HDD for this single fall day.

The benchmark 65 degrees represents an engineering convention that 65 degrees is a typical comfortable inside temperature. Every day in the year is summed up, so the total might be 2,000 HDD over the year for this California valley location.

Figure 7.1 represents the broad differences in heating requirements across the United States.[6] As expected, the northern regions are colder, with higher heating requirements. The figure shows the general relationship between geography and heating requirements. For actual values for representative cities in each state, see the Appendix, Table 7.A. (For example, Duluth is the second coldest with 9,800 heating degree days, and Miami Beach has the mildest winters with only 200 annual heating degree days.)

The map also shows an air conditioning zone where 'cooling degree days' (CDD) exceed 2,000. These cooling degree days are used to measure air conditioning requirements, and are determined in a manner similar to heating degree days.[7] However, as Table 7.1 shows, heating energy is more than 10 times as great as air conditioning energy, so heating costs will continue as the main focus.

The next term in the equation is 'HL' for heat loss for the home. This is the variable that reflects the individual characteristics of each house and apartment. It is expressed as the reduction in warmth per hour for each degree difference between inside and outside temperatures. The last part of the equation uses 24, the hours in a day, to link heat loss with HDD. Two examples can show the importance of these individual home factors in determining heat loss. First, the average new home is so much better insulated that it needs one-third less heat than a home built 50 years earlier, in spite of newer homes being 550 square feet larger.[8]

FIGURE 7.1 U.S. Climate Zones[6]

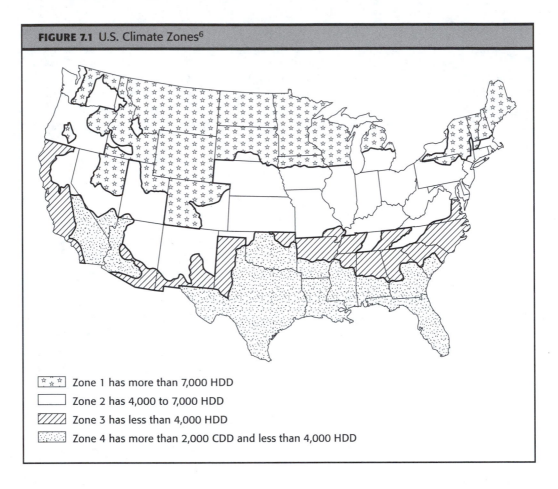

☆☆☆ Zone 1 has more than 7,000 HDD

☐ Zone 2 has 4,000 to 7,000 HDD

▨ Zone 3 has less than 4,000 HDD

▦ Zone 4 has more than 2,000 CDD and less than 4,000 HDD

Second, direct sunlight during a Northern U.S. winter can provide 100 percent of home heating for eight hours on a subfreezing day.[9] This is with a well-insulated home. As a consequence, two houses of the same size in the same location can have HL factors as far apart as a low of 350 to a high of 1,300. Table 7.3 describes some of the factors that influence heat loss for a particular home.

Consider a representative home in a cold climate. The climate has HDD of 7,000, and the home has a HL of 475 Btu/h for each degree of difference between indoor and outdoor temperatures. The application of the concept to these specific assumptions is

$$EH = 7,000 * 475 * 24 = 80 \text{ MBtu/y.} \tag{7-1b}$$

The next step, after estimating the heat energy requirement, is to calculate the amount of purchased energy. Purchased energy is usually larger than heat energy because of the energy loss in the furnace and chimney. Suppose the object is to estimate natural gas needs with a new furnace. The efficiency may be 80 percent. The relationship between EP (energy purchased) and EH (energy for heating the home) is simple. It is:

TABLE 7.3 Factors Affecting Home Heat Loss, Which . . .
A. . . . Increase Heat Loss 　windy location 　single-level ranch house 　bad carpentry with significant drafts 　no basement 　large size 　poor insulation 　one thermostat 　(HL = 650 to 1,300 Btu) B. . . . Reduce Heat Loss 　protected location 　windows on the south 　two-story box shape 　good carpentry with little warm air loss 　insulated basement 　moderate size 　good insulation 　several thermostats 　(HL = 350 Btu)

$$EP = \frac{EH}{eff} \qquad (7\text{-}2)$$

Since the efficiency of the furnace is 80 percent and EH is 80 MBtu per year, purchased energy is 100 MBtu.[10]

Finally, the annual heating bill (AHB) is simply the result of buying the fuel:

$$\text{Annual Heating Bill} = \text{Price} * \text{Energy Purchased} \qquad (7\text{-}3)$$

If the natural gas price is $7 per MBtu, for 100 MBtu annually, the annual heating bill is $700. This basic method is applicable to any residence in any climate zone, using the fuel energy chosen for the home.

There is an interesting difference for conventional electric resistance heating panels. In the home itself, 100 percent of the electrical energy is converted into heat energy. Consequently, the in-home efficiency is 100 percent. However, it should be kept in mind that, in general, 3 Btus of energy need to be burned in the power plant for each single Btu of energy delivered as electricity into the home. In spite of the in-home efficiency, the high energy losses in producing electricity result in the high price of electricity on an energy basis. In the last column of Table 7.4, electricity is the most expensive energy at $26 per MBtu.

TABLE 7.4 Typical Residential Energy Prices, Late 1990s

Energy Type	Price in Normal Measurement	Energy Content	Price in MBtus
Natural gas	$6.80/thousand ft³	1,027Btu/ft³	$7/MBtu
Electric panels	9¢/kWh	3,412 Btu/kWh	$26/MBtu
Fuel oil	90¢/gal	139,000 Btu/gal	$6.50/MBtu
Wood purchased	$120/cord	20 MBtu/cord	$6/MBtu
Propane	$1/gal	91,000 Btu/gal	$11/MBtu

Note: Table numbers are rounded off. Sources are HECE and *Monthly Energy Review*. Natural gas is sometimes measured in therms: each therm is 100,000 Btu. A cord of wood is formally defined as 128 cubic feet, typically a rectangle 16 feet by 4 feet, and 4 feet high. However, local custom may be to give smaller deliveries as cords. Typically, more firewood is cut by users than is purchased. Remember, there is significant variation above and below these prices in different regions.

TABLE 7.5 Annual Heating Bills (assume 80 MBtu in the home)

Energy Type	Annual Heating Bill $/Y
Natural gas	$700
Electric panels	$2,080
Fuel oil	$670
Wood purchased	$800
Propane	$1,100

Note: Assumed furnace or panel efficiency is .8 for natural gas and propane, 1.0 for electric panels, .775 for heating oil, and .6 for wood furnace boiler. Amounts are rounded off.

The annual heating bills are shown in Table 7.5, on the basis of Equations (7-1), (7-2), and (7-3). Both Tables 7.4 and 7.5 are typical U.S. values. There are very important regional variations. For example, electricity to residential customers in Washington State has an average price of 5¢ per kWh rather than 9¢, which is typical of the country. It also has unusually high heating oil prices. As a result, Washington uses more electric heat and less fuel oil heat.

The pattern of geographic differences in electricity, petroleum, and natural gas prices to customers is based upon cost differences in supply. Natural gas is least costly in areas where it is produced, and in major urban areas served by pipeline systems.

For electricity rates, large-scale hydropower generally is very inexpensive, so the Pacific Northwest has the lowest rates. In contrast, nuclear power has frequently become very costly, making electricity generally expensive in states with significant nuclear generation.

Petroleum products such as gasoline, diesel fuel, and heating oil are at their lowest costs and prices in urban areas near refineries. Costs and prices are higher in sparsely populated rural areas where petroleum products are transported to the area by truck from distant refinery or pipeline terminal facilities.

Consequently, New York State has the highest residential electric rates and very high natural gas and heating oil prices. Wood burning is very common in rural New York because of its much lower cost, whether purchased or cut by the users.[11]

These economic-engineering relationships help explain much of the economic influences on choices of heating and air conditioning systems. They can also be used to determine the cost-effectiveness of personal investments in energy conservation. As one example, consider the issue of deciding whether to add insulation to a very old, uninsulated large home. Suppose a $3,000 contract for installing more insulation will reduce total heating requirements and annual heating bills by 10 percent.

Now, consider a milder climate, 5,000 heating degree days. (This might be Northern California near the Sierra, or St. Louis, Missouri, or Long Island in New York.) The home is large, 2,500 square feet. The installation is to be paid by a home equity loan at 8 percent interest for 15 years.

According to Table 7.6, this insulation investment is cost effective with electric heating, but not with natural gas. In this example, then, the St. Louis and Long Island homes might have natural gas, and would forgo the new insulation. The Northern California home may not have natural gas, and with electric heating would be in circumstances where the new insulation pays for itself with lower electric bills.

As broad generalizations, additional insulation is more likely to be justified in terms of economics for colder climates, for very hot regions with heavy air conditioning use, for single owner-occupied homes, and for homes without access to inexpensive natural gas or heating oil. Remembering Table 7.3, however, there are many individual factors that cause heating energy to vary widely within the same locality. Nevertheless, the basic relationships are the same anywhere in the United States or anywhere on the planet, with metric or American units, with roubles, rand, and yen, as well as dollars.

It is this kind of individual household economics which resulted in the nationwide reduction in residential energy use that was discussed at the beginning of the

TABLE 7.6 Cost Effectiveness of Conservation

Type of Heating	Electric Panels	Natural Gas
Climate: heating degree days	5,000	5,000
Size of home	2,500 ft	2,500 ft
Home heating energy before insulation	200 MBtu/y	200 MBtu/y
Insulation contract cost	$3,000	$3,000
Levelized cost factor (8%, 15 yr)	.117	.117
Levelized annual cost	$351/y	$351/y
Reduced energy in home	20 MBtu/y	20 MBtu/y
Reduction in purchased energy	20 MBtu/y	25 MBtu/y
Price	$26/MBtu	$7/MBtu
Reduction in annual heating bill	$520/y	$175/y
Total saving per year	$169	−$176 (loss)

chapter. In fact, it is the only major category of energy use that has declined. It seems a fair conclusion to note that local economics related to cost-effective energy use provided the incentives for this large-scale reduction in energy consumption and the associated reduction in air pollution.

There are other important economic factors which influence home energy decision-making, particularly related to ownership. Before analyzing these factors, however, we will examine the economics affecting home and business lighting.

Economics and Lighting

Home lighting is not a significant part of residential energy use, according to Table 7.1, but it merits special consideration because of a new technology. Compact fluorescent bulbs offer the opportunity for very cost-effective energy conservation with related environmental benefits. Yet only 9 percent of U.S. homes use these bulbs. They are more common in owner-occupied houses and apartments, and less common in rented homes.[12]

The basic economics can be analyzed with the levelized cost approach. One typical decision would be the choice of bulbs to install in a new home. Suppose there are 50 light fixtures, with an average of 75 Watts in conventional lighting wanted for each fixture. Table 7.7 represents the basic data.

The technical term for the lighting ability of a lamp is 'lumen'; it measures the degree of illumination.[13] A typical 75-Watt bulb provides light equal to 1,170 lumens. The comparable compact fluorescent produces slightly more light, 1,200 lumens, but only needs 20 Watts to do this.

The expected lifetimes of the different lamps vary significantly. A standard bulb is designed for 750 hours' use, while a CF (compact fluorescent) is engineered for 10,000 hours. A typical year's use is considered to be 1,000 hours. On this basis, a standard bulb might have a 9-month average lifetime, and a compact fluorescent a 10-year life.[14]

Since the prices are so different, there is a large contrast in initial purchase cost: $1,100 for compact fluorescents, and only $30 for the standard bulbs. The conserva-

TABLE 7.7 Part A: Economics, Compact Fluorescents, and Conventional Incandescents		
	Standard Bulb	*Compact Fluorescent*
Light power (lumens)	1,170	1,200
Watts	75	20
Life (1,000 hours is one year), hours	750	10,000
Price	60¢	$22
Initial purchase cost (50 fixtures)	$30	$1,100
Levelized cost factor (10 years, 12%)	n.a.	.201
Annual cost of bulbs (ACB)	$40	$221

TABLE 7.7 Part B: Electricity Cost and Total Cost

	Standard Bulb	Compact Fluorescent
Hours used annually	1,000 hours	1,000 hours
Fixtures	50	50
Average watts	75	20
Total kilowatt hours	3,750 kWh/y	1,000 kWh/y
Electricity price	12¢/kWh	12¢/kWh
Annual lighting bill—electricity	$450	$120
Annual cost of bulbs (part A)	$40	$221
Total cost, electricity and bulbs, annual	$490	$341

tion option is so costly that a loan or credit-card purchase is a real possibility. To calculate the levelized annual cost,

$$\text{Annual Cost of Bulbs—CF} = \text{lcf}(10 \text{ years}, 12\%) * \$1,100 \qquad (7\text{-}4)$$

The levelized cost factor is .201, taking a credit card interest rate of 12 percent and the average 10-year lamp life. The levelized Annual Cost of Bulbs—CF is $221 each year.

In contrast, the standard bulbs on average last less than a year, and the purchase price is 60¢ each. The annual cost for them is

$$\text{Annual Cost of Bulbs—STND} = \frac{\text{Bulbs in Home}}{\text{Lifetime, Fraction of Year}} * \text{Price} \qquad (7\text{-}5)$$

The result here is $40 annually. This is obviously much less than the CF lamp cost, which is $221 if it is financed with a credit card–type interest rate.

The cost-effective energy conservation arises in Table 7.7B. Note the fourth entry, where the CFs have much lower electricity requirements. At a 12¢/kWh rate, the CFs are using $120 of electricity per year, much lower than the standard bulbs. In the last three entries, annual bulb cost and electricity bills are added together. The 50 CFs, even with the loan/credit card financing, save $150 yearly in total costs.

If electricity is very cheap, then the standard bulbs turn out to be cost-effective. Or, if interest rates are as high as 50 percent per year, as they can be in developing countries, the cost of CFs is higher.[15] In the industrialized countries, however, most households pay electric rates that are high enough and interest rates low enough so that CFs are cost-effective.

Since the per-household energy savings are so high, the national impact is significant. Referring again to Table 7.1, this cost-effective household policy would mean a proportional national reduction of 2Q in residential lighting energy, and a proportional reduction in power plant pollution.

Why, then, isn't this conversion taking place? Part of the problem is understandable customer preference for the standard bulbs. The conventional lamps have a color spectrum closer to sunlight, while some CFs have a green (or "cool") color to their light. Most people prefer light which is close to sunlight, which leads consumers away from CFs. Another problem is the 'warm-up': most people don't like the 'power curve' which CFs follow over a few minutes in reaching their full illumination. Finally, the new CFs don't easily fit many standard lamps, so households choose the standards.

These three problems are specific to the CFs, and will probably disappear slowly as technology solves the problems. However, there are significant economic problems which affect the use of CFs, and these economic problems are qualitatively similar to problems affecting cost-effective home heating.

Economic Obstacles to Cost-Effective Conservation

Home insulation and compact fluorescents are both capital-intensive. Each has a useful life measured in many years, and returns a favorable savings over many years while reducing air pollution and greenhouse gas emissions. In this respect, they represent many cost-effective energy conservation technologies.

The market problem arises when the cost of installation is separated from the economic benefits of use. For an owner-occupied home, with the household anticipating at least 10 years' residence, there is no problem.

One common situation where there is a problem is with renting, where the period of residence is fairly short. Consider a renting household that plans to live for two years in their current residence. If they invest $1,100 in CFs, the electric bill savings in those two years will only be $660. Although they can consider taking the CFs with them, this may create other problems with landlords, and handling or storing bulbs in an old or new residence. As a result, we can understand why essentially no mobile home renters own a CF, but more than 10 percent of owner-occupied houses use CFs.

For insulation, Figure 7.2 shows a similar pattern. Homeowners are more likely to have good insulation, and households renting houses are more likely to have poor insulation.

The result is a situation comparable to the Chapter 1 discussion: the social optimum and the market equilibrium may be noticeably different. The purchaser of insulation and CFs often does not receive the benefits of lower energy bills and less pollution. Consequently, the purchaser's personal evaluation of benefits and costs leads to what, from another perspective, is under-investment in cost-effective, less-polluting energy conservation techniques.

There are two main types of programs that have been designed to encourage cost-effective energy conservation. One is governmental, where federal or state employees counsel individual businesses or households to install CFs or install more insulation.[16]

The other program category is 'demand side management.' Here, a private electric utility assigns staff to advertise and promote CFs or other conservation techniques, and other company employees may visit individual households. A state regulatory commission typically allows the utility to earn a profit on utility company investment in the program. Supporters of demand side management believe

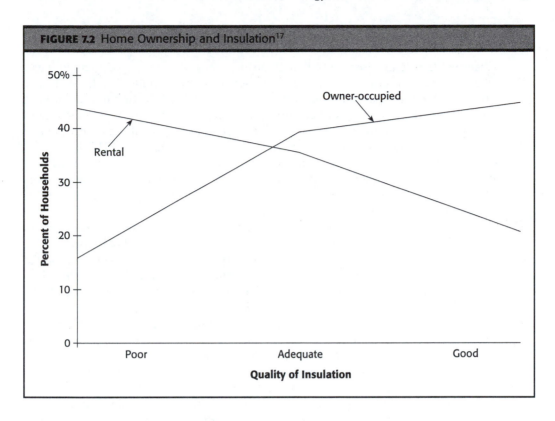

FIGURE 7.2 Home Ownership and Insulation[17]

that energy efficiency programs typically cost less than 3.5¢ for each kWh saved. This is generally much less costly than electricity from new generating plants. Nationwide, the Electric Power Research Institute has concluded that 20 percent of U.S. total electricity consumption could be saved at this price.[18] Since energy conservation means less pollution, advocates of these programs can make a persuasive argument that they are environmentally and economically efficient.

The main problem with both programs is the absence of incentives for efficiency. For example, the demand side management cost for a private utility for each CF placed in a home and actually used may reach $50 per bulb. The costs here include professional and technical salaries as well as equipment. When, as is usual, the program cost is included within the rate base for allowed profit, there is no incentive for proposing proper illumination levels or satisfactory color quality. In the absence of efficiency incentives, these programs may be a very costly approach to the problem.

There is no clear effective policy remedy for the divergence between paying costs and receiving benefits from energy efficiency. However, it is interesting to note that residential heating and lighting are two areas in household energy that have experienced lower levels of use. Perhaps market forces are working efficiently after all.

Air Pollution and Home Heating

Because of the clean nature of fuels and the efficiency of furnaces today, natural gas, oil, and propane produce relatively little conventional air pollution. In Table 7.8, natural gas heating does not produce significant amounts of the first four pollutants.

Electric panel heating produces zero pollution at the residence; the estimated amounts in the table are associated with electricity generation at the power plant.[19] For electric heating, only sulfuric acid is an important air pollutant. This is because sulfur released from coal-burning power plants is important in some regions. However, for electric heating with hydropower, the environmental impact is very different. There is no air pollution at the home or the power plant, but hydropower can be a significant threat to salmon and other fisheries.

The third column is important for rural areas where wood fuel use is common. Conventional pollutants are released in significant amounts. For health protection, residential lot size for wood-burning communities may need to be on the order of an acre per home. Communities in sheltered valleys would require larger lot sizes for safe pollution dispersal. These communities may also need to require use of catalytic pollution control systems in wood-burning furnaces and stoves.

The carbon dioxide entries are proportional to the carbon content of the fuel. Notice that wood use can have either the most CO_2 release, or zero. This depends upon whether wood fuel is harvested on a sustainable basis. If fuel wood is produced with sustained yield management, then the continuous growth of new biomass absorbs CO_2 on a level equivalent to the CO_2 from burning fuel wood. The area needed for sustained fuel wood use is 5–10 acres per household.[20]

Considering the gains made in air pollution control in the United States, the importance of CO_2 as a greenhouse gas may become greater in the future. Significant future gains in renewable energy use and in energy conservation (and associated pollution reduction) may be dependent upon some future period wherein real energy prices rise. This leads to the subject of a later chapter: is world petroleum a likely candidate to lead the way to higher energy prices, or will the low prices of the 1990s continue into the future?

TABLE 7.8 Air Pollution from Residential Heating (pounds per year, 120 MBtu inside heat energy)

Pollutant	Natural Gas	Electric Panels	Wood
Sulfuric acid	0	575	0
Soot-particles	0	5	455
Carbon monoxide	5	10	2,910
Organic compounds	0	5	315
Carbon dioxide	18,000	48,000	0; or 59,000

Source: See D. Chapman, Note on Air Pollution and Home Heating, March 27, 1996.

But first, Chapter 8 examines the economics of renewable energy, its low levels of current use, and the high expectations for the future.

Questions for Discussion and Analysis

1. Assume the average U.S. residence purchases 56 MBtu annually for home heating and releases eight tons of CO_2 each year from the fossil fuel burned for heating. With 100 million homes, what would be the annual U.S. total CO_2 released from residential heating? If annual home heating requirements were reduced by 7 MBtu for each residence, what would be the yearly amount of CO_2 emissions for heating U.S. homes?

2. Would significant increases in solar heating or nuclear power generation affect your conclusions in Question 1? Explain.

3. Consider Table 7.6. Suppose you lived in a region with the same climate and in the same house but electricity cost was only 4.5¢/kWh. What would be the total savings per year for investing in insulation?

4. In Table 7.7, if electricity cost 5¢/kWh, what would be the total annual cost of electricity plus the cost of using conventional bulbs? What would be the annual difference between standard bulbs and compact fluorescents?

5. You represent an environmental group lobbying in Washington. Outline five reasons why energy used in household heating should be taxed.

6. You represent a trade association of coal, oil, gas, and electricity producers. Outline five reasons why taxes on home heating energy should be kept at current levels or reduced.

7. Do you favor or oppose government programs to promote residential insulation, compact fluorescent lighting, and other home energy conservation programs?

Appendix

TABLE 7.A Heating Degree Days in U.S. Cities, Averages for a 30-Year Period, 1961–1990					
Alabama	Mobile	1,702	Nevada	Reno	5,674
Alaska	Juneau	8,897	New Hampshire	Concord	7,554
Arizona	Phoenix	1,350	New Jersey	Atlantic City	5,169
Arkansas	Little Rock	3,155	New Mexico	Albuquerque	4,425
California	Los Angeles	1,458	New York	Albany	6,894
	Sacramento	2,749		Buffalo	6,747
	San Diego	1,256		New York City	4,805
	San Francisco	3,016	N. Carolina	Charlotte	3,341
Colorado	Denver	6,020		Raleigh	3,457
Connecticut	Hartford	6,151	N. Dakota	Bismarck	8,968
Delaware	Wilmington	4,937	Ohio	Cincinnati	5,248
DC	Washington	4,047		Cleveland	6,201
Florida	Jacksonville	1,434		Columbus	5,708
	Miami	200	Oklahoma	Oklahoma City	3,649
Georgia	Atlanta	2,991	Oregon	Portland	4,522
Idaho	Boise	5,861	Pennsylvania	Philadelphia	4,954
Illinois	Chicago	6,536		Pittsburgh	5,968
	Peoria	6,148	Rhode Island	Providence	5,884
Indiana	Indianapolis	5,615	S. Carolina	Columbia	2,649
Iowa	Des Moines	6,497	S. Dakota	Sioux Falls	7,809
Kansas	Wichita	4,791	Tennessee	Memphis	3,802
Kentucky	Louisville	4,514		Nashville	3,729
Louisiana	New Orleans	1,513	Texas	Dallas	2,407
Maine	Portland	7,378		El Paso	2,708
Maryland	Baltimore	4,707		Houston	1,599
Massachusetts	Boston	5,641	Utah	Salt Lake City	5,765
Michigan	Detroit	6,569	Vermont	Burlington	7,771
	Sault St. Marie	9,316	Virginia	Norfolk	3,495
Minnesota	Duluth	9,818		Richmond	3,963
	Minneapolis	7,981	Washington	Seattle	4,908
Mississippi	Jackson	2,467		Spokane	6,842
Missouri	Kansas City	5,393	W. Virginia	Charleston	4,646
	St. Louis	4,758	Wisconsin	Milwaukee	7,324
Montana	Great Falls	7,741	Wyoming	Cheyenne	7,326
Nebraska	Omaha	6,300			

Source: 1995 Statistical Abstract of the United States, 115th edition (Washington, DC: U.S. Department of Commerce, Bureau of the Census), page 248.

Notes to Chapter 7

1. The reduction in household energy use is based upon changes from 1981 to 1993. The data on household energy use in 1981 are in D. Chapman, *Energy Resources and Energy Corporations, op. cit.,* pages 319–20. Current data are from U.S. Energy Information Administration, HECE: *Household Energy Consumption and Expenditures 1993* (Washington, DC: October 1995); HC: *Housing Characteristics 1993* (Washington, DC: June 1995); also, the summary in the August 1995 *Monthly Energy Review* (MER), pages v, vi.

2. According to HECE and HC, *op. cit.*

3. Sources for Table 7.1 are HECE, pages 10 and 71, and *MER,* both cited in Note 1.

4. For Table 7.2, energy use in the home (104 MBtu) is from Table 7.1. The household vehicle data is taken from HC, page 10. Fuel economy data is from *MER,* and "Fast Speeds and Big Cars Send Gas Consumption Up," February 15, 1996 *New York Times,* beginning page D1. Energy loss in power generation: *MER,* page 39.

5. A Btu is the amount of heat energy necessary to warm a pound of water by one Fahrenheit degree. MBtu is the American unit, meaning one million Btus. Britain is moving away from British thermal units and taking up metrics. The most comparable metric unit of energy is the kilojoule; one equals .948 Btu. Of course the economic methods in the text are applicable with both metric and U.S. units.

6. Adapted from HECE, *op. cit.,* page 275. HDD is heating degree days, and air conditioning potential is measured in CDD, cooling degree days.

7. Since a cooling degree day measures air conditioning requirements, it is equal to the day's midpoint less 65 degrees. Example: the day's high is 95 degrees, and the low is 75 degrees. The midpoint is 85 degrees, and the cooling degree days for this particular day are 20 (i.e., 85 degrees − 65 degrees = 20).

8. The average home size grew from 1,700 square feet to 2,250 square feet. From HECE *op. cit.,* page 88.

9. This observation is based upon the author's former home in Western New York, with a climate of 7,000 HDD annually. With the furnace off, on a sunny day with the outside temperature at 10 degrees F, open doors are needed to keep the temperature from reaching 90 degrees F. I calculate the passive solar heat contribution to be one-half MBtu per day. Because of the high insulation, no summer air conditioning is needed.

10. Older furnaces and furnaces using oil, coal, and wood will usually have lower efficiencies. A furnace heating hot water for radiators will generally have greater efficiency than a forced air furnace.

11. The sources for state data are *MER* and *Electric Power Monthly.*

12. U.S. Energy Information Administration, "Energy Highlights," 1996, Volume 3, page 3.

13. A lumen was historically defined as the amount of light from a small candle. See Phillips Lighting Company, *Lighting Handbook* (1984).

14. For compact fluorescents, *Consumer Reports* indicates a very high degree of difference above and below the 10,000-hour level (August 1994, page 492).

15. With the assumptions in Table 7.7, an electricity price of 6.5¢ per kWh or less will change the result in the text and make the standard bulbs the cost-effective choice. If the discount rate is 50 percent annually instead of 12 percent, the CFs become the preferred choice at 19¢ per kWh.

16. Examples of federal programs are described in "Energy Efficient Mortgages" and "Lighting Efficiency Program Gains Popularity" in Fall 1995 *Alliance Update,* and U.S. EPA, "Green Lights Program," December 1993.

17. HC, *op. cit.,* page 169.

18. The Electric Power Research Institute coordinates environmental and energy research for U.S. electric utility companies. It is financed by contributions from the companies. A good review article which supports these programs is "U.S. Electric Utility Demand Side Management: Trends and Analysis," May 1996 *Electric Power Monthly,* pages xi–xxvii. Typically, the companies' expenditures on demand side management are added into the rate base to earn profit, in a manner comparable to investment in generating equipment. As deregulation occurs, state regulatory commissions usually reduce or terminate these programs.

19. Oil heating pollution (not shown) is intermediate between natural gas and electric panel heating.

20. If the wood fuel is from cleared land which is then converted to non-forest use, the net CO_2 impact is very large. This is the basis for the large greenhouse gas effect from tropical deforestation, one of the subjects of the chapter on global climate change.

CHAPTER 8

RENEWABLE ENERGY ECONOMICS

BY MATTHEW SCHWARTZ AND
DUANE CHAPMAN

The economic context of renewable energy is important for the future of environmental policy. First, we assume that, at some future date, atmospheric environmental resources will become scarce; specifically, climate change and ground-level (tropospheric) air pollution will force us to rethink the historic growth in U.S. and global energy use. In addition, at some point in the middle or latter part of the 21st Century, crude oil depletion will deepen interest in renewable energy.

Finally, understanding economics is essential in order to understand why renewable energy gained very little ground relative to conventional energy in the latter part of the 20th Century. Cost effectiveness is a major part of the answer. Consequently, this chapter's review of renewable energy will conclude that considerable acceleration in technological innovation is needed before renewable energy forms can compete broadly on a cost or price basis with conventional energy.

Consider the projection of growth in global renewable energy in Figure 8.1.[1] It shows a dramatic growth in renewable energy use. The global level of renewable energy reaches 900 Q in 2060, when it becomes 61 percent of total energy of 1,500 Q. (Q is an American energy unit, representing one quadrillion Btus.[2])

The projection is named "Sustained Growth" by its authors, and supposes that global economic product grows 3 percent annually over the period. Its major assumptions are that economic growth requires energy growth, and that new renewable energy can displace or substitute for conventional energy on a cost-effective basis.

The author of this study? Shell International Petroleum.[3] As part of this analysis, they studied likely future patterns of petroleum and natural gas use. Their conclusion on this point: conventional oil and natural gas use will peak in the period 2025–2050 and remain high while declining slowly. (From a very different analysis, Chapter 9 has a surprisingly comparable trajectory of oil's growth and decline in the 21st Century.)

This is the background for renewable energy: it is expected to play a major role in the future.[4]

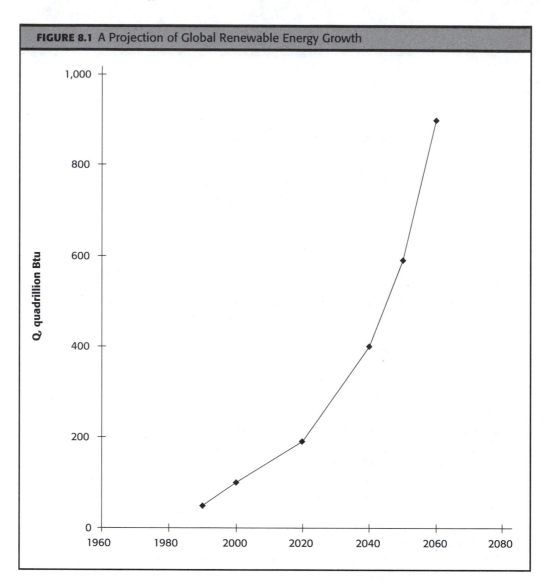

FIGURE 8.1 A Projection of Global Renewable Energy Growth

Solar Energy

Renewable energy comes in many forms, as represented in Table 8.1. Direct sunlight for heating homes and buildings is important because building design and location can significantly affect requirements for purchasing conventional heat energy. (Direct sunlight is often called 'passive solar energy.') For example, even in the Northern United States, passive solar heating can contribute 30 percent of the annual home heating requirement.[5]

Solar hot water heating has been used for decades in Israel and in Florida,[6] and is lower in cost than conventional electric hot water heating. If conventional energy

---

TABLE 8.1 Renewable Energy Sources

A. *Heating: Buildings and Hot Water*
  *1. Direct sunlight heat
  *2. Solar hot water
   3. Sustainable forestry fuelwood

B. *Electricity: Utility and Home*
   1. Hydropower
  *2. Solar photovoltaic
  *3. Solar thermal
  *4. Wind power
   5. Fuelwood/biomass

C. *Transportation*
   1. Biomass ethanol
  *2. Electric automobile, renewable electricity
   3. Electric public transit, renewable electricity
   4. Ox and horse power

Note: Asterisk indicates that some form of energy storage or conventional energy source back-up is required for use of the indicated type of renewable energy. Other potentially renewable energy forms not in the body of the table are tidal power, geothermal heat, and energy from geysers.

---

prices should increase, then use of solar hot water would rise globally in areas where it is suitable.

At the end of the 20th Century, however, neither direct solar space heating for buildings nor solar water heating were significant in the United States. In Table 8.2, they play a small role in household renewable energy use.

The major renewable energy sources are wood heat (analyzed in the previous chapter) and conventional hydropower for electricity. In each of these cases, the renewable source has been widely chosen in specific regions because of its low cost relative to conventional energy.

Throughout the last 25 years, solar electricity has received considerable interest and federal funding. If cost-effective, it could displace conventional coal, nuclear, and other generating sources. For example, a study by Drennen, Erickson, and Chapman estimated that competitively priced solar electricity could reduce global CO_2 emissions 32 percent below levels projected for the mid-21st Century.[7]

Solar electricity is technically capable of replacing gasoline as the power source for vehicles, as well as much of the conventional energy used in power generation. In the latter part of this chapter, the economics of ethanol and solar electric cars is explored. Here, we shall turn our attention to the major issues affecting solar electricity economics: (1) residential solar in high-income and developing countries; (2) large-scale utility-type power plants; and (3) the complex issue of research and development to promote technological innovation.

TABLE 8.2. Renewable Energy in U.S. Household Energy Use, Average for All Households, Mid-1990s[8]	
Ethanol in vehicles	0.6 MBtu
Direct solar heating	0.1 MBtu
Wood heating	5.7 MBtu
Solar hot water	0.5 MBtu
Electricity	
Hydropower	10.0 MBtu
Geothermal energy	0.2 MBtu
Wood and municipal waste	0.1 MBtu
Wind generation (less than .001 of 1%)	—
Photovoltaic generation (less than .001 of 1%)	—
Total average household renewable energy (rounded)	17 MBtu
Percent of total per household, 304 MBtu	6%

Residential Solar Electricity

Going "off the grid" has been a popular concept for three decades. It means that a household or business can produce its own electricity without reliance on power from an electric utility. Consider a small new home in rural Arizona, a mile from the electric utility's roadside power line. A very simple solar electric system would utilize the high solar energy levels there.[9] A large system would produce about 1,000 usable kWh annually, sufficient for wide use of compact fluorescent lighting and normal use of energy-efficient appliances. Suppose the complete cost is $7,000, as in Table 8.3. The levelized annual cost is $1,141 per year or about $1 for each kWh.

TABLE 8.3 Basic Photovoltaic Solar Electricity Economics for Households, U.S.[10]
A. *Assumptions*
1. Annual electricity use: 1,000 kWh/y
2. Solar electric purchase cost: $7,000
3. Levelized cost factor: .163, 10 percent interest for 10 years
4. Utility line to home, one mile: $20,000
5. Electricity rate: 9¢/kWh
6. Gasoline cost: $1.33 per gallon
B. *Results*
1. Annual solar cost—levelized: $1,141/y
2. Annual power line cost—levelized: $3,260/y
3. Annual purchased electricity cost: $900/y
4. Portable gasoline generator cost: $500/y

Of course this is much higher than the utility rate of 9¢ per kWh in the table. But when the new power line cost is included on a levelized cost basis, the total cost per year for both the purchased electricity and the power line is about $4,200 annually. It is a reasonable conclusion that household solar electricity is less costly for homes in sunny regions where the residence is at a distance from power lines.

The table also notes the cost of providing electricity by a portable gasoline generator, which is about $500. Although this is lower than the solar cost, the negative externalities arising from generator use lead many high-income households to choose solar electricity. Generators are noisy and emit local pollution arising from gasoline combustion.

Developing Countries and Residential Solar Electricity

Most of the solar electric equipment produced in the United States is exported to developing countries through the World Bank, USAID, and other aid programs.[11] In part, these programs are intended to promote renewable solar energy as a choice rather than conventional electricity sources.

However, there are circumstances in which households in developing countries will prefer solar electricity on a cost or environmental basis. The preceding section explained the cost advantage in the United States for solar power compared to electric utility service when the customer pays for long power lines. In developing countries, this advantage applies, but a second factor comes into play as well. A solar system is available at a lower capacity, and, at a modest cost for lights, radio, or television, the system can be fully utilized by a household. An under-utilized portable generator may actually have higher kWh costs compared to a solar system. (Note the section of Figure 8.2 to the left of 168 kWh/y that shows this.)

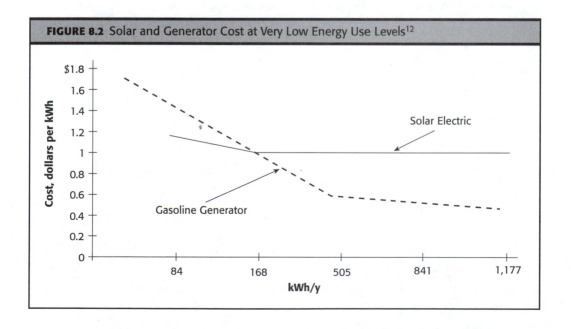

FIGURE 8.2 Solar and Generator Cost at Very Low Energy Use Levels[12]

A second factor favoring household preference for solar electricity in developing countries is the previously noted absence of the noise and smell of generator operation. Also, highly variable household monthly income may favor paying up front for solar power investment in place of frequent gasoline purchases. Finally, an inefficient state-run petroleum company or national government may be so unreliable as to lead a household to feel more secure with a solar unit because gasoline may be unpredictably unavailable.

Technological complexity may not be a major factor in the choice. A household with the expertise to wire and operate home electricity can handle PV or portable generators with equal facility. Field research suggests that components for both systems are usually equally available in countries where solar electric systems are in use.[13] In one region in the Dominican Republic, one individual who delivered gasoline for household portable generators also sold and maintained household solar systems.

Large Solar and Renewable Electric Plants

The leading technology for large-scale power generation is solar thermal, exemplified by the Solar Two unit in the California desert. Two thousand mobile mirrors follow the sun, and their reflected heat is absorbed by molten salt in a single tower. Steam is produced from the heat in the molten salt, and electricity is generated by conventional steam turbines. Some sources say the cost may be as low as 8¢/kWh; others give a much higher cost.[14] Regardless of the actual cost, solar thermal plants have proven their ability to work, and may become more widely used in high solar areas if energy prices increase in the future.

Figure 8.3 is a simplified representation of current costs of generation for large conventional and renewable power plants. (Remember that hydropower is both re-

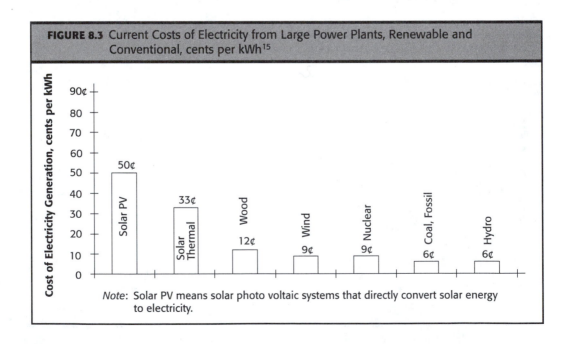

FIGURE 8.3 Current Costs of Electricity from Large Power Plants, Renewable and Conventional, cents per kWh[15]

Note: Solar PV means solar photo voltaic systems that directly convert solar energy to electricity.

newable and conventional.) In reality, these costs vary over significant ranges depending upon the size of the plant, and the cost and availability of regional fuel and energy.

Costs of generation have been following a learning curve, declining rapidly for the new power plant renewables, averaging 7 percent reduction annually.[16] Obviously, this rapid cost decline suggests that wind power is competitive now in some areas, and solar electricity will be competitive in the mid-21st Century if this rate of progress continues.

Research or Development? Scale Economy, Technological Innovation, and Policy

Economic logic implies that, in terms of optimal public policy, the implementation of solar energy technology should be promoted when the declining social cost of solar energy passes below the rising social cost of conventional energy generation. (Social cost here, as in Chapter 1, is the sum of market and externality costs.) Given the presumption that the externality cost of gasoline production and use is significantly greater than that for solar energy use, it should be expected that private market outcomes would defer solar implementation to later periods than would be socially optimal.

With respect to producer costs for solar installation, it is widely believed that significant scale economies reduce marginal and average cost as installations and capacity increase. This is another reason why the export of solar electric systems to developing countries is subsidized.

Figure 8.4 shows a highly simplified static representation of the complex interaction of these assumptions. Three curves are shown. Demand for solar, of course, increases with a lower price. The long-run market supply curve for solar ($LRMS_s$) shows scale economy, with the path of industry long-run cost declining as volume increases. There are two dynamic factors which shift this $LRMS_s$ downward.[17] These two factors are (1) the learning curve effect, over time and (2) the beneficial results of public investment in solar research.

The market equilibrium for solar systems has a high price, P^*_{MKT}, and a low output, Q^*_{MKT}. Given the sharply declining cost curve, solar advocates suggest that public policies to subsidize solar energy would reduce costs by capturing scale economies and enhancing environmental protection.

Is there economic justification for such a policy? Yes, at least partially. Conventional energy has considerable environmental externalities in the form of air pollution (see Chapters 1 and 11) and greenhouse gas emissions (see Chapter 18). These values could be as high as 10¢ per kWh.

In the figure, the external environmental cost of conventional power generation is represented by EEC_C. It is used to calculate the social cost of solar generation. The marginal social cost of solar (MSC_s) equals long-run market supply cost less the environmental benefit when solar electricity is used in place of conventional fossil power.

The desired social optimum (Q^*_{SOC}) needs to have a subsidized price P^*_{SOC} to induce sales at the higher socially optimal level. The subsidy per kWh equals the difference between the optimal price P^*_{SOC} and the higher cost to producers C^* of producing the desired amount.

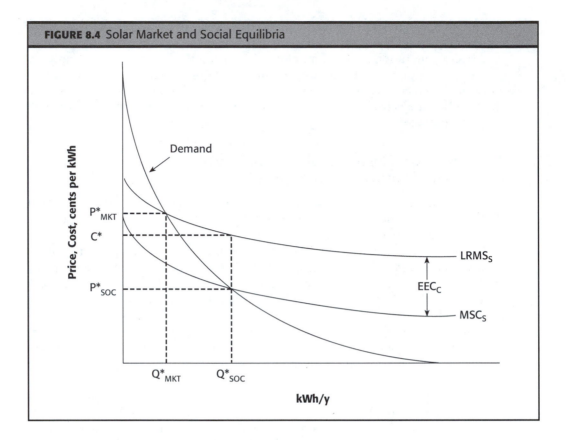

FIGURE 8.4 Solar Market and Social Equilibria

In summary, the joint existence of significant scale economies by producers as well as external social benefit from the use of solar electricity combine to offer a strong economic incentive for developmental subsidy of PV use. Under these conditions, government support and donor aid would clearly promote economic efficiency. Figure 8.4 is intended to represent the economic logic of current solar development policy.

In reality, donor aid does not always lower the solar cost curve. In one country that was analyzed extensively through field research of local installations, PV fabrication is supported by a network of international donors supplying materials, technical assistance, large scale promotion, and low-interest loans. The donor aid is probably some multiple of the cost charged to solar energy system users. Nevertheless, the cost to users appears higher than it might be in the absence of international donor aid in an efficient market.

In another small, developing country, the continued use of solar energy is heavily influenced by the dedicated commitment of a U.S. NGO (nongovernmental organization) run by an expatriate with a high level of technical and marketing skills. This NGO is supported by international aid.

Given the apparent importance in the near term of donor aid support for developing country applications, the question arises as to the best allocation of solar R & D (research and development). Is the return greater for a dollar invested in a uni-

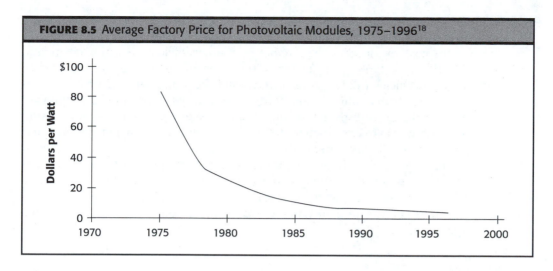

FIGURE 8.5 Average Factory Price for Photovoltaic Modules, 1975–1996[18]

versity laboratory on basic research, or for a dollar invested in placing a solar unit with a rural developing country business or household?

Figure 8.5 is a representation of the decline in PV costs over time. It is primarily the learning curve effect. It shows falling cost per kWh, but the rate of reduction is declining. This reduction in market cost is a reflection of a major basic research effort in the 1970s and 1980s. This university-industry-government program reduced panel costs from $80 to $4 per Watt (in 1995 dollars) while increasing conversion efficiency and operating lifetimes. By 1990, however, the Department of Energy had eliminated the university support program.[19]

Renewable and Alternative Transportation Fuels (by Matthew Schwartz)

There are two principal justifications for switching from conventional gasoline to alternative transport fuels: (1) to reduce air emissions; and (2) for the United States and some other countries to reduce their dependency on foreign petroleum sources.

First, motor vehicle use accounts for roughly 30 percent of all anthropogenic greenhouse gases in the United States.[20] In total, the transportation sector contributes 75 percent of carbon monoxide emissions and about one-third of total carbon dioxide releases. (Chapter 18 explores the 'greenhouse effect' in greater detail.) Alternative fuels, in particular those not requiring the combustion of fossil fuels, have the potential to significantly reduce deleterious vehicle emissions and improve ambient air quality levels in our major cities.

Second, the United States obtains one-half of its petroleum from imports,[21] and the transportation sector consumes 66 percent of the total petroleum products supplied to end-users. Motor gasoline use, in particular, represents 44 percent (the largest share) of these petroleum products. It is clear that growing vehicle use of gasoline in the United States is a significant factor in ozone pollution, climate change, and energy security policy.[22]

Over the past few decades, the number of motor vehicle registrations increased from 74 million in 1960 to more than 200 million in the 1990s.[23] In addition to adding more vehicles to the nation's roads each year, the total number of miles these vehicles traveled and the number of gallons of gasoline consumed climbed steadily as well. In this respect, the United States leads a global trend. As a result, the search for new sources of transportation energy that are clean and abundant has been seen as a priority and a necessity.

The remainder of this chapter explores three potential substitutes for conventional gasoline: ethanol, natural gas, and electricity. Each technology is available now. Table 8.4 presents the environmental benefits associated with these three alternative fuels in terms of their tailpipe and auxiliary power plant emissions relative to gasoline.

Ethanol

Farmers can distill agricultural crops to produce liquid ethanol, or grain alcohol, in a process similar to whiskey distillation. Almost all (95 percent) of ethanol used in the United States comes from corn, and an average bushel of corn yields approximately 2.5 gallons of pure ethanol.[24] (Figure 8.6 shows the sources of renewable and alternative vehicle fuels.) Other countries, such as Brazil, distill ethanol from sugar. Both

	Carbon Monoxide (CO) (grams/mi)		Nitrogen Oxides (NOx) (grams/mi)		Non-Methane Hydrocarbons (NMHC) (grams/mi)	
Fuel Type	Tailpipe	Power Plant	Tailpipe	Power Plant	Tailpipe	Power Plant
Gasoline	3.42	—	0.32	—	0.27	—
Ethanol	3.40	—	0.41	—	0.12	—
Natural gas	0.17	—	0.02	—	<0.01	—
Electric (from coal)	0.00	0.06	0.00	0.40	0.00	0.01
Electric (from solar)	0.00	0.00	0.00	0.00	0.00	0.00
California ultra low-emission vehicle (ULEV) standard	1.70		0.20		0.04	

TABLE 8.4 Alternative Fuel Vehicle Air Emissions[25]

FIGURE 8.6 Alternative Fuel Energy Sources

Petroleum

Gasoline Vehicle

Natural Gas

Natural Gas Vehicle

Corn

Ethanol Vehicle

Coal Plant

Solar Energy

Electric Vehicle

corn and sugar are agricultural products that farmers can harvest sustainably, providing vehicle owners with a dependable, domestic, and renewable fuel source. Ethanol used for motor vehicles typically appears as a gasoline blend: usually 85 percent ethanol to 15 percent unleaded gasoline (E85). In contrast, gasohol is typically 90 percent gasoline and 10 percent ethanol. The combustion of an ethanol blend fuel produces fewer tailpipe emissions than the combustion of motor gasoline.

Natural Gas

A plentiful domestic supply makes natural gas a potentially attractive substitute for gasoline. Natural gas, a nonrenewable fossil fuel extracted from underground reservoirs, can serve as a vehicle fuel in either its compressed form (compressed natural gas) or its liquid form (liquified natural gas). The combustion of natural gas is 'clean-burning,' that is, tailpipe emissions exist in smaller quantities than those associated with gasoline. This positive environmental benefit holds true for all of the emissions listed in Table 8.4, except for methane, a potent greenhouse gas. While natural gas may never completely replace gasoline, it shows promise as a partial transitional fuel, bridging today's gasoline use with tomorrow's use of renewable alternative fuels.

Electricity

Electric vehicles function in much the same way as rechargeable flashlights. When not in use, the vehicle is plugged into an electrical outlet for recharging. Large battery packs store the electricity used to power the vehicle's engine and electrical components during operation. Since electrical outlets are ubiquitous in the United States, the alternative fuel infrastructure for electricity providers already exists. Additionally, electric vehicles do not have combustion engines, thus eliminating the need for a tailpipe. A lack of noticeable engine exhaust earns electric vehicles the title of 'zero-emission' vehicles. Even though electric vehicles have no tailpipe emissions, coal-fired power plants (and those that burn oil and natural gas) release emissions during power generation.

The United States currently generates more than half of its electricity from coal.[26] As indicated in Table 8.4, electric vehicles obtaining power from coal-derived sources augment the emission of nitrogen oxides and sulfur oxides, primary precursors of acidic precipitation. Electric vehicle owners, however, can avoid coal's negative externalities by purchasing their electricity from renewable solar sources.[27]

Alternative Transportation Costs

Imagine that you are shopping for an alternative fuel vehicle. The previous section provided some background on several different types of alternative fuels, but as an informed consumer, you need to weigh environmental benefits with out-of-pocket costs. Similar to the costs of a conventional gasoline vehicle, the costs associated with owning and operating an alternative fuel vehicle fall into two categories: fuel cost and purchase cost.

Annual Fuel Cost

Calculating annual fuel costs requires two pieces of information: (1) the fuel cost 'at the pump' and (2) the fuel efficiency. Table 8.5 compares the fuel cost information of four alternative fuels to that of conventional gasoline.[28] Whether the alternative fuel comes in the form of a gas, liquid, or electrical current, the cost of each fuel can be expressed in terms of dollars per unit of fuel. These at-the-pump fuel costs range from $2 per gallon of ethanol to $0.08 per kWh of electricity. In addition to differing fuel costs, each alternative fuel has a unique fuel efficiency (i.e., how many miles a vehicle can be driven per unit of fuel). For liquid and gaseous fuels, the octane rating determines a fuel's relative efficiency.[29]

To arrive at an annual fuel cost figure, the consumer combines at-the-pump fuel cost and the vehicle's fuel efficiency. For example, an electric vehicle owner purchasing fuel from a solar power plant for 30¢/kWh incurs an operating cost of 8¢/mile (30¢/kWh * 1 kWh/4 miles = 8¢/mile). Applying this operating fuel cost to an annual vehicle use estimate of 12,500 miles yields an annual fuel expenditure of $1,000.

Total Annual Cost

Calculating total annual costs requires two pieces of information in addition to the fuel cost: (1) the initial purchase cost of the vehicle and (2) an estimate of the annual operation and maintenance (O & M) costs. Table 8.6 compares the annual cost information of four alternative fuel vehicles to that of a conventional gasoline vehicle. The initial purchase cost of the different vehicles under consideration ranges from $17,000 for a gasoline vehicle to $35,000 for an electric vehicle. In this

TABLE 8.5 Calculating Annual Fuel Cost[30]

Fuel Type	Fuel Cost 'At-the-Pump' ($/unit)	Fuel Efficiency (unit/mile)	Operating Fuel Cost ($/mile)	Annual Fuel Cost[a]
Gasoline	$1.20/gallon	1 gal/30 mi	$0.04/mi	$500
Ethanol	$2.00/gallon[b]	1 gal/9 mi	$0.22/mi	$2,750
Natural gas	$0.80/gge[c]	1 gge/31 mi	$0.03/mi	$375
Electric (from coal)	$0.08/kWh	1 kWh/4 mi	$0.02/mi	$250
Electric (from solar)	$0.30/kWh	1 kWh/4 mi	$0.08/mi	$1,000

[a]Assumes vehicle use of 12,500 miles/year
[b]Before subsidies
[c]gge = gallon of gasoline equivalent

TABLE 8.6 Calculating Total Annual Cost of Owning and Operating an AFV

Fuel Type	Initial Purchase Cost	Annualized Purchase Cost[a]	Annual Fuel Cost from Table 8.5	Annual O & M[b]	Total Annual Cost
Gasoline	$17,000	$2,414	$500	$1,000	$3,914
Ethanol	$25,000	$3,550	$2,750	$1,000	$7,300
Natural gas	$21,500	$3,053	$375	$1,000	$4,428
Electric (from coal)	$35,000	$4,970	$250	$900[c]	$6,120
Electric (from solar)	$35,000	$4,970	$1,000	$900	$6,870

Notes: [a]Annualized over 10 years at a discount rate of seven percent; lcf = 0.142. If a shorter vehicle life of 7 years instead of 10 years were to be used in the calculations, then the cost spread from conventional gasoline to renewable fuel vehicles would increase.

[b]Annual O & M includes the costs of routine maintenance, oil changes, insurance, etc.

[c]Electric vehicles require less routine maintenance (e.g., no oil changes) than do other alternative fuel vehicles.

example, the consumer finances the purchase cost of the vehicle over ten years at a car loan interest rate of 7 percent. In addition to car loan payments, a vehicle owner also incurs annual O & M costs. These costs typically cover routine maintenance, oil changes, and insurance.

To arrive at a total annual cost figure, the consumer simply adds the annualized purchase cost to the annual fuel cost and O & M estimates. For example, an electric vehicle owner obtaining fuel from a solar power plant incurs a total annual cost of $6,870 ($4,970 + $1,000 + $900 = $6,870).

Economic Incentives

To promote the use of true 'zero-emission' vehicles, government agencies could subsidize the costs of owning and operating an electric vehicle that acquires fuel from solar power plants. The logic is similar to the justification for subsidizing residential solar electricity. Figure 8.7 depicts the pre-subsidy marginal cost curve of the alternative fuel vehicle manufacturers (curve PMC). A government subsidy reduces industry costs and shifts the cost curve downward, from PMC to the new marginal cost curve, NMC. This shift moves the equilibrium point from A to B, resulting in lower alternative fuel vehicle prices to consumers and greater industry output. In other words, the subsidy encourages more automobile manufacturers to produce electric vehicles. A similar subsidy to electric utilities would promote a switch from fossil fuel power generation to solar and wind power.

Table 8.7 presents three potential government subsidy scenarios. In scenario #1, the government offers a $10,000 subsidy toward the initial purchase cost of the elec-

FIGURE 8.7 Theoretical Impact of Alternative Fuel Subsidy

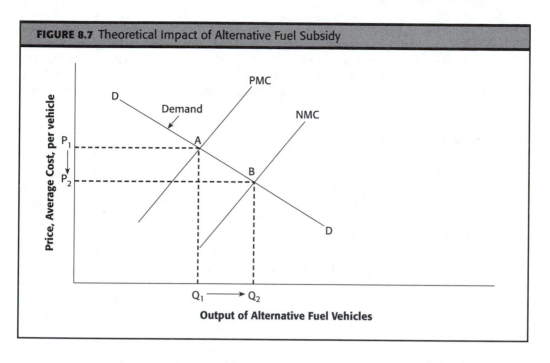

tric vehicle. This subsidy lowers the initial purchase cost from $35,000 to $25,000, resulting in a total annual cost figure of $5,450. In scenario #2, the government offers a $10,000 subsidy toward the initial purchase cost of the electric vehicle and a 10¢/kWh subsidy toward solar electricity cost. In this situation, the vehicle subsidy lowers the initial purchase cost from $35,000 to $25,000, and the fuel subsidy lowers the fuel cost from 30¢/kWh to 20¢/kWh, resulting in a total annual cost figure of $5,075. In scenario #3, the government offers a $15,000 subsidy toward the initial purchase cost of the electric vehicle and a 100 percent fuel cost subsidy. Under this offering, the vehicle subsidy lowers the initial purchase cost from $35,000 to $20,000, and the fuel subsidy lowers the fuel cost from 30¢/kWh to 0¢/kWh, resulting in a total annual cost figure of $3,740.

TABLE 8.7 Subsidy Scenarios for Electric Vehicles Receiving Fuel from Solar Sources

Subsidy Scenario	Initial Purchase Cost	Annualized Purchase Cost	Annual Fuel Cost	Annual O & M	Total Annual Cost
Scenario #1	$25,000	$3,550	$1,000	$900	$5,450
Scenario #2	$25,000	$3,550	$625	$900	$5,075
Scenario #3	$20,000	$2,840	$0	$900	$3,740

Only under subsidy scenario #3 does the total annual cost of an electric vehicle obtaining fuel from solar power compare satisfactorily with the total annual cost of a conventional gasoline vehicle ($3,740 versus $3,914). The underlying question of whether the environmental benefits of a true 'zero-emission' vehicle outweigh the cost of the combined subsidy in scenario #3 ($16,000 per vehicle) remains debatable.

Policies and Economics

As the concern about climate change and air pollution increases, interest in policies to promote renewable energy is rising. This chapter has reviewed the economic logic associated with the relatively high market cost of renewable energy, its slow growth in use, and the theoretical arguments which support U.S. subsidy programs.

Across the spectrum of renewable and alternative energy, from solar and wind electricity to biomass and fuel cell vehicles,[31] research is seeking technological innovations that can reduce the cost of renewable energy use while avoiding the greenhouse gas and pollution emissions of conventional energy use.

The types of policy proposals which are being considered are summarized in Table 8.8. In addition to those policies, consideration is being given to increased gasoline taxes, which change the relative market costs and prices of conventional and renewable energy.

Table 8.8 also shows several policy proposals affecting energy conservation and efficiency, the subject of Chapter 7 on household energy use. In Chapter 9, we examine the economics of petroleum production and use, and the issue of its potential depletion.

TABLE 8.8 Types of Policies to Promote Renewable Energy and Energy Efficiency[32]

A. *Research Investment*
1. Solar electricity
2. Appliance energy efficiency
3. Fuel economy
4. Fuel cell, new vehicle technology

B. *Building Tax Credits*
1. Energy-efficient homes
2. Renewable energy heating systems

C. *Automobiles and Trucks*
1. Tax credit for high fuel economy vehicles
2. Subsidy for ethanol

D. *Electric Utilities*
1. Tax credits for solar, wind power

Questions for Discussion and Analysis

1. From Table 8.3, calculate the levelized cost of solar electric power if the interest rate is 2 percent for 10 years.

2. Assume that annual electricity use is 1,000 kWh, and the levelized purchase cost of a portable generator is $250 per year. Fuel use is one gallon for 5 kWh. Gasoline costs $1 per gallon. What is the total cost per kWh?

3. Do you favor or oppose tax subsidies to promote solar energy and alternative energy vehicles? Explain your position.

4. In Figure 8.4, the price difference $P^*_{MKT} - P^*_{SOC}$ is greater than the possible subsidy EEC_c. Yet, in Figure 8.7, the subsidy if drawn is greater than the price difference $P_1 - P_2$. Why is this so?

5. What implications does the high production cost of renewable energy have for world oil price? For U.S. and global air pollution?

Notes to Chapter 8

1. The sources for Figure 8.1 are Shell International, "The Evolution of the World's Energy System 1860–2060," London, 1995. Also see "The Future of Energy," *The Economist,* October 7, 1995; this article discusses the Shell study. The Shell study defines three types of renewable energy: traditional biomass fuelwood, solar electricity, and wind power.
2. The standard large metric energy unit is the exajoule; this is the unit widely used elsewhere. In comparison, 1,000 exajoules equal 948 Q.
3. See Note 1 above.
4. Although Shell and others expect rapid growth in renewable energy in the future, it was essentially without growth from the 1970s to the 1990s. In the United States, non-hydro renewable energy was 3.2/3.3 Q in both 1990 and 1996. (From USEIA, *Renewable Energy Annual, 1995* and *1996*).
5. See the discussion in the preceding chapter and Note 9 to that chapter. For example, use the text value of 80 MBtu/y for the northern United States, and assume an average of one-sixth of a MBtu per day for six months for a direct sunlight heat impact. This reduces purchased energy by more than 30 percent.
6. Solar hot water heating is typically used in areas that do not experience winter freezing. Consider a simple solar heater integrated with an electric heater. For an investment of $1,700, the system could provide 3,000 kWh (about half) of hot water heating. From Table 8.6, assume an interest rate of 8 percent, a 15-year payment period, and electricity costing the household 9¢/kWh. Using the levelized cost method again, the cost per kWh of solar hot water would be 7¢, less costly than the conventional system. Source: J. Harrison, "Simple Solar Water Heating Systems," November/December 1997 *Solar Today* 11(6):26–29. As with space heat in Chapter 7, natural gas-heated hot water is less costly than electrically heated hot water.
7. T. E. Drennen, J. D. Erickson, and D. Chapman, "Solar Power and Climate Change Policy in Developing Countries," 1996 *Energy Policy* 24(1):8–16.
8. For Table 8.2, the sources are the Table 7.2 sources; February 1996 *Electric Power Monthly,* page 13; and Solar Energy Research Institute, *The Potential of Renewable*

Energy, March 1990. For 20 million households with heating from firewood, the average use is 27 MBtu from 1.3 cords. For the 3 million homes with primary wood heat, the average is 81 MBtu from 4 cords. Total solar hot water for all households: about 0.05 Q.

9. Solar energy impact is measured in 'solar hours,' kWh per square meter per average day. Northern and Eastern Arizona receive 6 solar hours daily; Northern New York is the lowest in the country at 3.3. As solar hours per average day increase, fewer batteries and solar panels are needed to supply a reliable home electricity source. Upstate New York cost for solar electricity might be about $2 per kWh.

10. The methodology used in Table 8.3 is described in D. Chapman and J. Erickson, "Residential Rural Solar Electricity in Developing Countries," April 1995 *Contemporary Economic Policy,* 13(2):98–108; and J. Erickson and D. Chapman, "Photovoltaic Technology: Markets, Economics, and Developing Countries," 1995 *World Development* 23(7):1129–1141. The solar system includes panels, control and inverter equipment, and batteries. A generator requires about one-fifth of a gallon of gasoline per kWh. The generator cost in the table includes estimated lubrication and repair costs. Also see "Remote Home Power System Packages," Spring 1997 *Real Goods News; J. Schaffer, Solar Living Sourcebook* (White River Junction, VT: Chelsea Green Publishing, 1996), and *Alternative Energy Engineering* 1997–98 Design Guide (Redway, CA, 1997).

11. J. Erickson and D. Chapman, "Photovoltaic Technology: Markets, Economics, Rural Development," 1995 *World Development* 23(7):1129–1141.

12. The source for Figure 8.2 is Chapman and Erickson.

13. J. Agras, "Solar Energy in Zimbabwe," seminar, Cornell University, March 14, 1994; J. Erickson, "PVs in the DR," memorandum, August 1993.

14. See the estimates of solar thermal cost in the discussion of solar electric vehicles later in this chapter.

15. Figure 8.3 is a simplified summary of Shell International, *op. cit.,* and *The Economist's (op. cit.)* analysis of the Shell study. The values in the figure here are midpoints, adjusted for inflation to 1997. As noted previously, solar PV and windpower require special engineering consideration because of the need to store energy. The Energy Information Administration projects future costs which are much lower for solar PV and solar thermal. See their *Challenges of Electric Power Industry Restructuring for Fuel Supplies,* September 1998. The Shell estimates in the figure are for current construction and operation.

16. For windpower and solar PV, Shell International, *op. cit.*

17. For simplicity, Figure 8.4 does not include short-run or long-run marginal and average costs for individual firms in the PV industry. The $LRMS_s$ curve in the figure represents a path of long-run marginal and average cost equilibrium points.

18. The source for Figure 8.5 is L. Brown *et al., Vital Signs 1997* (New York: Norton, 1997), page 55.

19. J. Erickson, *Sustainability and Economics,* Ph.D. Dissertation, Cornell University, 1997, page 183.

20. USEIA, *Describing Current and Potential Markets for Alternative-Fuel Vehicles,* March 1996.

21. Net imports as a source of petroleum are rising slowly, from 35 percent in 1973 to 49 percent in 1997. November 1997 *Monthly Energy Review,* page 15.

22. These are the central topics in Chapters 9, 11, and 18.

23. USEIA, *Annual Energy Review: 1995*, July 1996.

24. Carless, J., *Renewable Energy: A Concise Guide to Green Alternatives* (New York: Walker, 1993); and D. Chapman, "New Technologies and Microeconomics," *Energy Resources and Energy Corporations* (New York: Cornell University Press, 1983), pages 284–290.

25. For Table 8.4, the gasoline and electric (from coal) emission data came from Q. Wang, "Emission Impacts of Electric Vehicles," *Air and Waste Management Association* 40(9), September 1990. The ethanol emission data are based on the Ford Taurus Sedan LS, which is certified as a California Transition Low-Emission Vehicle (TLEV). These emission data and the California ULEV data came from U.S. EPA, *Exhaust Emission Standards for Light-Duty Vehicles and Trucks,* personal fax from Ms. Mary Manners, Office of Mobile Sources, June 1997. The natural gas emission data are based on the Honda Civic Sedan EX, which is certified at a level of 1/10 that of the California standards.

26. *Annual Energy Review: 1995, op. cit.*

27. The Sacramento Municipal Utilities District in California uses photovoltaic cells to supply electric vehicle charging stations. For more information see A. Schwartz et al., *Chemistry in Context* (Dubuque, IA: Brown Communications and the American Chemical Society, 1994). In addition, the Southern California Edison Company currently operates Solar Two, a solar thermal power plant capable of producing 10 megawatts of electricity—enough to supply power to 10,000 homes. For more information see Electronics Now staff, "Solar Success Story," November 1996 *Electronics Now,* page 8.

28. The fuel and vehicle cost information listed in Tables 8.5 and 8.6 represent the costs of currently available alternative fuel vehicles. The gasoline vehicle is based on a Honda Civic Sedan EX with a four-speed automatic transmission. The ethanol vehicle is based on a Ford Taurus Sedan LS with a four-speed automatic transmission. The natural gas vehicle is also based on a Honda Civic Sedan EX with a four-speed automatic transmission. The electric vehicles are based on a General Motors EV1 Coupe with a one-speed automatic transmission. For more information on these vehicles see Memorandum to Duane Chapman, Cornell University, from Matt Schwartz, Industrial Economics, Inc., "Sources of Alternative Fuel Vehicle Information," May 3, 1997.

29. Typical gasoline octane ratings range from 85 for regular gasoline to 95 for premium gasoline. Ethanol has an octane rating of 105 and compressed natural gas has an octane rating of 120. The low fuel efficiency of the ethanol vehicle described in Table 8.6 is attributable to the six-cylinder engine in the Ford Taurus Sedan LS, versus the four-cylinder engine in the Honda Civic Sedan EX. For more information on alternative fuel octane ratings see J. Carless, *Renewable Energy: A Concise Guide to Green Alternatives* (New York: Walker Publishing, 1993).

30. The $2/gallon ethanol cost in Table 8.5 is an estimate of at-the-pump price before any subsidies. Ethanol has been heavily subsidized in Brazil and the United States. See *The Economist,* October 7, 1995, page 24, and D. Chapman, *Energy Resources, op. cit.,* pages 284–287.

31. Other new vehicle technologies will probably have purchase costs comparable to the ethanol and electric automobiles in Table 8.6. Consider a fuel cell electric vehicle using gasoline as the source of hydrogen: it would have one-half or less of the gasoline usage of the gasoline car, but, because of the high purchase price, its total annual cost would be in the $5,000 to $6,000 per year range.

32. These Table 8.8 proposals were initiated in early 1998; *New York Times,* January 31, 1998.

PART III

THE QUESTION OF GLOBAL RESOURCE LIMITATIONS

CHAPTER 9

WORLD OIL: A STRATEGIC LIMITED RESOURCE?

The presumption is that petroleum, created in previous geological eras, is limited in its conventional form as crude oil brought to the earth's surface. Yet this seemingly straightforward proposition is the subject of considerable controversy. If oil is scarce, some argue, its price will rise over time as it is depleted and becomes more costly to produce. Yet Figure 9.1 shows no obvious pattern pointing toward rising price. In fact, that price at the end of the 20th Century was below the real inflation-adjusted annual average prices during most of the long period from 1950 to the end of the century.

The early industrial history of petroleum does not fit comfortably with the popular concepts of monopoly. The first well produced oil in 1859 in Pennsylvania. As production increased, John D. Rockefeller and associates gained significant

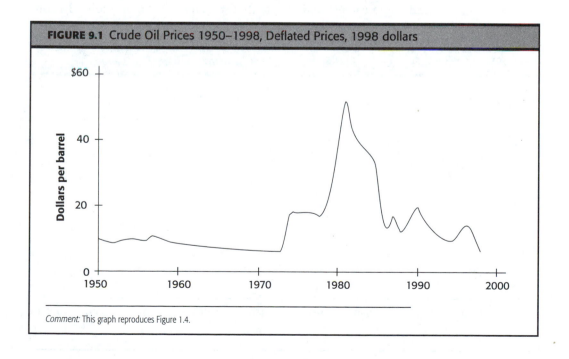

FIGURE 9.1 Crude Oil Prices 1950–1998, Deflated Prices, 1998 dollars

Comment: This graph reproduces Figure 1.4.

influence in the industry through lower costs, better organization, and imposing technology. At one point, the Rockefeller Standard Group held 84 percent of the market for refined products in the United States. In contrast to Chapter 1's explanation that monopoly restricts production and raises prices, however, it must be emphasized that the Rockefeller organization accelerated production and sales and lowered prices.[1]

As we move into the 21st Century, oil and gasoline prices are at historically low levels. Gasoline prices in the United States are at the lowest levels ever experienced. (See Figure 9.2.) At the same time, world oil use as well as U.S. gasoline consumption are rising to new record levels each year.

Why does this matter? Transportation, in the United States and worldwide, relies on inexpensive petroleum. In the United States, petroleum products supply 99 percent of the transportation energy. In other countries without major electric rail service, the dependence of transportation on inexpensive petroleum is similar. The partial exceptions are Europe and Japan, where nuclear power provides electric rail energy.

If petroleum does become scarce, then electrified transportation will become more important. This, in turn, will clearly lead to an increased magnitude of environmental problems in two areas: nuclear power and climate change (see Chapter 18). If and when oil becomes more costly, coal-burning power plants will accelerate the growth in greenhouse gases because there is more carbon dioxide for a unit of energy in coal than in petroleum. An alternative to coal and nuclear substitution for petroleum, of course, is, theoretically, the possible development of solar-based renewable transportation energy (see Chapter 8).

M. A. Adelman and many other energy economists believe that a stable period of low prices and rising use for oil indicate that scarcity is not a problem.[2] In con-

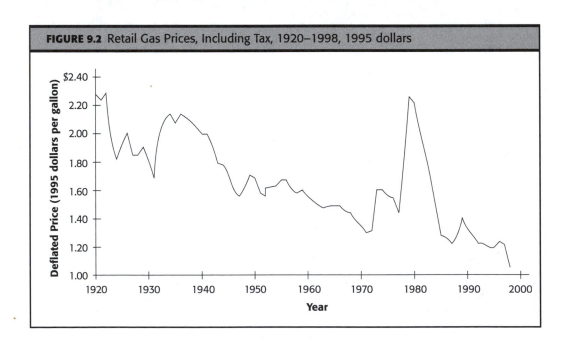

FIGURE 9.2 Retail Gas Prices, Including Tax, 1920–1998, 1995 dollars

trast, geologists generally believe that petroleum is the most likely energy resource for which scarcity and depletion will become a problem. How can we reconcile these apparent contradictions?

The Geologists' Approach

Geologists measure earth's history in billions of years, and their telescope for the future is long term. The geological estimates in Table 9.1 were developed by experts familiar with regional geologic data. They are typically based upon knowledge about current production and proved reserve data, and on extrapolation to identified geological regions. The techniques employed include underground sound testing, satellite data, and computer imaging. As we shall see, these estimates of remaining resources have grown significantly.

The significant aspect of Table 9.1 is the difference between coal and petroleum. Coal exists in great quantities. Petroleum is our most important fossil energy,[3] and is the energy type most carefully studied. It is also the one that appears to be most limited. Even if all values in the table double, it seems very likely that crude oil will experience depletion effects before natural gas or coal. Future coal use is measured in millennia; future oil use is measured in decades.

Throughout much of the 1980s and 1990s, a group originating with C. D. Masters estimated the earth's total endowment of conventional crude oil, dividing their calculations of remaining oil into two broad categories, identified reserves and undiscovered resources. These are the first two definitions in Table 9.2.

TABLE 9.1 Geological Estimates of Remaining Conventional Energy Resources (U.S. tons, barrels, or Btu)[4]

	Geological Estimate of Remaining Resources	*Current Annual Use*	*Ratio*
Coal	15 trillion tons	5 billion tons	3,000 years
Crude oil	1.9 trillion barrels	23 billion barrels	80 years
Natural gas	15 quadrillion cubic feet	76 trillion cubic feet	200 years

Note: The coal figure is from the latest source cited by Sundquist. On an energy basis, coal would have 4,000 years remaining of current use levels. The petroleum and natural gas data are from Masters et al., 1994. Numbers are generally rounded to two digits. Oil and gas data are from Masters, but at the upper 5 percent level as discussed in the text.

C. J. Campbell and J. H. Laherrere come to a more conservative estimate of one trillion barrels of remaining resources in their "The End of Cheap Oil," March 1998 *Scientific American,* pages 78–83.

TABLE 9.2 Conceptual Definitions of Oil Resources[5]

1. *Identified Reserves:* Economically recoverable crude oil at known reservoirs and fields with expected technology. Similar to an inventory concept.
2. *Undiscovered Resources:* Geological extrapolation of potential crude oil based upon application of knowledge of occurrence of geological formations and relationships of crude oil to geological formations. A probabilities concept.
3. *Remaining Resources:* An estimate of total conventional crude oil available for recovery, the sum of the probabilistic undiscovered resources and the inventory concept of identified reserves.
4. *Cumulative Production:* The amount of conventional crude oil produced to date. Analogous to an accounting concept.
5. *Original Resources:* The estimated amount of undiscovered resources, identified reserves, and cumulative production. Consequently, it combines the probabilistic and accounting definitions.

It is important to realize that identified reserves are essentially an inventory. (Many geologists use a similar but narrower concept, "proven reserves.") The companies or governments that hold the reserves know that this oil can be produced. In turn, oil refining and distribution activities can be scheduled because the "inventory" of identified reserves is available.

Of course, this summary has simplified a very complex technology. Estimates of identified reserves can be adjusted significantly in response to higher prices for crude, new lower-cost production technology, cooperative production agreements, revisions in field size, and enhanced recovery. Some of these subjects are taken up later in this chapter; the main idea to this point is that identified reserves are a useful planning concept. Table 9.3 uses these geological concepts to identify the major components of remaining reserve estimates on a geographical basis. Of particular interest is the stakeholding in proven reserves of countries that have been the object of military threat by Iraq. If Iraq had been successful in its invasions of Iran, Kuwait, and perhaps Saudi Arabia, it would have controlled 55 percent of proven world reserves.

Probability plays an important role in these estimates. The U.S. Geological Survey authors favor a lower estimate of undiscovered resources. They prefer a "most likely" approach, a lower value of 471 billion barrels rather than the 938 value in the table. The Geological Survey uses a cost concept of $50 per barrel as defining the upper limit of feasible production. However, if prices rise above this level in the next century, there will be more enhanced recovery, and the definition of economically recoverable oil will be enlarged.

It is interesting to note that, over the 9-year period 1983–1993, the Geological Survey estimate of the most likely amount of undiscovered crude oil declined

TABLE 9.3 Geologists' Upper Probability Estimates of Regional and World Crude Oil (billion barrels)[6]

	Identified Reserves	Estimated Undiscovered Resources	Estimated Total Upper Probability Remaining Resources
Persian Gulf	660	217	877
Former Soviet Union	57	234	291
United States	23	55	78
North Sea— Western Europe	17	34	51
World	1,000	938	1,938

Note: On identified reserves: Iraq 100; Iran 89; Kuwait and Neutral Zone 99; Saudi Arabia 259. World totals include other regions. Total four countries: 547; or 55 percent. See U.S. Geological Survey and other sources in Note 6. For 1995 production, the amounts were Persian Gulf 7; FSU 2.5; U.S. 2.5; North Sea and Western Europe 2; world total 22; all in billion barrels.

from 550 billion barrels in 1983 to 471 billion in 1993. The 5 percent upper probability estimate declined by a much larger difference of 400 billion barrels.[7] Three factors were at work: (a) estimates of total original endowment increased, (b) undiscovered oil as of 1983 had been transformed into identified reserves by 1995, and (c) continuing growth in world consumption used 215 billion barrels in the 10-year period. Weighing both positive and negative factors, the geological perspective is that there was more oil than was anticipated 10 years ago, but less remains now.

The Economists' Approach

The geologists' perspective is not popular with economists. In particular, in Table 9.1, the ratio of 80 years remaining crude oil to current production is typically rejected. Economists are generally more comfortable with the implications of Figures 9.1 and 9.2: prices are declining and consumption is growing. Where is some manifestation of depletion?

A careful review of oil production cost data offers some insight into this question. A warning is necessary: the results show field production costs and transportation costs to be much lower, by dramatic proportions, than the reader anticipates.

In its simplest form, the full cost of delivering crude oil from the Persian Gulf to Japan, the United States, or elsewhere can be divided into three parts: development, operations, and shipping. It can be represented as:

$$\begin{array}{ccccccc}
\text{Crude} & & \text{Investment} & & \text{Operations,} & & \\
\text{Oil} & = & \text{in} & + & \text{Lifting} & + & \text{Shipping} \qquad (9\text{-}1) \\
\text{Cost} & & \text{Development} & & & &
\end{array}$$

The investment in development cost is the most complex part of the equation. Here, it is taking in exploration, field testing, field equipment, and investment specific to the well. The simplest approach is the same as was introduced in Chapter 4, in analyzing the levelized annual cost of acid rain scrubbers near the Grand Canyon.[8] Initially, let's assume the same 10 percent interest rate and 30 year operating life that was used in that case. The levelized cost factor is the same, 0.106 per year.

$$\begin{array}{ccccc}
\text{Simple} & & & & \\
\text{Investment} & & \text{Total} & & \\
\text{in} & = & \text{Initial} & * & \text{lcf} \qquad (9\text{-}2) \\
\text{Development} & & \text{Investment} & & \\
\text{per Barrel} & & & &
\end{array}$$

$$26.5\text{¢/bl} \; = \; \$2.50\text{/bl} \; * \; 0.106 \qquad (9\text{-}3)$$

Adelman's work suggests, for Saudi Arabia, that $2.50 per barrel should be used as the total initial investment.[9] Equation (9-3) shows the results. The first calculation shows 26.5¢ per barrel for development cost. However, this is too simple. We will make one other step used in petroleum economics. We will make a special adjustment for the risky nature of the oil business, and for the decline and exhaustion of oil flowing from an individual well. The simplest process is to add together three rates: the interest rate, the risk factor, and the production decline rate. We are already assuming a 10 percent interest rate. We add another 10 percent risk factor. Finally, a 2 percent decline rate reflects declining production as an oil reservoir is depleted. The result is a total of a 22 percent 'oil discount rate.' Now, the 'oil discount rate' should be used to calculate the 'oil levelized cost factor.'

But since the oil discount rate is high, and the production period is a long 30 years, it would be acceptable to use this adjusted method:[10]

$$\begin{array}{ccccc}
\text{Adjusted} & & \text{Total} & & \\
\text{Investment} & = & \text{Initial} & * & \left(\dfrac{\text{Interest}}{\text{Rate}} + \dfrac{\text{Risk}}{\text{Factor}} + \dfrac{\text{Depletion}}{\text{Rate}} \right) \quad (9\text{-}4a) \\
\text{in Development} & & \text{Investment} & &
\end{array}$$

$$55\text{¢/bl} \; = \; \$2.50\text{/bl} \; * \; (.10 + .10 + .02) \qquad (9\text{-}4b)$$

Since the total investment is $2.50 per barrel, and we've set the interest rate at 10 percent, the risk factor at another 10 percent, and the decline rate at 2 percent, the result is 55¢ per barrel. This is more realistic than the simple 26.5¢ figure that was first calculated.

This concludes the illustration of the difficult first step in calculating crude oil cost. The other two parts are very straightforward. In Saudi Arabia, the operations and lifting cost may be about 25¢ per barrel, and the tanker shipping cost about $1.50 per barrel.[11] The result may be surprising, and it may be helpful to restate Equation 9-1 to show the resulting cost of $2.30 per barrel for Saudi Arabia.

$$\begin{array}{lclclcl}
\text{Illustrative} & & \text{Adjusted} & & \text{Operations,} & & \\
\text{Crude Oil} & = & \text{Investment} & + & \text{Lifting} & + & \text{Shipping} \quad (9\text{-}5) \\
\text{Cost for} & & \text{in Development} & & & & \\
\text{Saudi Arabia} & & & & & & \\
\end{array}$$

$$\$2.30/\text{barrel} \;=\; (55\cent) \;+\; (25\cent) \;+\; (\$1.50)$$

This outline of costing will seem simplistic to petroleum engineers, and complex to students of environmental economics. But a feel for the methodology is helpful to grasp the reality: at the turn of the century, crude oil production cost in the Persian Gulf is about $2.50 per barrel. And this includes an allowance for risk. Generally, the same cost would be expected to deliver crude oil to Japan or Europe.

The comparable figure for the North Sea or Alaskan oil fields is on the order of $15 per barrel.[12] This is because geography and climate impose higher technological requirements with higher costs. Many years ago at the peak of production in Texas and nearby states, crude oil costs may have been as low as $5 per barrel in 1995 dollars in some fields.

If we consider the geographic data and the cost data together, it appears that oil production has increased in the regions with high cost and lower reserves. Simultaneously, production has fallen in the Persian Gulf where reserves are high and costs are low.

At the same time, with respect to Figure 9.1, it is clear that crude prices have fallen sharply from their 1980 and 1990 peaks, but world prices remain far above the apparent Persian Gulf production costs.

To compare the economics reviewed here with actual data, Persian Gulf oil prices for crude landed in the United States was between $15 and $20 per barrel for 10 of the 11 years between 1986 and 1998. The price for crude in the United Kingdom is similar. In the United States, the world's largest petroleum consumer, the domestic well-head price averaged $16 per barrel over the same period.[13] Why, then, are some costs near price, and Persian Gulf costs so far below price? Can economists help clarify this situation?

Competition, Monopoly, or a Hybrid?

Again referring to Chapter 1 and Figure 1.1, recall that the competitive theory resulted in an optimal price of $16 per barrel and output of 22 billion barrels annually. In contrast, the monopoly theory (Figures 1.2 and 1.3 in that chapter) called for output to be restricted to 12.69 billion barrels and the price of a barrel of crude raised to nearly $35. Clearly, this material reflects the assumption that the oil market is primarily competitive; the illustration of the competitive theory gives a price and world output typical of this period.

In fact, many economists and policy analysts in the 1970s and 1980s mistakenly confused monopoly and depletion. When OPEC successfully raised prices in the mid-1970s and again in 1980, these analysts thought that the suddenly higher price reflected depletion. In fact, from 1970 to the mid-1990s, the geological estimates of original global oil resources have continued to increase.

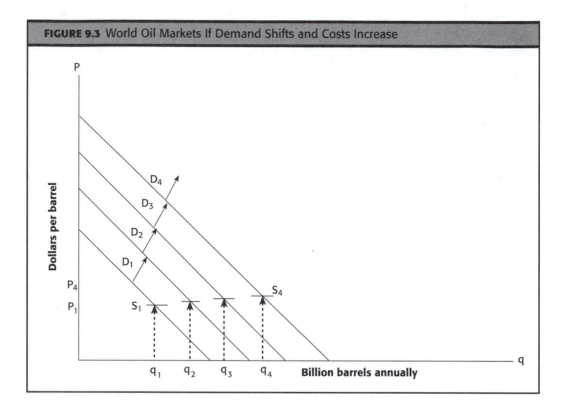

FIGURE 9.3 World Oil Markets If Demand Shifts and Costs Increase

The price (see Figures 9.1 and 9.2) reflected OPEC's ability at that time to impose monopoly pricing. However, as new production emerged in the North Sea, Alaska, Mexico, and elsewhere, the price spikes collapsed.

Is it possible to reconcile the geologists' and economists' perspectives? The answer is a qualified yes. Consider the prospect of growing world population and income. Ten years from now, if the prices of crude oil and gasoline were unchanged in real dollars, demand and consumption would be higher. This is reflected in the upward-shifting demand lines[14] in Figure 9.3.

Suppose that production costs were also rising, but more slowly. These are slowly rising supply costs S_1 to S_4. The equilibrium world output levels q_1–q_4 are growing rapidly, and crude price is growing slowly.

The economic theory of depletion was introduced in Chapter 6. It shows how maximum economic rent or producers surplus can be determined for the full period of use of a finite resource. Equation (9-6) simply applies Equation (6-17) to world oil in a competitive framework. Fortunately, the results of this mathematical theory can be expressed simply:

$$Q_t = QC_t - (1 + r)^t * DF \tag{9-6}$$

Turning to Figure 9.4, the upper curve of triangles shows how world oil use would grow if oil were to be limitless. This is the same track as the intersections of supply and demand in Figure 9.3.

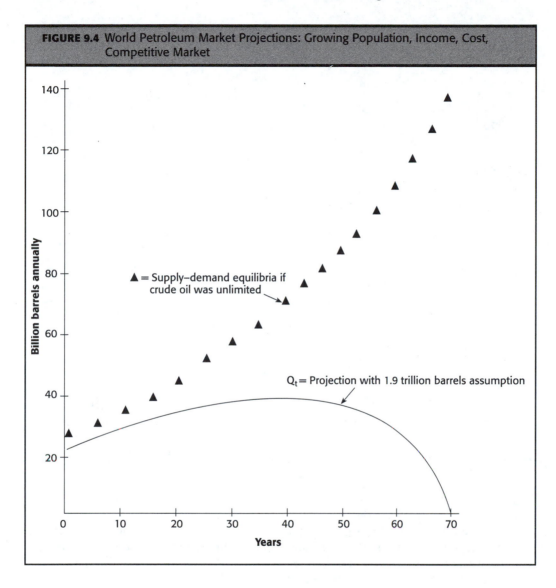

FIGURE 9.4 World Petroleum Market Projections: Growing Population, Income, Cost, Competitive Market

But the lower curve, the upside-down bowl, shows what the result is when the resource limitation is taken into account. This curve for conventional crude oil use, which ultimately falls to zero, reflects Equation (9-6). The Q_t term on the left is the projected supply-demand equilibrium.

The first term on the right is QC_t. This is what the rising supply-demand equilibrium would be. It is analogous to the competitive market from Chapter 1, but projected outward over time as world population and income grows.

The last pair of factors on the right have a negative sign. As time passes, this negative term grows larger, and, as oil is depleted, it eventually forces Q_t to zero. DF is a depletion factor, which is defined mathematically by the relationship between demand and remaining resources.[15]

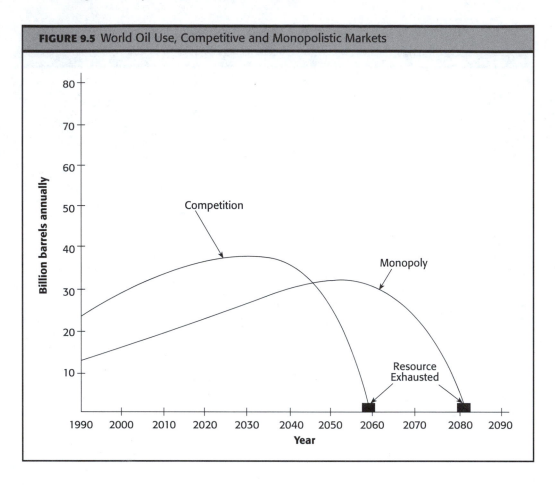

FIGURE 9.5 World Oil Use, Competitive and Monopolistic Markets

While Adelman's expectation of stable prices near current levels seems likely to be true for the near future, it is dependent on the continuation of the present hybrid competitive market. In part, this is a question of political economy, addressed briefly in the last section of this chapter.

If world monopoly were to become established in the future, there would be a shift to higher petroleum prices and lower production and consumption levels. However, these higher prices would stretch out the period to exhaustion of conventional crude oil. Both competitive and monopolistic paths are shown in Figure 9.5.

The discussion here of depletion theory is simplified, but Equation (9-6) and the concepts used here are potentially applicable to finite resources, whether fossil energy or metals.[16]

Can the future price of crude oil be predicted from economic theory? Chapter 6 (and especially Figure 6.6) introduced some of the broad possibilities as concepts. In a later section of this chapter, we return to the subject of future oil and gasoline prices. But first, it is necessary to see how global geopolitics interacts with economics in world oil markets.

The Security Dimension, Hybrid Competition, and Game Theory

In the early period of the Persian Gulf conflict, then-President Bush and Secretary of State James Baker were very explicit about the economic motivations for reversing the Iraqi attempt to dominate the Persian Gulf. Remember, Table 9.3 indicates that Iraq sought control over 55 percent of proved reserves. This quotation was typical:

> *Our jobs, our way of life, our own freedom and the freedom of friendly countries around the world would all suffer if control of the world's greatest reserves fell into the hands of Saddam Hussein.*[17]

Iraq was defeated (as it had been in Iran), and its world production in the 1990s was reduced to only 20 percent of its 1989 level. There are important unresolved issues that need to be addressed. They include: (a) the political motivation on the part of low-cost Persian Gulf producers to shelter expensive Northern Hemisphere oil, (b) the powerful economic incentive for continuing instability, and (c) the military cost to the United States of guaranteeing access to low-cost Persian Gulf oil. Finally, are there now or should there be international mechanisms to address the incentives for seizure and the global problems of growing energy use?

If Persian Gulf production costs are as low as the data in the first part of this chapter suggest, why do the Persian Gulf producers not seek monopoly power by first driving high-cost competitors out of the industry? Adelman's work leads him to conclude that $5 per barrel could have been an equilibrium competitive price in the 1980s and 1990s.[18] He had noted that this price would have been profitable for OPEC, and could have led to major increases in OPEC production and world oil consumption. At the same time, a price of $10 or below would have reduced capacity in the United States and in the North Sea.

It is this latter point which should be given considerable attention. If Saudi Arabia and Persian Gulf governments keep prices in the $15 to $20 range, they support high-cost oil production in the countries that provide military security for Persian Gulf governments.

This important point is emphasized by George Bush's meetings with Saudi government ministers and the King in 1986. Bush, then Vice President, publicly and privately sought Persian Gulf support for higher crude oil prices. The price at that time was below $10.[19]

The economic logic is roughly as follows. U.S. net imports of petroleum have reached one-half of total use.[20] The U.S. production is costly; production in the Persian Gulf is not. Consequently, low crude oil prices increase U.S. dependence on imports, in two ways. Obviously, high-cost U.S. production has to be shut down when crude prices are near or below $10. Second, U.S. consumption of oil increases with lower prices. The end result is that crude prices in the $15–$20 range avoid financial loss for American oil producers, slow the decline in U.S. production levels, and encourage U.S. political support for Persian Gulf governments threatened by Iraq or other forces seeking monopoly power of Persian Gulf oil. The result of those discussions was an agreement (in 1986) to set $15–$18 as a world goal.[21] As already noted, that price level has endured. The Persian Gulf War added strength to the existing political relationships.

Consider Japan's position of supporting the military defense of Kuwait by the U.S.-led operation. Japan imports essentially all of its petroleum. Three-fourths of its crude oil has originated in the Persian Gulf.[22] In the short run, it would benefit from a $10 world price. But, if Persian Gulf oil drives out U.S. and North Sea producers, the resulting monopoly-influenced price would probably exceed the current $15–$20 range. With a long-run perspective, Japan can depend upon stable prices with political stability supported by the United States.[23]

The concepts developed in *game theory* can help explain these global interactions. Game theory in economics analyzes the consequences of strategic decisions made by decision-makers. The theory considers both cooperative and self-interest strategies and their interactions. A neighborhood poker game is an example of a 'zero-sum' game: the profit to winners equals the loss to losers.[24]

But world oil, viewed through the perspective of game theory, is a complex 'positive sum' game for producing governments and companies. The potential annual winnings, as we have seen, are measured in tens of billions of dollars in possible economic rent.

Table 9.4 summarizes global petroleum economics and politics in a game theory framework. Both Persian Gulf and OECD (Organization for Economic Cooperation and Development) governments have been accustomed to the $15–$20 stable price range. Either group, acting alone, could for a short period force prices in either direction from this range. Remember the logic of Figures 1.2 and 1.3; the Gulf governments know that either too-low prices or too-high prices can reduce profit and rent.

This game theory outcome in one narrow facet resembles a competitive market: world price is about at the level where it equals the marginal cost of high-cost producers.

At least for the near term into the very early 21st Century, both groups have incentives to keep prices in their current range. This is similar in meaning to the economic concept of 'Nash equilibrium': a status quo where neither side can improve its overall situation by changing its strategy. This $15–$20 level is far below a true monopoly price. It is also far above a truly competitive world price.

In the absence of a widely accepted economic term to reflect the political and economic reality of world oil markets, the phrase 'hybrid competition' is used here. It is intended to represent the interaction of politics, military defense, and economics.

The second security issue has already been noted: the Persian Gulf's holdings of extensive amounts of low-cost reserves is an incentive for continuing instability. The magnitude of potential gain is evident from the analysis. With a competitive world market, the economic rent accruing to the owners of the resource has a present value on the order of $15 to $20 trillion.

If a monopoly were unexpectedly to reassert control, the economic rent estimate would be a higher $20 to $25 trillion. This petroleum rent, or profit above cost, is comparable in magnitude to the planet's total Gross Economic Product.[25]

On a short-run basis, the annual Persian Gulf production was typically in the neighborhood of 5 billion barrels. Recalling the discussion in this chapter of Saudi Arabian crude oil costs, the rent, the difference between price and cost, is typically between $10 and $15 per barrel. We can assert that, with the current market framework, Persian Gulf governments earn at least $50 billion annually in rent above cost.

TABLE 9.4 General Economic Impact of Crude Oil Price Decision in Game Theory Framework

Price Per Barrel	*OECD Countries*	*Persian Gulf Oil Producers*
$10 or less	▲ Higher GNP growth ▲ Shut domestic production ▲ Greatly increased oil consumption ▲ More imports ▲ More pollution, climate change ▲ End Persian Gulf political support	▲ Loss of OECD political support ▲ Lower revenue, greater volume ▲ Higher market share ▲ Faster depletion
$15–$20	▲ Stable GNP growth ▲ Stable near-term oil production ▲ Slow growth in oil consumption ▲ Slow growth in import share ▲ Stable prices ▲ Continue Persian Gulf support	▲ Continued OECD political support ▲ Stable revenue, profit, rent
$30	▲ Decline in GNP ▲ Rapid near-term growth in production ▲ Stable or declining consumption ▲ End Persian Gulf support	▲ Loss of OECD political support ▲ Less market share ▲ Less production, more profit, rent ▲ Greater payoff to successful Iraq-type action

The tremendous magnitude of these amounts continues to offer incentives for groups outside the current framework to gain some part of this value through arms and political coercion. Consequently, continuing political instability is a possible consequence of the high levels of economic rent.

This leads to the third security issue: what is the military cost to the OECD countries of protecting the current market framework and continued access to the extensive Persian Gulf reserves? Economists generally do not consider this point to be relevant for calculations of external cost. Table 1.2 in Chapter 1 noted the exception, Darwin Hall.

Hall's statistical analysis finds a relationship between oil imports and U.S. defense spending. Translated into simple terms, each barrel of imported oil adds $10 to defense expenditures. This outweighs a trend variable which would be reducing military spending by $17 billion annually, in the hypothetical absence of oil imports. Hall also concludes that the U.S. Strategic Petroleum Reserve adds another $2 to federal expenditures for each barrel of imported oil.[26]

During the Cold War era of competition between the Soviet Union and U.S. allies, there was considerable concern about Soviet influence acquiring a voice in Persian Gulf decision-making. In 1920 and again in the 1940s during World War II, the Soviet Union actively supported short-lived soviet republics in Iran. In 1950, the U.S. Central Intelligence Agency provided short-term leadership to the effort to change Iran's government.[27] The collapse of the Soviet Union ended this competition in the early 1990s.

It must be noted that Hall's approach is not widely accepted among environmental economists. For example, none of the studies of external social cost of energy in Chapters 1 and 3 consider oil and military security, and none of the 30 general texts in environmental economics cited in Chapters 1–5 consider the subject. Outside the field of environmental economics, energy economists are somewhat more interested. But even among analysts concerned with petroleum and military/political security, there is reluctance to take Hall's literal dollars-and-cents approach.[28]

Can the Price of Oil Be Predicted?

Economic theory in Chapter 6 suggested very neat possibilities for projecting future prices for finite resources. In contrast, the preceding discussion in this chapter introduced the complex world of geopolitics, which created a decade-long era in which crude oil prices were generally in the $15 to $20 per barrel range.

'Oil shocks' that create rapid price increases are dramatic, as occurred briefly in the 1970s, 1980s, and 1990s. However, unexpected events can also reduce petroleum prices. One such surprise took place in 1998. Even though world oil consumption continued to increase, oil prices dropped sharply. Figure 9.6 helps explain this.

First, note that actual oil consumption increases from the first period to the second period: Q_{2A} is greater than Q_{1A}. (Q_{1A} is actual quantity in the first period, and Q_{2A} is actual quantity consumed in the second period.)

But, actual prices have fallen sharply, and P_{2A} is much lower than P_{1A} in spite of the increase in world oil consumption. How did this happen? It was a result of surprising shifts in both demand and supply curves. The world oil industry had expected the global demand curve to continue to shift upward, to move from D_{1A} (actual first period demand curve) to D_{2E} (expected second period demand curve). Oil production capacity was adequate, and the graph shows the same supply curve for the first period (SC_{1A}), and the expected supply curve for the second period (SC_{2E}). If everything had gone as expected, the expected second period price (P_{2E}) would have been about the same, and the expected second period market equilibrium for quantity (Q_{2E}) would have increased. Both are shown.

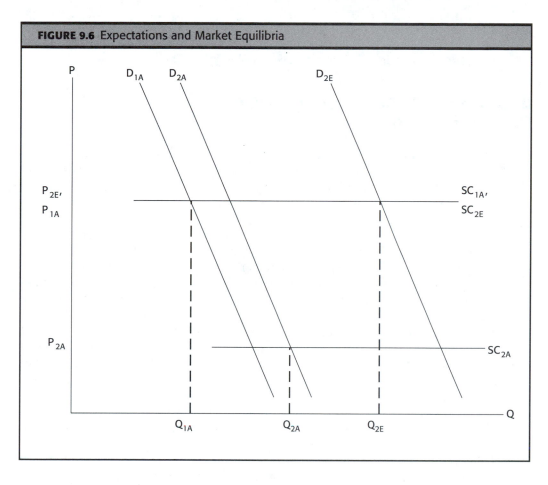

FIGURE 9.6 Expectations and Market Equilibria

However, there were two major surprises. First, the economic downturn in Asia in 1998 made the actual global demand curve D_{2A} much less than the expected D_{2E}. Second, Iraq nearly doubled its sales in 1998, so more oil was available. The actual global supply curve SC_{2A} was greater than the expected SC_{2E}.

The results? Q_{2A} increased from the previous year's actual Q_{1A}, and actual price dropped sharply from P_{1A} to P_{2A}.[29]

Suppose the low crude oil prices of 1998 were to have continued. We know from the preceding analysis that there would be significant reductions in high-cost U.S. oil production. There would be a restructuring of the U.S. oil industry as shut-down production required new corporate networks organized around low-cost Persian Gulf oil.

Alternatively, the strategic game theory equilibrium might return crude prices to the $15 to $20 range.

It should not be supposed that there is sufficient information here to make a precise forecast of the price of oil at some future date. We do know, however, that in this and earlier chapters, we have identified the factors which influence those future prices.

Personally, I expect continued low crude oil and gasoline prices (in real dollars) in the early beginning of the 21st Century. Very much further into the future, I think the children of today's students will see the emergence of continuously growing real prices for petroleum products and ultimately the emergence of new energy sources to substitute for today's petroleum technologies.[30]

In Conclusion: A Summary and a Very Brief Opinion-Editorial

The long period of low gasoline and crude oil prices in association with growing world and U.S. consumption seem persuasive evidence for the absence of any economic problems associated with the concepts of scarcity or depletion. Reviewing the estimates of geologists on availability of coal suggests that this resource can be used at low production costs for many centuries.

However, an examination of the geographic and economic bases of geological petroleum estimates raises new problems for economics. Economic theory can forecast a long period of growth in world oil consumption at stable prices. But the theory also defines—in the absence of economic substitutes—an ultimate decline in petroleum use associated with a future period of rising prices. (This is obviously a simple summary, and the material in this chapter as well as Chapter 6 should be recalled as relevant.)

Current costs of production and transportation of Persian Gulf oil to Europe, Japan, and the United States is low, on the order of $2.50 per barrel. Comparable figures for North Sea and Alaskan crude oil are roughly $15 per barrel. The geographic distribution of conventional crude oil is such that current world production comes disproportionally from high-cost, lower reserve regions.

Economic theory related to competition and monopoly helps explain some dimensions of the policies of OECD and OPEC countries, but game theory helps incorporate the political factors which support a stable status quo for the near term. 'Competitive hybrid' is one possible description of current markets: the term reflects the interactions of economics, politics, and military considerations.

Given the magnitude of economic rent and geological resources in the Persian Gulf region, the incentives for the use of military force to gain or defend access will continue. As the region continues to increase its proportional share of remaining petroleum resources, the potential for armed conflict will grow.

Both conservative and liberal economists have contributed valuable analyses and perspectives. George Bush articulated a view that international military force is appropriate to defend this world resource against monopolistic control by aggressive invaders. However, the combination of the growing economic importance of Persian Gulf oil, and the role of petroleum as a source of greenhouse gases, will define a new challenge. At some future period in the 21st Century, international taxation as well as military protection may be considered for application to Persian Gulf oil.

Questions for Discussion and Analysis

1. Describe at least three factors that could lead to a sudden drop in crude oil prices. Use supply and demand curves to illustrate your discussion.

2. Similarly, describe at least three factors that could increase crude oil prices in the short run. Again, use supply and demand curves to illustrate your discussion.

3. In the mid-1980s, then Vice President George H. Bush went to the Persian Gulf to support higher crude oil prices. In the early 1990s, President Bush strongly supported UN military action to terminate Iraq's occupation of Kuwait and Iraq's potential to raise Persian Gulf oil prices. How can you reconcile this apparent contradiction?

4. First, assume these costs for gasoline:

Price to customers:	$1.20/gallon
Taxes:	$0.43/gallon
Refining, marketing:	$0.41/gallon
Tanker shipment:	$2.10/barrel

Second, if Persian Gulf production cost is $2.50 per barrel, what is the 'economic rent' per barrel?

Third, if Alaskan production cost is $15 per barrel, what is the 'economic rent' for these producers?

5. Do you think there is a relationship between current oil price and long-term estimates of the amount of remaining conventional crude oil? Explain your reasoning; perhaps use a graph.

Notes to Chapter 9

1. Chapman, 1983, pages 103–105, especially Figures 6.1 and 6.2.
2. Edward Erickson articulates the Adelman view that extensive low-cost supplies will restrain world oil prices in his "What Does It All Mean?" pages 349–356 in *The Changing World Petroleum Market*, Special Issue, Helmut J. Frank, editor, *Energy Journal*, 1994. Adelman articulates his own perspective in "The World Oil Market: Past and Future" (same issue); "Modelling World Oil Supply," *Energy Journal*, David Wood Memorial Issue, 14(1):1–32, 1993; and "No OPEC," Winter 1997 *IAEE Newsletter*, pages 14, 15. Cutler Cleveland expects depletion to be a problem in his "An Exploration of Alternative Measures of Natural Resource Scarcity: The Case of Petroleum Resources in the U.S.," April 1993 *Ecological Economics* 7(2):123–157.
3. Fossil energy is a term used to describe fuel that originated with the geological deposit of plant and other organic material millions of years ago. In addition to coal, oil, and natural gas, the term also applies to oil from shale rock, and to natural gas liquids, and some other similar energy forms. Methane from sewage or urban landfills is technically not a fossil fuel, but is treated as if it were because of its chemical identity with natural gas.
4. Sources for Table 9.1 are USEIA *International Energy Annual 1993*, May 1995 and *Monthly Energy Review*, November 1995; C. D. Masters, E. D. Attanasi, and D. H. Root, "World Petroleum Assessment and Analysis," in *Proceedings of the 14th World Petroleum Congress*, Wiley 1994. Also, Eric T. Sundquist, "Geological Perspectives on Carbon Dioxide and the Carbon Cycle," in *The Carbon Cycle and Atmospheric CO_2: Natural Variations Archean to Present*, E. T. Sundquist and W. S. Broecker, eds., American Geophysical Union Monograph 32, Washington, DC, 1985.

5. Discussion of reserve definitions is in Masters, *op. cit.*

6. Table 9.3 sources are Masters 1994 *op. cit.,* and *Oil and Gas Journal*, December 1995. The Masters estimates, given as of January 1, 1993, have been adjusted for production from that date to 1996. Also see Chapman 1983 *op. cit.,* Chapters 3–10, and Duane Chapman, "World Oil: Hotelling Depletion or Accelerating Use?" *Nonrenewable Resources*, Journal of the International Association for Mathematical Geology (2)4:331–339, Winter 1993, and, with N. Khanna, "World Oil: The Growing Case for International Policy," January 2000 *Contemporary Economic Policy*, in press.

7. See Masters 1994 *op. cit.,* and C. D. Masters, D. H. Root, and W. D. Dietzman, U.S. Geological Survey, "Distribution and Quantitative Assessment of World Crude-Oil Reserves and Resources," Open-File Report 83-728, 1983.

8. Equations (4-1a) and (4-1b) in Chapter 4.

9. In this chapter the term 'development cost' is used to include both exploration and development. Industry professionals separate them, and disaggregate each into appropriate subcategories. Adelman 1993, page 15, uses $502 in 1990 as an estimate of daily capacity development cost, excluding exploration cost recovery. I adjusted this with the GDP inflation index, added 50 percent to represent exploration, divided by 365.25 to have a per-barrel figure, and rounded to the $2.50 used in the text. The methodology used in calculating the 'oil discount rate' and its risk and depletion factors is explained in detail in M. Adelman, "Crude Oil Production Costs," Chapter 3 in his *The World Petroleum Market* (Baltimore: Johns Hopkins, 1973). Also see Adelman 1993, *op. cit.*

10. As either T, r, or both become very large, the levelized cost factor approaches the value for the discount rate. This is the same principle used in Chapter 4 for Equation (4-2).

11. For lifting cost, Adelman's figure (1993, page 14) was adjusted to 1995 prices. The shipping cost is computed as the average U.S. difference between FOB and landed Saudi crude for 1992–1995, rounded to $1.50. From *Monthly Energy Review*, various issues.

12. Again as illustration, use Adelman's U.K. value (1993 *op. cit.*) of $14,400 per daily capacity. Now, assume this includes exploration cost. For the 'oil discount factor,' use 10 percent interest, 10 percent risk, and 5 percent decline. Assume $5 per barrel for both operations and delivery to a European port refinery. The result is $15 per barrel production cost for crude oil for the U.K. Incidentally, the British Petroleum Company owns 53 percent of the Alaskan Prudhoe Bay field. It is also active in the North Sea, and in shipping Persian Gulf oil to Europe. In this global respect it is similar to the other major global oil companies, Exxon and Shell (Chapman 1983, Chapters 5 and 6).

13. *Monthly Energy Review*, December 1998.

14. Remember that a curve can be a line, and a 'demand curve' is frequently a line.

15. QC_t, the trajectory of supply-demand equilibria in the absence of a resource constraint, is $(\beta_2 e^{\theta t} - C_0 e^{\theta t})/\beta_1$. These terms represent demand and cost function parameters. Marginal cost starts at initial C_0 and grows at θ. The demand function is $P_t = \beta_2 e^{\theta t} - \beta_1 Q_t$. The θ term is the sum of income demand elasticity and growth, and population demand elasticity and growth (i.e., $\theta = \theta_1 \nu + \theta_2 \epsilon$). The 'depletion factor' DF in the text is $(S - \beta_4)/m(r)$. In this latter expression, S is the 1.9 trillion barrels of assumed remaining reserves. β_4 is the integral (or sum) of QC_t; it is the amount of oil that would be consumed by time T if there were no limitation. $m(r)$ is an accumulation factor: $m(r) = (e^{rT} - 1)/r$.

    This gives the exact solution to the problem in the text of defining a competitive solution, and also provides for optimal T. See, for detailed mathematical discussion, D. Chapman, "World Oil: Hotelling Depletion or Accelerating Use?" *Nonrenewable Resources*, Journal of the International Association for Mathematical Geology, Winter 1993(2)4:331–339, and Chapman and Khanna, *op. cit.,* Note 6.

16. In the 1970s, this subject of the economically optimal approach to depletion was extensively discussed by economists. Two well-known papers were J. E. Stiglitz, "Monopoly and the Rate of Extraction of Exhaustible Resources," September 1976 *American Economic Review* 66:655–661; and R. S. Pindyck, "Gains to Producers from the Cartelization of Exhaustible Resources," May 1978 *Review of Economics and Statistics* 60:238–251. A pair of well-known texts that introduce this theory are Tietenberg *op. cit.* Chapters 6 and 7, and A. C. Fisher, *Resource and Environmental Economics* (New York: Cambridge University Press, 1981).

    The material here in the text is somewhat different; it builds on the theory to apply it to geological data. The economic concepts developed in this discussion are generally applicable to finite geological resources.

17. *New York Times*, August 16, 1990, page A14. Also quoted in Daniel Yergin, *The Prize* (New York: Simon and Schuster, 1991), page 773.

18. Adelman 1993 page 25, and Adelman, "The Competitive Floor to World Oil Prices," October 1986 *Energy Journal* 7:9–31. Sheikh Zaki Yamani suggested $5 per barrel might be appropriate so OPEC producers could increase market share by closing down high-cost European and North American producers. Yamani is a former petroleum minister in Saudi Arabia. *Oil & Gas Journal*, December 28, 1998, page 5.

19. Yergin, pages 755–761. Yergin's commentary notes one OPEC oil minister discussing $5 as a possible market price (page 759).

20. There is some disagreement on the point as to whether import dependency should be measured by imports alone, or net imports defined as imports less exports. On the net import basis, the U.S. percentage is about 50 percent of the 6–7 billion barrels of annual consumption. Both U.S. annual consumption and the net import percentage are slowly increasing. The Persian Gulf has supplied about 20 percent of imports over a quarter of a century.

21. Yergin, pages 755–761.

22. US-EIA, *International Energy Annual 1992*, page 52.

23. Yergin, pages 759–760.

24. See the introduction to "Game Theory" in Byrns and Stone, *op. cit.,* pages 593–596, and "The Nash Equilibrium Concept," in Robert H. Frank, *Microeconomics and Behavior*, 1994, New York: McGraw-Hill, page 532. The concept is attributed to John Nash, mathematician. In economic thought, the world petroleum market in some ways resembles oligopolistic competition. But that theory does not include a case where OECD buyers encourage prices significantly above OPEC average cost!

25. In 1990, the present value of competitive rent was $15.7 trillion and of monopoly rent was $21.5 trillion. These values are adjusted by the 13 percent increase in the GDP deflator. Chapman 1993, page 338, and Chapman and Khanna 2000, *op. cit.* World Gross Economic Product was $28 trillion in 1995 (*World Development Report* 1997).

26. The Strategic Petroleum Reserve is maintained at nearly 600 million barrels. Hall's estimates were in 1985 dollars; the text values are in 1995 dollars. From Darwin C. Hall, "Oil and National Security," November 1992 *Energy Policy*, pages 1089–1096.

27. Kermit Roosevelt coordinated this effort. His *Countercoup: The Struggle for Control of Iran*, New York: McGraw-Hill, 1979 is very informative. He later became a Gulf Oil Corporation vice president and director of the company's Washington office. A brief history of the Cold War in oil is in Chapman 1983, pages 83–86.

28. Some other sources on the economics of petroleum and national security are Adelman 1993, pages 27–28; Douglas R. Bohi and William B. Quandt, *Energy Security in the 1980s: Economic and Political Perspectives*, 1984, The Brookings Institution; Harry G. Broadman and William W. Hogan, "Is an Oil Tariff Justified? An American Debate—The Numbers

Say Yes," *Energy Journal*, July 1988, 9(3):7–30; John H. Lichtenblau, "Oil Imports and National Security: Is There Still a Connection?" in *The Changing World Petroleum Market, Energy Journal*, Special Issue, 1994, H. J. Frank, ed., pages 329–346; Amory Lovins and Joseph Romm, "Fueling a Competitive Economy," *Foreign Affairs*, Winter 1992/93; Earl C. Ravenal, *Defining Defense: The 1985 Military Budget*, Cato Institute, 1984, Washington, DC, and "Defending Persian Gulf Oil," *Intervention*, 1984. Shibley Telhami and Michael O'Hanlon attribute $50 billion annually to U.S. military spending related to the Persian Gulf; see *New York Times*, December 30, 1995, and September 18, 1996.

29. Of course, Figure 9.6 is not drawn to scale; it shows the economic logic of shifting demand and supply curves causing price reductions while consumption increases.

30. In addition to the alternative renewable transportation fuels discussed in Chapter 8, new technologies may bring such sources as tar sands, oil shale, and coal liquefaction into commercial gasoline production. Much higher prices would bring these sources into production. Backstop technologies are part of the depletion theory used in this chapter; see D. Chapman *Nonrenewable Resources*, Note 15.

CHAPTER 10

THE LIMITS TO GROWTH QUESTION: INDUSTRIAL RESOURCES, DEPLETION, RECYCLING, AND POPULATION

The economic markets and politics for world oil resources are likely to continue to be characterized by low and generally stable prices for the near future. According to the last chapter, conventional crude oil markets may not be affected by scarcity and long-term cartel pricing until well into the 21st Century.

In the 1970s, as we noted, the brief periods of very high OPEC crude oil pricing and production restraints were misinterpreted as reflecting impending exhaustion, a limitation restricting economic growth. As competitive forces created the new equilibrium levels of prices and consumption in the 1990s, concern about possible near-term exhaustion of oil disappeared.[1]

The concern about petroleum depletion was part of a general interest in the question of resource depletion and its potential impact on reducing economic growth and perhaps forcing reductions in U.S. and world living standards. Economists have studied this scarcity question carefully, with results that can seem surprising.

Recycling economics, of course, influences the need for the products of mines and forests. Many raw materials already depend upon recycling as a source, and this can continue to increase.

Pollution prevention and source reduction also influence resource use and depletion. As pollution prevention is increased, resources can be used more efficiently, requiring less virgin material to be extracted. Less material becomes waste, and fewer resources are required for any production level.

Population growth affects resource availability in an obvious way: a global population of 20 billion people would on the whole use twice the resources of 10 billion people with the same incomes. Perhaps this should be restated: if population doubles, demand curves would rise, and the actual levels of resource use would be determined by prices, incomes, technology, and environmental policy.

Each of these issues (depletion, recycling, pollution prevention, population growth) affects the question of the existence or absence of limits on economic growth. This chapter addresses those subjects, and begins by examining the debate which originated with the 'Club of Rome' and the Meadows group at MIT.[2]

The "Limits to Growth" Theory

The Club of Rome drew its name from the city where they met. Originally an international group of 30 business leaders, civil servants, and academics, they defined an ambitious goal, to (in their words) establish their "Project on the Predicament of Mankind." Their ambitious goal was to use the then-new technique of computer modelling to investigate the sustainability of agricultural, industrial, environmental, and other resources.

FIGURE 10.1 The Standard Limits to Growth Model Run: Resource Depletion and Economic Collapse[3]

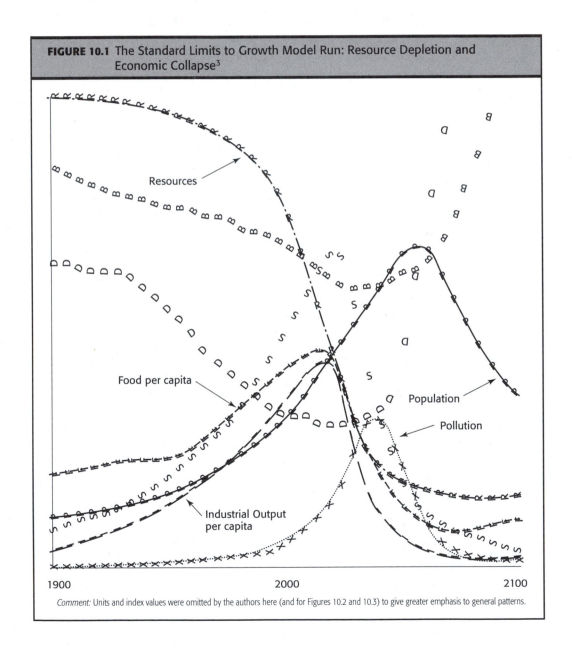

Comment: Units and index values were omitted by the authors here (and for Figures 10.2 and 10.3) to give greater emphasis to general patterns.

The base case in the Limits to Growth model is shown in Figure 10.1. Usually a variable in the model is a conceptual or hypothetical index. For example, consider the variable "resources" that originates in the upper left of the figure as "R," and is designated by an arrow. The Meadows group simply assumed 900 billion units remaining in stock for every kind of finite resource: coal, oil, iron, aluminum, and so on. The next step was to assume that these hypothetical or imaginary units were being used at a rate of one each per person per year in 1970. Finally, each variable is linked to other variables through simple equations similar in form to those used throughout this text. Thus, the resources index R is reduced by growth in another index, the material living standard index. The rest of the Limits to Growth model is similar in nature.

Now return to the base case in the figure. The results show global natural resources for industry (the curve R) approaching depletion in the first half of the 21st Century. Industrial output per capita (marked with an arrow) peaks at 2015 and then declines sharply. Agriculture is immediately affected because industry can no longer provide agriculture's need for energy, fertilizer, and other requirements. As a result, food per capita (F) falls.

With material living standards and food supplies both collapsing, health services (partly represented by S in the figure) also collapse. These factors, in turn, cause a rapid acceleration in death rates (D). As death rates rise above birth rates (B), world population (the heavy line marked "population") begins to decline in 2056.

In summary, according to the models and the authors' interpretation of their work, the basic case for the world has industrial resource exhaustion creating cascading negative effects on industrial and agricultural production and on services such as health care. Death rates rise and the population falls. So, in these circumstances, resource depletion causes economic and social collapse.

When this work was introduced into academic and public debate in the 1970s, it was in the period of OPEC's reductions in oil output and very high petroleum prices. This congruence between the Limits to Growth work and the problems in oil markets enhanced the credibility of the analysis.

However, as we shall see below, it has become clear that most basic energy and metal resources are unlikely to be depleted in the foreseeable future. This 1972 analysis is not viewed as credible now.

Unfortunately, the great debate about resource depletion deflected attention from the second major component of the Meadows group's work. Consider Figure 10.2: in this case the resource depletion curve (again starting upper left) shows only a small decline over the two-century interval. Because industrial resource use is now unlimited, pollution (the heavy dotted line starting lower left, which connects the Xs) grows exponentially. This pollution curve, in turn, damages crop yields and increases disease and death rates.[4]

In this second case, population and living standards collapse from unrestrained pollution and its impact. In summary, the two basic cases were (1) economic and population collapse caused by resource depletion and (2) economic and population collapse caused by pollution with unlimited resources.

History has treated the resource depletion case poorly, and it is no longer viewed seriously. Joel E. Cohen states the current consensus with acerbity: "[This work] reflected no more than [their] intuitive view of how the world works. It should be shelved with . . . *Brave New World,* even though Forrester (and Meadows) used the

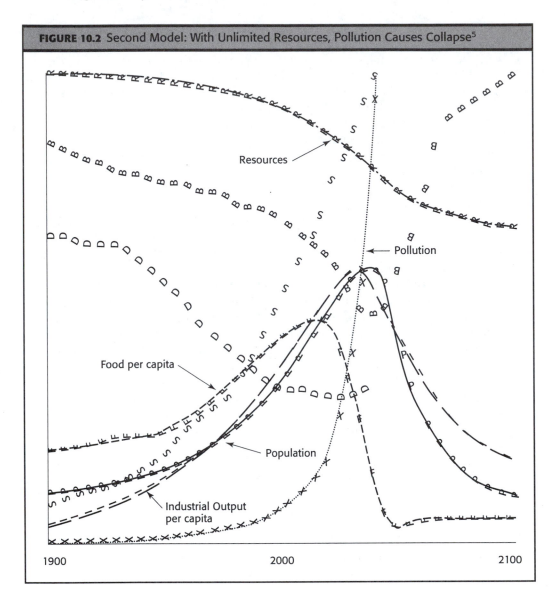

FIGURE 10.2 Second Model: With Unlimited Resources, Pollution Causes Collapse[5]

literary device of the computer to work out details of the plot."[6] In other words, although sharply put, Cohen says the Limits to Growth work is fiction.

Unfortunately, the second case (unlimited resource use and accelerating pollution) disappeared from the debate about their work. In 1992, the Meadows group used their new book *Beyond the Limits* to update the analysis.[7] The emphasis is upon pollution, climate change, and policies that they believe promote sustainability. They advocate an average family size of two children, stabilizing living standards one-third above the 1990 global average, and making significant investments in pollution control and the protection of agricultural land. The optimistic result is shown

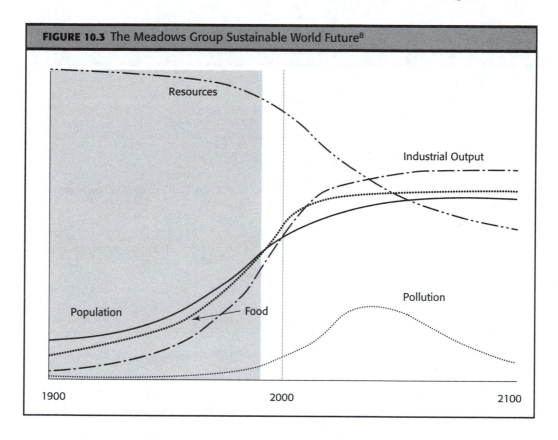

FIGURE 10.3 The Meadows Group Sustainable World Future[8]

in Figure 10.3. With this introduction to the Limits to Growth work, it is clear why both scientists and economists have given considerable attention to empirical data relevant to the issue of resource availability. This, in turn, leads to the question of industrial resource availability for metals and energy.

Scarcity or Abundance: Metals and Energy Fuels

The economist's perspective on resource depletion has been strongly influenced by the theory that was introduced in Chapter 6 and in Chapter 9 on world oil.[9] A simplified view of this economic theory predicts that, as use of a resource leads to approaching exhaustion, its price will rise rapidly. Figure 10.4 shows this general idea; it represents the logic in the 1970s version of the Limits to Growth model.

The problem with this simple theory is that it assumes that technology is stagnant, and recycling unimportant. Consider this relationship in Equation (10-1):

| This Year's Marginal Cost | = Last Year's Cost | + Higher Cost from Scarcer Resource | − Lower Cost from Improved Efficiency | − Lower Cost of Increased Recycling | (10-1) |

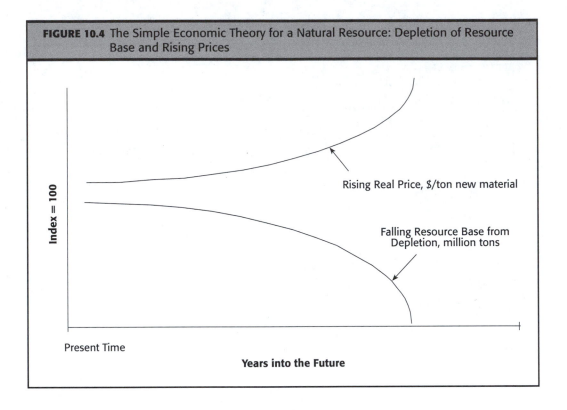

FIGURE 10.4 The Simple Economic Theory for a Natural Resource: Depletion of Resource Base and Rising Prices

Higher costs from increased scarcity may or may not be matched or exceeded by improvements in technology and production which work to lower costs. Since the global markets for the basic industrial resources are generally competitive, we can expect market prices to approximate actual marginal costs. So, if marginal costs are moving upward over time, we expect prices for these materials to move in the same direction. But, in contrast to the simple theory in Figure 10.4, we can see that this year's cost and price can be part of a downward trend. (This is the same point introduced mathematically by Figure 6.6 and its discussion.) The historical evidence is mixed. Figure 10.5 shows that mineral resource prices were declining in the last half of the 20th Century.[10]

Although the economic perspective gives mixed results on the scarcity issue, the geological picture is more straightforward. Table 10.1 shows the most important industrial metals: aluminum, copper, and iron/steel. The first and second rows define estimates of remaining world ore resources and current consumption. (The definitions are the same as those in Chapter 9 for energy resources.)

If consumption stays constant, then there is no need for concern in the near future. As with coal (see Table 9.1), there would be adequate resources well into the third millennium.

However, the uncertainty about future resource availability arises because of uncertainty about both demand and supply factors. On the demand side, global eco-

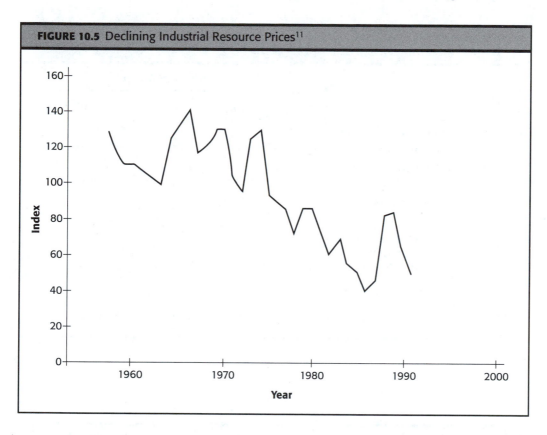

FIGURE 10.5 Declining Industrial Resource Prices[11]

nomic and population growth could increase metal consumption. In the fourth row, consumption grows at 2.7 percent each year, the same rate as a widely cited projection of world economic growth.[12] In this case—with no technological gains—exhaustion of all three industrial metals would occur in roughly a century.

On the supply side, there is uncertainty about the direction of the type of factors in Equation (10-1). Metals recycling, technological improvement in mining efficiency and resource use, and substitution[13] of other cost-effective materials will grow as alternatives to current mining of metals.

In the final case, the "Years Remaining" have become infinite. If we assume that recycling, mining efficiency, pollution prevention, and substitution of new materials reduce resource use, and that these gains grow on average at 1 percent annually, then the resources of remaining ore metal may never need to be exhausted.

Consider Figure 10.6: it summarizes in a simple form the processes in steel, copper, aluminum, and other metals, and focuses on iron and steel. If necessary, nearly all iron and steel could be recycled, extending the life of the global iron ore resource even further than already described.

In summary, there seems to be no empirical basis for resource limitations in metals or total energy in the near future. While this seems clear today, it was the subject of an interesting disagreement between economist Julian Simon and ecologist Paul

TABLE 10.1 Years Remaining with Current Geological Estimates, Global Basis (rounded to nearest 25 years)[14]

	Industrial Metal		
	Aluminum	*Copper*	*Iron/Steel*
Estimated remaining resources, metric tons	65 billion	1.6 billion	800 billion
Current consumption level, metric tons	110 million	10 million	1 billion
If consumption stays constant	600 years	160 years	800 years
If growth in consumption equals growth in world economy, no improvements	105 years	62 years	115 years
If technology gains in mining, recycling, and substitutes are significant	infinite	infinite	infinite

FIGURE 10.6 The Basic Iron and Steel Process

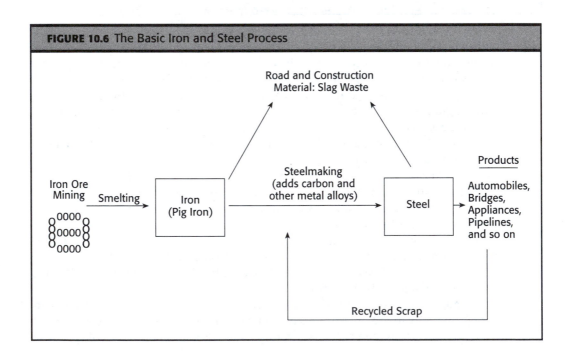

Ehrlich. Ehrlich believed that resources were becoming scarce, and Simon thought the opposite. They each thought, according to economic theory, that prices would reflect scarcity or abundance.

Consequently, in 1980, they wagered that the real prices of five metals would be higher in 1990 (Ehrlich), or lower in 1990 (Simon). The results: all the prices declined, an average of 38 percent.[15]

Recycling and Waste Disposal Economics

Recycling has grown to be a significant source of material for metal production in the United States. As Figure 10.7 illustrates, scrap contributes about as much as primary smelting from ores.

The basic economics of recycling can be complex. With scrap metals, recycling and ore sources are both well integrated without significant government intervention. Recycling processors will often collect large items such as autos and appliances, and process the material for sale to a smelter. In this case, Figures 10.8A and 10.8B outline the basic markets.

The supply of recycled metal (S_R) is initially less costly than metal produced from ore (S_O) in panel A. The supply curve for metal from ore, in contrast, is more stable in cost, starting at a higher level but increasing more slowly.

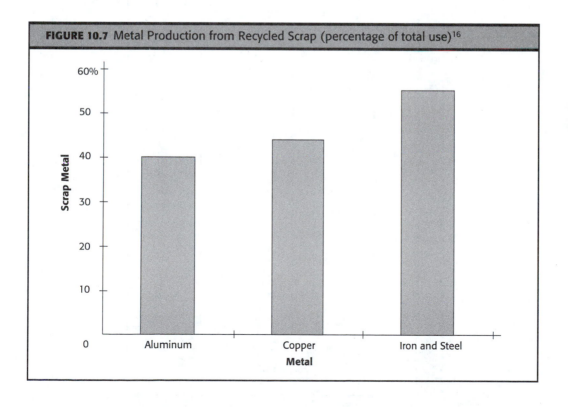

FIGURE 10.7 Metal Production from Recycled Scrap (percentage of total use)[16]

FIGURE 10.8 Market Economics: Metal from Recycling and Ore Smelting

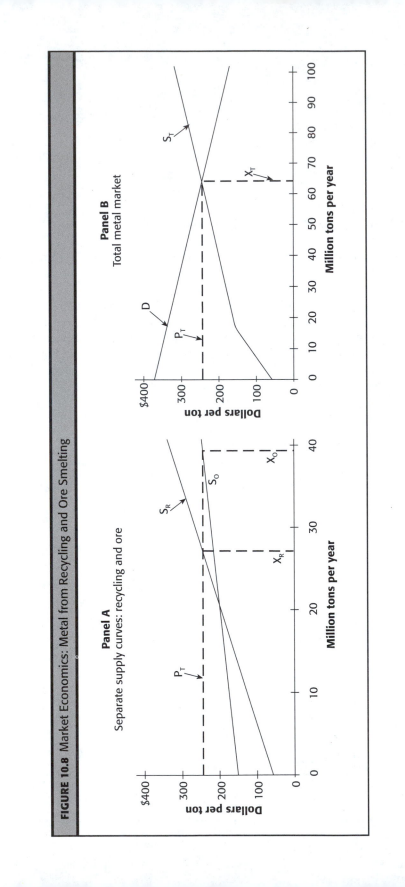

Panel A
Separate supply curves: recycling and ore

Panel B
Total metal market

TABLE 10.2 Municipal Recycling and Waste Disposal per Capita United States, 1990[17]

Item	Waste, Pounds per Person	Recycle Proportion	Disposal Proportion
Paper	587	28%	72%
Glass bottles	95	22%	78%
Aluminum cans	13	63%	37%
Steel cans	22	23%	77%
Steel applications	75	13%	87%
Plastic milk jugs	3	24%	76%
Plastic soda bottles	3	41%	59%
Food waste	106	0%	100%
Yard waste	280	12%	88%
Other	382	5%	95%
Total/average	1,566	19%	81%

In the next panel, B, the total supply curve for the metal S_T adds together the supply curves for recycled and smelted metal. In this simplified case, the demand curve (D) does not differentiate between recycled metal and metal refined in a smelter from ore. The market price P_T defines total metal use X_T, and the amounts of recycled metal (X_R) and metal from ore (X_O).

The economics of managing household and small business waste is more complicated; choices must be made between recycling materials collected in small amounts or disposing of the material. The average amounts per capita of this material are shown in Table 10.2. While some items have passed the 33 percent level in the proportion recycled, most material remains waste for disposal in landfills or incinerators.

It is very clear that recycling can be increased. But it is not clear which policies and options are efficient, either in a market or social context. The economic problems arise because of the externality values, public policy choices, and consumer options outlined in Table 10.3.

Negative externality values from recycling are possible. For example, battery recycling in developing countries may cause serious health and ecosystem damage from lead exposure.[18]

The positive externality values are straightforward and influence the business and household choice of options. Consider the logic of Figure 10.9. Begin with the upper curve representing the original purchase of consumer materials that become waste or recyclables. As disposal costs decline, the household feels free to purchase packaged goods with less regard for disposal cost. At waste disposal cost C, the purchase of disposable material is Q_T.

The second curve represents a household with no external values associated with its disposal or recycling decision.[19] This is in a community with optional recycling. So this family, for example, may choose to dispose of dirty cans rather than cleaning them for recycling. The charge to the household for municipal solid waste disposal is C, which defines a quantity Q_{DN} of disposed waste in this second case. (Q_{DN} is the quantity disposed as waste by the household with no positive external values for recycling.) The general recycling quantity and ratio is

$$Q_{RN} = Q_T - Q_{DN} \text{, the amount recycled}$$

$$r = Q_{RN}/Q_{DN} \text{, the ratio of recycled material to total material}$$

(10-2)

Note in the figure that if recycling is optional and there is no unit charge, then recycling becomes zero for this household. (In other words, if C = 0, then $Q_{DN} = Q_T$, and $Q_{RN} = 0$). As the unit charge for disposal increases, this household moves up the middle curve and starts reducing its total materials purchased, and it makes a greater reduction in its waste disposal quantity. So, as the garbage price rises, the proportion recycled grows. Of course, we are assuming no 'bandit dumping.' (This is illegal roadside or vacant lot waste disposal.)

The third and lowest curve is very different. It represents a household with significant positive externality value for recycling. This might be a different household, or the same household with changed values from one year to another. Note that even if C is at zero, this 'green' household would still have a very small waste disposal quantity Q_{DS}, and would recycle most of its material.

The focus here has been on the household, but the logic would be the same for the owners or employees of a small business.

TABLE 10.3 Municipal and Household Waste: Externality Values, Policy Choices, Consumer Options

A. *Externality Values*
1. Recycling encourages positive feeling by the consumer for protecting the environment
2. Recycling reduces the external social cost of landfills and incinerators
3. Recycling often reduces energy requirements, thereby reducing pollution and greenhouse gasses
4. Negative environmental externality can arise from pollution-intensive recycling, and from household and bulk recyclables transport

B. *Policy Choices*
1. Advance disposal fee paid at purchase
2. Refundable deposit
3. Recycle subsidy
4. Annual property tax or fee
5. Tipping fee for waste haulers at landfill, recycling center, or incinerator
6. Charge household and business a unit price, $/load or $/pound

C. *Consumer Options*
1. Minimum cost in response to policies
2. Voluntary recycling
3. Home incineration or dumping
4. Bandit dumping in parks, roadways, and woods

FIGURE 10.9 Complex Economic Framework of Household Recycling

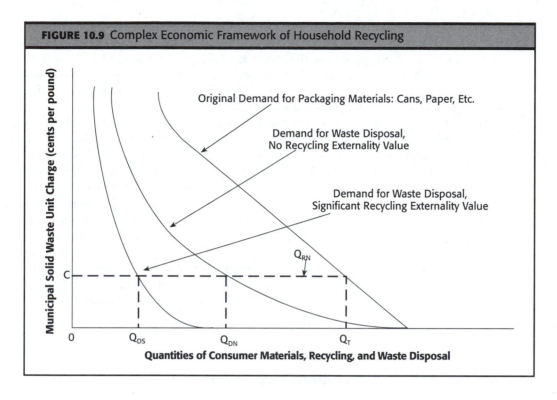

In order to manage their waste disposal problems, the municipalities (city, village, or county)[20] must take into account the household economics in Figure 10.9, as well as incorporate the policy choice factors from Table 10.3. For example, if the waste disposal fee is too high, bandit dumping may become a severe problem. If the fee is too low, then increased material use is encouraged, as well as reduced recycling ratios.

Another complication arises from recyclables which may require a subsidy to be paid to the collector by a local government. Suppose that landfill costs are high, but recycling markets are depressed. In these circumstances, efficiency might support a subsidy to the recyclables collectors if total costs to the local community were reduced.[21]

Economists have begun to examine these issues empirically. Given the great variability in the externality value and market costs relevant to both household and municipal decision-making, there is no one policy which will be preferred in all locations. The Palmer group[22] concluded that deposit/refund programs are the most efficient. However, they emphasize significant differences in program administrative costs. The Massachusetts program worked through retail stores, and required the retailers to sort returns by brands for bottlers to collect. The Massachusetts retailers paid the refund to the consumer. In contrast, the California system used recycling centers, and did no brand sorting or return to bottlers. Since almost all recycled bottles and cans are melted for remanufacturing, the California program administration cost only 1¢ for five containers, while the Massachusetts administrative costs were a much higher 11.5¢ for five containers. With high administrative costs for brand deposit/refund programs, recycling center programs may be the best choice for municipalities.

In evaluating waste disposal fees, several studies concluded that unit prices on the order of 5¢ per pound would be efficient.[23] This would be equivalent to a charge of 80¢ for the curbside pickup of the contents of a typical household garbage can. Fees at this level might be expected to reduce overall waste quantities by 15–20 percent. However, in a locality where bandit dumping is a problem, municipalities may want to consider paying residents for their trash!

But, returning our attention to the question of material limitations on global economic growth, it is clear that any major increases in costs and prices of both metal production from ore and paper from wood can be expected to work through the household and municipal waste and recycling markets. The significant increases in recycling amounts and proportions would feed back to our earlier discussion (Table 10.1), and extend the global periods of use of these basic industrial resources. Our detailed introduction to the complex economics of recycling and waste disposal supports the conclusion that recycling can further extend industrial resource use far into the future.

This review of recycling economics has focused on policies and economic studies in high income countries. In developing countries, the perspective can be very different. Old plastic bottles and cans may be modified for other uses, and even broken umbrellas are repaired.[24]

Population, Economics, and Environment

Paul and Anne Ehrlich with John Holdren,[25] a physicist and two ecologists working together, popularized a simple relationship that links pollution, population, and income:

$$\text{Pollution Total} = \text{Population} * \text{Consumption per Capita} * \text{Pollution per Unit of Consumption} \qquad (10\text{-}3)$$

For example, they attributed nearly a century's twelve-fold increase in U.S. energy use to the interaction of a three-fold growth in energy consumption per capita and a four-fold increase in population.

As it stands here, the logic is non-economic and perhaps anti-economic. Economists generally dismiss this approach.[26] However, we can redefine the components of Equation (10-3) as a set of more complex and realistic economic relationships:

$$\text{Pollution per Unit of Consumption} = \text{Environmental Policy and Practice} * \text{Initial Pollution Intensity per Unit of Consumption} \qquad (10\text{-}4A)$$

$$\text{Consumption per Capita} = A * Y^{\alpha} * P^{\beta} \qquad (10\text{-}4B)$$

$$\text{Pollution Total} = N * A * Y^{\alpha} * P^{\beta} * PUC \qquad (10\text{-}4C)$$

The new symbol is 'PUC', pollution per unit of consumption. As used in other chapters, N represents total population, Y is per capita income, P is the general price level of consumer goods, and A represents geographic, cultural, and time factors. The last equation here (10-4C) is a more complex restatement of the original Ehrlich-Holdren concept. Nevertheless, the impact of population growth on total pollution still has a one-to-one effect. In economic terminology, it is assumed that the elasticity of pollution with respect to population is one.[27] The equations (10-4) are still hypothetical, but they provide an economic context for the Ehrlich-Holdren relationship.

It is the strong impact (the assumed elasticity of one) which has contributed to the economist's interest in the interaction of environment and population. This interest has included two related subjects: (1) The demographic transition to stable population levels as incomes rise and (2) the carrying capacity of the earth.

The theory of the demographic transition is based upon the concept of a general relationship between birth and death rates as incomes grow over time.[28] As summarized in Figure 10.10, each stage is defined by birth and death rates and their interaction. The first stage was characteristic of human society before the development of agriculture and industry.

In the second stage, modern medicine and public health policies combine with greater food availability to reduce death rates, while birth rates stay high. As a consequence, population grows rapidly. In the third stage, education, rising incomes, birth control, and formal employment opportunities for women all interact to reduce the birth rate and population growth.

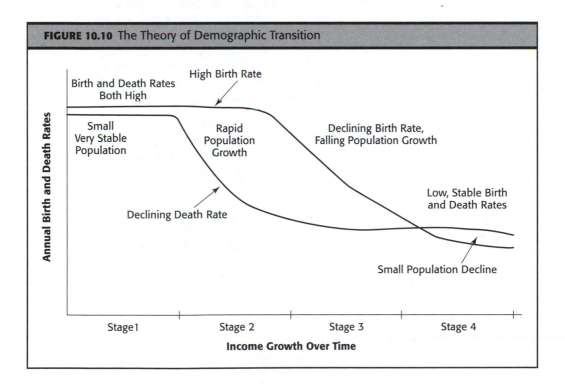

FIGURE 10.10 The Theory of Demographic Transition

Japan and the other OECD countries are in the fourth stage, where birth and death rates are both low.[29] Senior citizens in this stage become a significant proportion of the population. Population growth apart from immigration may actually be negative as is represented in the figure.

'Fertility rate' is an important concept. It summarizes the average number of children born to each woman. A fertility rate value of 2.1 is in the range that is expected to stabilize population levels. Both China and the United States are near this rate.

The demographic transition concept can be illustrated with income and fertility data in the United States. In Table 10.4, note that fertility in the highest income category is below the sustainable population level. Fertility in the lowest income group is considerably above the stable population level.

The theory of demographic transition is helpful in a broad way in understanding the history of population growth in some regions, especially the high-income OECD countries. But China, for example, has the same low population growth rate as the United States, although its rapidly growing per capita income remains much smaller.[30] In the future, population growth may be more influenced by family and national family planning than in the past.

Joel Cohen's *How Many People Can the Earth Support?* rekindled interest in this subject in the late 1990s.[31] Cohen makes several important points. First, he notes that carrying capacity is itself changing as a result of technology, culture, and economics. Consequently, it may not be possible for us now to project future global carrying capacity levels with satisfactory accuracy.[32]

Second, his review of 66 global carrying capacity studies results in his cautiously phrased conjecture that the population carrying capacity may be in the range of 8 to 12 billion people.[33]

Third, Cohen's examination of agriculture, water availability, energy, and industrial resources (as discussed in this chapter) do not lead him to his own numerical value, but in a general way support his cautious conclusion of a possible range. Finally, these points are combined in his conclusion:

The human population of the Earth now travels in the zone where a substantial fraction of scholars have estimated upper limits on human population size. These estimates are no better than present understanding of humankind's culture, economic and environmental choices and constraints. Nevertheless, the possibility must be considered seriously that the

TABLE 10.4 The Demographic Transition Theory in the United States: Fertility and Income, 1987[34]	
Family Income	*Fertility: Estimated Total Births per Woman*
Less than $10,000	2.66
$20,000 to $25,000	2.00
Above $35,000	1.53

number of people on the Earth has reached, or will reach within half a century, the maximum number the Earth can support in modes of life that we and our children and their children and their children will choose to want.[35]

Summary and Conclusion

Two centuries ago Thomas Malthus argued that population growth potential exceeds the maximum growth in food production. More precisely, he noted the human potential for exponential population growth, but he believed that innovation in agricultural production increases at a constant and lower rate. Consequently, he concluded that war, famine, and disease would periodically bring human populations back into the range permitted by food output.[36]

While world population and agricultural output have both continued to grow, the modern concern about possible limits to growth and sustainability reflect the Malthusian concern. Cohen's review of global carrying capacity emphasized water, energy, and industrial resources as well as agriculture. His conclusion is that the current level and growth[37] are moving into the range where the question needs to be considered.

It remains to be seen whether or not the demographic transition will lead to the disappearance of population growth as incomes rise.

The Ehrlich-Holdren relationship defines environmental impact as being the multiplied sum of population, consumption, and pollution and environmental intensity per unit of consumption. Although non-economic in its original form, the impact concept can be restated to emphasize the pollution elasticities associated with population, incomes, prices, and the interaction with technology and policy. In this economic reformulation, environmental impact has (other things being equal) an elasticity of one with respect to population level.

Household and municipal waste is already experiencing significant recycling. On average, about 20 percent by weight is recycled and the remainder placed in landfills. For several consumer items (paper, cans, plastic soda bottles) the proportion is much higher.

Economists have concluded that unit disposal charges encourage recycling and reduce landfill waste. This is a simplification of a complex issue: some households experience positive externality values from recycling regardless of the disposal charge. Some few households, at the other extreme, engage in bandit dumping.

For industry, metals recycling has already reached a level where it is the source of about 50 percent of new metal products, and economic logic suggests that, if supply curves for metals from ore shift, becoming more costly, then market demand for recycled metal will grow further.

Taking together the economics of consumer and industrial recycling, the conclusion is that recycling can extend industrial resource use for longer periods.

The availability of traditional industrial resources from mines and smelters is extensive. Estimating future availability and consumption on a conservative basis, metals from ore could only be used for roughly a century. However, if technology and recycling continue to produce new innovations, then the lifetimes of metal use become almost infinite.

The Limits to Growth debate in the latter part of the 20th Century was based upon pessimistic assumptions in each of these areas, and for agriculture as well. In the most widely discussed case, the availability of resources for industry was projected to peak in the second decade of the 21st Century, and to decline rapidly to depletion. Consequently, in this projection, food supplies and living standards declined, causing death rates to rise and global population levels to fall. As our knowledge of global resource availability, recycling, and population growth has improved, we now know that this scenario is unlikely. Resource prices have remained low and stable, and economic growth has continued.

The second major projection in the Meadows group's work focused on pollution. In this projection, living standards fall as does population, as a result of the damaging effects of pollution and climate change. This second case has been much less widely discussed, and remains a challenging theory, neither proven nor rejected in the broad context of the 21st Century.

Questions for Discussion and Analysis

1. First, summarize and contrast the two basic Limits to Growth cases. Second, indicate your response to Joel Cohen's criticism.

2. Study Figure 10.9. Use it to show the impact of a higher waste disposal charge on (a) original demand for packaging materials, (b) demand for waste disposal for the household with no perceived externality value for recycling, and (c) the change in recycling for this household.

3. Which version of the Ehrlich-Holdren equation do you prefer, Equation (10-3) or (10-4)? Why?

4. Restate (briefly) Cohen's concept of carrying capacity. Indicate the basis of your judgment in accepting or rejecting this concept.

5. For students with intermediate microeconomics: consider this possibility. The future demand curve for metal in Figure 10.8 increases because of growth in population and income. In Panel B, the future demand curve becomes $X_D = 250 - .5 * P$. The ore smelting curve remains unchanged at $X_O = .4 * P - 60$. However, recycling becomes somewhat less costly, and the new recycling supply curve is $P_R = \$25 + 7.5 * X_R$. Calculate the new total market quantity and price, the production levels from ore and recycling, and recycling as a percentage of the total supply. Illustrate with a graph if helpful.

How has this percentage changed as a result of the shift in the demand curve?

Notes to Chapter 10

1. See Figures 9.1 and 9.2 in the previous chapter.
2. The early 1970s Meadows group included the several individuals in Note 3 below. The 1990s team was the two Meadows and J. Randers; see Note 7.

3. Figure 10.1 represents the "World Model Standard Run," Figure 35, as reported in Donella Meadows, Dennis Meadows, Jørgen Randers, and William W. Behrens III, *The Limits to Growth* (New York: Universe Books, 1972), pages 124, 125. This is similar to the "Basic Behavior of the World Model," Figure 4.1 in J. W. Forrester, *World Dynamics* (Cambridge, Mass: Wright-Allen, 1971), page 70. Forrester worked closely with the Meadows group.

4. Figure 10.2 reflects Figure 37 in Meadows (1972), and Figure 4.5 in Forrester.

5. Meadows et al. (1972), page 132.

6. Joel E. Cohen, *How Many People Can the Earth Support?* (New York: Norton, 1995), pages 126, 127.

7. D. H. Meadows, D. L. Meadows, and J. Randers, *Beyond the Limits* (Post Mills, VT: 1992). Figure 10.3 shows Scenario 10, page 199.

8. Meadows et al. (1992), page 199.

9. Especially the concepts of monopoly, competition, and depletion introduced in both Chapters 6 and 9.

10. A contrasting view was suggested by P. Berck and M. Roberts, "Natural Resource Prices: Will They Ever Turn Up?" July 1996 *Journal of Environmental Economics and Management* 31(1):65–78.

11. C. A. Hodges, "Mineral Resources, Environmental Issues, and Land Use," June 2, 1995 *Science* 268:1305–1311.

12. The Wharton econometric forecast, as cited in USEIA, *International Energy Outlook 1995*, page 7.

13. Copper competes with aluminum in electrical and cooling equipment. Optical fiber is used in place of copper in electronics, and plastics are used in plumbing. For iron and steel: aluminum and plastics compete in motor vehicles; wood and cement compete in building construction; and glass, aluminum, and plastics are substitutes for beverage and food cans. Aluminum can be replaced by steel and copper as already noted. In addition, wood competes with aluminum in construction; and, in packaging, glass, paper, and plastics are substitutes.

   If managed properly, wood is a renewable resource, and glass, although finite, is nearly inexhaustible, especially with recycling. Source is *Mineral Commodity Summaries, op. cit.*

   These economic substitutes are clearly capable of performing as an additional factor in extending the duration of the period of use of the three metals.

14. The data in the first three columns is from U.S. Geological Survey, *Mineral Commodity Summaries 1996*. The "Years Remaining" with constant use divides the resource column by the current use column. The fifth column, with use growing at 2.7 percent annually, is found by solving for T in

$$\int_0^T C_0 e^{mt} dt = S$$

C_0 is the current use in column 3, m is the 2.7 percent growth in use, and S is the remaining resource estimate in column 2.

   Finally, in the last column, if mining efficiency, recycling, and substitution grow faster in combination than does the demand for the metal, conventional world ore resources will never be depleted. The growing interest in the concepts of pollution prevention and industrial ecology may contribute new technologies to reducing materials use in industry, thereby adding to the available lifetimes of industrial resource use.

   The 2.7 percent growth in total GDP of the global economy could be assumed to reflect both population growth and per capita income growth.

15. J. Tierney, "Betting The Planet," December 2, 1990 *Sunday New York Times Magazine*, starting page 52.

16. See Hodges *op. cit.*

17. Table 10.2 is based upon data by Franklin Associates, U.S. Bureau of the Census, *Recycling Times,* and *Resource Recycling,* in K. Palmer, H. Sigman, and M. Walls, "The Cost of Reducing Municipal Solid Waste," June 1997 *Journal of Environmental Economics and Management* 33(2):128–150. 1993 recycling estimates were used for some entries in this table. The U.S. population was 249.9 million in 1990, with a national total of about 200 million tons of municipal waste.

18. See brief summary of lead health hazard in Table 11.4.

19. Logically, Figure 10.9 should be more complex than is discussed in the text. The demand for original packaging Q_T will be influenced by C, of course, but also by the households' recycling preferences. D. Fullterton and W. Wu have developed a somewhat similar model; it is both more comprehensive and complex. See their "Policies for Green Design," September 1998 *Journal of Environmental Economics and Management* 36(2): 131–148.

20. Waste incinerators have not been included in this discussion. They are generally more costly (even with energy sales credits) than a good landfill. Also, incinerators face uncertainty with respect to toxic pollutant emissions. They are not a significant part of the waste disposal system.

21. Palmer et al. analyze recycling subsidies and find them less efficient than the deposit/refund policy. Subsidies lead to greater recycling but do not reduce total disposable waste.

22. Palmer, Sigman, and Walls: see Note 17. For their discussion of costs, see their page 142, citing F. Ackerman, et al., "Preliminary Analysis: The Costs and Benefits of Bottle Bills," Tellus Institute, Boston, MA, 1995.

23. In addition to Palmer *op. cit.,* recent empirical work includes R. Jenkins, *The Economics of Solid Waste Reduction: The Impact of User Fees* (Brookfield, VT: Elgan, 1995); T. C. Kinnaman and D. Fullerton, "How a Fee per Unit Garbage Affects Aggregate Recycling," in A. L. Bovenberg and S. Cnossen, eds., *Public Economics and the Environment in an Imperfect World* (Dordrecht, Holland: Kluwer, 1995); D. Fullerton and T. C. Kinnaman, their "Garbage, Recycling, and Illicit Burning or Dumping," July 1995 *Journal of Environmental Economics and Management* 29(1):78–91, and "Household Responses to Pricing Garbage by the Bag," September 1996 *American Economic Review* 86(4):971–984.

 The level of unit charge in the text (80¢ per garbage can; 5¢ per pound) is the general magnitude of unit charge from the preceding studies in this Note. In his analysis of rural New York cities, Reidhead concludes that a unit price of $7 per household trash container would be efficient, almost 10 times the value discussed in the text; P. W. Reidhead, *Environmental Costs and Optimal Unit Pricing for Municipal Solid Waste Services*, master's thesis, Cornell University, 1996. Reidhead incorporates significant externality values in his work, resulting in the higher unit price for disposal.

 D. Nestor and M. Podolsky find that bag charges lead households to make greater reduction in household waste than do garbage can charges. But, they find neither charge reduces total demand for original packaging, the Q_T used in the text here. See their "Assessing Incentive-Based Environmental Policies for Reducing Household Waste Disposal," October 1998 *Contemporary Economic Policy*, 16(4): 401–411.

24. T. Naughton and C. Kirchoff, "Recycling in Africa," June/July 1997 *Keeping Track*, pages 26–28. This environmental magazine is published in South Africa.

25. P. R. Ehrlich, A. H. Ehrlich, and J. P. Holdren, *Ecoscience: Population, Resources, Environment* (San Francisco: Freeman, 1970), page 720.

26. Partha Dasgupta describes the Ehrlich-Holdren relationship as illuminating, descriptive, but not analytical; "The Population Problem: Theory and Evidence," December 1995 *Journal of Economic Literature* 33(4):1879–1902.

27. Remember the economic definition of elasticity: see Chapter 1 Appendix.

28. This discussion makes use of the definitions of Cohen *op. cit.* Chapter 4, Tietenberg *op. cit.* Chapter 5, and M. P. Todaro, *Economic Development in the Third World* (New York: Longman, 1989), Chapters 6 and 7.

29. See the low rates of population growth in A. Maddison, *Monitoring the World Economy 1820–1992* (Paris: OECD, 1995), pages 102–103.

30. In 1996, China's per capita GNP, adjusted for purchasing power as explained in Chapter 2, was $3,330. The U.S. figure was $28,020, the world's highest. The annual population growth rate was 1.1 percent in China and 1.0 percent in the United States. See World Bank, *World Development Report 1997*, Tables 1 and 4.

31. J. Cohen, *How Many People Can the Earth Support?* (New York: Norton, 1995). Also see an interesting discussion of the book by Bill McKibben, "Reaching the Limit," May 29, 1997 *New York Review of Books* 44(9):32–35. In a developing country context, the demographic transition as well as the Ehrlich-Holdren pollution relationship is reviewed in P. W. Reidhead, L. F. Qureshy, and V. Narain, "Population, Environment, and Development," pages 45–68 in R. K. Pachuri and L. F. Qureshy, eds., *Population, Environment, and Development* (Delhi, India: Multiplexus for the Tata Energy Research Institute, 1997).

32. Cohen, Appendix 3, and pages 368–369.

33. This is my interpretation of Cohen's discussion on pages 367 and 444–445 in Appendix 6.

34. Table 10.4 is estimated from data in U.S. Census Series P-20, Report No. 427, assuming 28 years childbearing potential for women.

35. Cohen, page 367.

36. A good summary of Malthus' theory is in R. Costanza, J. Cumberland, H. Daly, R. Goodland, and R, Norgaard, *An Introduction to Ecological Economics* (Boca Raton, FL: St. Lucie Press, 1997), pages 25, 26.

37. Current world population is about 6 billion, increasing at a rate of 1.5 percent annually. This growth rate continues to decline slowly.

RENEWABLE ENVIRONMENTAL RESOURCES: AIR AND WATER QUALITY, AGRICULTURE, AND FORESTRY

CHAPTER 11

AIR POLLUTION CONTROL: ECONOMICS AND POLICY

A Success Story: Reduced Pollution Emissions

Air pollution problems have a long history. A royal order from England's King Edward I in the early 14th Century is shown in Table 11.1. His successor, King Edward II, is said to have tortured polluters.[1] Nevertheless, for much of U.S. and world history, the dominant attitude has considered air pollution a visible symbol of industrial strength and economic prosperity.

It was not until the decades following World War II that the United States and Europe experienced air pollution episodes with severe impact on mortality.

A 1948 event is often cited as an important milestone in developing U.S. policy. In Donora, Pennsylvania, in October of that year, 20 people died from pollution-induced causes, and several thousand people had respiratory problems. This occurred in a five-day period, in a pollution episode caused by industrial emissions. In London, in December 1952, more than 3,500 deaths were caused by air pollution and fog trapped in a temperature inversion. The pollution was primarily particulates and sulfur dioxide, and caused death through heart disease, pneumonia,

---

TABLE 11.1 Early Problems with Air Pollution[3]

1. England's King Edward I, A.D. 1307, to the Sheriff of Surrey: "[Coal-fired kilns] from which is emitted so powerful and unbearable a stench that, as it spreads throughout the neighbourhood, the air there is polluted over a wide area, to the considerable annoyance of said prelates, magnates, citizens and others dwelling there, and to the detriment of their bodily health. [Kiln operators] should henceforth make absolutely no use of coal . . . under pain of heavy forfeiture."

2. Board of Health of Massachusetts, 1869: "We believe that all citizens have a right to the enjoyment of pure and uncontaminated air, and water, and soil; that this right should be regarded as belonging to the whole community; and that no one should be allowed to trespass upon it by his carelessness or his avarice, or even by his ignorance."

TABLE 11.2 U.S. Air Pollution Control Success[4] (amounts are in million tons, unless indicated)

Pollutant	1970 Actual Amount	1995 Actual Amount	Projected Emissions 1995 w/o CAA	1995 Actual Amounts, Percentage Reductions	
				From Actual 1970	From 1995 Projected w/o CAA
Carbon monoxide	128.1	92.1	219.5	−28%	−58%
Nitrogen oxide	20.6	21.8	36.0	+6%	−39%
Volatile organics	30.6	22.9	78.2	−25%	−71%
Sulfur dioxide	31.3	18.3	40.4	−42%	−55%
Particulate matter	12.2	2.5	8.8	−80%	−72%
Lead	219.5	5.0	465.0	−98%	−99%
Average change			+119%	−45%	−66%

Note: Particulate matter is PM–10, in thousand tons. Lead is also in thousand tons. Excludes agriculture, road dust, natural sources.

and bronchitis.[2] These and similar events initiated the modern era's concern, and subsequent research programs and policies which have reduced air pollution and its consequences.

The United States has been very successful in this regard. Six pollutant emissions are shown in Table 11.2. Five of them have decreased dramatically since 1970, on average by 45 percent. It is also possible to use EPA (Environmental Protection Agency) calculations to see what pollution emissions would have been in the absence of the 1970 Clean Air Act. These amounts are in the third column in the table. On average, pollution would have doubled without the Clean Air Act.[5]

It is difficult to determine global air pollution trends outside the United States because no international organization regularly reports world data on these basic pollutants. In Western Europe, sulfur oxide emissions have apparently been reduced significantly, and nitrogen oxide emissions have been stabilized. European Union rules are following the United States in air pollution control requirements for automobiles and in eliminating lead from gasoline. However, emissions in the developing world are growing rapidly.[6]

Concentration Levels and Health Standards

In 1970, the U.S. Environmental Protection Agency was established and charged with implementing the new Clean Air Act of that year.[7] The Agency developed the

TABLE 11.3 Typical Primary Health Standards

Pollutant	Representative Time Period for Standard	Standard for Concentration in Air
1. CO—carbon monoxide	8-hour average	9 ppm
2. NO_2—nitrogen dioxide	yearly average	.053 ppm
3. O_3—ozone	8-hour average	.08 ppm
4. SO_2—sulfur dioxide	yearly average	.03 ppm
5. PM—particulate matter	daily average	
Small particles ($PM_{2.5}$)		65 $\mu g/m^3$
Large particles (PM_{10})		150 $\mu g/m^3$
6. Pb—lead	3-month average	1.5 $\mu g/m^3$

Notes: m^3 = cubic meter; μg = microgram, one millionth of a gram; ppm = parts per million; 1 oz = 28.4 grams.

Source: USEPA, *National Air Quality and Emissions Trend Report, 1995*, page 7. There are daily standards, hourly standards, annual standards, and secondary standards. The particle size of 2.5 microns is the benchmark for small particulates (which are smaller than this) and larger particulates. PM_{10} means particles between 2.5 and 10 microns in size. These standards are frequently described in terms of the number of exceedances per year.

first National Ambient Air Quality Standards in the following year, 1971. Table 11.3 shows a typical set of these standards.

The relationship between emissions in Table 11.2 and concentrations is complex. Emissions arise from automobiles, factories, and mines (for example), and become absorbed in the air. The amount of a pollutant in the air is termed its 'ambient concentration,' or simply 'concentration.' Emissions are measured in tons per year, and the resulting concentrations are measured in parts per million. (This latter term is abbreviated ppm.) In Table 11.3, the last column shows $\mu g/m^3$ (micrograms per cubic meter) as well as ppm as a measure of pollutant concentration.

These primary health standards are defined only on the basis of protecting human health. While valuation and benefit-cost analysis are assuming an increasing importance in air pollution control policy,[8] the primary standards remain focused on health protection to the exclusion of economic consequences.

The actual concentrations in any location depend upon local emissions, pollution blown from distant and nearby locations, wind direction and velocity, sunlight, air temperature, and chemical interactions between pollutants. Ozone (abbreviated O_3) is particularly complicated. This pollutant requires three major ingredients: sunlight as a catalyst, volatile organic compounds, and nitrogen oxides. This pollution "soup" creates ozone. When ozone concentrations rise above normal levels, it begins to become hazardous.[9]

The six pollutants with representative standards are in Table 11.3.[10] There is an important difference between the six in Table 11.2 and the six in Table 11.3. Volatile organics in Table 11.2 are a significant pollutant emission because of their role in ozone formation, but are not by themselves given the status of a major health threat in Table 11.3.

Ozone is listed only in Table 11.3 as important for its concentration level, but not in Table 11.2 as an emission. This is because ozone results from other pollutants as explained.

In summary, pollutant emissions result in pollutant concentrations in the air. Table 11.3 reflects the focus on protecting human health for the primary standard.

Although the emphasis of the standards is placed upon health, they also are intended to protect against damage to ecosystems, historical and Native American sites, buildings and cars, and visibility.[11]

The nature of the relationship of each pollutant to different illnesses constitutes the major scientific problem in defining the primary standards. Are there threshold levels below which no damage occurs? How does the presence of multiple pollutants affect the response of health to pollution? Should identifiable groups (people with asthma, infants, etc.) be analyzed separately? Are responses linear, or accelerating? Figure 11.1 shows just two examples. The accelerating curve was used to show ozone concentration and mortality in St. Louis, and is frequently used in ozone studies. Carbon monoxide, in contrast, was studied with the straight line concept for heart attacks in Medicare populations.[12] These two curves in the figure do not represent actual numerical relationships, but they do show the conceptual difference between linear and accelerating health responses to air pollution.

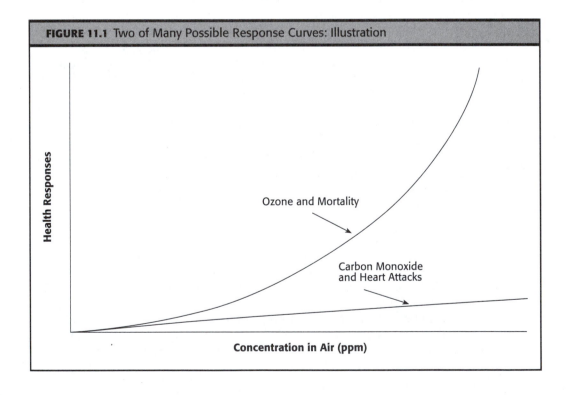

FIGURE 11.1 Two of Many Possible Response Curves: Illustration

---

TABLE 11.4 Human Health Effects of the Criteria Pollutants[13]

Pollutant	*Known Health Effects*	
Ozone	Inflammation in the lung Mortality Restricted activity Decreased income resulting from decreased performance	Reduced lung capacity Respiratory illness Hospital admissions Asthma attacks Emergency room visits
Particulate matter, sulfates	Reduced lung capacity Acute bronchitis Mortality Worse asthma for asthmatics	Hospital admissions Respiratory illness Restricted activity Work loss, lost income
Carbon monoxide	Angina (intense suffocating pain that affects breathing)	
Nitrous oxides	Respiratory illness, including flu and pneumonia	
Sulfur dioxide	In asthmatics: changes in lung capacity, respiratory illness	
Lead	IQ loss Hypertension (high) blood pressure) Heart disease	Mortality Neonatal mortality Fetal effects Strokes

Note: In other countries with higher pollutant concentrations in the air, human health can be more severely affected than in the United States.

The proven health effects of these pollutants are identified in Table 11.4. The following table, 11.5, shows the major sources of the pollutants.

Improvement in Pollution Concentration and Exposure

The EPA uses these health standards to develop an overall pollution index to indicate the daily health hazard for individual urban areas. Table 11.6 explains the basic format. However, it should be emphasized that the PSI (Pollutant Standards Index) is not an average. It is defined by the highest value for any one of the pollutants.

For example, suppose on a spring day at noon New York City has "Good" readings for SO_2, CO, PM-10, and NO_2. But, the City has ozone at the .3 ppm level. The PSI will take the level of the highest hazard. Since ozone is in the very unhealthful range, the PSI takes this hazard level, and the PSI for this day has an index value of 250.

The index shows the severity of the health hazard. A PSI level of 200 indicates a first-stage alert. In this New York City example, then, senior citizens and people with asthma and emphysema are encouraged to remain inside and to avoid physical activity. The other stages and the recommendations are shown in Table 11.7.

Fortunately, the success in reducing U.S. pollution emissions has brought about a reduction in pollution concentrations and exposure in urban areas. Figure 11.2

TABLE 11.5 U.S. Criteria Pollutants and the Major Emissions Sources[14]

Pollutant	Primary Sources of Each Pollutant	
Ozone	Chemical reaction to NO_2 and VOC with sunlight as a catalyst (See entry for nitrous oxides below.)	Major VOC sources are solvent use, vehicles, gasoline-powered equipment, and waste disposal.
Particulate matter TSP Sulfates	Coal Gasoline Oil Firewood (See entry for sulfur dioxide below.)	
Carbon monoxide	Vehicles and gasoline equipment Firewood locally	
Nitrous oxides	Electric utilities Vehicles	Industrial fuel use Diesel equipment
Sulfur dioxide	Electric utility coal use Industrial coal use	
Lead	Gasoline Lead and copper smelting Lead recycling	

Note: Other countries may have different emissions sources than is currently the case for the United States. For example, in Mexico and Africa, copper smelting is a major source of sulfur emissions.

shows the number of times people in large cities were exposed to days with unhealthy levels of air pollution.[15]

The data used to compile the PSI show two important trends. First, ozone continues to be a problem causing unhealthy urban air pollution. A very large 92 percent of the unhealthy PSI days in the mid-1990s is directly linked to high ozone concentrations. The other major pollutants have been reduced below the unhealthy levels most of the time in most U.S. cities.

A second important trend is geographic. California alone accounts for more than one-half of the unhealthy air pollution days in the United States, and this is primarily in Southern California.[16]

The first three sections in this chapter have introduced the scientific background for U.S. health standards and the major reductions in air pollution emissions, as well as pollution concentration levels in the air. The following sections begin to review the economics of air pollution. First, we survey a benefit-cost analysis of the national program. Then, after the benefit-cost analysis, we examine

TABLE 11.6 Pollutant Standards Index Values[17]

Index Value	Air Quality Level	PM-10 (24-hr) μg/m³	SO₂ (24-hr) μg/m³	CO (8-hr) ppm	O₃ (1-hr) ppm	NO₂ (1-hr) ppm	Health Effect Descriptor
500	Significant harm	600	2,620	50	0.6	2.0	Hazardous
400	Emergency	500	2,100	40	0.5	1.6	Hazardous
300	Warning	420	1,600	30	0.4	1.2	Very unhealthful
200	Alert	350	800	15	0.2	0.6	Unhealthful
100	NAAQS	150	365	9	0.12	nd*	Moderate
50	50% of NAAQS	50	80	4.5	0.06	nd*	Moderate
0		0	0	0	0	0	Good

Note: No benchmark values are defined for these concentration levels. Also see Table 11.7. NAAQS means National Ambient Air Quality Standard, comparable to Table 11.3 on health standards where similar time intervals are used in both tables (i.e., PM-10, CO).

the innovative program of marketable permits used to make major gains in reducing the acid rain problem.

Benefits and Costs of the Clean Air Act

The EPA is now required by Congress to evaluate the economic costs and benefits of air pollution control. The first evaluation covers the period beginning with the Clean Air Act of 1970, to 1990.[18] The benefit-cost analysis began with a review of the major gains in reduced pollution emissions and lower pollution concentration levels. The analysis uses basically the same methodology introduced in this chapter, but it is necessarily broader and more sophisticated. The benefit valuation draws upon estimated health response relationships (as in Figure 11.1), and the techniques that were surveyed in Chapters 3, 4, and 6. Some of the important factors are noted in Table 11.8.

The effectiveness of pollution control technology in implementation of the Clean Air Act is very impressive. For power plants as well as new cars, 95 percent reduction is typically achieved for all pollutants. However, the costs of pollution control can be very high in some circumstances. In new cars, for example, emissions control constitutes about $2,000 of the cost, and safety another $1,600. With the typical new car selling at about $20,000, pollution control and safety costs are about 18 percent of a new car purchase price.[19] For new power plants, two-thirds of the capital investment in both coal and nuclear power is associated with environmental protection and safety.[20]

TABLE 11.7 Health Warning Stages for the Pollutant Standard Index Levels[21]

Air Quality Health Level	Health Effects	Health Warning
Hazardous, significant harm	Premature death of ill and elderly. Healthy people will experience adverse symptoms that affect their normal activity.	All persons should remain indoors, keeping windows and doors closed. All persons should minimize physical exertion and avoid traffic.
Hazardous, emergency	Premature onset of certain diseases in addition to significant aggravation of symptoms and decreased exercise tolerance in healthy persons.	Elderly and persons with existing diseases should stay indoors and avoid physical exertion. General population should avoid outdoor activity.
Warning, very unhealthful	Significant aggravation of symptoms and decreased exercise tolerance in persons with heart or lung disease, with widespread symptoms in the healthy population.	Elderly and persons with existing heart or lung disease should stay indoors and reduce physical activity.
Alert, unhealthful	Mild aggravation of symptoms in susceptible persons, with irritation symptoms in the healthy population.	Persons with existing heart or respiratory ailments should reduce physical exertion and outdoor activity.
Moderate or good	All pollutant levels are below primary health standard levels.	

Fortunately, these two cases (automobiles and power plants) are unusual. In aggregate, for the whole economy, costs of pollution control total $29 billion annually, only about one-half of one percent of GDP. According to the EPA, the benefits are a much higher $457 billion annually. (Figure 11.3 shows benefits and costs.)

In summary, national economic benefits considerably exceed costs for the Clean Air Act since 1970. This reflects the success in reducing emissions and improving air quality in the United States.

A similar positive conclusion is appropriate for the region with the greatest success in air pollution control, Southern California. In the last third of the 20th

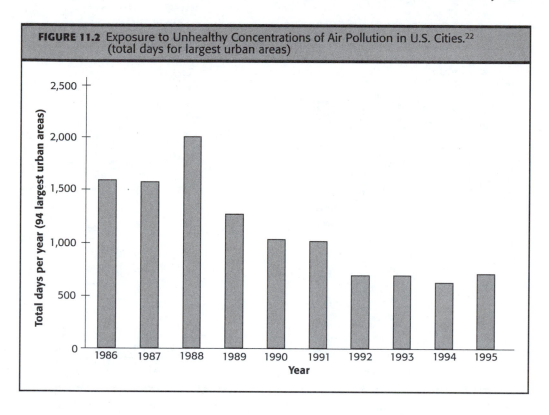

FIGURE 11.2 Exposure to Unhealthy Concentrations of Air Pollution in U.S. Cities.[22] (total days for largest urban areas)

TABLE 11.8 Benefit Values from Reduced Air Pollution in the Clean Air Act Analysis[23] (1990 dollars; 1990 annual data)

Type of Benefit from CAA	Benefit Values	Change in Yearly Number of Cases (or crop yield)	Annual Benefit
Avoided death	$4.8 million	79,000	$379 billion
Avoided strokes	$587,000 each	10,000	$6 billion
Avoided heart attacks	$587,000 each	18,000	$11 billion
Avoided loss in IQ	$5,550 each IQ point	na	$550 million
Increased agricultural yield	na	1% to 18%	$67 million

Note: 'na' means not available. Yield change is for wheat, cotton, peanuts, corn, soybeans, and sorghum.

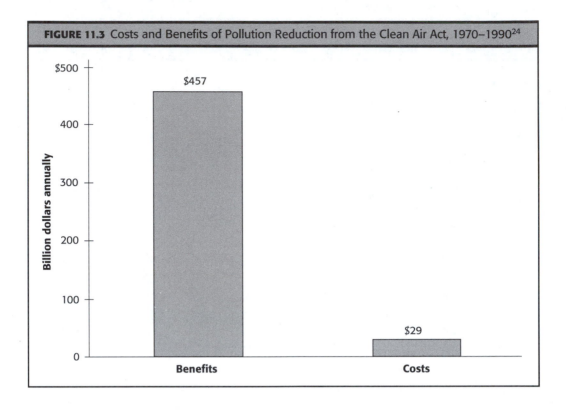

FIGURE 11.3 Costs and Benefits of Pollution Reduction from the Clean Air Act, 1970–1990[24]

Century, air quality was improved by 50 percent, while population and cars tripled, and income increased.[25]

Perhaps the least-recognized contributor to this success is business. The actual installation of air pollution control technology in factories, homes, cars, and elsewhere, is on the whole handled by business and private contractors. In industry, most monitoring is self-monitoring undertaken by business. It is verified through inspection and other means by the EPA and by state agencies.[26]

The significant degree by which national benefits exceed costs for air pollution programs is very different from the results of benefit-cost analysis of national water quality programs. In Chapter 12, economic analysis finds that future increased water pollution control expenditures may exceed benefits unless health benefits are more accurately estimated.

Regulation and Marketable Permits: The Acid Rain Case

Acid rain has been a major problem in pollution control. The name itself simplifies a complex problem. 'Acid rain' means the fallout of sulfur and nitrogen oxides which are transformed into acids when they interact with water. The acid rain concept includes acidic rainfall, of course, but also applies to acid fog, acid snow, and dry deposition which eventually becomes wet and acidic. As with ozone pollution, acid rain emissions often originate in distant locations, and are transported long

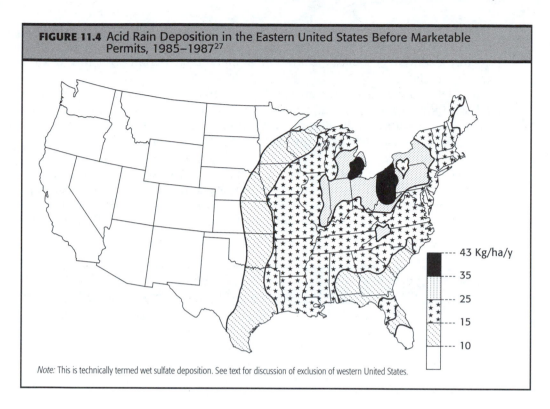

FIGURE 11.4 Acid Rain Deposition in the Eastern United States Before Marketable Permits, 1985–1987[27]

43 Kg/ha/y
35
25
15
10

Note: This is technically termed wet sulfate deposition. See text for discussion of exclusion of western United States.

distances before deposition occurs. The technical term 'acid deposition' means the total fallout on the ground, buildings, cars, vegetation, and so on of wet or dry pollutants which become acidic. Acid deposition is primarily caused by SO_2 emissions.[28]

Notwithstanding the successful reduction in SO_2 which is shown in Table 11.2, acid rain continues to be a problem. The pattern of sulfuric acid deposition in the eastern United States in the 1980s is shown in Figure 11.4. One area of major concern is the Adirondack and White Mountain region of the Northeast. Although this area is not in one of the high-fallout regions, it is unusually susceptible to damage because of the interaction of soil, climate, and natural ecosystems with acid rain. In Chapter 14, we will see the controversial findings on acid rain impact on the area's forest ecology. However, it is lakes and streams that are known to be particularly sensitive, and 20 percent of large Adirondack lakes are not suitable for brook trout and the other sensitive aquatic species: minnows and salamanders.[29]

The 1990 Amendments to the Clean Air Act established a national goal of significant additional reductions in SO_2 emissions and acid rain damage. The legislation established a maximum of 8.95 million tons of sulfur emissions for electric utilities in 2010.[30] The economic innovation in this legislation is to introduce marketable permits as a policy option. These acid rain marketable permits offer an opportunity for business to make cost-effective decisions about pollution control.

Ultimately, the acid rain marketable permit system will allocate a basic pool of 8.95 million SO_2 allowances to electricity producers, and companies will be required to pay heavy fines if their SO_2 emissions exceed their allowances.[31]

If the program succeeds, it may be expanded to other sources of SO_2 emissions such as copper smelters and oil refineries. Also, a successful SO_2 program would probably lead to the establishment of similar marketable permit programs for CO_2 and other pollutants.

In order to illustrate the features of the marketable permit system, we use here an illustration which may be appropriate for the future: multi-industry permits for SO_2 emissions. Although the illustrative case uses an air pollution context, the marketable permit concepts are equally applicable to water quality and other environmental policies.

Suppose a region now experiences 200 million pounds of acid rain emissions from two companies. One operates a large power plant, and the other company operates a smelter. The goal is to reduce this level to 100 million pounds annually in the most cost-effective manner possible. Cost data are in Table 11.9. Which will be

---

TABLE 11.9 Cost Assumptions for Sample Analysis of Acid Rain, Markets, and Regulation

	Annual Amounts, Million Pounds	
Company and Control Costs per Pound of Sulfur Removed	*Additional Amount Removed*	*Amount Remaining*
A. Power Company (original emission is 110)		
A1. 10¢/lb acid rain reduction from use of low-sulfur coal	50	60
A2. 50¢/lb acid rain reduction from 68 percent scrubbing	25	35
A3. 80¢/lb acid rain reduction from 91 percent scrubbing	25	10
A4. $2/lb cost for 95.5 percent scrubbing	5	5
B. Copper Smelter (original emission is 90)		
B1. 2¢/lb net cost for recycling sulfuric acid	25	65
B2. 75¢/lb cost for 83.3 percent scrubbing	50	50
B3. $1.75/lb cost for 94.4 percent scrubbing	10	5
C. Total Regional Pollution Before New Policy: 200 million pounds of sulfur emissions annually. The percent scrubbing entries always take each company's original emissions as the 100 percent base.		

more cost-effective, a 50 percent reduction by each company or a marketable permits program?

50 Percent Regulatory Rollback for Both Companies

For policy reasons related to employment and other factors, the EPA might consider an equal reduction for both industries. Suppose this takes the form of a 50 percent rollback for each company.

Now, the power company is required to cut 55 million of its original 110 million pounds of emissions. It switches to low-sulfur coal for a 50 million reduction, and scrubs (at 68 percent) another 5 million. The cost to the power company is $7.5 million.

The copper company reduces 45 million of its original 90 million pounds emissions. It does this by recycling 25 million and scrubbing 20 million pounds. The total cost to the copper company is $15.5 million.

For both companies for the region, the combined cost is $23 million. This turns out to be much higher than the combined cost with marketable permits to meet the same goal.

Achieving the Same Reduction with Marketable Permits

The EPA issues an initial 50 tradeable permits to each company. Each permit represents one million pounds of released sulfur, and sells at $600,000. The two companies will seek the minimum cost combinations of technology and permits. The power company decides to switch to low-sulfur coal, and goes to 68 percent scrubbing. It is removing 75 million pounds, and uses 35 of its 50 permits to cover the remaining emissions. It offers 15 permits for sale to the copper company at $600,000 each, totalling $9 million. So, the power company has its own pollution control cost of $17.5, but offsets this with the $9 million from permit sales.

The copper company decides to do sulfur recycling only for 25 million pounds, a cost of $0.5 million. It buys the 15 permits from the power company for $9 million, and adds these 15 permits to its own 50 to cover the remaining pollution. Its total cost is $9.5 million.

The combined costs of pollution control and permit sale will be $8.5 million for the power company and $9.5 million for the copper smelter: a total of $18 million. And emissions are reduced by the same 100 million pounds. (The power company eliminates 75 million, and the copper smelter 25 million pounds.)

In fact, there is only one solution which is the least expensive and most cost-effective for the region, and it is shown in Figure 11.5. The "50 percent regulatory rollback for both companies" costs more because it doesn't use this least-cost solution to meet the regional goal. In theory, the marketable permit system is best: the companies themselves have been given economic incentives to use the best solution.

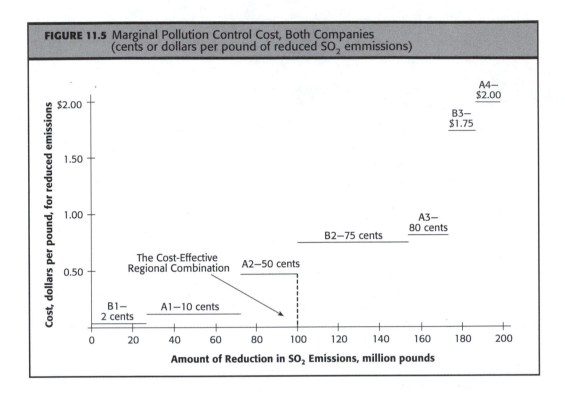

FIGURE 11.5 Marginal Pollution Control Cost, Both Companies (cents or dollars per pound of reduced SO₂ emmissions)

The illustration shows the strengths and weaknesses of a permit system. If properly executed by the companies, it is more efficient and less costly than rollback regulation. But it is very complicated. The first major test of tradeable permits is taking place in the United States for acid rain control and power plant emissions. Preliminary data show that switching to low-sulfur coal is the policy preferred by electric utilities, followed by installation of SO_2 scrubbers, and then use of permits.[32] (These, of course, are the power company options in the illustration.) The overall results are not yet available.

This case shares an assumption with actual policy: we assume that damage is the same regardless of the source of the sulfur emissions. Consequently, we assume the same benefit from one less pound from the power plant, or from the copper smelter.

The validity of this assumption depends upon the specific response curves (Figure 11.1) for the geographic area and its pollution sources. In reality, for sulfur emissions, the actual distribution of acid deposition (Figure 11.4) emphasizes the importance of this assumption. Future research is certain to examine these issues of location, damage, and the effectiveness of marketable permits.[33]

Even this highly simplified illustration of marketable permits and rollback regulation seems complex. It does, however, represent the simplicity and potential political attractiveness of rollback regulation, and the difficulty and potential efficiency of marketable permits.

On a smaller, regional geographic scale, the RECLAIM program in Southern California also seeks to use the market incentives of tradeable permits. The goal is to encourage significant reduction in nitrogen and sulfur oxide emissions in a cost-effective way. In its first four years, $30 million in permits have been traded by participating businesses while reducing overall emissions in the region.[34]

Regional policies using tradeable permits are growing in importance in the United States. For the eastern United States, EPA is developing a program to reduce nitrogen oxide emissions in 22 states. The goal is to reduce ozone concentration levels by reducing nitrogen oxide emissions. It would make extensive use of the economic incentives of marketable permits, and focus on electric utilities. One factor encouraging the regional approach is meteorological: winds often move air pollution from the Midwest and South to the East.[35]

The future may see the evolution of "Pigouvian" taxation as well; it has the same focus of using economic incentives to arrive at cost-effective solutions.[36] Since the tax is based upon external social cost associated with the commodity, the price to consumers now reflects its external social cost. For the near future, however, marketable permits are the approach preferred by economists, perhaps because the permit system does not increase the overall tax burden on affected industries. Appendix 11.A gives the complete numerical solutions in detail for pollution taxation as well as marketable permits and rollback regulation.

Conclusion

In formulating pollution control policy, it is common for Congress to work with the EPA, state environmental agencies, business, and environmental groups. Congress and the President establish federal legislation, the EPA defines a regulatory framework, and implementation is usually accomplished by business and state agencies. The actual system is very complex. The American process is messy and frustrating, but the result in air pollution control is a cause for considerable commendation.

Since the enactment of the Clean Air Act in 1970, U.S. emissions of major air pollutants have declined by one-half. Considering the magnitude of economic growth since that time, pollution emissions are two-thirds lower now than would have been expected in the absence of air pollution control.

Air pollution primary standards for the concentration levels of pollution in the air are intended to protect human health. They are based upon scientific studies of the relationships between pollution concentration and illness. The most important national measure of overall exposure (the Pollutant Standards Index) shows that the number of days of unhealthy air has fallen by one-half since the 1980s.

Both pollution emissions and concentration levels have shown considerable improvement. As a consequence, a major study of the economic benefits and costs of air pollution control finds benefits far in excess of costs, and this is primarily because of reductions in mortality and illness from air pollution.

On average, air pollution control costs are less than one percent of GNP. However, in power generation and automobile manufacture, environmental protection costs are significant.

Ozone and acid rain continue to be a focus for new policy initiatives. In cities, remaining significant problems are overwhelmingly linked to ozone, and concentrated in Southern California.

Acid rain deposition (meaning the fallout of sulfur and nitrogen oxides in rain, snow, fog, or as dry particles) is particularly important in forests and lakes in the mountains of the Northeast. An innovative new program in marketable permits is intended to reduce SO_2 from power generation to 9 million tons annually. The plan has the virtues of decentralized decision-making coupled with minimum cost, but is very complex. Pollution taxation (referred to as 'Pigouvian taxation' by economists) is another market-oriented policy which may be used in the future.

Historically, the two decades following 1970 were a period in which, on the whole, the EPA, business, states, and environmental groups worked out a cooperative framework to achieve very considerable economic benefits from pollution control at a generally reasonable cost.

Since 1990, as further gains become more difficult and more costly, the emphasis in policy is shifting from regulation to market-based incentives to attempt to increase economic efficiency.

At the end of the 20th Century, the emphasis in air pollution policy was more closely focused on efficiency and market incentives, as noted. Attention is also turning to transportation, as in Chapter 8. That same chapter outlines the current high cost of new energy technologies. However, the growing air pollution levels in the developing world, coupled with the slow emergence of the climate change problem, may lead to new efforts to find cost-effective, less polluting technological substitutes for conventional energy use.

The macroeconomic consequences of air pollution control may be uncertain, but overall living standards, reflecting health and environmental protection benefits, are higher. Chapter 17 reviews our current knowledge about the relationship of pollution to income, employment, and living standards, and also examines trade and environment.

This chapter has focused on the status and economics of the major air pollutants. (Chapter 5 introduced the problem of other air pollutants known as 'air toxics' in the context of the environmental justice debate.) In Chapter 12, the economic status of the analysis of water quality appears to be quite different.

Questions for Discussion and Analysis

1. Explain the relationship between emissions and ambient concentration. Why does ozone appear in Table 11.3 but not in Table 11.2?

2. Suppose your city has these readings on a summer day: PM-10 at 350 μ/m^3, SO_2 at 1,600 μ/m^3, and the other three pollutants are in the "moderate" category. What would be the PSI value and the health effect descriptor?

3. The main component of the national benefits from the Clean Air Act is reduced mortality. Compare the benefit value used here to the conclusions reached in the review of the Value of a Statistical Life in Chapter 3.

4. Suppose for the acid rain case (Table 11.9 and Figure 11.5) that the marginal cost of moving to 91 percent sulfur scrubbing for the power plant becomes $1 per pound reduced emissions instead of 80¢ per pound. How does this affect the results for the four policies in Table 11.A?

5. Give at least one advantage of each of the four types of policies considered for acid rain reduction. Which do you prefer, and why?

Appendix 11.A: Complete Solutions to the Power and Copper SO$_2$ Reduction Problem

In reading the summary in Table 11.A, remember the impact of economic incentives on company cost. For the marketable permits case, the Power Company has a direct cost of $17.5 million which it offsets by permit sales of $9 million to the Copper Smelter. The Copper Smelter, in turn, has direct cost of $0.5 million, plus its cost of purchasing $9 million in permits.

For the tax case, the Power Company pays $21 million and the Copper Smelter $39 million. Of course, any tax rate between 50¢/lb and 75¢/lb would provide the same incentives for pollution reduction.

TABLE 11.A Appendix Table for Solutions (emissions in million pounds)

Policy Company	50% Rollback for Each Company	Marketable* Permits 60¢/lb SO$_2$	Pollution* Taxation 60¢/lb SO$_2$	Perfect Regulation
Power company eliminated emissions	55	75	75	75
Remaining emissions	55	35	35	35
Total company cost	$7.5 M	$8.5 M	$38.5 M	$17.5 M
Copper smelter eliminated emissions	45	25	25	25
Remaining emissions	45	65	65	65
Total company cost	$15.5 M	$9.5 M	$39.5 M	$0.5 M
Regional eliminated emissions	100	100	100	100
Remaining emissions	100	100	100	100
Total regional cost	$23 M	$18 M	$78 M	$18 M

* See the accompanying text for a discussion of the financial impact of the permit system and the tax.

Also shown as the fourth column in the table is a "Perfect Regulation" case, where regulators, having perfect knowledge of actual technology and costs in Table 11.9, have issued regulations setting maximum sulfur emissions at 75 million pounds for power and 25 million pounds for copper.

In each of these four cases, each company seeks the policy with minimum cost of compliance for itself.

Notes to Chapter 11

1. R. Wilson et al., *Health Effects of Fossil Fuel Burning* (Cambridge, MA: Ballinger, 1980), page 2.
2. USEPA, *National Air Pollutant Emissions Trends*, 1900–1995, page 4; and Wilson *op. cit.*, page 163.
3. Wilson, *op. cit.*, pages 1 and 316.
4. In Table 11.2, nitrogen oxide emissions rose steadily throughout the 20th Century, stabilizing in the 20–25 million ton range since 1970. Lead emissions peaked in 1972, and then declined sharply. PM-10 peaked in 1950 and has declined since. (PM-10 in this table is particulate matter less than 10 microns in diameter.) The other three criteria pollutants (SO_2, VOC, CO) peaked within the interval 1966–1973. Sources are USEPA, *The Benefits and Costs of the Clean Air Act, 1970 to 1990*, October 1997, Appendix B; and USEPA, *National Air Pollutant Emissions Trends, 1900–1995*, October, 1996, Appendix A.
5. Since the average increase from 1970 would have been 119 percent, this means the average pollutant's increase would have slightly more than doubled.
6. *New York Times*, "Europe Bans Leaded Gas: Tighter Air Pollution Rules," July 3, 1998. For an analysis of worldwide data, see the Worldwatch Institute, *Vital Signs* (New York: Norton, 1996), pages 70, 71, the reports on global sulfur and nitrogen oxide emissions from fossil fuel burning. By taking these global totals and subtracting the U.S. values, the rest-of-the-world figures show rapid growth, nearly doubling since 1970. Also see Figure 2.3 in Chapter 2.
7. Several sources provide good summaries of the development of air pollution control policy. They include *National Air Pollutant Emission Trends* (*op. cit.*), pages 4, 5; Paul Portney, *Public Policies for Environmental Protection* (Washington, DC: Johns Hopkins for Resources for the Future, 1990); and Field, *op. cit.*, Chapter 15. Also, Arthur Stern, "History of Air Pollution Legislation in the United States," January 1982 *Journal of the Air Pollution Control Association* 32(1):44–61.
8. See the historical introductions to Chapters 3 and 4, and Erickson's Chapter 19. Also, see the references in the preceding note. Note 11 below gives the references for current and proposed revisions in the standards in Table 11.3.
9. Upper-atmosphere ozone (termed 'stratospheric ozone') is the focus of the ozone depletion problem. Natural ozone from trees and plants exists at low, harmless concentration levels. In this chapter, the type of ozone considered is ground-level ozone which can affect humans, animals, and plants. Even the text description of ground-level (tropospheric) ozone formation risks oversimplification. It is the petroleum hydrocarbons in the VOCs which participate in ozone formation. Natural gas combustion is another ozone precursor, as is carbon monoxide.
10. These six are sometimes called 'criteria pollutants' because they were the first to have standards defined in quantitative terms to protect human health.
11. The concept of a secondary standard reflects the intention to protect these non-health values. Only sulfur dioxide has a secondary standard which is differentiated from the pri-

mary standard. Up-to-date versions of the standards are reported annually in USEPA, *National Air Quality and Emission Trends*. It is available from the EPA's Research Triangle Park office in North Carolina. The EPA Web site provides up-to-date information on current and proposed new standards.

12. USEPA, *The Benefits and Costs of the Clean Air Act, 1970–1990*, 1997, pages D27 and D37.
13. The source for Table 11.4 is *Benefits and Costs, op. cit.*
14. The source for Table 11.5 is *Emission Trends, op. cit.* (see Note 11).
15. Figure 11.2 shows the total number of days when the PSI reached 100 or higher, summed for the 94 largest urban areas.
16. Southern California cities (Bakersfield, Fresno, Los Angeles–Long Beach, Orange County, Riverside, San Diego, Ventura) have 46 percent of the U.S. total. (See *National Air Quality and Emission Trends, op. cit.*, Table A-18.)
17. Table 11.6 is adapted from *Emission Trends, op. cit.*
18. *Benefits and Costs, op. cit.*
19. American Automobile Manufacturers Association, *Motor Vehicle Facts and Figures 1996*, pages 60 and 87.
20. Chapman, *Energy Resources op. cit.*, page 267.
21. The source for Table 11.7 is USEPA, *Measuring Air Quality: The New Pollutants Standards Index*, 1978, pages 4–5.
22. Figure 11.2 is adapted from Figure 6.1 in the 1995 edition of *National Air Quality and Emission Trends, op. cit.*
23. The values in Table 11.8 are taken from *Benefits and Costs op. cit.*, pages xvi, 38, 265. The report's present value estimate of $10 billion for agriculture has been converted to an annual equivalent amount of $67 million in Table 11.8. Midpoint values are used here. The $550 million benefit for avoided IQ loss is from USEPA, *Costs and Benefits of Reducing Lead in Gasoline*, February 1985, pages IV–55, adjusted by the GDP deflator.
24. Figure 11.3 is adapted from the present value graph Figure 3 in *Benefits and Costs op. cit.* The conversion from present value to annual value uses 20 years at 3 percent, or a levelized cost factor of .0672. 1990 dollars are used.
25. Southern California's success in combining economic growth and pollution reduction is discussed in the macroeconomics, trade, and environment chapter.
26. M. L. Cropper and W. E. Oates, "Environmental Economics: A Survey," June 1992 *Journal of Economic Literature*, 30:696. C. S. Russell's review in depth is his "Monitoring and Enforcement," Chapter 7 in P. R. Portney, ed., *Public Policies for Environmental Protection* (Washington, DC: Resources for the Future, 1990). Also J. D. Harford, "Self-Reporting of Pollution and the Firm's Behavior under Imperfectly Enforceable Regulations," September 1987 *Journal of Environmental Economics and Management (JEEM)* 14(3):293–303; and in the May 1993 *JEEM* 24(3), the articles by H. L. Gabel and B. Sinclair-Desagne, "Managerial Incentives and Environmental Compliance," and by A. S. Malik, "Self-Reporting and the Design of Policies for Regulating Stochastic Pollution."
27. The source for Figure 11.4 is *National Acid Precipitation Assessment Program op. cit.*, page 182. A kg/ha is equivalent to .9 pounds per acre; so, for example, 35 kg/ha (the lower boundary for the heaviest deposition category) equals 31 pounds per acre.
28. *Benefits and Costs op. cit.*, page 245. There are two comprehensive technical reports on acid rain: *National Acid Precipitation Assessment Program*, 1990, and its successors; and USEPA, *Acid Deposition Standard Feasibility Study Report to Congress*, 1995.
29. This is a simplified summary of a very complex scientific issue. Two examples of the complexity of identifying the impact of acid deposition: (1) other human actions may have eliminated more fish species in Adirondack lakes than has acid deposition, and (2) small lakes tend to be more acidic because of decaying organic material. See *National Acid Precipitation Assessment Program op. cit.*, Chapter 2.

30. The policy also calls for reducing nitrogen oxide emissions from power plants by 2 million tons. See U.S. Energy Information Administration, *Electric Utility Phase I Acid Rain Compliance Strategies for the Clean Air Act Amendments of 1990*, March 1994, Chapter 2, which has a detailed review of specific regulations and legislation. Also, U.S. Energy Information Administration, *The Effects of Title IV of the Clean Air Act Amendments of 1990 on Electric Utilities: An Update*, March 1997.

31. See Note 30.

32. March 1997 *Monthly Energy Review*, page vii.

33. Initial evaluation of the acid rain marketable permits program suggests that it has lowered the costs of reduced emissions for utilities, but has been less widely utilized than expected. See R. Schmalensee et al, "An Interim Evaluation of Sulfur Dioxide Emissions Trading," and R. N. Stavins, "What Can We Learn from the Grand Policy Experiment?" Symposium, Summer 1998, *Journal of Economic Perspectives* 12(3):53–88. Also see A. D. Ellerman and J.P. Montero, "The Declining Trend in Sulfur Dioxide Emissions: Implications for Allowance Prices," July 1998 *Journal of Environmental Economics and Management* 36(1):26–45. D. Burtraw et al, "Costs and Benefits of Reducing Air Pollutants Related to Acid Rain," October 1998 *Contemporary Economic Policy* 16(4):379–400, conclude that net benefits have been significant.

34. The RECLAIM name is taken from the more formal Regional Clean Air Incentives Market. A valuable popular summary of Southern California's progress is "The Southland's War on Smog" (South Coast Air Quality Management District, Diamond Bar, CA: 1997). The District was formed in 1977 through incorporation of four counties' programs into one unified agency. The District has been an innovative leader in regional approaches to reduce air pollution.

35. *Environment Reporter*, "NOX Cuts of 1.1 Million Tons Annually Sought in Rule on Transported Pollution," October 2, 1998, pages 1093–1098. Also, *New York Times*, "U.S. Orders Cleaner Air in 22 States," September 25, 1998. One study of the Northeast concluded that current control policy may not be efficient in the sense that regulations are, at the margin, requiring more costly policies for electric utilities and industry than for vehicles. See G. W. Dorris, *Redesigning Regulatory Policy: A Case Study in Urban Smog*, Ph.D. dissertation, Cornell University, 1996.

36. Pigou's innovative development of the concept of pollution taxation was described at the beginning of Chapter 4. Acid rain emissions (especially sulphur dioxide) are taxed in five European countries and in Japan; see D. Cansier and R. Krumm, October 1997 *Ecological Economics* 23(1):59–70.

CHAPTER 12

WATER QUALITY ECONOMICS

Water Quality and the Environmental Kuznets Curve

Chapter 5 examined the importance of New York rural farming to the quality of New York City's municipal water supply. Coase Theorem concepts in that situation led to an understanding that cities and rural areas can work together. The case reflects a national trend: as municipalities and industry have reduced water pollution significantly, agriculture has become the leading overall source of water pollution. In Table 12.1, human activity in forests and other rural sources along with agriculture contribute 69 percent of water pollution.

In Chapter 13 (Agriculture, the Environment, and Economics), water quality is a major emphasis. However, in this chapter, the focus is on the externalities of non-agricultural water use.[1]

In their original work, Shafik and Bandyopadhyay found interesting results when they applied Chapter 2's Environmental Kuznets Curve to international data on water quality.[2] The Curve was significant for fecal material in rivers: this pollutant increased as income approached the $2,000 per capita level, and then this measure of water pollution declined as income increased beyond the $2,000 mark.[3]

Two other water quality variables (access to clean water and access to urban sanitation) both showed continuous improvement with rising income.

TABLE 12.1 Sources of Water Pollution in the United States.[4]	
Agriculture	41 percent
Forests	15 percent
Other rural	13 percent
Industry	8 percent
Municipal	17 percent
Other urban	6 percent
Total	100 percent

Jean Agras, Andrea Kreiner, and Matt Schwartz are thanked for their comments on this chapter.

TABLE 12.2 Environmental Externalities and Water Quality

1. Human Health
    Drinking water
    Fish, shellfish, meat
    Recreation (swimming, fishing, boating)

2. Ecosystem Protection
    Algal blooms
    Fish kills

3. Direct Economic Effects
    Water treatment costs because of absence of waste-treatment: human, industrial, animal, irrigation
    Productivity loss in labor force from waterborne illness
    Tourism loss
    Fishing loss

4. Reduction in Stewardship, Existence Values

In general, their work seems to show weak but positive support for the concept that per capita income is a significant factor in improving water quality. In the later discussion on developing countries in this chapter, the relationship between water quality expenditure and income levels helps explain the basis for the curve.

From a broad perspective, water quality externalities can be organized into three types: human health, ecosystem protection, and direct economic effects. These are summarized in Table 12.2.

The EPA uses a complicated methodology to determine water quality for U.S. rivers and lakes. The methodology first involves defining designated uses for each mile of river and each lake, then evaluating whether or not the water meets its designated use. Designated uses include drinking water supply, fish and aquatic organism suitability, safe swimming, and wildlife habitat.[5] On this basis, the current status of U.S. rivers and lakes is an approximate 60 percent rating in terms of being acceptable for their designated uses. However, recent trends are negative, as Figure 12.1 indicates. The decline from 1988 to 1992 is about 2 percent annually for rivers and 3 percent annually for lakes.

Human Health

For the United States, 85 percent of the water supply is safe to drink after treatment.[6] This is after removing or treating drinking water for the broad array of contaminants in Table 12.3. The microbiological threat to health has been a traditional

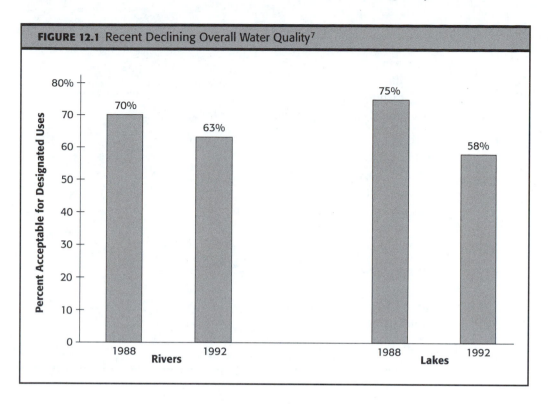

FIGURE 12.1 Recent Declining Overall Water Quality[7]

concern, and some of the major waterborne microbiological diseases are shown in Table 12.4. All of these illnesses are transmitted by human waste entering drinking water from infected individuals. In addition, some of these microbiological organisms are transmitted to humans through animal waste. Giardia, for example, is widespread in beaver, salmonella in chickens, and pfiesteria in swine waste.

TABLE 12.3 Water Quality Contaminants[8]

Oil and gasoline
Pesticides and herbicides
Chemicals
Metals (lead, copper especially)
Radionuclides
Microbiologicals (pfiesteria, cryptosporidium, etc.)*
Animal waste
Human waste
Sediment

*Cholera, typhoid have been eliminated from U.S. waters.

TABLE 12.4 Leading Biological Hazards in Drinking Water[9]

A. Protozoans
   Giardia
   Cryptosporidium
   Amoebic dysentery (developing countries)

B. Bacteria
   Salmonella
   Cholera (developing countries)
   Typhoid (developing countries)
   E. Coli
   Shigella
   Campylobacter

C. Viruses
   Hepatitis
   Polio (developing countries)
   Rotavirus

D. Dinoflagellates: pfiesteria

Several of the major waterborne illnesses have been eliminated from the United States and other high-income countries. Polio, cholera, and typhoid, for example, continue to be problems in developing countries but not high-income countries.

Nevertheless, the United States experiences 100,000 cases of gastrointestinal illness in a typical year. Occasionally more severe problems arise: in 1993, Milwaukee experienced a cryptosporidium epidemic, with 400,000 persons ill and 100 fatalities.[10]

In developing countries, gastrointestinal illness is the second leading cause of disability. (Later in the chapter, the economic problems linked to water quality in developing countries are reviewed.)

Ecosystem Protection and Wetlands

While concern about protecting human health has been a continuing priority, Table 12.2 also notes the importance of ecosystem protection. Figure 12.2 shows the severity of the problem. More than 60 percent of freshwater crayfish and mussel species are at risk of extinction.[11] This is the greatest degree of risk for any group of U.S. plants or animals.

These ecological problems arise not only because of contaminated water bodies, but also because of loss of ecosystem habitat. Wetlands are particularly important: although they represent only 5 percent of the U.S. surface area, one-third of the endangered species depend upon them.[12]

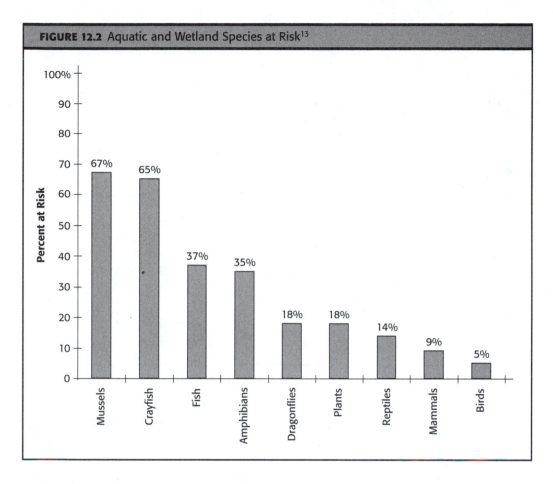

FIGURE 12.2 Aquatic and Wetland Species at Risk[13]

'Wetland' is a scientific term, meaning an area that is periodically covered with water and has developed soil and ecosystem characteristics related to periodic water coverage.[14] In popular terminology, a wetland might be a swamp, marsh, bog, pond, or a large "wet spot" in a farm field. Geese, ducks, herons, pelicans, and other waterfowl depend upon them as they migrate across North America each spring and fall. Because wetlands are so prolific in the growth of plant and fish life, they are home to many of the water-based carnivores: mink, weasel, and otter, and of course beaver and bear.

Besides the ecosystem value, wetlands support fishing, hunting, and recreation, and provide a natural method of water purification. Wetlands also contribute to groundwater by serving as recharge areas; surface water is absorbed by wetlands, which transfer their water to groundwater flows and aquifers.

In the 1700s, wetlands covered 221 million acres, primarily in the eastern and prairie states. The conversion of wetlands to agriculture and urban development probably peaked in the period 1950–1975, with 11 million acres lost in that quarter of a century. At the end of the 20th Century, concerted efforts by agriculture, government, and conservation groups nearly halted the decline. With 100 million acres still remaining, the loss of 80,000 acres annually is a rate of less than one percent.[15]

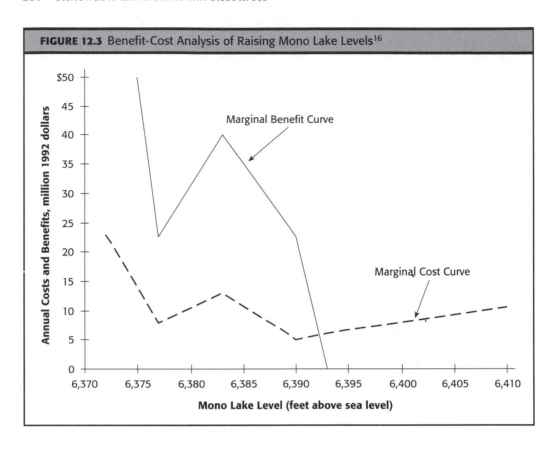

FIGURE 12.3 Benefit-Cost Analysis of Raising Mono Lake Levels[16]

The Mono Lake problem is a particularly interesting case study of economics applied to wetland management. For 60 years, most of the Sierra Nevada drainage flow into Mono Lake has been transported 300 miles south for Los Angeles's water supply.

The Lake itself is unusually salty and alkaline, but its shrimp and insects support millions of migratory birds as they move across the continent. The water diversion has lowered the lake 40 feet and reduced surface area by one-fourth.[17] In addition to the reduction in populations of shrimp, insects, and birds, the exposed salt flats result in massive salt dust storms.

Figure 12.3 summarizes the work of the Wegge group.[18] They used a contingent valuation survey to determine WTP (willingness to pay) for the increased wildlife and reduced salt storms that would follow from a restoration of Mono Lake. They included nonvisitors in the survey as well as visitors to the lake. By including nonvisitors, they address the issues of option, existence, and bequest values, which are discussed in more detail in Chapter 15 on biodiversity.

Their calculations of the cost of lake restoration are based upon estimates of the costs to Los Angeles of finding different sources of water supply and power generation. The Mono Lake level was 6,375 feet above sea level when the study was undertaken. The results, summarized in the figure, indicate that maintaining a Mono

Lake level at about 6,393 feet may be the best policy, balancing water supply needs and environmental values.[19]

Economic Benefits of Water Quality Improvement in the Willamette Basin and in National Water Supply

The Willamette River flows along the west side of the Cascade Mountain Range in Oregon, through Eugene, Salem, and Portland, where it meets the Columbia River on its way to the Pacific Ocean. In the 1950s, it was "grossly polluted," unsafe in many areas for drinking or recreation.[20]

Since that period, municipalities have invested nearly $1 billion in wastewater plants, and another $75 million in operating those facilities.[21] Paper mills also now treat wastewater, and agriculture and public and private forest managers have adopted practices that reduce contaminated runoff.

As with many regions, the effort has been successful. Notwithstanding the growth in population in Oregon and this basin, water quality has improved significantly.

Table 12.5 shows estimates of the benefits of that improved water quality. There are two problems with the results. First, although fecal and chemical contamination have been reduced, the impact on human health was not fully considered in the study of benefits. The magnitude of reduced gastrointestinal illnesses from water contact and fish consumption could be significant, but this health improvement benefit is not estimated.

A second problem is the range of benefits: the high estimate is more than twice the lower estimate in the table.

TABLE 12.5 Economic Estimates of Improved Water Quality in Willamette River Basin in Oregon[22] (1995 dollars; annual benefits, rounded to nearest million dollars)

	Lower Estimate (in million dollars)	Upper Estimate (in million dollars)
Fishing	$61	$84
Swimming	19	30
Beach use	9	56
Windsurfing	5	9
Water skiing	9	10
Jet skiing	1	2
Power boating	3	9
Sailing	1	1
Wildlife watching	9	44
Option, existence, bequest values	31	72
Total benefits	$148	$318

Note: The nine recreational categories account for nearly 80 percent of the benefit estimates. Individual items do not sum to total because of rounding.

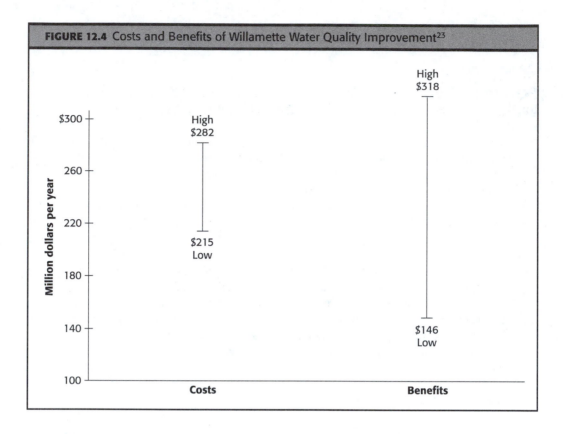

FIGURE 12.4 Costs and Benefits of Willamette Water Quality Improvement[23]

The consequence of these two problems is evident in Figure 12.4, which compares cost and benefit estimates. With the high estimates, benefits are greater than costs, and the benefit-cost ratio is 1.1. But, with the low estimates, costs exceed benefits, and the benefit-cost ratio is 0.7.

The report emphasizes the absence of health benefits in the study, and cautiously concludes that if they had been estimated, benefits "could exceed related pollution abatement costs."[24] In fact, given the widespread willingness to pay for improved water quality, I think this is correct.[25]

A national study of Clean Water Act costs and benefits was similar to the Willamette analysis. In one scenario, the 1972 fecal removal rate of 62 percent (a national average) was maintained while population increased. The annual cost of treatment was estimated to be between $15 billion and $20 billion annually. However, the benefit range of estimates was very large: from $16 billion down to a low estimate of $800 million annually.[26] Obviously, taking the midpoints of both benefit and cost estimates, national benefits would be less than costs. However, as with the Willamette study, the benefits of reduced gastrointestinal illness were not explicitly considered in the national study.

Given these results, some economists believe that expansion of water pollution control efforts will have costs in excess of benefits.[27] But this is uncertain unless the EPA incorporates health benefits in its water quality evaluations, as it already does in air pollution control analyses.

One possibility is that federal grants for construction of local treatment facilities have unintentionally encouraged local agencies to build expensive plants. This may have been more costly than would be the case if economic incentives placed greater emphasis on efficiency. In the New York City–Catskills example (Chapter 5), an imaginative program for managing rural animal and human waste is less costly than construction of a municipal filtration plant.

Marketable permits have already been implemented in acid rain and ozone pollution reduction programs, as the last chapter explained. This new innovation is beginning to be used in water quality policy. In New Jersey, effluent trading is being developed by the Passaic Valley Sewerage Commission.[28] This is a significant test because of the complexity of the water quality problem in the valley. The Commission is responsible for the industrial and domestic wastewater from 1.3 million people and 306 major industrial plants. As operator of a large treatment plant, the Commission seeks to simultaneously reduce its treatment cost and improve water quality.

Water Quality Economics and Developing Countries

The beginning of the chapter pointed to the relationship between international income levels and water quality contamination. The problem for low-income developing countries is severe. More than 2 million deaths and billions of illnesses are attributed to waterborne diseases that could be prevented with water and sewage treatment.[29] Without effective policies or income growth, the World Bank projected a "business as usual scenario" in which the global population without adequate sanitation would double to 3 billion people by 2030.[30]

The problem is particularly difficult because of the expense of good water and sanitation relative to low incomes. Whether for individual household systems, or community water and sanitation, the cost of U.S. levels of water quality is on the order of $1,000 to $2,000 per household. For countries and communities with incomes of less than $2,000 per household per year, this is too expensive. Figure 12.5 illustrates this problem. The first panel in the figure helps explain the Environmental Kuznets Curve. At income level I_m, households are able to begin to reduce water pollution by paying fees or taxes for sewage treatment, or constructing their own septic systems. The upper curve shows pollution growing without prevention or control. But, after income level I_m has been passed, water and sewage pollution prevention and control begin to reduce pollution, as in the lower curve.

The lower graph in Figure 12.5 shows rising expenditures above I_m to secure clean water and sanitation, again through fees, taxes, or household systems. As incomes rise above the I_m level, expenditures grow, causing the reduction in pollution in the top graph. This explanation in Figure 12.5 helps explain the logic behind the Environmental Kuznets Curve (from Chapter 2) as it relates to water quality.

But the implication for very low income countries is unpleasant. As their populations grow and their rising incomes are still less than the I_m level, water pollution and related disease may continue to increase.

FIGURE 12.5 Income, Expenditures, and Water Quality

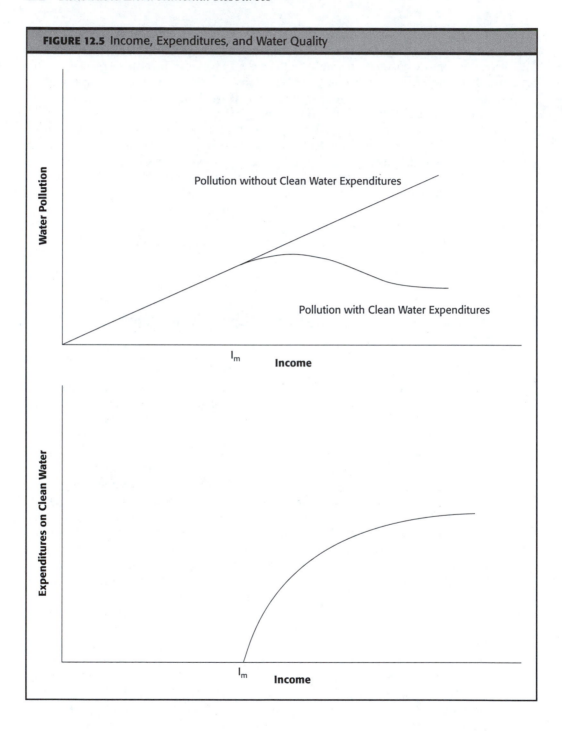

Conclusion

For developing countries, health problems from water quality contamination can be severe. Current waterborne disease causes an estimated 2 million deaths and more than a billion illnesses each year in the developing world. The Environmental Kuznets Curve theory suggests that for countries with low incomes, this problem may become more serious. The World Bank believes that $600 billion should be spent on water and sewer facilities in developing countries.[31]

Can water be considered a public good, in the sense introduced in Chapter 1? The answer is a qualified yes. If everyone (households, industry, municipalities, agriculture, and so on) cooperates in programs which permit appropriate reuse, and if prices charged for water supply and for wastewater treatment reflect both marginal cost and scarcity, then, possibly, water might be a public good. With these assumptions, it can be widely accessible to multiple users, at given prices.

Increasingly, repurification as well as water supply management will be considered in regions where fresh water resources are wholly committed. In San Diego, planning is underway to construct a facility to process sewage to such quality levels that it will be drinkable. All of the contaminants in Tables 12.3 and 12.4 will be reduced to health standard levels by filtration and disinfection. The city anticipates costs to be on the order of $750 per acre-foot (about 2¢ for 10 gallons). This is comparable to the opportunity cost of acquiring water rights from agricultural water users. It is less costly than seawater desalination.[32]

The overall picture of water quality in the United States is positive, but the recent trends appear to be slightly negative. Rivers and lakes are both declining in their attainment of designated uses. Wetland loss is still continuing, but the rate of loss has been lowered significantly.

Benefit-cost analyses of both the national gains from the Clean Water Act and the regional improvement in the Willamette River basin find that benefits and costs are of comparable size, and perhaps the net benefits of expanded water quality programs may be negative. However, this generalization must be qualified by noting that health benefits from clean water were not calculated in the analyses.

There are at least two implications of these results. First, the empirical findings in water quality benefit-cost analyses are very different from similar work in air pollution control. The air pollution studies make extensive use of estimates of the health benefits of air quality, as seen in Chapter 11, and typically find significant net benefits.

Second, it is possible that there should be a change in emphasis, with less capital-intensive treatment facilities, and greater use of cost-effective conservation and pollution prevention technologies and policies. New developments in the use of tradeable permits in the Passaic Valley in New Jersey may help define policies that result in improved water quality at lower cost.

Questions for Discussion and Analysis

1. From Figure 12.4, calculate the median costs and benefits of Willamette River Basin water quality improvement. What are the annual net benefits and the benefit-cost ratio? Do you think these results are valid? Why?

2. Does the Environmental Kuznets Curve for developing country water quality depend upon income and policy or income only?

3. It is widely believed by economists that federal subsidies for municipal treatment plants are too high and promote inefficiency. Explain this argument.

4. Consider these federal subsidies. Discuss the significant economic justification that arises from externalities.

5. Should protection of aquatic and wetland species be valued in benefit-cost analysis of water quality improvement?

6. What are two arguments on each side, pro and con, with respect to treating sewage to supply drinking water? Can these arguments be placed in an economic framework?

Notes to Chapter 12

1. The question of water supply economics (as distinct from water quality) is addressed in many textbooks, including D. C. Hall, ed., *Advances in the Economics of Environmental Resources, Volume I, Water* (Greenwich, CT: JAI, 1996).

2. N. Shafik and S. Bandyopadhyay, "Economic Growth and Cross-Country Evidence," World Bank Policy Research Working Paper WPS 904, Washington, DC, June 1992. They also studied air pollution, deforestation, and CO_2 emissions. In their work, they used the international purchasing parity method described in Chapter 2.

3. They reported a surprising statistic: a second turning point of $15,600. When per capita income passes this level, fecal material in rivers shows increases. The income statistics have been adjusted to 1997 real dollars.

4. In Table 12.1 the percentages represent mean values for five pollutants related to biological (and also chemical) oxygen demand, suspended solids, nitrogen, and phosphorus. Based on data in R. M. Lyon and S. Farrow, "An Economic Analysis of Clean Water Act Issues," January 1995 *Water Resources Research* 31(1):213–223.

5. Other designated uses are safe fish and shellfish consumption, possible water contact from boating, irrigation and livestock use, groundwater recharge, and Native American use for ceremonies, religion, or subsistence. See USEPA, *National Water Quality Inventory: 1994 Report to Congress,* pages 9, 10.

6. As of 1994. USEPA, "Environmental Indicators of Water Quality in the United States," 1996, page 12.

7. Figure 12.1 is based upon data in Figure 3 in *Inventory op. cit.,* page 152. The U.S. Public Interest Research Group is very critical of the toxic chemical releases into U.S. waters. See their "Troubled Waters: A Report on Toxic Releases into America's Waterways," 1998.

8. Table 12.3: See *Inventory op. cit.,* page 136.

9. Table 12.4 doesn't include waterborne parasitic worms such as schistosomiasis. The table lists organisms by their common rather than scientific names. Sources are *Inventory op. cit.,* Appendix E, "Public Health and Aquatic Life Concerns"; USEPA, "Strengthening the Safety of Our Drinking Water," 1995, pages 57–60.

10. USEPA, "Strengthening the Safety of Our Drinking Water," March 1995; and "Water," November-December 1996 *Backpacker.*

11. "Indicators" *op. cit.,* page 11.

12. USFWS, "Status and Trends of Wetlands in the Conterminous United States," 1997.

13. Figure 12.2 is based upon the EPA's Indicator 8 in "Indicators" *op. cit.*

14. The definition used by the U.S. Fish and Wildlife Service is a page long, and includes lands which are periodically water saturated as well as covered. See Appendix A, "Wetlands," *op. cit.*

15. See "Indicators" *op. cit.*, page 11. Agriculture is eliminating 80,000 acres annually, but restoring 15,000 acres each year.

16. Figure 12.3 is adapted from T. Wegge, W. M. Hahnemann, and J. Loomis, "Comparing Benefits and Costs of Water Resource Allocation Policies for California's Mono Basin," pages 11–30 in Hall *op. cit.* (See Note 1). The fluctuation in the marginal benefit curve may arise from the topography of the lake bed and from normal variation in contingent valuation survey results.

17. The discussion about Mono Lake is based upon the work of Wegge, *op. cit.*

18. Wegge, Hahnemann, and Loomis, *op. cit.* Their study also analyzes other nearby lakes.

19. Notice the negative marginal benefits above 6,393-foot level. Benefits become negative above this point because the lake's unique salt formations (tufa) would be submerged, and some shore bird habitat would be lost.

20. Industrial Economics, Inc., "Costs and Benefits of Water Quality Improvements in Oregon's Willamette Valley," prepared for USEPA, December 1997.

21. "Willamette," Chapter 2.

22. Table 12.5 is adapted from "Willamette" *op. cit.*, Chapter 3.

23. Figure 12.4 is derived from Exhibits 1-1 and 1-2 in "Willamette," *op. cit.* The costs in the figure are levelized at a 2 percent discount rate. As discussed in Chapter 4, a higher discount rate would have reduced the benefit-cost ratios.

24. "Willamette," pages 1–5.

25. Two 1993 opinion surveys report that more than 75 percent of U.S. residents are willing to pay higher water rates or taxes to improve water quality. In four years, *Money* magazine finds clean water to be the most important factor in determining the best places to live. "Drinking Water," *op. cit.*, pages 5, 6. Also, W. H. Desvousges, V. K. Smith, and A. Fisher, "Option Price Estimates for Water Quality Improvements," September 1987 *Journal of Environmental Economics and Management* 14(3):248–267.

26. USEPA, "Impacts of Municipal Wastewater Treatment," September 1995. The scenario discussed here in the text is scenario number 2 in the report.

27. Lyon and Farrow, *op. cit.;* also Richard Carson and Robert Mitchell come to the same conclusion in their "The Value of Clean Water: The Public's Willingness to Pay for Boatable, Fishable, and Swimmable Quality Water," July 1993 *Water Resources Research* 29(7):2445–2454.

28. The program is a partnership between the Commission, the EPA, and the New Jersey Department of Environmental Protection. See USEPA, "Sharing the Load: Effluent Trading for Indirect Dischargers," May 1998. An overall perspective on economic incentives is given in K. Stephenson, P. Norris, and L. Shabman, "Watershed-Based Effluent Trading: The Nonpoint Source Challenge," October 1998 *Contemporary Economic Policy* 16(4):412–421.

29. World Bank, *World Development Report 1992, Development and the Environment*, pages 4, 5.

30. *Ibid.*, page 112.

31. G. Gardner, "Recycling Human Waste: Fertile Ground or Toxic Legacy?" January/February 1998 *Worldwatch* 11(1):28–34.

32. Paul Gagliardo, Research Center, San Diego Metropolitan Wastewater Department, personal communication, April 13, 1998.

CHAPTER 13

AGRICULTURE, THE ENVIRONMENT, AND ECONOMICS

BY BRENT SOHNGEN AND
DUANE CHAPMAN

Introduction

Agriculture evokes powerful images in America: family farmers toiling from dawn to dusk; fields of golden wheat flowing in the wind; combines churning their way through row after row of corn; cattle grazing grassy hillsides. Despite the rustic image, environmental concerns and their economic consequences affect agriculture just as they do other industries. These concerns range from the potential effect of air pollution on agricultural production to the contribution of agriculture to water quality problems.

Before beginning our examination, however, the terms 'point source' and 'nonpoint source' pollution must be defined. Point source refers to sources of pollution that have well-defined outlets (i.e., pipes) into the environment. Examples include pipes into streams and rivers, storm sewers, or industrial smokestacks. Nonpoint source pollutants are those arising from dispersed or diffuse sources. These include agricultural fields that have many pathways for water to enter a stream (i.e., along the surface, underground, or through old wells), or automobiles. Most regulations to date have focused on point source pollution.

This chapter begins with an examination of the potential impacts of air and water pollutants on farms. It then explores the impacts of agricultural externalities on human health and ecological resources. Several interesting environmental issues are raised, including risk assessment, the relationship between farmers and the growing suburban population, and policy mechanisms for mitigating potential environmental damages.

The Effect of Air Pollution on Agriculture

Most of this chapter focuses on externalities arising from farming, but air pollutants, such as ozone and acid rain, can also damage agriculture and affect our food supply. Acid rain was a significant part of Chapter 11 on air pollution. It is a mixture of sulfuric or nitric acid with rain, snow, or fog. It occurs when sulfur dioxide (SO_2) or nitrogen oxide (NOX), arising from fossil fuel burning, mix with water and oxygen in the atmosphere.

Studies of the impact of acid rain began in the 1970s and early 1980s, when concern over damages to human and ecological resources led to the National Acid Precipitation Assessment Program (NAPAP). This program was charged with linking the science of acid rain formation with impacts on human and ecological systems and structures.[1] These studies found that, while acid rain could affect growth of crops through a variety of pathways, yields would not be altered substantially by existing concentrations.

Another pollutant, low-level (tropospheric) ozone, also can reduce agricultural production. (Ozone is also part of Chapter 11.) Low-level ozone occurs on hot, sunny summer days, when a complex chemical interaction converts nitrogen oxides (NOX) and volatile organic compounds (VOCs) into low-level ozone. Both chemicals result from burning fossil fuel. When low-level ozone contacts crops, it may reduce photosynthesis and nutrient uptake, both of which can decrease crop yields. Lower crop yields entail economic damages because they lead to lower profits for farmers and, potentially, to higher prices for consumers.

Despite these concerns, NAPAP and recent economic analysis of the Clean Air Act suggest that the economic damage to agriculture from acid rain and low-level ozone is actually quite small.[2] The Clean Air Act, for example, is credited with reducing low-level ozone by 15 percent between 1976 and 1990. The average annual benefits to agriculture of the Clean Air Act during this time range from $0.4 to $1.8 billion (1990 USD). Compared to the annual value of agricultural production in the United States, which is approximately $110 billion, this is only 0.3 percent to 1.7 percent of the annual value of agriculture in the United States.

In Chapter 11, the overall problem of economic incentives to reduce acid rain impacts is reviewed in the context of the marketable permit program. However, agriculture, as we have seen, is not a major consideration in U.S. policy at the generally low levels of air pollution now attained.

Environmental Impacts of Agriculture

Although farming may not be heavily affected by air pollution, there is concern that pollutants from agricultural activities cause human and ecological health damages. As Chapter 12 explains, agriculture is now the leading source of water pollutants (Table 12.1). Agricultural pollution is considered a nonpoint source externality because we generally cannot determine which farm or field is causing the downstream damage. This leads to several complications for policy that are discussed below. We begin, however, by considering a few particular externalities that arise from farming.

The Hydrologic Cycle, Soil Erosion, and Nitrogen

In order to understand the effects of agriculture on water quality, it is necessary to understand what happens to rainwater when it falls on agricultural land. At the beginning of a rainstorm, most water will enter the soil and travel through small openings between soil particles. As soil becomes saturated, rainwater flows across the land. While some surface water may evaporate, most water flows either into underground aquifers or aboveground waterbodies. Because flowing water may pick up soil particles, nutrients, pesticides, or other effluents from farm operations, the hydrologic cycle inadvertently transports harmful residuals from farm fields to downstream populations.

Soil sediments are one example of an environmental externality carried by water. While the focus of our discussion is on off-site impacts, soil erosion can also affect farm productivity. This occurs because soil is used like a nonrenewable resource in growing crops, and its erosion is similar to resource depletion as introduced in Chapter 6 and applied to world oil in Chapter 9. Soil erodes during rainstorms when plowing has left it bare. Because essential nutrients are lost with the eroded soil, crop yields may decline. Despite these losses, soils can be replenished over time by fertilizers or decomposing plant materials. In addition, some cropland receives productive net deposits of upstream soil in spring floods. In the United States, however, the average rate of soil erosion occurs faster than replenishment rates, so that, on the whole, farmers are effectively mining the soil.[3]

Estimates of the economic costs to farmers of soil losses are highly variable. One study, by a David Pimentel group, estimates that the costs are as much as $146 per hectare per year, while another study by Xu and Prato finds that they are a much lower $8 per hectare per year.[4] (A hectare is about 2.5 acres.) The wide range of estimates occurs because researchers measure productive inputs, such as nitrogen fertilizer, differently. Despite the potential costs, most farmers do not appear overly concerned with soil erosion because the most detrimental effects of soil mining will not occur for many years in most regions.

Perhaps the most potent downstream effect of soil erosion arises from nutrients like phosphorous, which are carried with soil particles. High levels of phosphorous in streams causes eutrophication, which occurs when phosphorous fertilizes the rapid growth of algae. As algae grow, they use large quantities of oxygen, depleting the oxygen resource for fish or plants. Other effects of soil erosion include loss of biodiversity when sediments cover important aquatic habitat, or the loss of capacity in downstream lakes and reservoirs when sediments fill them. Table 13.1 presents estimates of likely damages from off-site impacts of soil erosion.

A related externality is nitrogen contamination. Nitrogen can lead to eutrophication as phosphorus does, but there are other contamination issues as well. Although nitrogen is an essential component of life, when it reacts with water, nitrate is created. Nitrate is harmless to most people, but it can harm infants under the age of six months. In young infants, for example, nitrate may be converted to nitrite, which will reduce the body's ability to assimilate oxygen. The resulting "blue baby" syndrome can be deadly for these infants. Nitrogen contamination can be a problem for both public water supplies and private wells near agricultural fields.

To address nitrogen contamination, the EPA requires public water supplies to remove the nitrogen. The equipment to do this, however, is very expensive, and it may only be necessary during times of heavy runoff from agricultural fields, maybe 1–5 days a year. As an alternative, some cities can issue nitrogen advisories that caution residents to use bottled water. For private well owners, many states have developed

TABLE 13.1 Estimates of the Off-Site Damages Caused by Soil Erosion[5]

Production Region	1986 dollars per metric ton
Appalachia	$1.42
Corn Belt	1.15
Delta	2.45
Great Lakes States	3.74
Mountain	1.12
Northeast	7.06
Northern Plains	0.57
Pacific	2.48
Southeast	1.92
Southern Plains	2.02

testing programs to help alert owners to nitrogen contamination problems. Well owners may be able to avert some of the problem by altering behavior on their own land, but if the nitrogen source is farther upstream, they may have no recourse but to find alternative water supplies.

While nitrogen fertilizer rates have stabilized in recent years, nitrogen contamination from animal wastes may be increasing. Regulators are concerned that as agriculture continues to industrialize, livestock operations are becoming more concentrated. High concentrations of animal waste may result, with few precautions to minimize contact with water in some areas. The USEPA and USDA are currently developing regulations to address these issues with large livestock operations, and this emerging issue will probably continue to increase in importance.

Pesticides and Risk Assessment

Over the last few decades, the use of pesticides has grown in the United States, although it has stabilized. Although pesticides are used to eliminate harmful bugs and weeds in order to increase crop yields, the public perception of pesticides is negative. For example, the concerns raised by Rachel Carson in her famous 1960 book *Silent Spring*[6] vividly illustrate the potential harm that synthesized chemical compounds can bring to humans and the natural environment. This dread of pesticides, along with health and ecological effects, leads directly to the public policy dilemma confronting the use of pesticides in agriculture.

Pesticides are regulated in two ways. First, the federal government regulates pesticide registration with the Federal Insecticide, Fungicide, and Rodenticide Act (FIFRA). Regulating registration means that pesticides cannot be sold on the market until they are registered and approved by the EPA. Second, the EPA regulates pesticide concentrations through laws like the Food, Drug, and Cosmetic Act, the Safe Drinking Water Act, and the Food Quality Protection Act of 1996 (FQPA). The Food Quality Protection Act is a powerful new tool implemented in the late 1990s by the federal government and discussed more thoroughly later in this chapter.

In order to understand how pesticides are regulated, one must understand the concept of 'risk assessment,' as established in FIFRA. Risk assessments attempt to balance the health and other risks of toxic substances with the benefits, such as increased food production and greener lawns.

In order to see how risk assessment works in practice, let's examine the recent registration of acetochlor. Acetochlor is a corn herbicide used to control weeds and grass. The Monsanto Company originally applied to register acetochlor in 1983, but did not receive approval from the EPA until March 1994, and then only under restrictive conditions that require a large reduction in the use of other corn herbicides in the United States, such as atrazine (discussed more thoroughly below).

The first step in the risk assessment was to use laboratory experiments on animals to test whether or not acetochlor is a human carcinogen. On finding it to be a likely carcinogen, further experiments were conducted to determine the relationship between dose and the likely response in humans. With this information, the additional risk of cancer in humans could be calculated by assuming average consumption patterns, 100 percent use on all corn crops, and the highest possible residue levels. Under these conditions, acetochlor was determined to add a one in two million chance of contracting cancer for a person in the general population.

The risk assessment also considered the risks of acetochlor to farm workers, birds and mammals, insects, aquatic invertebrates, and fish. Farm workers would be exposed to additional risks in the range of 2 to 40 in one million. Ecosystems were not found to be affected significantly.

The main benefit of acetochlor is that it is a substitute for other, more risky, corn herbicides. Under stringent reduction goals for these herbicides, to which industry agreed, the EPA determined that using acetochlor would provide a net reduction in overall health risks from pesticides. Strict testing and monitoring guidelines of ground and surface water, as well as strict reduction goals for other pesticides, will ensure that these reduction goals are met.

While risk assessment provides a powerful tool for assessing the potential benefits and damages of toxic substances, it is difficult in practice. For example, using laboratory animals for toxicological experiments provides some evidence about the carcinogenic effects of compounds, but the effects in humans may differ substantially. Furthermore, most tests occur in a laboratory under controlled conditions. When pesticides enter the environment, the dose is not controlled at all, and there are usually many other chemicals present. Scientists may have little knowledge of the possible synergistic effects of many different chemicals on humans.

As discussed in Chapter 3, assessing the economic value of health risk is complex. Economists have employed a variety of tools to estimate the benefits of reducing risks, but we are still faced with the difficult prospect of valuing risk objectively. Objectively valuing risk is difficult because people have different levels of risk aversion, health or genetic histories, ages, and trade-offs between risk and income.

Turning now to the second method of regulating pesticides, we consider the case of the Safe Drinking Water Act and atrazine.[7] Atrazine is used by farmers to reduce weeds in corn fields. Federal regulations in the Safe Drinking Water Act require drinking water companies to provide water with less than 3 parts per billion atrazine to their customers. Despite this, some areas in the United States have experienced levels of atrazine in the water at higher concentrations, leading to the current policy dilemma.

Ribaudo and Bouzaher consider four options for reducing the risks to drinking water posed by atrazine. First, atrazine could be banned altogether. Second, water companies can install technology to remove atrazine. Third, one might ban atrazine only at certain times of the year, when it has the greatest probability of getting into water supplies. (This scenario is called "banning certain treatments.") Finally, a targeted approach involves localized strategies to reduce atrazine only in watersheds where standards are in danger of being broken.

Deciding among these alternatives is an interesting economic exercise where the costs of alternatives must be compared. Table 13.2 presents these estimates for the Midwest, as calculated by Ribaudo and Bouzaher. Without considering economic analysis, the risks of atrazine may suggest that a complete ban is justified. Ribaudo and Bouzaher, however, point out that risks can be significantly reduced, but not eliminated, at a lower cost. Society must determine whether or not the added costs of alternative strategies are worth the certainty of eliminating risk.

Finally, the new Food Quality Protection Act amends existing laws in many ways, perhaps the most important of which is that it sets a single health-based standard for pesticide residues in food. Under the new standards, the EPA will reassess safety tolerances for these pesticide residues over the next 15 years. These tolerances attempt to provide "reasonable certainty that no harm will result from aggregate exposure."

In addition, the Food Quality Protection Act clarifies conflicting messages in previous laws, the most potent example being the Delaney Clause of the Food, Drug and Cosmetic Act of 1958. The Delaney Clause effectively banned many pesticides in processed foods, while allowing these same pesticides in unprocessed foods. It also grandfathered many existing pesticides, while banning new pesticides, so that new pesticides with lower health risks could not be substituted. By setting a single health-based standard on cumulative, lifetime exposure, the Food Quality Protection Act attempts to minimize risks over all pesticides, regardless of the end product.

Another important component of the law is that it focuses heavily on the diets of infants and small children by allowing additional safety margins to be used in setting tolerances on foods used heavily by this segment of society. The safety of children is now explicitly considered in setting safety tolerances. Finally, the act considers the benefits of pesticide use more directly. Under circumstances where pesticide regulations would adversely affect national food security, or reduced tolerances would increase other risks, tolerances could be adjusted to balance costs and benefits.

TABLE 13.2 Estimates of the Costs of Complying with Safe Drinking Water Act Standards for Atrazine in Midwestern United States[8]

Proposal	Annual Cost of Compliance
Ban on atrazine	$517 to $665 million
Treating atrazine	$400 million
Ban on certain treatments	$224 to $295 million
Targeted atrazine reduction	$328 to $389 million

At this point, it is too early to understand fully the implications of this new law. The law, however, is likely to have profound implications for pesticide regulation in the United States. Economists will continue monitoring the process of resetting tolerances to see how costs, risks, and benefits are balanced.

Agriculture and the NIMBY Syndrome

The NIMBY, or "Not-In-My-Backyard," syndrome is most often applied to hazardous or nuclear waste sites. In recent years, however, it has entered the dialogue between farmers and their non-farm neighbors. Two trends here appear to be in conflict. First, Americans continue to flee cities, seeking refuge in rural areas. Second, agriculture is becoming more industrialized, leading to larger operations, particularly livestock operations. New residents in the country are therefore faced with a whole new set of unfamiliar conditions, such as the smell of pesticides and animal manure.

Perhaps the first question to address is whether or not there really is a conflict between farmers and their neighbors. A study by Thomas Stout and others at Ohio State University in 1990 and repeated in 1996 surveyed farmers and non-farm rural residents in seven Ohio counties at the urban-rural fringe to assess their attitudes about the potential conflict.[9] The study found no exceptional conflicts between farmers and non-farmers. While non-farmers rated chemicals, dust, and animal odors as the most objectionable agricultural externalities, 91 percent in 1980 and a similar 89 percent in 1996 reported that neighborhood conflicts were not normally related to farming. Only 9 percent in 1990 and 11 percent in 1996 reported that they were. When these same non-farmers were asked if they in particular had conflict with farmers, none of them responded affirmatively.

Conflict between farmers and neighbors can be investigated with economic analysis. For example, economic analysis of housing values in North Carolina by Raymond Palmquist and others found that hog operations located near rural residences had a measurable impact on the value of houses.[10] This study found that house values could be depressed by up to 9 percent, depending on their proximity to hog operations and the number of hogs. Despite these effects, the researchers found that the marginal impact of additional hogs decreased as more and more hogs were added, as suggested by economic theory. In contrast to the Palmquist study, Richard Ready and others found that Kentucky residents were willing to pay from $5 to over $200 per year to keep horse farms in the state.[11] Horse farms therefore appear to be a positive externality for residents in that state.

These three studies appear to have mixed results, but on closer examination, they tell an interesting story. On one hand, the evidence suggests that we place a high value on environmental amenities near our homes. The pastoral setting provided by crop or horse farming can help provide these benefits. Conversely, there is evidence that certain types of farming such as large livestock operations, as found in the study by Palmquist and others, can have a detrimental effect on house values and our quality of life.

The hogs and horse farm externalities in Figure 13.1 show this point. In the top graph, MPC (marginal producer cost) intersects the demand curve at hog output H_M, the market-determined level. But odor and health effects constitute negative

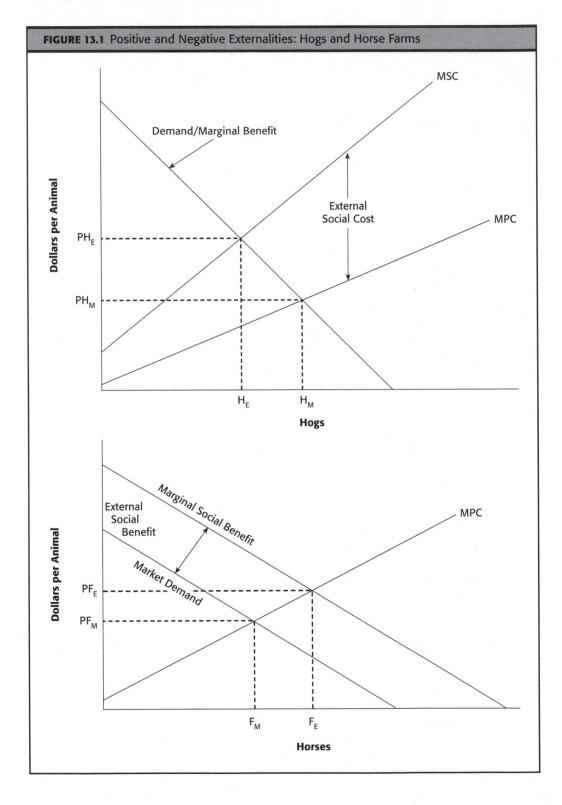

FIGURE 13.1 Positive and Negative Externalities: Hogs and Horse Farms

external social costs. The MSC (marginal social cost) reflects both the externality cost and MPC. But MSC intersects demand at H_E. Therefore, H_E is efficient in the sense that it optimizes net social value (Chapter 1 concepts again).

In contrast, the lower graph depicts a community with a positive externality: horse farms. Neighbors and casual drivers appreciate the aesthetics of grazed fields, fence rows, well-kept barns, and horses. Here the efficient social output level is F_E, higher than the market outcome.

Farm operations with severe regional negative externalities motivate the NIMBY syndrome and policies to reduce pollution. In contrast, farms with positive externalities may benefit from local tax protection programs, the federal EQIP program, and state programs such as the New York City–Catskills program. (The latter two programs are taken up later in this chapter.)

Food Safety: A Risk Assessment of the Benefits and Costs of Meat Inspection

Food safety is a major environmental concern, and this is particularly important for meat and poultry products. In the mid-1990s, the U.S. Department of Agriculture concluded that pathogenic contamination of these food products caused between 1.4 and 4.2 million cases of illness per year.[12] The mortality rate was small, but fatalities attributed to these illnesses were estimated to be on the order of a few thousand each year.[13]

The general source of contamination for these illnesses was in meat and poultry slaughter, processing, and product manufacture.[14] In order to reduce up to 90 percent of the pathogens, the Department of Agriculture's Food Safety and Inspection Service developed a new regulatory approach that focuses on a safe process.

This new system is described as the Hazard Analysis and Critical Control Point program, which will be referred to as "Hazard Control" here.[15] Its annual cost to industry is reflected in the flat line in Figure 13.2. (This is equivalent to one-fifth of one cent per pound of meat.) The possible economic benefits from better meat processing are shown in the two higher lines. Both the high and low benefit use the "value of a statistical life" methodology as described in Chapter 3. Unlike the Chapter 3 discussion, however, life's value as used in the Hazard Control study ranged from $1.6 million (for a young person with full earning power awaiting him or her), to a low of $12,000 (for retired persons with earning power behind them.)[16]

The difference between the two rising lines in the figure reflect variations in a complex assumption about the dose-response effect. Simplified, the high line shows that there may be a strong relationship between contaminated meat and illness, while the low line shows a possible weak relationship.[17]

The main result from this simple summary of a complex study: under the worst assumptions, benefits will exceed costs with 20 percent effectiveness. Under the higher assumption in the figure, the value of net benefits may exceed $2 billion annually through reduced illness.

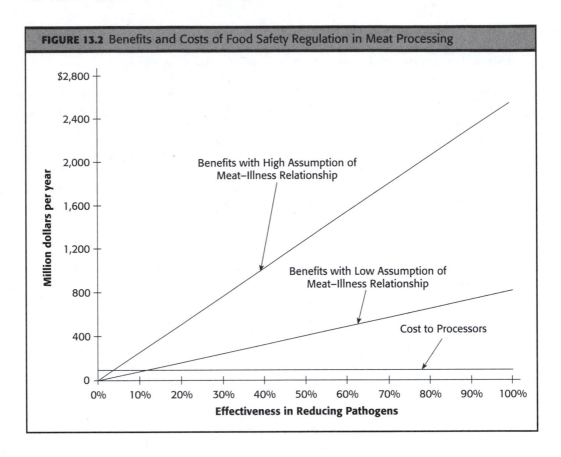

FIGURE 13.2 Benefits and Costs of Food Safety Regulation in Meat Processing

Reducing Agricultural Pollution: Policy Approaches in an Economic Framework

Finding policies to reduce pollution from agriculture presents many challenges to society. Economists often argue that incentive-based mechanisms such as taxes or pollution markets are more efficient than more traditional command and control. This section examines several approaches for reducing the effects of agricultural pollution.

Economic Approaches

Economists have tended to consider agricultural pollution problems as problems in information. With most point sources of pollution, regulators can observe the actual level of emissions. With agriculture, however, the regulator has less information about the number of firms, the technology employed by each firm, and the level of pollution from each firm. Furthermore, weather is highly variable, with a significant influence on pollution impact. This variability also affects the informational burden placed on regulators.

Economists describe nonpoint source pollution in terms of two economic problems known as 'adverse selection' and 'moral hazard'. Consider a regulator who would like to institute an efficient pollution penalty that penalizes farmers by making them pay the marginal cost of abatement. However, regulators do not know who the heavy and light polluters are, and therefore cannot determine the optimal penalty for each farmer. This is the problem of adverse selection, and it is similar to insurance markets where companies do not know good and bad risks in advance. One solution might be to use an average penalty across all farmers, but this means that regulators force light polluters to pay too much and heavy polluters to pay too little.

Moral hazard considers the problem from the farmer's point of view. Even if regulations are in place, why would a profit-maximizing farmer undertake pollution-reduction activities? Farmers realize that regulators do not know whether they are heavy or light polluters, so they engage in risky behavior by maximizing profits without regard for environmental externalities. As before, this is similar to insurance markets where individuals with insurance policies have incentives to engage in risky behavior. Thus, a lack of information on good and bad polluters leads to non-optimal pollution levels from a societal perspective, but optimal pollution levels from the farmer's perspective.

Economists have derived a host of theoretical mechanisms to deal with these informational problems. Kathleen Segerson, for example, proposes a scheme where farmers pay the full marginal damages, rather than their share. Anastasio Xepapadeas, on the other hand, proposes a system of subsidies and random fines. If aggregate pollution levels are optimal, each farmer receives a share of the net social benefits. If, however, aggregate pollution levels exceed the social optimum, one random farmer is penalized, while all others are subsidized. This mechanism may work in theory, but it is not likely to be accepted in practice because random fines may affect both heavy and light polluters. Another mechanism is the tournament of Govindasamy, Herriges, and Shogren. Such a tournament ranks farmers based on their input use or their pollution abatement effort. If pollution levels are higher than socially optimal, then the lowest-ranking firms are penalized. If, on the other hand, pollution levels fall below the social optimum, the highest-ranking firms are given a subsidy.[18]

While interesting, these theoretical mechanisms are difficult to institute in practice. Although they each require a different level of information, such information is costly for regulators to obtain. Furthermore, there is considerable political pressure against levying fines, and in particular, random fines. Regulation of non-point source pollution has instead focused on direct government subsidies and other mechanisms to mitigate water quality problems associated with agriculture.

The Conservation Reserve Program

The Conservation Reserve Program (CRP) is one such program. CRP is a voluntary incentive program aimed at removing highly erodible land from crop production. Annual incentive payments provide farmers financial support to remove land from crop production and plant it in species that provide year-round cover. Of the approximately 360 million acres of land in the United States that are cultivated every year, between 40 percent and 50 percent are estimated to be eligible for CRP, based on erosion criteria. To date, 33 million acres have been enrolled in the CRP program, with most acres enrolled west of the Mississippi River.

While CRP has enjoyed success in removing soils that are classified as highly erodible from crop production, it is not obvious how well the program has worked to reduce the downstream effects of soil erosion. Earlier in this chapter, we addressed the issue of risk assessment. The concepts of risk assessment can be applied to soil erosion, suggesting that if downstream effects are the public policy problem with which we are faced, efforts should be targeted to regions where the greatest damages are occurring due to soil erosion. The numbers in Table 13.1 suggest that the largest damages from soil erosion occur in the Northeastern United States, yet states in that region have the lowest percentage (in fact, it is often zero percent) of eligible acres enrolled in CRP.

EQIP: A New Program

The Environmental Quality Incentive Program, or EQIP, is a new program to reduce the environmental impacts of agriculture. EQIP was established in the 1996 Farm Bill, and it defined federal cost-share payments for farming practices aimed at reducing the environmental impacts of agriculture. Such practices range from reduced-impact tillage methods to better systems for handling livestock waste.

The economics of cost-share programs like EQIP are shown in Figure 13.3. The horizontal axis shows the number of acres that might be included in EQIP, while the

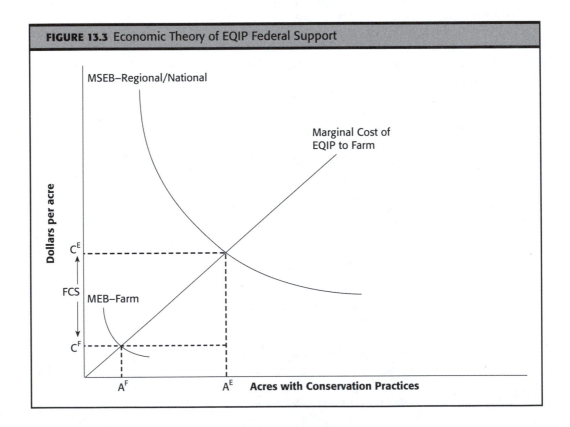

FIGURE 13.3 Economic Theory of EQIP Federal Support

vertical axis shows the cost for each acre with conservation practices. Costs per acre are rising as more and more acres enter the program.

When farmers enroll in EQIP, they receive some direct environmental benefits from the supported practices, such as improved health and quality of life from less dust or fewer smells, or the feeling of environmental stewardship. These benefits to a farm household are represented by the marginal environmental externality benefit curve (MEB–Farm) in the lower left hand corner. Without financial incentives, farmers will manage only a small number of acres with EQIP practices. This is A^F. The economic logic here may explain why few farmers adopt conservation practices on their own.

When society is considered, however, the marginal social environmental benefits are much higher, as shown in the middle of the figure by the MSEB–Regional/National curve. In some cases, where local farm practice affects better consumer health or migrating bird mortality over thousands of miles, the benefits of conservation practices are national or global. The MSEB–Regional/National curve intersection with marginal cost defines a much higher desired level of acres, A^E, for the EQIP program. It represents the environmental optimum, at least conceptually.

Theoretically, in order to obtain the efficient level of external environmental benefits, the federal cash incentive subsidy per acre (FCS) should equal $C^E - C^F$. These cash payments induce farmers to do more than what they would do voluntarily (A^F). Taxpayer costs are the area of the rectangle, $FCS*(A^E - A^F)$, while farmer costs are the area underneath the marginal cost curve up to the point A^F. Farmers, therefore, are likely to receive some surplus, or profit, from enrolling in EQIP.

The EQIP program is very new, and we have little experience from which to judge it, but farmers will probably take advantage of EQIP because it is being phased in as traditional price support programs are being phased out. The economic surpluses shown in Figure 13.3 may provide additional incentives for them to become involved in conservation management. It will be interesting over the next few years to see if EQIP meets its goals.

Incentive programs are only one way of addressing environmental concerns related to agriculture and non-point source pollution. State and local governments appear to be taking a very different tack from the federal approach just discussed. They are addressing problems from a watershed perspective, tackling local problems, often with unique solutions. In this section, we examine two such solutions, both of which have substantial agricultural components.

Economic Analysis of Voluntary Incentive Programs

As voluntary incentive programs, such as CRP and EQIP, have been used widely in agricultural-environmental policy, two key economic questions should be asked. First, one might ask if these programs will provide enough protection against environmental damages. Remember that the socially desirable level equates marginal benefits with marginal costs. Although voluntary incentive programs may spend substantial sums of money, if they do not spend the money on the cheapest alternatives, they will not achieve the social optimum.

Kathleen Segerson and Thomas Miceli recently found that the degree of environmental improvement in voluntary incentive programs depends on the strength of the threat to impose regulation. Behind all voluntary agreements lies the specter of traditional, heavy-handed government intervention. When this concern is credible and strong, firms will reduce pollution to the socially optimal level voluntarily. Further, Segerson and Miceli found, they will not require a subsidy. Where the government has a weak threat of regulation, which is likely to be the case in agriculture, firms may agree to make some reductions in pollution. Segerson and Miceli argue, however, that although some environmental improvements will occur, they will be much less than the social optimum. Thus, voluntary programs can be a useful component of environmental regulation, but they may not obtain optimal reductions in pollution in all cases.

A second question involves the details of voluntary incentive programs: are these programs designed to be successful? Sandra Batie and David Ervin suggest that this may not be the case in their current form, for several reasons. First, they do not always have clear objectives in terms of environmental goals. Many existing programs appear to have components of traditional farm subsidies that focus on income enhancement rather than environmental benefits. Consequently, government agencies have difficulty implementing these programs efficiently.

Second, voluntary incentive programs may not be flexible enough to provide the type of gain in social welfare that is desired. Batie and Ervin argue that many incentive programs force producers to use best-management practices that are desirable for farm profits, but may not be all that effective in reducing pollution outputs. Finally, Batie and Ervin point out that even if programs were made to be highly flexible, they would still entail high transactions costs. Institutions, including the USEPA, USDA, and producers, would have to undergo substantial change and education to learn how to use flexible programs in order to reduce costs enough to make the programs cost-effective.[19]

The Coase Theorem in Action: The Example of the New York City Water Supply

The case of the New York City–Catskills program was discussed in Chapter 5. From that discussion, we saw how the Coase Theorem might work in practice. The downstream party, in this case New York City, will pay for the prevention of future degradation in water quality. In the context of this chapter, the example illustrates an alternative to regulatory command and control, taxes, or tradable permits: a partnership.

The partnership occurred after New York City threatened to use its legal right under existing New York State law to regulate land use practices in the Catskills in order to maintain the quality of its water supply. After a backlash among residents of the Catskills, the partnership plan emerged between residents of the Catskills, the State of New York, the EPA, and the City of New York[20]. Rather than using eminent domain, New York City is purchasing environmentally sensitive land at its market prices. In addition, the City will continue to pay property taxes to local communities on this land. While the City and the State will develop a new set of watershed protection regulations, these regulations will only be implemented with the consent of the partnership council. New York City will provide funds to upgrade sewage treatment plants and individual septic systems, to build new sewage systems, to enhance storm water management, and to develop other stream corridor protection plans.

As described here and in Chapter 5, two important lessons can be learned. First, while the City must spend a significant amount of money on watershed protection, the partnership allows it to spend less than if it had relied solely on the new technology required by the EPA. Second, the partnership focuses on local acceptance rather than command and control. Acceptance will be obtained partly by monetary transfers, but these costs are apparently worth bearing.

Tradable Water Pollution Permits: The Example of the Tar-Pamlico Basin in North Carolina

The Tar-Pamlico basin in North Carolina drains an area of approximately 4,550 square miles into the Pamlico Sound of the Atlantic Ocean.[21] The environmental issues in the basin differ substantially from those in the New York City watershed. The main reason is that natural resource concerns encompass not only drinking water quality (there are many municipalities drawing water within the basin), but also damages to commercial and recreational fisheries, recreational boating and swimming, and other water uses.

Nutrient loading concerns revolve around industry, development, and agriculture. Nonpoint sources contribute 66 percent of phosphorus and 84 percent of the nitrogen loads to the surface water, much of which arises from the crop, hog, dairy, chicken, and turkey operations. The remaining loads arise from point sources of pollution, such as wastewater treatment plants and other industry. The resulting nutrient loads lead to algal blooms and fish-kills downstream.

With the designation of the watershed as Nutrient Sensitive Waters in 1989, the state developed a strategy that focused on strictly limiting new and expanding point sources of nitrogen and phosphorous loads to the watershed. These dischargers, in turn, developed the Tar-Pamlico Basin Association to negotiate with the state.

The Association feared that the costs of complying with nutrient load limits unfairly focused on them. It proposed a trading scheme that would allow firms to purchase nitrogen and phosphorous reduction practices from farmers, while at the same time meeting total nutrient reduction goals within the watershed. Like the marketable permits discussed for SO_2 reduction in Chapter 11, if the costs of reducing nitrogen and phosphorous loads from nonpoint sources are lower than installing new technology into wastewater treatment facilities, then firms can buy nutrient reductions from farmers more cheaply. Such a plan would fulfill the nutrient reduction goals, while allowing new plants to enter the basin, as long as they were willing either to install new technology or to purchase the necessary BMPs.

The Tar-Pamlico case illustrates several difficulties with water pollution trading programs. Perhaps the most difficult aspect of implementing such a system involves pollution measurement. This involves defining the baseline quantity of pollution from which future reductions will be measured. The baseline provides both regulators and trading partners with the necessary information to measure performance, but it also must be measured scientifically, and is subject to some debate.

A related issue involves determining who produces the pollutants that eventually enter the stream, point or nonpoint sources. This is important because all trading parties must be able to track whether or not they achieve their goals. A final measurement issue involves determining what pollutant, nitrogen or phosphorus, has the most impact downstream. Understanding this will provide regulators and policy-makers with information to better target activities that reduce pollution.

While pollution trading is an exciting new area in regulation, there are not likely to be many trades in the early years of the Tar-Pamlico program. Standards were not set all that tightly, so firms did not have to reduce emissions significantly. This may change in the future, however, as standards are projected to tighten over the life of the agreement. Another reason there will be few trades is that the agreement required the participating municipal wastewater treatment plants to determine if they are operating in the most efficient manner. If not, they must make minor capital improvements that would reduce nitrogen and phosphorous emissions. Nevertheless, the infrastructure exists so that industry and farming can continue to grow as water quality standards become more strict in the region.

Sustainable Agriculture: What Is It?

Many farmers, researchers, and policy-makers see 'sustainable agriculture' as an alternative to the industrialized farming that has dominated most of the post–World War II era. Proponents of sustainable agriculture have three concerns. First, they are concerned that industrial agriculture is using too many chemical and technological inputs, such as fertilizer and pesticides, and harming the ecological balance in soils. Second, they fear that, as farms become larger and larger, they are eroding the fabric of rural communities. Third, they suspect that farm profits are declining as farmers invest heavily in chemical and technical agriculture. Production costs may be reduced, they argue, if farmers invest more heavily in understanding and taking advantage of basic ecological processes.

Many individuals maintain that sustainable agriculture involves a philosophical change. A more inclusive definition says that sustainable agriculture is a set of agricultural practices that involve the intersection of the three key areas: farm profits, agro-ecosystems, and local communities. The primary goal of sustainable agriculture is to develop farming systems that promote each of these areas equally, rather than just one or the other alone. Previous practices, it is argued, often focused solely on farm profits, at the expense of ecosystems, farming communities, and externalities.

To give us a better sense of what is meant by sustainable agriculture, consider an example. When unwanted bugs, weeds, or diseases affect crops, many farmers turn to pesticides. An alternative to heavy pesticide use, however, is 'integrated pest management' (IPM). IPM involves a set of farming practices that use a mix of biological and chemical controls, as well as other methods, to control pests. Rather than spraying a farm field with the suggested mix of chemicals on the label, practitioners of IPM may choose instead to scout their fields before spraying, and spray only in certain areas where pests are evident. Alternatively, they may use reduced rates of pesticide application, or introduce new crop rotations, new pest-resistant varieties, or new crops altogether.

While a committed set of farmers embraces sustainable agriculture, an equally committed set of farmers is concerned that it implies that farmers should "move back in time." Despite these different views, we might ask if sustainable agriculture provides important lessons for all agriculture. Indeed, many large farms appear to have adopted these practices in recent years. They use IPM, reduced pesticide applications, conservation tillage, or a whole host of other sustainable agricultural practices. New technologies such as Geographic Positioning Systems, or GPS, may enable farmers to further refine these methods by targeting pesticide and nutrient applications to particular areas of farm fields, rather than applying a continuous amount over the entire field.

From an environmental-economic perspective, sustainable agricultural practices provide profitable alternatives to farmers who are increasingly asked by society to reduce externalities. With incentive programs such as EQIP (discussed above), we are likely to see continued adoption of sustainable practices in many areas of the country. In certain watersheds, such as New York City or Tar-Pamlico, they can also play an important role in reducing agricultural effluents. These practices are therefore an important tool to use for convincing farmers to shift practices to those that produce fewer externalities. They are not likely by themselves to be sufficient to eliminate water quality problems associated with agriculture, but they can be useful tools that help policy-makers and farmers deal with important environmental problems.

Summary

Air pollution as acid rain and ground-level ozone affects agriculture, but not significantly in most regions. Water pollution is important not because of its impact on agriculture, but because agriculture is now the leading source of water pollution problems. (The good news here, of course, is that municipalities and industries have done so well in the United States that they are now less important sources of water pollution.)

Precipitation runoff is an important factor in two aspects of water pollution. Soil erosion reduces farm yields, and animal waste and fertilizers add unwanted nitrogen to water supplies, with resulting health effects.

Risk assessment is being used to evaluate the costs and benefits of pesticide control and meat inspection. In both cases, health protection (sometimes using the "value of a statistical life" methodology from Chapter 3) is a paramount priority.

Theoretically, the economic externalities arising from agriculture are positive and negative. For positive externalities, federal and state programs create financial incentives for environmentally benign agricultural practices. In the negative case, policies include fines, regulation, and the NIMBY syndrome.

New initiatives involving both process and economic incentives are developing throughout the United States. Sustainable agriculture seeks to balance and protect farm income, agro-ecosystems, and local communities. IPM is an important approach arising from sustainability concepts; it uses modern technology to reduce chemical pesticide usage.

Two regional conservation programs are of particular interest: the New York City–Catskills plan invokes some of the concepts of the Coase Theorem, while the Tar-Pamlico Basin Association is attempting to utilize tradeable permits in order to reduce agricultural pollution in an efficient manner. In these and other programs, economics is making a contribution to solving the problem of promoting environmental protection while maintaining economic growth.

Questions for Discussion and Analysis

1. Describe whether the following are point or nonpoint sources of pollution:

   a. A wastewater treatment plant

   b. A 200-acre soybean field

   c. A 35-cow dairy operation

   d. A 2 million-bird egg-laying operation

   e. A construction site for a bridge over a stream

   f. A timber harvest

2. Suppose that a certain hypothetical pesticide named Garbazine is used by corn farmers and is linked to morbidity and mortality in humans who drink water tainted with the substance. In recent years, daily loads of this chemical in the Scootsol river basin has averaged 4.0 million tons. Because Garbazine happens to be the most effective pesticide known for reducing the damage caused by certain pests, environmental regulators have been reluctant to ban its use. A recent study, however, showed that the marginal benefits (in dollars per ton) and the total benefits of abating this chemical by million tons in the Scootsol river basin are:

$$MB = 100 - 25 * A, \qquad TB = 100 * A - 12.5 * A^2$$

   a. What level of pollution abatement do you think would be desired by hardcore environmentalists? What would be the dollar value of the total benefits of this level of abatement?

   b. The farmers who use this chemical have compiled information on their costs of abatement. They claim that the aggregate marginal and total cost functions for pollution abatement are:

$$MC = 10 + 20 * A, \qquad TC = 10 * A + 10 * A^2$$

   Given these marginal benefit and marginal cost functions, how many tons of Garbazine pollution should be abated for the economically optimal solution? What are the net benefits at this level?

3. Suppose that the TransNational Egg Company wants to install a two million chicken egg-laying operation in your rural, agricultural community. Can you describe three economic impacts of this new operation on the local community? Use marginal benefit and marginal cost curves to describe the situation.

4. If a large chemical company has a new weed-killing product that they would like to market, what steps would they need to take in order to bring this chemical to market? What is this process called?

5. You are the coordinator of a task force that is attempting to improve water quality in your 50-square-mile watershed. This area has three wastewater treatment plants, several large industrial wastewater treatment plants, and a land area that is 75 percent agricultural. Assume that 30 percent of the nitrogen pollution comes from the wastewater treatment plants and 70 percent comes from the agricultural fields. Can you think of two or three practical policies you could suggest to reduce nitrogen pollution in this watershed?

Notes to Chapter 13

1. Summaries of the research supported by the NAPAP process can be found in *Acidic Deposition: The State of Science and Technology*: Volumes I–IV, National Acid Precipitation Assessment Program. (Washington, DC: U.S. Government Printing Office, 1990 and later editions).

2. These results can be found in two studies, the first of which is the NAPAP results noted above. Another useful study is U.S. Environmental Protection Agency, *The Benefits and Costs of the Clean Air Act, 1970 to 1990*, 1997. This report as well as acid rain and ozone are major subjects of Chapter 11. Also: D. A. Westenbarger and G. B. Frisvold, "Air Pollution and Farm-Level Crop Yields," October 1995 *Agricultural and Resource Economics Review* 24(2):156–165. They estimate that the response in yield to ozone exposure is represented by elasticities of -0.19 for corn and -0.54 for soybeans.

3. For example, David Pimentel and others present evidence that average soil loss from crop production in the United States is 0.15 cm per year, while soil formation on this same land ranges from 0.0025 cm per year to 0.013 cm per year. See D. Pimentel, C. Harvey, P. Resosudarmo, K. Sinclair, D. Kurz, M. McNair, S. Crist, L. Chopritz, L. Fitton, R. Saffoury, and R. Blair, "Environmental and Economic Costs of Soil Erosion and Conservation Benefits," February 24, 1995 *Science* 267:1117–1123.

4. Feng Xu and Tony Prato, "Onsite Erosion Damages in Missouri Corn Production," 1995 *Journal of Soil and Water Conservation* 50: 312–316. The Pimentel study is cited in the preceding note.

5. Marc O. Ribaudo, "Water Quality Benefits from the Conservation Reserve Program," *Agricultural Economic Report Number 606* (Washington, DC: Resources and Technology Division, Economic Research Service, United States Department of Agriculture, 1989).

6. Rachel Carson, *Silent Spring* (Boston: Houghton Mifflin, 1962).

7. The information for this example comes primarily from Marc O. Ribaudo and Aziz Bouzaher, "Atrazine: Environmental Characteristics and Economics of Management," *Agricultural Economic Report Number 699* (Washington, DC: U.S. Department of Agriculture, Economic Research Service, 1994).

8. Table 13.2 is from Ribaudo and Bouzaher *op. cit.*

9. Thomas Stout, "Relationships Between Farm and Rural Non-farm Residents in Ohio: A Preliminary Summary," *ESO 2386* (Columbus: Department of Agricultural Economics,

The Ohio State University, 1997). Also, Thomas J. Bollinger, Pamela J. Brown, Thomas T. Stout, Gino M. Tosi, "Conflict in the Countryside? Farm and Nonfarm Neighbors Sharing the Land," *Ohio's Challenge* (Columbus: Department of Agricultural Economics, Ohio State University, 1990).

10. The results of this study can be found in "Hog Operations, Environmental Effects, and Residential Property Values," by Raymond B. Palmquist, Fritz M. Roka, and Tomislav Vukina, in the February 1997 *Land Economics* 73(1): 114–124.

11. Richard C. Ready, John C. Whitehead, and Glenn C. Blomquist, "Contingent Valuation When Respondents Are Ambivalent," 1995 *Journal of Environmental Economics and Management* 29:188–196.

12. U.S. Department of Agriculture, Food Safety and Inspection Service, "Pathogen Reduction; Hazard Analysis and Critical Control Point (HAACP) Systems; Final Rule," July 25, 1996 *Federal Register* Part II, 9CFR Part 304, et al.:38,806–38,989, especially page 38,956.

13. T. Roberts, J. C. Buzby, and M. Ollinger, "Using Benefit and Cost Information to Evaluate a Food Safety Regulation: HAACP for Meat and Poultry," December 1996 *American Journal of Agricultural Economics* 78(5):1,297–1,301. Specifically, the fatality estimate was 740 to 3,800 deaths annually. The four pathogens are scientifically known as Campylobacter jejuni/coli, Escherichia coli OH157:H7, Listeria monocytogenes, and salmonella. The Hazard Control program will add microbiological testing and treatment (and many other innovations) to the utilization of visual inspection. The Food and Drug Administration is pursuing a different solution to these food-borne illnesses, and has authorized meat irradiation to reduce pathogens.

14. USDA *op. cit.,* page 38,807.

15. The original benefit cost analysis is presented in present values. The text and figure here use annual values, with the usual methods; a 20-year, 7 percent present value factor of .1059 will reproduce the original USDA published values.

16. The Roberts group (Note 13) argues that the benefits of the Hazard Control program are much higher than shown in Figure 13.2.

17. See *Federal Register op. cit.,* especially page 38,965.

18. The Segerson and Xepapadeas proposals and other policy mechanisms are described more thoroughly in a recent book edited by Cesare Dosi and Theodore Tomasi, *Nonpoint Source Pollution Regulation: Issues and Analysis* (Boston: Kluwer Academic Publishers, 1994).

19. Sandra S. Batie and David E. Ervin, 1999. "Flexible Incentives for Environmental Management in Agriculture: A Typology." In C. F. Casey, A. Schmitz, S. M. Swinton, and D. Zilberman, eds., *Flexible Incentives for the Adoption of Environmental Technologies in Agriculture.* Boston: Kluwer Academic Publishers (forthcoming, 1999).

20. *The New York City Watershed Draft Memorandum of Agreement,* Sept. 10, 1996. See Chapter 5.

21. *Tar-Pamlico River Nutrient Management Plan for Nonpoint Sources of Pollution* (North Carolina Division of Environmental Management, Water Quality Section, December, 1995).

CHAPTER 14

FORESTRY ECONOMICS

A century ago, forestry in the United States was very different. Although the eastern forest had been largely cleared, the forests of the western states seemed inexhaustible. Each giant redwood, fir, or spruce was conquered individually by manpower and hand tools and moved by horsepower, steam engines, and flowing rivers.

As the 21st Century begins, environmental values increasingly influence forest economics. As we have seen (Chapter 10), recycled paper is competitive with new wood pulp as raw material. Another example of the new significance of these values is contingent valuation (from Chapter 3) of old-growth trees and endangered species. In addition, environmental considerations are influencing on-the-ground logging practices, with, for example, some individual trees now being removed by helicopter to protect environmental quality. Wilderness and recreation have always been part of federal and state forest policy; today, these traditional noncommercial values have been joined by new environmental dimensions in making forest policy.

However, in this chapter, the subject is the commercial aspects of forestry. Chapter 17 examines more specifically the macroeconomic influence of forestry policy on housing construction. Chapter 15 explores the economic dimensions of the emerging field of biodiversity. We see how benefit-cost analysis has been used to illuminate the national debates about endangered species in general and the spotted owl program in particular. Part of the focus at the end of the present chapter is the complex interaction of commercial and environmental goals.

This chapter's focus is upon the forest itself and the ecological and economic aspects of modern management. The main emphasis for application is the Douglas fir forests of Washington and Oregon, and the forests of the eastern United States to a lesser extent. As with other subjects, the basic economic and ecological principles are relevant to understanding forestry management anywhere in the world.[1] Table 14.1 defines some of the basic terminology.

Acknowledgment: To Richard Haynes, Gary Goff, Don Schaufler, Chuck Keegan, Roger Fight, Jon Erickson, Brent Sohngen, and Tim Fahey for their invaluable assistance in reviewing and suggesting material for this chapter.

TABLE 14.1 Basic Forestry Definitions

Board foot: a measure of the volume of timber and lumber equal to 144 cubic inches. It can be conceived as a board 12 feet in length and one inch in width and depth. See "cubic foot," and "recovery rates."

Clear-cut: as a popular term, it can mean that all the commercially valuable trees in an area are removed in one season. However, in actual forestry practice, it is strongly influenced by public policy and the owner's management philosophy. Professional foresters consider periodic clear-cutting to be sustainable yield management. In addition, clear-cutting can be undertaken to promote wildlife habitat.

Cord: a measure of volume usually used for firewood or pulpwood, but not lumber. It is 128 cubic feet; equivalent to a firewood stack 4 feet wide, 4 feet high, and 8 feet long.

Cubic foot: volume equal to a box of one foot in length on every side. It is used to measure both pulpwood and timber: abbreviated as "ft^3".

DBH: tree diameter measured at 4.5 feet above ground. The term means "diameter at breast height." Foresters use this measure rather than circumference.

Harvest: timber cut for use as lumber, veneer, firewood, paper pulp, etc.

Hectare: a metric unit of measuring land, approximately equal to 2.5 acres; precisely, 2.47 acres. It is frequently abbreviated as "ha."

Old Growth: there are many definitions. One arbitrary but simple definition is a stand of trees undisturbed by natural or human causes for 100 years or more. In the western United States, old growth may mean forest never logged.

Recovery rates: the proportions of a log that are processed into different products: lumber, pulp, fuelwood, panel, etc. Lumber is a high proportion for Douglas fir, and lower in the east.

Rotation period: a concept defining a management goal where harvesting is scheduled regularly at nearly constant intervals on a long-term basis.

Selective harvesting: refers broadly to a harvest that is intentionally less complete than clear-cutting.

Sustainable yield: the primary definition refers to a policy that yields an ongoing stable harvest indefinitely into the future.

Take: percent of standing timber cut for harvest.

Thin: reduce the number of trees in a stand to encourage growth of high-quality trees.

Two-by-four: a basic size of construction lumber. It is actually 1.5" × 3.5", rather than 2" × 4". (This is specific to planed, finished lumber, not rough-sawn lumber.)

What Is Sustainable Yield?

In the mid-1970s, the innovative work of Colin Clark revolutionized economic theory as it relates to natural resources. He succeeded in developing a multidisciplinary theory that integrated economics, biology, and mathematics.[2] One of his contributions is a definition of 'sustainable yield': it is the amount that can be harvested while maintaining a fixed population level for a biological population.

Obviously, this general definition is appropriate to most renewable biological populations, fish and pasture as well as forest. (Chapter 6 used a fictitious ecofin fishery to introduce modern economic thinking about sustainable harvests and environmental values.) In the forestry context, Figure 14.1 represents a typical natural growth curve for a Douglas fir stand[3] and is the basis for the subsequent discussion of profitability and sustainability.

Although the growth curve looks attractively predictable, there are so many interactive influences that the typical curve might be considered to be a theoretical concept. Soil, water, sunlight, and storm and insect damage can all influence year-to-year

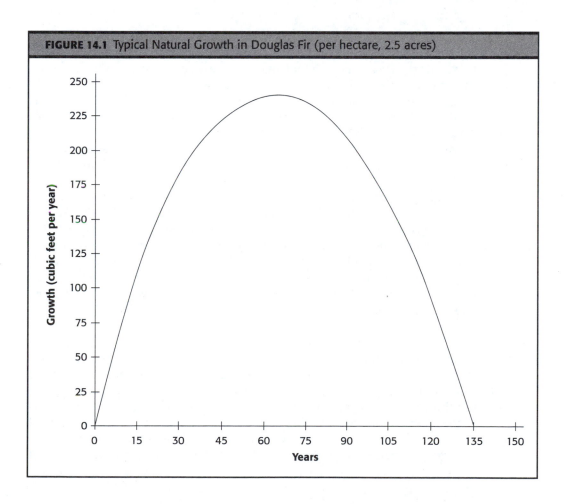

FIGURE 14.1 Typical Natural Growth in Douglas Fir (per hectare, 2.5 acres)

250 Renewable Environmental Resources

TABLE 14.2 Typical Stages of Douglas Fir Growth (on 2.5 acres)[4]	
A. *Natural Seeding:*	2,500 original natural seedlings; those remaining at age 30 may be growing as much as 2 feet annually.
B. *Mature, 100 Years:*	On a typical site, 400 trees, average 130 feet tall, circumference 4–5 feet, growing 6 inches annually. Average 500 board feet; very good sites can have 50 percent more volume, and very poor sites may have only one-third as much.
C. *Giant Old Growth:*	500 to 1,000 years old, 250 feet tall, circumference 19 feet. Oldest tree was 1,400 years when cut; 330 feet is record height.

fluctuations above and below this curve. In addition, the history of the original seeding will influence subsequent growth for centuries. A plantation of Douglas fir on old pasture will average better growth than in the figure. In contrast, natural seeding on an eroded hillside clear-cut will have much lower growth.

But the theoretical concept is that a typical plot would resemble Figure 14.1. Even without significant outside disturbance, the Douglas fir stand undergoes considerable evolution. Table 14.2 illustrates the development of forest stands. Of 2,500 naturally seeded sprouts on an average site, 400 (more or less) would remain a century later. Timber cutting at this time would produce about 200,000 board feet.

Consequently, the ideal growth curve in the figure represents growth in commercially usable wood, based upon the kind of evolution that is outlined in the table. It must be emphasized that both the table and figure represent typical values in the absence of major disturbances. Douglas fir has some natural dominance over competing species such as hemlock, cedar, and true fir. In addition, management practices may seed only Douglas fir, or involve herbicide application to other species. As a result of both natural and human factors, Douglas fir now exist in very large areas of even-aged stands.[5] This, of course, is very different from the natural multispecies successions in eastern forests.

The standing volume of trees is shown in Figure 14.2.[6] It represents the on-the-ground amount of commercial Douglas fir timber. Both growth and standing volume are also shown at 10-year intervals in Table 14.3, in the second and third columns. The figures are nicely smooth, but there is considerable debate about the shape of the volume and growth curves at very long growing periods. This uncertainty arises because the long growing period of Douglas fir and other commercial lumber species exceeds the experience acquired in the 20th Century. Some researchers expect a period of negative growth prior to a stable climax. Others expect

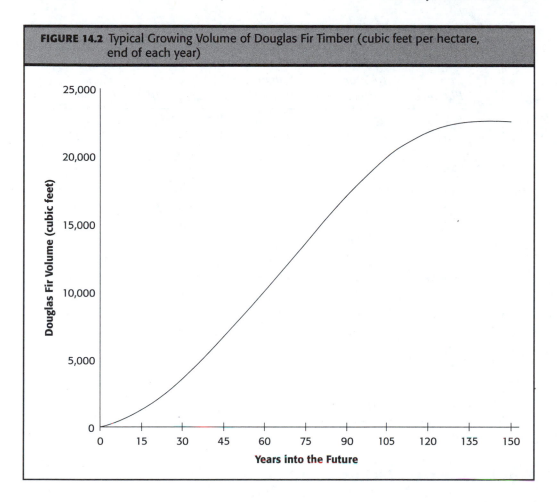

FIGURE 14.2 Typical Growing Volume of Douglas Fir Timber (cubic feet per hectare, end of each year)

a very long period of slow growth over a millennium. But the figures represent the simplest widely held views.[7]

In theory, there are many approaches to sustained yield forestry. For example, suppose the owner waited for 30 years of growth, to a total volume of 3,558 cubic feet. In that year, 1,646 cubic feet are harvested, bringing the standing volume down to 1,912 cubic feet in Table 14.3. From that point, every 10 years 1,646 new cubic feet would grow, and that same amount can be harvested each period. This is sustainable yield harvesting, because the same amounts are grown and cut on a continuing basis. (As we shall see, although this would be a sustainable plan, it is not the most profitable sustainable plan.)

In fact, any time period, in theory, can be selected for sustainable yield as long as the volume harvested matches the volume grown. In the table, the maximum sustainable physical yield for 10-year intervals is at year 70. At that point, 2,398 cubic feet are cut in each period. It is the maximum amount possible among many sustainable choices.

TABLE 14.3 Typical Douglas Fir Growth, 2.5 Acres (shown in Figures 14.1, 14.2)				
Years from Planting	*Growth 10-Year Periods (ft³)*	*Volume (ft³)*	*Price +1.1%/y (dollars per ft³)*	*Future Value (dollars)*
1	—	0	4.00	—
10	694	694	4.42	3,065
20	1,218	1,912	4.93	9,424
30	1,646	3,558	5.50	19,574
40	1,978	5,536	6.14	33,993
50	2,214	7,750	6.85	53,115
60	2,354	10,104	7.65	77,293
70	2,398	12,502	8.54	106,746
80	2,346	14,848	9.53	141,503
90	2,198	17,046	10.64	181,320
100	1,954	19,000	11.87	225,582
110	1,614	20,614	13.25	273,174
120	1,178	21,792	14.79	322,330
130	646	22,438	16.51	370,437
135	94	22,532	17.44	392,991
140	0	22,532	18.43	413,798

Note: Actually, price increases annually at 1.105%, tripling in 100 years. The last time intervals are 5 years.

Profit and Forest Management

As we saw in Chapter 10, real prices for finite metals and energy have actually declined. In contrast, the real prices for lumber in the United States generally increased throughout the 20th Century.[8] This introduces a complex problem for forest managers of both small woodlots and industrial forest plantations. The fourth column in Table 14.3 shows price in dollars per cubic foot rising at 1.1 percent annually into the future. This leads the price to increase fourfold in 135 years.

In the last column, the future value of harvesting is based upon the future price as well as the timber expected to be available for harvesting. How realistic is this growth value? It is based upon two separate trends. One trend is quality: older wood if unaffected by disease or other disturbance is of higher quality, and earns a premium above the price of younger timber. Second, and quite independently, the long-term trends of rising prices for wood products will continue. Actual prices in the 21st and 22nd Centuries will probably be higher than those in the table.

To find the most profit, the owner theoretically wishes to use the Net Present Value (NPV) concept again, as introduced in Chapter 4. The traditional approach is to use this definition of profit:

$$\text{NPV}_t = \frac{\text{FV}_t}{(1 + r)^t} \qquad (14\text{-}1)$$

The goal is to plan the timber harvest at the year that gives the highest present value profit. One way to do this is by a trial-and-error approach. We simply apply the Net Present Value equation to several different periods and look for the largest NPV. Table 14.4 does this for several possible waiting periods. It shows how Net Present Value changes as the owner anticipates a future date for harvesting timber. (The assumed interest rate is 10 percent, and Equation 14-1 is used with Future Values, as in the last column in the Table 14.3.)

The same method can be utilized to calculate the Net Present Value curve in Figure 14.3. This NPV curve is analogous to the profit curve in Chapter 1. Here, the owner seeks the optimum years to wait for harvest. In that first chapter, oil producers sought the optimum production level for maximum profit.

The curve is reflecting the declining growth rate in timber interacting with the rising price, and this Future Value (from Table 14.3) is discounted. The maximum NPV is at 18 years, at $1,414.60.[9]

In Figure 14.4, note that the optimum for 10 percent interest is also at 18 years, in a different context. This figure is showing the marginal revenue and the marginal cost of waiting. As each year passes, the standing trees are growing in volume, and the price is rising as well. This is the marginal revenue of waiting a year to harvest.

The interest rate shows the 'opportunity cost' (another Chapter 1 concept) of waiting. As each year passes, the owner loses the opportunity of investing the revenue from the timber sale. The owner loses the opportunity of a 10 percent annual return in some other investment. So, in Figure 14.4, it is always worthwhile to wait as long as the marginal revenue curve is above the 'opportunity cost' of 10 percent. But the maximum profit will be the year at which marginal revenue equals opportunity cost.

TABLE 14.4 Net Present Value (NPV) for Several Waiting Periods, Years to Timber Harvest (at 10 percent interest)

Years from Planting to Harvest (t)	Future Value (FV)	Discount Factor $(1 + r)^t$	Net Present Value (NPV_t)
10	$3,065	2.594	$1,181.60
15	$5,801	4.177	$1,388.80
*18	$7,865	5.560	$1,414.60
20	$9,424	6.727	$1,400.90
25	$13,944	10.835	$1,291.60

Comment: Net Present Value is calculated using Equation (14-1), an interest rate of 10 percent, and Future Value as shown in Table 14.3. (While Table 14.3 is primarily in 10-year intervals, Future Values can be calculated for all years.) The Net Present Value calculations are rounded to the nearest 10¢. The maximum NPV is at 18 years, as in Figure 14.3.

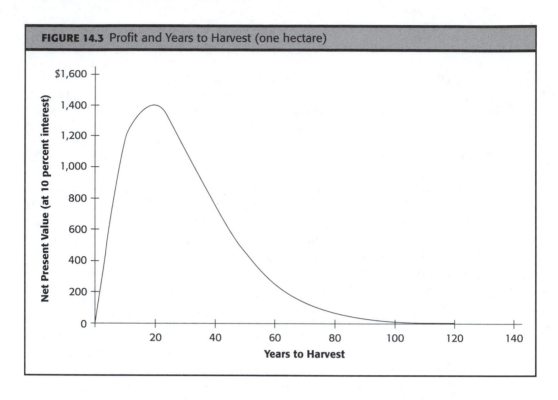

FIGURE 14.3 Profit and Years to Harvest (one hectare)

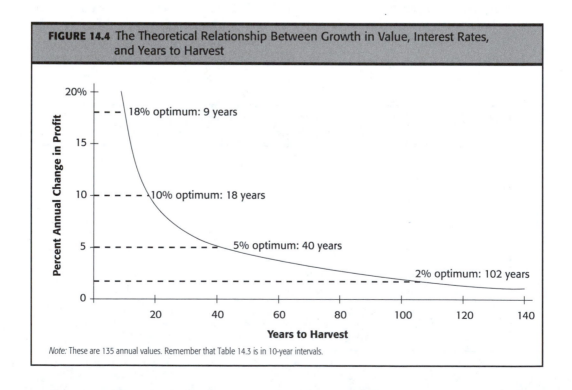

FIGURE 14.4 The Theoretical Relationship Between Growth in Value, Interest Rates, and Years to Harvest

Note: These are 135 annual values. Remember that Table 14.3 is in 10-year intervals.

Figure 14.4 shows the basic economic theory for selecting the growing period to harvest. The maximum profit will occur when the declining growth rate in value falls to the interest rate appropriate to the decision-maker. This is a simplified version of the Faustmann rule.[10]

For example, a high interest rate of 18 percent might be appropriate to a small operator with expenses charged to a credit card. The NPV is $590 for a 9-year period to harvest. Trees this size might be marketed as Christmas trees.

The next illustration is the 18-year optimum for 10 percent interest. This might represent an established company with reliable low-cost credit. The NPV here (with Equation (14-1) again) is $1,415. Obviously, lower interest means higher profit in the sense of NPV. These trees might be used for pulp.

Third, a 5 percent interest rate might reflect the finances of a wealthy family corporation. Here, the decision-maker can "afford" to wait until appreciation in value has fallen to this discount rate after 40 years. For this low-interest case, the maximum NPV ($4,829) occurs by waiting for the trees to reach lumber value.

Finally, 2 percent represents a hypothetical public forest agency concerned with long-term social values, as discussed in Chapter 4. Now, the decision-maker is maximizing NPV by waiting 102 years to harvest. (NPV is $31,162.)

The realism of these illustrations is uncertain. Historically, the harvesting of low-cost, old-growth Douglas fir dominated prices for all ages of Douglas fir and much of the lumber industry. This picture is clearly in the process of changing as the era of large-scale old-growth cutting is slowly drawing to a close.

As we move into the 21st Century, commercial forestry increasingly turns to new-growth lumber species, and the Faustmann rule (incorporating future trends in housing, exports, and environmental protection) may have a broad qualitative applicability.

In reality, year-to-year management decisions for individual owners are influenced by cash needs, mill requirements, sales, fluctuations in current prices, and even individual retirement decisions.

It is appropriate to end the discussion of profitability and Douglas fir by examining the economics of the choices available to an owner of old-growth forest in good health. The two broad choices under consideration are (a) cut everything now for a maximum value today, or (b) cut back the old growth to a less dense forest to encourage maximum physical sustainable yield.

From Table 14.3, the old-growth stand of 2.5 acres (approximately one hectare) has 22,532 cubic feet of standing timber, and net growth has stopped. At this age, there might be a 50 percent price premium over the initial $4/ft^3 stumpage price; assume $6/ft^3.

For Option A, the net present value of cutting everything is simply $6 * 22,532. (Note that the $6 appropriate to cutting today is a quality growth premium, and does not include the additional future trend growth. Both factors are added together in Table 14.3.) The result for clear-cutting today is NPV = $135,000. This is the first entry in Table 14.5.

Option B is more complex. First, the owner cuts 10,000 cubic feet. This brings the stand back to about the 12,500 cubic feet volume level, the maximum physical sustainable yield amount. In other words, theoretically, the owner is cutting back to the same growth level that Table 14.2 shows to be typical of the 70-year growth. Now

TABLE 14.5 An Old-Growth Stand: Clear-Cut Now, or Sustainable Yield in the Future?

Option A: Cut all 22,532 cubic feet now, valued at an average $6/ft^3. Net present value is $135,000 for 2.5 acres.

Option B: Cut back 10,000 cubic feet now, then operate on a sustainable yield basis of 240 cubic feet of harvesting every year. Total present value is $89,000, using the 5 percent interest rate.

Note: Dollar values are rounded to nearest thousand.

the owner can harvest on an indefinite basis about 2,400 cubic feet every 10 years, or perhaps 240 feet annually.[11]

For Option B, NPV has two components. The first segment of NPV is the immediate cash from cutting 10,000 cubic feet at $6/ft^3. This yields $60,000. The second segment represents the Net Present Value of a permanent future annual return. Every year, 240 cubic feet are harvested and sold, earning $1,440 annually. Conceptually, it is the present value equivalent of the "eternal" levelized cost[12] introduced in Chapter 4. At the 5 percent interest rate, NPV is $1,440 ÷ 5 percent.

$$\text{For } n \div \infty, \text{NPV} = \frac{C}{r} = \$29,000 \qquad (14\text{-}2)$$

Therefore, the Net Present Value for the sustainable yield plan is the sum of the two components: first, the one-time large cutback to the maximum growth rate forest, and second, the value of the ongoing sustainable yield. The two together are worth $89,000. This isn't fully realistic, because the clear-cut will have lower labor and equipment costs on a per cubic foot basis. However, the two options in Table 14.5 show, at least in a general way, why clear-cutting in old-growth Douglas fir has historically been much more profitable than moving to sustainable yield management.

But—and this is important—if the trend in growth in prices continues or accelerates in the future, then this situation will be dramatically reversed. Converting old-growth inventory to sustainable yield would become the profitable choice for many forest owners. To grossly simplify this point, a predictable regular annual increase in real inflation-adjusted prices of at least 5 percent would make sustainable yield management a practical and profitable option in many situations.

The Eastern Forest[13]

Since the peak of agriculture in the Northeastern United States in the 1800s, much of the former cropland and pasture has returned to woods. New York State, which many people may see as an urban state, is now more than 70 percent woods. All of the New England states and Pennsylvania are more than 50 percent woodland.[14] For the South, there has been a comparable return to forest.

As a result, many regionally extinct or scarce wildlife species in the East have returned in large numbers to their prior forest homes. This not only includes bear and deer, but also coyotes, bobcats, beaver, moose and wolves (in some areas), turkeys, grouse, wood and hermit thrushes, and even salamanders.

Throughout the 20th Century, the Western United States dominated the lumber industry. However, because of the return of much Eastern farmland to forest, there is a growing forest industry outside its traditionally strong areas in the South and in Maine.

The concepts of profitability, the Faustmann rule, and sustainable yield are equally applicable to the forests of the Eastern United States as they are to the Pacific Northwest. However, the natural ecology of forests differ, so the interaction of ecology and economics has different results for commercial forest management in the East.

In the Northwest, we saw that nearly single-species stands of Douglas fir are common. In the East, an old-growth forest may have 50 tree species with the dominant economic value associated with oaks, maples, ash, and sometimes black cherry.

With prices equal to $5/ft^3, the stumpage value of a hectare of 100-year-old Western Douglas fir might be $100,000. For a hectare of typical hardwoods in the East of similar age, the value might be $5,000. (On a per-acre basis, these values are $40,000 and $2,000.)[15]

In terms of physical sustainable yield, the preceding representative maximum value for Douglas fir was 240 ft^3 annually. In the East, 100 ft^3 would be typical.

The financial values are very different between the two regions. Table 14.6 shows estimates of commercial value for two 70-year-old stands in a managed forest in a rural area in Western New York. Stand B of planted red pine has essentially no commercial value. Stand A nearby is more typical, with $1,250 in lumber and firewood value. If Stand A were allowed to grow another 30 years, it could reach a value of $2,000 at age 100. But this very small increase in value would not be financially

TABLE 14.6 Commercial Forest Value, Two New York Stands (one acre each, 70 years old)

Type	Representative Value, Mixed Hardwoods	Low Value, Red Pine
Trees per acre	405	460
Lumber:	Red oak 1,425 BF White ash 1,055 BF	No lumber quality; planted red pine
Total Lumber Value:	$1,050	None
Firewood	$200 (20 cords)	$120 (12 cords)
Pulpwood aspen	None	$40 (20 tons)
Total Commercial Value:	$1,250	$160

Source: Gary Goff and Don Schaufler, Cornell University, personal communication, April 20, 1996.

profitable; it represents only 1.6 percent increase in value annually, and does not include any charges for property taxes or mortgage payments.

There can be important local exceptions to the earlier generalization about the financial feasibility of commercial forests in the East. A well-protected site with good soil can have much higher values at 70 and 100 years. Black cherry veneer, or furniture-quality oak and maple can have higher growth rates as well as a quality premium in price. These factors would significantly raise values on a good site.

In general, however, forest ownership in much of the Eastern United States was not economically viable in terms of commercial forestry in the 20th Century. Much of the growth in forest on unused farmland in the East has taken place simply because farming is not as financially feasible in as many areas as it was previously.

There are three major economic incentives for private ownership in this region. First, income can be gained from cabin leases or hunting fees. Second, there has been a widespread anticipation of rising property values which is independent of current forest cover or use. Third, nonmarket benefits can be significant. Small woods owners or corporations may derive satisfaction from the wildlife and plant life that inhabit a forest, and its aesthetic existence value.

The option and existence externality value of forests has become increasingly important in the East. In New York, for example, small woodlots and industrial forests can attain significant local property tax exemptions if the owners agree to commit the property to timber harvesting on a long-term basis. In addition, the growing use of conservation easements may result in property tax reductions.

As with Douglas fir in the West, there is considerable uncertainty in the East about the long-term trends in wood product prices. However, the declining availability of old-growth Western trees may in the 21st Century accelerate price growth for lumber and wood products. Commercial forestry is important now in many areas in the East. That importance will increase, and sustainable yield forestry may become profitable on a commercial basis.

Commercial Forestry and the Environment: Externalities, Air Pollution, and the Spotted Owl

Since the Wilderness and Multiple Use–Sustained Yield federal legislation of the 1960s, forest management has become increasingly influenced by environmental considerations. Private forest owners as well as the U.S. National Forest Service must weigh these factors in making management decisions.

From an economic perspective, the environmental influences can be divided into two broad categories. Both categories are externalities as introduced in Chapter 1. The positive externalities arise because a forest provides as a byproduct to its commercial value a broad array of public benefits. Several of these are listed in Table 14.7.

The negative externalities have the opposite source-effect direction: forest growth is harmed as an unintentional byproduct of other economic activity. Emerging research on air pollution damage has introduced new findings on the magnitude of pollution impact on the type of growth curve introduced as Figure 14.1. In contrast to that figure, Figure 14.5 shows a significant hypothetical reduction in growth

TABLE 14.7 Economic Externalities and the Commercial Forest

A. *Positive Externalities Arising from Forest Growth*
Existence value of old-growth trees
Wilderness protection
Endangered species' use of forest habitat
Use value: recreation, hiking, hunting and fishing
Absorb atmospheric CO_2, reduce climate change
Improve water supply

B. *Negative Externalities Affecting Forest Growth*
Ozone, acid deposition, and heavy metal pollution
Possible climate change[17]
Local areas: recreation overuse

because of air pollution. It is based upon the work of Gene Likens, Donald Buso, and Charles Driscoll.[16] In the most detailed scientific research on this problem to date, they report that forest growth at their New Hampshire study site slowed in the mid-1980s. They attribute this to the cumulative impact of acid deposition. Notwithstanding the dramatic gains in air pollution control and the reduced sulfur

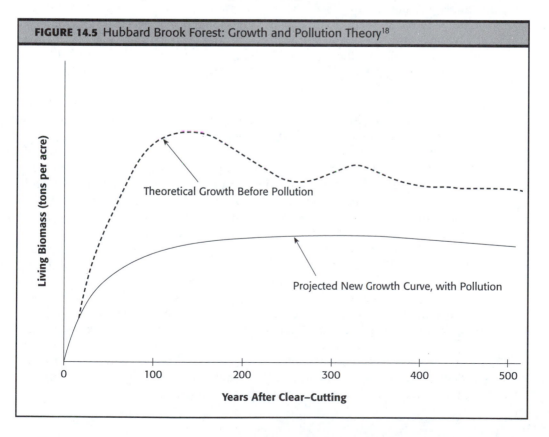

FIGURE 14.5 Hubbard Brook Forest: Growth and Pollution Theory[18]

Living Biomass (tons per acre)

Theoretical Growth Before Pollution

Projected New Growth Curve, with Pollution

0   100   200   300   400   500

Years After Clear–Cutting

emissions reported in Chapter 11, even today's dramatically lower pollution levels are too high to permit natural recovery, according to the Likens group.

However, it must be pointed out that the Likens work has not received full acceptance. It may be the case that the "before pollution" curve is simply wrong, and the lower curve may be correct regardless of acid deposition levels.

In earlier work prior to the Hubbard Brook findings, Kaiser et al. estimated the effects of air pollution damage at about $1 billion annually, and increasing. They assumed growth reductions in the East on the order of 5 percent to 10 percent. There is clear evidence of air pollution damage on some forests, and in general this is occurring in natural areas not now suitable for commercial forestry.[19]

Positive externalities are being recognized in new forestry policies. The protection program for the spotted owl, for example, requires selective harvesting, in that fixed percentages of living trees must be left on stands approved for logging. Regulations prescribe the size of down logs and standing dead trees that are to remain after logging.[20] (The next chapter on biodiversity reviews the benefits and costs of the spotted owl program.)

The growing use of selective harvesting on public land has an impact on commercial forestry. For example, one policy might allow the harvesting of the best 20 percent of the trees on each hectare.[21] Another approach would mark the best 20 percent for retention, but allow maximum take on the remaining 80 percent.

These environmentally beneficial selective harvesting policies affect the commercial logger in two ways. First, there is less timber harvested from each stand, so revenue is reduced. Second, the greater care in logging raises cost per cubic foot. The obvious result is less revenue, higher cost, and less profit per log. This, in turn, translates into higher lumber and construction prices. In a theoretical sense, the cost of environmental protection becomes internalized in the price for lumber in the same way that pollution control costs have become internalized in electricity rates and automobile prices.

As externalities assume a growing role in forest management and harvesting policies on public lands, the role of 'stakeholders' is being increasingly recognized. The U.S. Forest Service (as well as the Bureau of Land Management) is tentatively working with local groups to map out management plans for National Forests. The basic ideas may be cooperation and compromise: environmentalists, timber mills, and local businesses each acknowledge that their particular goals will not be wholly accommodated. Starting from this acknowledgment, the cooperative management group works out specific agreements of the kind outlined in Table 14.8.

The Quincy Library Group takes its name from the Library in Quincy, California, a town with 5,000 residents in the Sierra Nevada Mountains in Northern California. The group of 20 or so townspeople began meeting in the Library in 1993; it includes environmentalists, lumber industry employees, local business people, and U.S. Forest Service staff. Their success in working out a common proposal as summarized in the table has had significant impact on Congressional and Forest Service policy.[22]

These two new developments in forest management (the recognition of environmental externalities, and the emergence of cooperative management groups) are being paralleled by new research findings in economics.

TABLE 14.8 Quincy Library Group Management Plan, 1998[24] (major features)	
A. *Land Categories for the National Forests*	
Timber management	1.6 million acres
Botanical and special areas	148,000 acres
Back-country recreation including vehicles	346,000 acres
California spotted owl protection	125,000 acres
Wilderness	101,000 acres
Total national forest area in plan	2.3 million acres
B. *Major Management Policy Change*	
Clear-cut zones reduced to 2 acres, from 40 acres	
Expanded river protection zones	
50,000 acres cleared annually of dead wood, small trees	

It is increasingly clear that every forest area cannot be managed simultaneously for profit-maximizing clear-cuts and nontimber biodiversity and nonmarket values.[23] The current trend is to continue rotating clear-cuts, but in smaller plots, and to increase the areas with selective harvesting while reducing the areas on which clear-cutting is used.

Special areas for endangered species are being created (as with the spotted owl), and no-cut areas on steep hillsides and river banks are being defined.

Backpackers, offroad vehicles, and horses are each being assigned to areas restricted to one or two of these recreational uses.

This is still multiple use for national forests, but increasingly it means, essentially, zoning the national forests. Federal forest policy is interacting formally with local groups, continuing its historical cooperation with the timber industry, and recognizing the importance of environmental values.

From this chapter, it should be clear that competitive markets favor clear-cutting because this practice results in greater profit, lower wood product prices, or both. Consequently, the existence of positive environmental externalities from forest management is the basis for public policies affecting commercial forestry. In the next chapter on biodiversity, the nature of these externalities is explored in greater detail. The northern spotted owl protection program is examined as it relates to the economic valuation of species protection as well as the impact on employment.

Questions for Discussion and Analysis

1. Suppose you are a forester helping your neighbor manage her 1,000-acre stand of Douglas fir. If she says to you that she can maximize the value of her land by harvesting trees when they are 120 years old because this would maximize sustained yield, how would you respond?

2. As trees age, a profit-maximizing landowner is said to compare the marginal benefits with the marginal opportunity costs of waiting one more year to harvest trees. Describe the marginal opportunity costs of waiting to harvest trees.

3. Assess how the following changes in market conditions would affect the optimal economic period to harvest a 50 year old stand of Douglas fir.

    a. An increase in interest rates from 5 percent to 10 percent

    b. A decrease in timber prices

    c. A new owner who values elder timber stands, including old growth

    d. An increase in the demand for old timber

4. As the owner of a 500-acre plot of Eastern mixed hardwoods that are approximately 70 years old, you can cut and regenerate your stand now for $1,250 profit. Alternatively, you can wait 30 more years and gain $2,000 at harvest.

    a. If your interest rate is 5 percent, what should you do?

    b. If you can also get $500 per year in hunting fees without timber harvesting, would this change your answer?

    c. Suppose you can also get high-quality veneer logs in 30 more years, so your stand would be worth $10,000 then. How does this affect your answer?

5. Prices for nonrenewable resources have generally declined recently, while prices for timber, a renewable resource, have increased 1 percent to 4 percent per year. Can you provide any logical reasons for this?

Notes to Chapter 14

1. There are two helpful texts with additional introductory material on forestry and environmental economics. They are Tietenberg's (*op. cit.*) Chapter 11, and Chapters 10 and 11 in J. R. Kahn, *The Economic Approach to Environmental and Natural Resources* (Orlando, FL: Dryden Harcourt Brace, 1995). There are several good texts that offer a detailed introduction to forestry: one is G. W. Sharpe, C. W. Hendee, and W. F. Sharpe, *Introduction to Forestry* (New York: McGraw-Hill, 1986). Also, see the references in Note 10 below.

2. C. W. Clark, *Mathematical Bioeconomics: The Optimal Management of Renewable Resources* (New York: Wiley, 1976 and 1990).

3. Figure 14.1 is the forestry adaptation of the growth curve introduced with Figure 6.1 and ecofins. This forest growth figure is based upon Tietenberg's growth equation (Tietenberg, page 249), which is in turn based upon the work of Marion Clawson, "Decision Making in Timber Production, Harvesting, and Marketing," Research Paper R-4 (Washington, DC: Resources for the Future, 1977). The growth function in the figure is $G = 40 + 6.2t - .048t^2$, and the volume function is $V = 40t + 3.1t^2 - .016t^3$.

4. The sources for Table 14.2 are USDA Agriculture Handbook 654, *Silvics of North America* (Washington, DC, 1990), and 271, *Silvics of Forest Trees of the United States* (Washington, DC, 1965). Remember that a metric hectare is approximately 2.5 acres and precisely 2.47 acres.

5. There has been modest controversy about the taxonomic name of Douglas fir. Although its morphology is quite similar to both fir (apies) and spruce (picea), it occupies a separate genus, *Pseudotsuga* (or false hemlock—a misleading designation that further complicates elucidation), within the Pinaceae (pine family). For historical information see D. C. Peattie, *A Natural History of Western Trees* (Boston, MA: Houghton Mifflin, 1953), pages 170–181, and W. M. Harlow, E. S. Harrar, J. W. Hardin, and F. M. White, *Textbook of Dendrology*, eighth edition (New York, NY: McGraw-Hill, 1996), page 173.

6. Table 14.3 and the figures are intended to represent a "west side" stand. This is to the west of the Cascade peaks, to the Pacific Ocean. The stumpage initial price of $4 per cubic foot represents lumber, pulp, panel, and other values. The lumber mill recovery might be 8 board feet per cubic foot, with a price of 45¢ per board foot for lumber alone. The intention is to give a simplified but logical picture; it might be helpful to imagine the table reflecting volume and prices on a west side stand that is fairly flat, easily accessible, and allows a maximum take. Compare this Figure 14.2 for Douglas fir to Figure 6.2 and ecofins.

7. F. H. Borman and G. E. Likens favor a transition phase in which biomass declines slightly from its peak and then stabilizes; see their *Patterns and Process in a Forested Ecosystem* (New York: Springer-Verlag, 1979), especially pages 166–167. Jon Conrad ("Old Growth Forests and Jobs," unpublished, Cornell University, 1996) favors a growth function which asymptotically approaches zero. His conclusion is based upon the Douglas fir yield data of R. E. McArdle, "The Yield of Douglas Fir in the Pacific Northwest," Technical Bulletin 201 (U.S. Forest Service, Pacific Northwest Experiment Station, 1930). Clark (*op. cit.,* page 261) favors a growth curve that simply falls to zero, similar to Figure 14.1 in the text.

8. From the 1920s to the 1990s, inflation-adjusted Douglas fir stumpage prices increased nearly fourteenfold. There is very significant seasonal and year-to-year variation around this trend. Brent Sohngen and Richard Haynes, "The Great Price Spike of '93: An Analysis of Lumber and Stumpage Prices in the Pacific Northwest," PNW-RP-476 (U.S. Forest Service, Pacific Northwest Research Station, 1994).

9. The FV is $7,865 for year 18, discounted at 10 percent, to $1,414.60. See the growth and volume functions in Note 3.

10. The complete Faustmann rule incorporates a theoretical infinite planning period of harvesting cycles, and is typically expressed as $(dV/dt)/V = r/(1 - e^{-rT})$. It is named after Martin Faustmann. See Clark *op. cit.* page 259; Claire A. Montgomery and Darius M. Adams, "Optimal Timber Management Policies," Chapter 17 in D. W. Bromley, ed. *The Handbook of Environmental Economics* (Cambridge, MA: Blackwell, 1995); William A. Duerr, *Introduction to Forest Resource Economics* (New York: McGraw-Hill, 1993), Chapter 22; and Peter H. Pearse, *Forestry Economics* (Vancouver: University of British Columbia Press, 1990), Chapter 7.

11. Table 14.3 shows hypothetical data at 10-year intervals for the growth equation in Note 3. The yearly annual value is 240 ft^3 at maximum annual growth.

12. In Chapter 4, when $n = \infty$, NPV = C/r. "C" is the constant annual income stream. This is the inverse of $C = r * NPV$ when $n = \infty$.

13. Professional foresters would use different terms; some refer to New England, New York, and the Upper Great Lakes as the "Northern Forest." Others exclude the Great Lakes from this concept. The geographic area of the "Central Forest" is approximately the Midwest. See Sharpe *op. cit.,* Chapter 5.

14. B. F. Stanton and N. L. Bills, "The Return of Agricultural Lands to Forest," EB 96-3 (Ithaca, NY: Cornell University, February, 1996). One very readable general article is Bill McKibben, "An Explosion of Green," April 1995 *Atlantic Monthly* 275 (4):61–83.

15. Jon Erickson, Cornell University, personal communication, May 8, 1996.

16. The work of Likens, Buso, and Driscoll is reported in 12 April 1996, *Science* 272, page 240. It is discussed in *The New York Times,* April 16, 1996, page C4.

17. Some economists conclude that climate change may increase U.S. timber production while changing the composition of species in U.S. forests. See B. Sohngen and R. Mendelsohn, "Valuing the Impact of Large-Scale Ecological Change in a Market: The Effect of Climate Change on U.S. Timber," September 1998 *American Economic Review*, 88(4):686–710.

18. Likens, et al.

19. This work by Kaiser, Haynes, and Rosenthall is reviewed in U.S. National Acid Precipitation Assessment Program, *1990 Integrated Assessment Report* (Washington, DC: November 1991), page 162. Also, see the *Assessment Report* (*op. cit.*) for a summary, pages 162–163 and pages 301–324. Affected regions include red spruce in the East, loblolly pine in the South, and ponderosa pine in the West.

20. The preferred alternative for spotted owl protection specifies for each area the following requirements: two standing dead snags; 8–12 down, dead logs; and 15 percent live trees. See page 18 in U.S. Forest Service and U.S. Bureau of Land Management, *Record of Decision; Standards and Guidelines* (Portland, OR: April 1994).

21. This approach, taking only the superior trees, is often called 'high grading' by foresters, and is generally not recommended.

22. *High Country News*, September 29, 1997, "The Timber Wars Evolve into a Divisive Attempt at Peace." Also see the Quincy Library Group's Web site at qlg.org.

23. S. Swallow, P. Talukdar, and D. N. Wear, "Forest Eco-System Management," May 1997 *American Journal of Agricultural Economics* 79(2):311–326; and H. Önal, "Structural Diversity and Forest Management," same journal, 79(3):1001–1012.

24. See Note 22.

PART V

THE GLOBAL ENVIRONMENT

CHAPTER 15

BIODIVERSITY AND ENDANGERED SPECIES

Introduction

In the previous chapter on forestry economics, the major emphasis is on economic sustainability in timber harvesting and management. As with Chapter 6, which surveyed the basic theory of sustainability in the use of environmental resources, nonmarket externalities are seen as contributing a new dimension to economic management. In contrast, in this chapter on biodiversity, nonmarket environmental values take the dominant role in economic thinking.

The economics of biodiversity and endangered species protection is evolving rapidly, matching the rapid growth of scientific understanding. Biodiversity as a major concept emerged in 1980, closely following development of concern in the 1970s about endangered species.[1] The first three sections of this chapter review the scientific background of the definition and measurement of biodiversity and endangered species. It is necessarily on an introductory level.

This is followed by a review of the current thinking in economics about biodiversity, which is both conceptual and empirical. In this discussion, it is shown that nonmarket externalities are a significant part of the economic calculus. From the work done to date, it is apparent that biodiversity protection can have contrasting impacts for different groups and localities. Although net benefits from protection are frequently positive, it is not uncommon for one area or group to experience a negative impact, while another location or group sees a positive impact.

As an economic case study, the Pacific Forest Plan for protection of the northern spotted owl concludes the chapter.

Scientific Background; the Importance of Biodiversity

From viruses to insects to mammals, over the whole range of earth's life, scientists now estimate that the total number of species of every type of life is on the order of 14 million. Estimates are as low as 4 million and as high as 112 million, but the working number is 13.6 million.[2] Figure 15.1 plots the relationship between identified species and estimated total species. The 8 million estimated species of insects well exceeds the figure's scale.

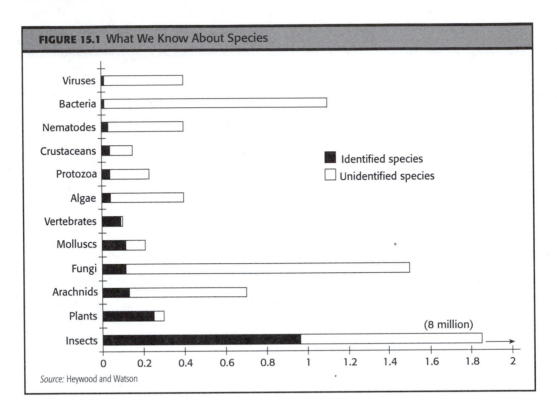

FIGURE 15.1 What We Know About Species

Source: Heywood and Watson

As might be expected, the greatest degree of knowledge has been obtained for those species most directly related to human use and interest: vertebrates and plants. Of approximately 50,000 vertebrate species there are only 30 to 40 mammals and birds which are of significant agricultural use. Taken together, the populations of the three domesticated species each of cattle, sheep, and pigs total 3.3 billion. In addition, there are an estimated 10 billion chickens worldwide.

The concentration of human use of plant species is also strong but not as extreme. Ninety percent of food plant supplies come from only 103 plant species, primarily grains and legumes.

Given this strong concentration in a few species for economic uses of animals and plants, it would be natural to suppose that human society is no longer dependent upon the extent of biodiversity from which these products originated. However, we continue to find important and new benefits from the world's biodiversity.

For example, the Pacific yew illustrates the importance of unanticipated discovery value, an economic concept taken up later in the chapter. The discovery of a cancer-fighting chemical in the yew is very recent. This substance, taxol, is produced from the bark of the Pacific yew for use in the treatment of cancer. It works by attacking rapidly dividing cancer cells and prevents them from replicating. Estimates of the number of ovarian cancer patients who could potentially benefit from the drug approach 60,000 a year.[3] The National Cancer Institute and Bristol-Meyers Squibb have harvested millions of dry pounds of yew from federal lands.[4] It is understandable, then, that the Pacific yew has been an important part of the policy debate between environmentalists, loggers, and government agencies. The yew (itself an endangered species) thrives in old-growth forest such as the Douglas fir type. But, as the preceding forestry chapter shows, clear-cutting is more profitable than selective harvesting in an old-growth forest.[5]

The Pacific yew case illustrates another facet of the biodiversity policy issue. How do we place economic value on biodiversity? Is quantitative measurement possible?

The Measurement of Biodiversity; the Definition of Endangered Species

Species diversity has always been a significant component of the study of biology and ecology. Nevertheless, concern for and study of the conservation of biodiversity is more recent.

Biodiversity is a complex concept; it is often perceived as having three dimensions:[6]

1. *Genetic Diversity*: variations in gene structure within and between species.
2. *Species Diversity*: within an area, a measure of the number of species. As with genetic diversity, species diversity can be defined across broad or narrow categories, and with very small or large geographic areas.
3. *Ecological Diversity*: variability in ecosystem habitat types.

Biologists and physical scientists have been developing empirical measures for biodiversity since the work of Shannon and Weaver in 1948.[7]

Economists have also worked to place biodiversity in a format that is subject to quantitative analysis. Of particular note is the work of Weitzman and Solow. Their work develops mathematical models of the genetic distance between different species in the crane family.[8] Without undertaking an in-depth review of these complex methodologies, it is worthwhile to illustrate the difficulty with three fairly simple potential measures for biodiversity. By doing so, we can see the difficulty in developing broadly acceptable methods of measurement.

Consider a hypothetical protected area of 1,000 acres with two of the carnivore families now present. Two management options are being considered. One is to maintain the status quo, which is shown as Option A in Table 15.1. In this option, foxes, coyotes, and raccoons (but not wolves) are established at their maximum carrying capacity.

Under Option B wolves are introduced and there is a major impact on other species within the carnivore group. This is because wolves prey on other carnivores, as well as upon rodents, turkeys, and grazing animals. Consequently, Option B has a representative reduction in foxes, coyotes, and raccoons resulting from the introduction of wolves.

Now consider the simple biodiversity criteria by which we might judge the two options. Under the first criterion listed in Table 15.2, we examine the maximum number of carnivores per acre as a measure of biodiversity. This first criterion,

TABLE 15.1 Biodiversity for Carnivores in a Hypothetical Area of 1,000 Acres

| | Canine Family | | | | *Total* |
	Foxes	*Coyotes*	*Wolves*	*Raccoons*	*Carnivores*
OPTION A (No Wolves)	40	20	0	40	100
OPTION B (Wolves Introduced)	25	10	5	30	70

Option A, with 100 animals on 1,000 acres, yields 0.1 carnivores per acre. By implementing Option B, the total number of animals per acre is reduced to 0.07. According to the first criterion, the status quo with no wolves would be preferred.

The second criterion in the table is species per acre. Under the status quo, there are three species. Under Option B, with the introduction of wolves, there are now four species. Species per acre is clearly higher in the second option with the wolf introduction. Consequently criterion 2 leads to a preference for Option B.

With the third criterion (total family types of carnivore per acre), two families, the canine family and the raccoon family, are both represented regardless of whether wolves are present or absent. Therefore, according to criterion 3, we would be indifferent between the two options.

In summary, the no-wolf Option A is chosen under the maximum number of animals per acre criterion. A maximum number of species per acre criterion would prefer Option B with wolf reintroduction. Under criterion 3, total family types of carnivores is indifferent between the two options.

This has been a simplified discussion, considerably less complex than the analyses of Weitzman and Solow that were noted above. However, the difficulties of using even simple measures can be emphasized by looking at the possibility of still another option. Suppose that this hypothetical area is in a warm-winter section of the United States similar to the veldt of Southern Africa. Now consider a third option in which not only North American wolves are reintroduced, but hyenas are brought from Southern Africa to live in this biodiversity preserve in the southwestern United States.

Certainly, according to both criterion 3 and criterion 2 it would appear that biodiversity is enhanced by the introduction of this third family of carnivores. Yet,

TABLE 15.2 Three Biodiversity Criteria

1. Maximum Number of Carnivores per Acre
2. Species per Acre
3. Total Family Types of Carnivore per Acre

TABLE 15.3 Biodiversity Survey

Divide 100 points total among each of the categories.

———— Laboratory Genetic Material

———— Laboratory Animals

———— Private Collections

———— Public Zoo

———— Private Ranch

———— Special Area: Endangered Species Protected from Predators with Food as Needed

———— Special Area: Endangered Species in Natural Ecosystem with Predators

while our biodiversity measures may appear to lead us to consider the hyena introduction as the superior choice, on other grounds this choice would clearly not be preferred. Another dimension of biodiversity, distinct from the three components of our definition above, overrides the others: a "naturalness dimension."

Table 15.3 represents a survey intended to emphasize this naturalness dimension, and its relationship to valuation. Each individual surveyed takes 100 points, and divides them among each of the categories of potential biodiversity. For example, with respect to wolf preservation we might consider simply storing wolf genetic material (DNA), keeping wolves in laboratories and reproducing them for scientific use, relying on private collections of individuals, or providing wolves for public zoos. You are invited to allocate your 100 points amongst those seven options. Then compare your judgment values to those shown in Appendix A. If all the concepts were of equivalent value, then each category would receive comparable points. Typically, however, because of the importance of naturalness, the last category, "endangered species in a natural ecosystem with predators," receives the highest total ranking. On this basis, if we were to consider this as a fourth criterion, it would clearly support the introduction of wolves, but the continued exclusion of African hyenas.

The definition and measurement of biodiversity is providing a serious intellectual challenge to both biologists and economists. It might seem that working on the species level would be simpler, but endangered species definition is also complex, and some of the economic issues arising from endangered species protection arise from definitions. Table 15.4 lists the basic definitions in the United States.

In the United States, the primary implementation of the Endangered Species Act is the responsibility of the Fish and Wildlife Service. On a secondary basis, the National Oceanic and Atmospheric Administration (NOAA) is responsible for protecting marine mammals such as whales and dolphins under the act. Globally, two international organizations complement NOAA and the Fish and Wildlife Service, and each of these international organizations publishes widely used lists of endangered species. These two international organizations are the CITES (Convention on

TABLE 15.4 The Definition of Endangered and Threatened Species[9]

1. 'Species' means any species, subspecies or distinct population of fish or wildlife. It means any plant subspecies.

2. 'Endangered' means in danger of extinction throughout all or a significant portion of its range.

3. 'Threatened' means likely to become endangered.

Note: Observe that a subspecies or local population is defined as a species.

International Trade in Endangered Species) Secretariat in the United Nations Environment Program, and the International Union for the Conservation of Nature. Each of these organizations uses definitions comparable to those in the United States. These parallel terms are given in Table 15.5.

Consequently, although much of the discussion in this chapter is on U.S. material, the concepts used internationally are almost identical. Usually the three organizations agree on the degree of problem for a particular species or variety. However, disagreements do arise. For example, in the mid-1990s, the United States considered the African elephant to be merely threatened, while CITES listed this animal in Appendix I, its most concerned category. But in 1997, CITES moved the African elephant populations in Botswana, Namibia, and Zimbabwe to Appendix II status, comparable to the U.S. "threatened" category. Other nations' African elephants as well as all Asian elephants remained in Appendix I. This seemingly illogical approach, however, is explained by the interaction between CITES and ivory trade, explained in the next chapter.

In 1995, the U.S. National Academy of Sciences completed its review of the Endangered Species Act. This review had been requested by both the U.S. Senate and House of Representatives, and the first issue was the definition of species.[10] In the

TABLE 15.5 Comparing International Terminology[11]

The U.S. Concept Of...	Is Comparable to This IUCN Red Book Term	And This CITES Term
'Species' includes subspecies and local populations	Same	Same
Endangered	Endangered	Appendix I listing
Threatened	Vulnerable	Appendix II listing

Note: IUCN means International Union for the Conservation of Nature; CITES is an acronym for the Convention on International Trade in Endangered Species.

Academy's report, the scientists conducting the study firmly endorsed the broad definition in Table 15.4.

The scientific issues, however, continue to be contentious because of their economic implications. The U.S. National Biological Survey was formed in 1993 to provide the scientific basis for data and policy on biodiversity and endangered species. It was terminated in 1996, and its work transferred to the Biological Resources Division in the U.S. Geological Survey.

Economic Assessment of Biodiversity and Protected Species

Economists studying biodiversity evaluation have made contributions in four areas: (1) Expanding the traditional concepts of economic theory in the context of non-market valuation; (2) Using empirical techniques in contingent valuation to estimate nonmarket preservation values; (3) Identifying the types of equity issues that arise in biodiversity protection; and (4) Applying benefit-cost analysis to specific policies, such as the northern spotted owl protection plan. This section reviews some of the work in the first three areas, and the chapter concludes with an examination of the economic analysis of spotted owl protection.

Traditional economic theory is being revised by economists working in biodiversity research. As shown in Table 15.6, these relationships reflect the work of the Heywood and Watson report on *Global Biodiversity Assessment* for the United Nations.[12] These terms are more advanced concepts that arise from the definitions in Chapters 1–6, particularly in their development of positive nonmarket externalities. The Equations (15-1)–(15-4) help summarize the interactions between the concepts.

$$TNV = NHV + TEV \tag{15-1}$$

$$TEV = DUV + IUV + OV + DSV + BV + EV \tag{15-2}$$

$$UV = DUV + IUV + OV + DSV \tag{15-3}$$

$$PNV = BV + EV \tag{15-4}$$

Total environmental value (TNV), the first equation, carries a controversial assumption. Do nonhuman species have value separate and distinct from the human perception of value? Erickson's Chapter 19 later in the text argues that species such as owls can have *nonhuman value* (NHV) in their own right. This is intriguing, but economists have not generally accepted this viewpoint. Equation (15-1), then, asserts a new idea that environmental value not only includes economic values (TEV), but also this concept of nonhuman value. It remains to be seen whether NHV will find favor with economists.[13]

The definition of *total economic value* (TEV) in the second equation is traditional. It has six components. The first, *direct use value* (DUV) arises from the consumption of market commodities as described in Chapters 1 and 2. It can be measured by consumers' surplus. *Indirect use value* (IUV) is also related to a traditional concept, the positive economic externality. It defines the importance of an environmental resource such as a forest in the production of a direct use marketing

TABLE 15.6 Economic Definitions Relevant to Biodiversity Adapted from *Global Biodiversity Assessment* (see text)

BV: bequest value, the value of preserving a resource for future generations.

DSV: discovery value, the unknown value of presently undiscovered dimensions of a biological resource; for example, the unknown value in the 1980s of Pacific yew as a future source of taxol.

DUV: direct use value, the market value of consuming a biological resource such as fish or lumber.

EV: existence value, the value conferred by the survival of a biological resource.

IUV: indirect use value, the role an environmental resource plays in the production of a market commodity. For example, a forest preserve enhances water quality and reliability.

NHV: nonhuman value, the value of living biological species in their own right, distinct from their value to human society. In *Assessment*, this is termed "non-anthropocentric instrumental value."

OV: option value, the value of opportunity to utilize a resource in the future.

PNV: passive nonuse value, the sum of bequest and existence value. Also see "UV" below.

POC: private opportunity cost, the market value of opportunities foregone.

SOC: social opportunity cost, the total environmental or economic value of opportunities foregone.

TEV: total economic value, the sum of direct, indirect, option, discovery, bequest, and existence values. It includes both use and passive nonuse values.

TNV: total environmental value, the sum of nonhuman value (NHV) and total economic value (TEV).

UV: use value, the sum of direct use value, option value, and discovery value. Total economic value (TEV) can be defined as the sum of use value and passive nonuse value.

Source: Heywood and Watson, page 830. (See Note 1.)

activity such as fishing. This IUV assumes considerable importance in the illustration of the benefits and costs of forest preservation in the Philippines that follows.

Option value (OV) was introduced in Chapter 4, in the context of willingness to pay for the protection of the Grand Canyon from air pollution. In Table 15.6, I have added the term *discovery value* (DSV). The purpose of this concept is to reflect the significance of future values which we do not presently understand. Just as taxol and many pharmaceutical chemicals originated from the Pacific yew and other biological resources, so too will future discoveries be made from preserved species.

Taken together in a group, the first four terms in total economic value have been defined as *use value,* or UV. It means that each concept applies to the human utilization of an environmental resource. Use value implies that the nature and character of biological resources and ecosystems may be changed in the process of use by human society.[14]

The remaining two terms in total economic value in Equation (15-2) are both components of passive nonuse value. Each concept (bequest value and existence value) implies that the current generation values a resource, but does not change its character. *Existence value* (EV) means we place positive value on an environmental resource even if we do not now or in the future plan to utilize the resource. *Bequest value* (BV) is somewhat different; it may include an intention for possible future utilization, but not today. Thus, if someone believes that petroleum may need to be produced in the future from the Alaskan National Wildlife Refuge, but not currently, this would reflect bequest value.

Stephen Swallow offers two main criticisms of this set of concepts.[15] First, if nonhuman value (NHV) is truly independent of human valuation, how can it be additive with respect to TEV, total economic value? In Swallow's view, Equation (15-1) is incompatible with the definition of nonhuman value.

His second criticism is that 13 conceptual definitions are excessive. He believes that double counting (embedding bias, see Chapter 3) is inevitable. This is important because contingent valuation plays a major role in biodiversity economics in the assessment of existence and bequest value. Necessarily, this work must contend with the kind of empirical problem discussed in that chapter. For example, consider the selected annual values shown in Table 15.7. Is a bog in the United Kingdom really worth 75 times the value of Swedish forests? Or consider the grizzly bear values, $19 per animal per year in the United States and $15 in Norway. These latter values seem surprisingly similar.

On a different theoretical topic, biodiversity economics recognizes the difference in incidence in the costs and benefits of biodiversity protection. Consider a recent analysis of a Philippines bay, where the authors found a strong link between logging, species destruction, and losses in tourism and fishing. They estimated that logging results in soil erosion of 100 million metric tons per square kilometer.[16] In a down-river ocean bay, this caused one additional coral species each year to become extinct. As a result of coral loss, fishing declined. The economic estimates are summarized in Table 15.8.

Suppose Village A is the upstream logging location. They may prefer the status quo; with a logging ban, these villagers would see their annual income fall from $10 million to nothing. If Village B is downstream by the ocean, then the ban would result in coral protection, with economic benefits from an enhanced fishery and increased tourism revenue for the village. This group would favor the proposed logging ban. Obviously, there would be conflict between the villages, which might involve other levels of regional and federal government.[17] Although this example is set in the Philippines, it has the same characteristics as the spotted owl protection program in the United States.

TABLE 15.7 Global Biodiversity Selected Estimates of Value (dollars per year, 1990 dollars)

United States

Humpback whales	$51
Northern spotted owl in old-growth forest	$21
Bald eagle	$19
Grizzly bear	$19
Wild turkey	$11
Blue whale	$9
Salmon	$8
Coyote	$5
Grand Canyon visibility	$27

Europe

Norwegian grizzly bear; wolf	$15
Swedish forests, recreational and old growth	$4
UK bog	$300

Source: Heywood and Watson, page 875.

TABLE 15.8 Biodiversity, Species Loss, and Logging Versus Fishing and Tourism (millions of 1986 dollars)

	Tourism Revenue	Fisheries Revenue	Logging Revenue	Total Revenue
Status quo: continued logging	$6M	$9M	$10M	$25M
Logging ban	$26M	$17M	0	$43M
Impact of change	+$20M	+$8M	−$10M	+$18M

Note: From *Global Biodiversity Assessment*, page 883. Net Present Value is calculated at a 10 percent interest rate.

Spotted Owl Protection: Economic Dimensions

From the prior discussion in this chapter, several general points emerge which are relevant to understanding economic analysis for the spotted owl case. First, the biological definition of endangered species and biodiversity can be complex and controversial. Second, the economic values of protection are frequently nonmarket externalities, such as option, bequest, and existence values. Third, although net

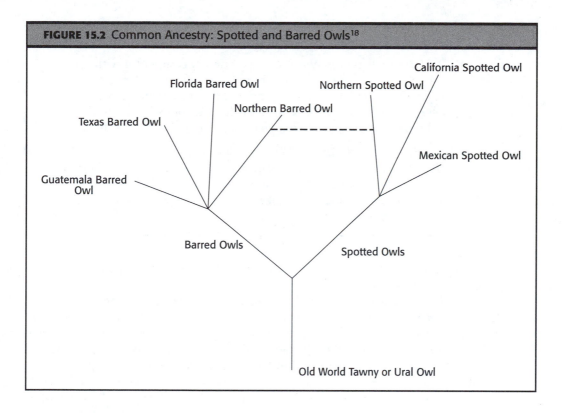

FIGURE 15.2 Common Ancestry: Spotted and Barred Owls[18]

benefits from protection are often positive, the distribution may be very different between localities and groups. It is not uncommon for one area to experience a negative economic impact while another area perceives positive benefit. This can be particularly important when significant externality values are relevant. Finally, given each of these points, policy making often is difficult and controversial.[19]

Illustrating the definitional problem, the northern spotted owl is officially listed as "threatened" by the Division of Endangered Species in the U.S. Fish and Wildlife Service.[20] However, Figure 15.2 represents the biological background of this listing. The northern spotted owl is, according to the Endangered Species Act, a threatened variety. There are two other varieties of the spotted owl species which are neither endangered nor threatened.

Another problem for the northern spotted owl is biological: its two greatest hazards are other owls. The great horned owl, of larger size, preys upon the northern spotted owl for food.

However, the northern barred owl is even more significant because it outcompetes the northern spotted owl, driving the spotted owl away from territories both prefer. It is interesting to note that both the spotted owl and the barred owl evolved from a common species, and now, as related species, are competing for the same ecological niche. Two very different opinions are quoted in Table 15.9.

In analyzing biological issues, Greg Easterbrook strongly criticizes the federal program to protect northern spotted owl nesting areas in old-growth Douglas fir.

TABLE 15.9 The Northern Spotted Owl versus the Northern Barred Owl[21]

1. *D. H. Johnson, serious concern:* "The primary competitor with spotted owls is the barred owl. The barred owl outcompetes in several ways; takes a wider variety of prey; and defends home ranges more vigorously. Barred owls seldom lose in interactions with spotted owls, and have continued to expand their range in the Pacific Northwest."

2. *J. W. Thomas et al., limited concern:* "Barred owls are uncommon in many upland Northwest areas, and it remains to be seen whether they will displace significant numbers of spotted owls. There is little the forest management agencies can or should do to influence the eventual outcome of this competition."

He argues that the other spotted owl subspecies are doing fine, especially the California variety in cut-over forests.[22]

Given this biological background, the economic significance of the definitions in Table 15.4 begin to come into focus. Although the northern spotted owl is a subspecies population, it traditionally prefers the old-growth forest such as the Douglas fir, a main focus of the preceding chapter on timber harvesting. Working from the legal definition which characterizes a threatened subspecies or distinct population as a threatened species, the northern spotted owl is by designation a threatened species. Consequently, forest management must incorporate both the sustainability concepts of timber harvesting and the nonmarket values of endangered species protection.

With this legal mandate, the Bush and Clinton administrations established the Pacific Forest Plan.[23] As a consequence of this approach to protecting northern spotted owls through the protection of the old-growth Douglas fir ecosystem, hundreds of associated plant and animal species receive greater protection. The Pacific yew (discussed earlier in the chapter) of course is now given greater protection, but several species now on the Endangered and Threatened Species list also will gain. These include the wolf, bald eagle, grizzly bear, and chinook salmon.[24]

In an economic analysis of the plan, Hagen, Vincent, and Welle emphasize these ecosystem benefits.[25] In economic terminology, the Hagen group seeks to determine willingness to pay for existence, option, and bequest values for the old-growth Douglas fir habitat favored by the northern spotted owl and other endangered species. Their contingent value survey of 1,000 U.S. households had a 41 percent return rate. As we saw in Chapter 3, the contingent valuation results are very sensitive to methodology. They reported three different calculations of the average value per household, shown in Table 15.10. In the midrange calculation, for example, they assumed that 590 nonresponding households derived zero value from the plan, and that the average for all 1,000 households is a benefit of $86 per household.

The Hagen study is a useful source of information on the benefits of the protection program. To understand the economic costs of the plan, we turn to the work of the Montgomery, Brown, and Adams group.[26] They take into consideration the probability of survival of the owl under different amounts of reserved Douglas fir forest. Their work used owl population modelling to derive Figure 15.3. It shows the

TABLE 15.10 Benefit-Cost Summary of Old-Growth Douglas Fir Ecosystem Protection for Northern Spotted Owls (annual estimates, to nearest billion dollars, 100 million households)

A. *Benefits:*		*Total Benefits, per Year*
1. If WTP = $144 per household		$14 billion
2. If WTP = $86 per household		$9 billion
3. If WTP = $48 per household		$5 billion
B. *Cost of Plan:* $5 billion annually		
C. *Net Social Value:*	Either	+$9 billion
	or	+$4 billion
	or	$0

Source: See text; adapted from Hagen et al. and Montgomery et al. Apparently 1990 dollars for both studies. Assume 100 million households. The high benefit value of $144 assumes that survey nonrespondents had positive value. The median benefit estimate ($86) assumes that nonrespondents had zero value for the plan. The lowest dollar value ($48) assumes that this amount has a 98 percent probability of the true value being higher; it is the lower bound of the 98 percent confidence interval.

FIGURE 15.3 Northern Spotted Owl Survival Probability[27]

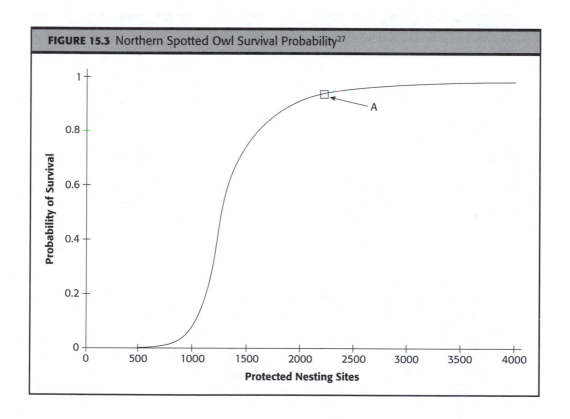

relationship between protected nesting sites and the probability of continued sur-vival for the northern spotted owl. Note that, if fewer than 500 sites are reserved, it is expected that extinction will occur.

The opportunity cost in terms of foregone timber is significant. Each pair of owls requires at least 3,000 acres of protected forest. The relationship between lost tim-ber and protected nests is almost linear, and the 2,400 protected nests require fore-going a projected 2.3 billion board feet each year.[28] In the figure, this gives a 95 percent probability of survival.

By combining data from both the Hagen and Montgomery studies, we can ana-lyze a representative benefit-cost analysis. Table 15.10 is a highly simplified rep-resentation of a complex picture. The willingness to pay (WTP) for ecosystem protection depends upon the interpretation of the Hagen survey results. Recall the three levels of calculation above: each defines a different benefit estimate per household. Each value implies a different national benefit level.

The social cost of the plan is based upon an analysis of the losses to consumers of wood products from higher prices,[29] and the net losses to timber industry busi-ness and employees from reduced production. In Figure 15.4, a simplified graph is used to introduce the Montgomery group's analysis.

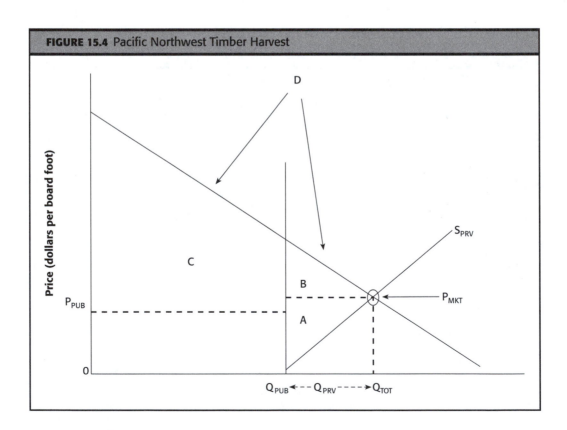

FIGURE 15.4 Pacific Northwest Timber Harvest

First, consider the market for timber on privately owned land on the right side of the figure. The supply curve is S_{PRV}, and represents the costs of production from private lands.[30] It intersects the demand curve D, and the intersection defines the equilibrium market price (P_{MKT}) and total timber sales (Q_{TOT}). Private forest owners' producer surplus is the "A" triangle, and consumers' surplus (for the timber buyers) is the "B" triangle.

The quantity of board feet cut from private land and from foreign sources is Q_{PRV}. The left hand side of the graph represents timber sales from public land. This amount is fixed by policy, at Q_{PUB}. The price charged to timber buyers is P_{PUB}, an amount fixed by federal and state forest agencies to cover their costs. Consequently, in this case there is no producer surplus or loss on public land. The consumer surplus is the awkward polygon labeled "C."

Given the basic outline in the figure, now imagine that for the Douglas fir spotted owl program the allowable cut on public land Q_{PUB} is reduced. We can anticipate the new intersection for demand and supply (where D intersects S_{PRV}) will move left. The likely result: higher market price P_{MKT}, less public sales Q_{PUB} as noted, a smaller increase in private timber sales Q_{PRV}, and a decline in total sales Q_{TOT}. We expect a small increase in producer surplus "A," but larger declines in consumer surplus from the public timber sales "B."

With this framework, the Montgomery group calculates the cost of the plan's negative impact on producers' and consumers' surplus. It is equivalent to $5 billion annually,[31] and is used as the cost of the plan in Table 15.10.

With the three different assumptions about the Hagen contingent valuation work, net social value benefits are $0, or $4 billion annually, or $9 billion annually.

Critics of the plan argue that each pair of protected owls has an economic cost of $2 million annually. As with the Philippines example, much of the cost is incurred by one region, while the passive nonuse benefits are national. Advocates of the plan emphasize the potential significant positive benefits, the enhanced character of the ecosystem, and the endangered species it includes. The U.S. Secretary of the Interior Bruce Babbitt summarized this position: "The biocide of clearcutting has been abandoned in favor of new forestry's selective logging, leaving behind sufficient forest structure to maintain biological connections and to sustain natural forest regeneration."[32]

Economics has a role to play in biodiversity analysis. As the spotted owl case shows us, it can partially illuminate some of the facets of major policy issues.

Emerging Issues

The Philippines and spotted owl cases share one important characteristic: the cost of biodiversity protection is largely incurred by a regional or local group because of the opportunity cost of foregone economic activity. In contrast, the benefits, although frequently much larger than the costs, are distributed to different groups.

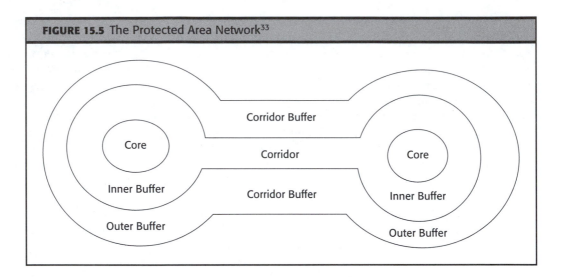

FIGURE 15.5 The Protected Area Network[33]

Economists have been working on two types of approaches to remedy this problem: buffer zones and local participation. Stephen Swallow places these approaches in an economic framework that draws upon the new findings of conservation biology. Swallow's reserve network[34] in Figure 15.5 might allow intensive resource utilization in the outer buffer: logging, for example. The inner buffer would be more restrictive, prohibiting clear-cuts but allowing selective logging. Both buffers might allow hunting and regulated firewood harvesting. But the core would be traditionally managed wilderness area, without logging and perhaps roadless. The Adirondack Park in New York has these characteristics, although the geographic boundaries are necessarily much more complex than those in the figure. The continuous network of National Parks and National Forests in the Sierra Nevada Mountains in California and Nevada also provide a real-world illustration of this network concept.[35]

The motivation for new approaches is not only because of the political importance of equity and local participation. There is also concern that biodiversity protection in traditional protected areas does not provide sufficient protection for endangered species.

The National Park Service is home to 123 endangered species, only about 15 percent of the U.S. total. Most of the currently endangered species are on private or state land.[36] There are two opposing interpretations of this fact. One viewpoint perceives these statistics as emphasizing the need for protection outside of protected areas. This is part of the basis for the growing role of the Nature Conservancy and other private organizations which purchase private land for biodiversity protection.

A contrasting perspective notes that the relative absence of endangered species in large U.S. National Parks is a reflection of their success. Empirical work by biologists shows that the number of species in a protected area increases with the size of the area. In one study of North American mammals and parks, this 'elasticity' was nearly 0.1. In other words, each 1 percent increase in area is associated with a one-tenth of 1 percent increase in mammalian species.[37]

There is probably insight in both perspectives. National Parks and Wilderness Areas have provided a basis for successful protection of species and ecosystems within their boundaries. However, the emerging need is for protection of endangered species and ecosystems on nonfederal U.S. land, and in other countries. Consequently, the future emphasis in biodiversity protection may be focused on new forms of private and public activity.

A different set of problems arises from the legal issues in ownership of biodiversity. Does, for example, an individual or corporation have standing to patent and own biological material with commercial value? Could I find a new plant or mushroom in Africa with cancer-fighting abilities like taxol, and patent it in the United States and elsewhere? While these types of legal issues are not strictly economic, they are of sufficient importance to mention here and to note other sources for substantive information.[38]

Summary

While science, public opinion, and politics are important in defining policy for biodiversity and endangered species protection, economics has a significant and growing role as well. At the beginning of this chapter, we saw how understanding the difficulties of definition and measurement are useful in comprehending the complexity of economic issues. Biodiversity always has dimensions of genetic, species, and ecosystem diversity, and its valuation may also have a naturalness dimension. 'Species' as used by conservation biologists and in U.S. law and treaties is defined to mean local individual populations of subspecies and varieties.

Economists working on biodiversity have built upon traditional theory of externality, and have emphasized newer concepts such as passive, existence, and option value, and the value of nonhuman biological populations in their own right.

The spotted owl case illuminates several aspects of biodiversity economics. The passive nonuse benefits are national, but the economic cost is local. The definition of endangered species comes into play, and requires the protection of the habitat of a subspecies, the northern spotted owl. This, in turn, provides for enhanced protection of the ecosystem for many other threatened and endangered species.

Contingent valuation identifies a significant passive nonuse value for the northern spotted owl ecosystem. The benefits compare favorably with the opportunity cost of foregone timber harvesting.

In the subjects of two other chapters, biodiversity and endangered species concepts are taking greater importance. Forestry economics (Chapter 14) must give growing recognition to biodiversity as well as traditional environmental values. In Chapter 16, the Kruger National Park must balance the social consequences of its history with economic development and biodiversity protection. For wealthy nations as well as developing countries, these chapters also analyze the divergence between private market solutions and public policy that incorporates externality values. It is this divergence that creates the justification for government support, whether today within the United States alone, or internationally in the future for African parks. Economics cannot answer all of the important questions, but it has an important role to play in understanding problems and framing policies and their consequences.

Questions for Discussion and Analysis

1. In the context of Table 15.1, consider a third *Option C*. Five wolves are reintroduced but penned and fed by the protected area reserve managers. Foxes, coyotes, and raccoons would remain at their original levels. Now use the three biodiversity criteria (Table 15.2) to compare *Options A, B, C*, and present the results in a table. Do you agree with the results as a basis for policy?

2. How do your biodiversity survey results (Table 15.3) compare to Appendix A at the end of the chapter?

3. Consider the WTP for protection of the existence of the eight U.S. species in Table 15.7. These values are per person per year. In round numbers, the U.S. population is 300 million people. Summing up the existence values for all eight species, what is the aggregate U.S. WTP? Review the pros and cons of accepting this number for policy.

4. Do you agree or disagree with Stephen Swallow's criticisms of the biodiversity economic concepts? Explain.

5. What is your own conclusion with respect to the desirability of the Pacific Forest Plan to protect the northern spotted owl and its ecosystem? Use at least three economic arguments to support your opinion.

Appendix: Biodiversity Survey: One Class Response

Divide 100 points total among each of the categories.

- __6__ Laboratory Genetic Material
- __4__ Laboratory Animals
- __4__ Private Collections
- __11__ Public Zoo
- __6__ Private Ranch
- __20__ Special Area: Endangered Species Protected from Predators with Food as Needed
- __49__ Special Area: Endangered Species in Natural Ecosystem with Predators

Source: See discussion of Table 15.3 in this chapter.

Notes to Chapter 15

1. V. H. Heywood, Executive Editor, and R. T. Watson, Chair, *Global Biodiversity Assessment*, United Nations Environmental Program (Cambridge, UK: Cambridge University Press, 1995); pages 5 and 6 summarize the emergence of biodiversity as a major scientific concept in the last two decades of the 20th Century. The Endangered Species Act became U.S. law in 1973. The Convention on International Trade in Endangered Species (CITES), an important treaty, was established the same year.

2. *Ibid.,* page 120.

3. U.S. General Accounting Office, *Cancer Treatment: Actions Taken to More Fully Utilize the Bark of Pacific Yews on Federal Land* (Washington, DC: USGPO, August 1992).

4. U.S. Department of Agriculture, Forest Service, Bureau of Land Management, and Federal Drug Administration, *Pacific Yew: Final Environmental Impact Statement* (Washington, DC: USGPO, September 1993).

5. See Table 14.5 in the forestry chapter.

6. This definition of biodiversity represents those given by the UNEP project, Barbier, Wilson, and others. For additional reading, see Heywood and Watson, *op. cit.,* Chapter 2; Edward B. Barbier, Joanne C. Burgess, and Carl Folke, *Paradise Lost? the Ecological Economics of Biodiversity* (London: Earthscan, 1994); E. O. Wilson, ed., *Biodiversity* (Washington, DC: National Academy Press, 1988).

7. The Shannon-Weaver mathematical formula was originally derived by Claude E. Shannon, a mathematician for the Bell Telephone company. He published his findings in the *Bell System Technical Journal* in 1948, and again with Warren Weaver in 1964 with *The Mathematical Theory of Communication* (Illinois: University of Illinois Press, 1964). In the late 1950s, ecologists started using this formula because it provided a way to measure both richness and evenness, and could be applied to plants and animals. The index is defined in Bruce Campbell and Elizabeth Lack, *A Dictionary of Birds* (Bath, UK: Ditman, 1985), where $i = i^{th}$ species; NS = number of species; Ni = total individuals in i^{th} species; and N = total individuals all species:

$$H = -\sum_{i=1}^{NS} \frac{Ni}{N} \log \frac{Ni}{N}$$

8. See Martin L. Weitzman, "What to Preserve? An Application of Diversity Theory to Crane Conservation," February 1993 *The Quarterly Journal of Economics* 108(1):157–184; Martin L. Weitzman, "On Diversity," May 1992 *The Quarterly Journal of Economics* 107(2):363–406; and Andrew Solow, Stephen Polasky, and James Broadus, "On the Measurement of Biological Diversity," January 1993 *Journal of Environmental Economics and Management* 24(1):60–68. A good current review of biodiversity measurement from a biological perspective is in Malcolm J. Hunter, Jr., *Wildlife, Forests, and Forestry: Principles of Managing Forests for Biological Diversity* (New Jersey: Regents/Prentice Hall, 1990). See especially "Diversity Indices," Appendix 3, by Katherine Elliott.

9. The definitions are taken from U.S. House Committee on Merchant Marine and Fisheries, "Endangered Species Act of 1973," Committee Print, 1988, pages 3, 4. The broad U.S. definition of species in Table 15.4 is similar to that in CITES, Article 1. The African CITES listing is particularly complicated because it is closely linked to trading rules for ivory and elephant products. See the next chapter on the Kruger National Park. A good popular history of the Act is J. P. Cohn, "How the Endangered Species Act Was Born," Winter 1997–1998 *Defenders* 73(3):6–13.

10. The letter from Congress requesting the study is Appendix A in the report, U.S. National Research Council, Committee on Scientific Issues in the Endangered Species Act, *Science and the Endangered Species Act* (Washington, DC: National Academy Press, 1995). The Act is included as Appendix B to the report.

11. The background sources for Table 15.5 are (1) "Endangered Species Act," *op. cit.*, (2) IUCN, *1994 Red List of Threatened Animals* (Cambridge, UK: IUCN, 1993), and (3) "Convention on International Trade in Endangered Species of Wild Fauna and Flora (CITES)," pages 9–27 in *International Wildlife Trade: A CITES Sourcebook*, Ginette Hemley, editor (Washington, DC: Island Press, 1994).

12. Heywood and Watson, *op. cit.,* Note 1.

13. Also see Chapter 5's discussion and criticism of ethical criteria and the natural rights concept.

14. Note that biodiversity economists have made a significant distinction between use value (UV), and one of its components, direct use value (DUV).

15. Stephen Swallow, personal communication, February 1998.

16. One hundred million metric tons per square kilometer is equal to 306 million U.S. tons per square mile of soil loss to the bay from logging. The study is discussed in Heywood and Watson, pages 882–883.

17. The discussion in the text assumes that the revenue from each activity is earned by villagers. In fact, significant proportions of revenue may, in particular circumstances, be earned by owners and employees from other areas and other countries.

18. Taxonomic information is from Richard Howard and Alick Moore, *A Complete Checklist of the Birds of the World* (Oxford: Oxford University Press, 1984). For further information on the probable ancestry of Strix, see Karel H. Voos, *Owls of the Northern Hemisphere* (Cambridge, MA: MIT Press, 1989), especially pages 225–236, and Allan W. Eckert and Karl E. Karalus, *The Owls of North America* (New York: Weathervane, 1987). The dashed line in Figure 15.2 shows that some very limited hybridization from interbreeding may be occurring.

19. Many ranching families and organizations have been particularly opposed to the implementation of the Endangered Species Act. *Range* magazine has been particularly forceful in expressing this viewpoint. See, for example, the articles on the kangaroo rat (Spring 1994), wolf reintroduction (Spring 1995), and the National Biological Survey (Summer 1995). However, their report (Winter 1996) on a cooperative ferret protection program is positive. See also Jon H. Goldstein, "Private Property Rights and the Endangered Species Act," Second Quarter 1996 *Choices*. A good collection of nine articles on "Regulatory Takings and Compensation for Environmental Damage" is in the October 1997 *Contemporary Economic Policy* 15(4):28–122.

20. U.S. Fish and Wildlife Service, "Endangered and Threatened Wildlife and Plants," August 20, 1994.

21. See J. W. Thomas et al., *Variability Assessments and Management Considerations for Species Associated with Late Successional and Old-Growth Forests of the Pacific Northwest* (Washington, DC: USGPO, 1993), pages 189–190. D. H. Johnson, "Predators, Competitors, and Mobsters: Interspecific Interactions Involving Northern Spotted Owls," is quoted in the Annotated Bibliography, Appendix 4-B in Thomas, pages 231–232. The quotations in the table are exact but shortened.

22. Greg Easterbrook, *A Moment on the Earth: The Coming Age of Environmental Optimism* (New York: Viking 1995), pages 220–224.

23. Bruce Babbitt, then Secretary of the Interior, provides a concise policy statement on spotted owl protection, the Douglas fir ecosystem, and the broader issues of biodiversity

and endangered species protection in "Science: Opening the Next Chapter of Conserva-tion History," March 31, 1995 *Science* 267:1954–1955. See also Thomas *op. cit.*, page 7, and the publications in the following note.

24. U.S. Department of the Interior, *Recovery Plan for the Northern Spotted Owl* (Washing-ton, DC: USGPO, 1991), Appendix D. U.S. Interagency SEIS Team, U.S. Forest Service and Bureau of Land Management, *Record of Decision and Standards and Guidelines* (Portland, OR: 1994), page 5.

25. D. A. Hagen, J. W. Vincent, and P. G. Welle, "Benefits of Preserving Old-Growth Forests and the Spotted Owl," April 1992 *Contemporary Policy Issues* 10(2):13–26.

26. C. A. Montgomery, G. M. Brown, Jr., and D. Adams, "The Marginal Cost of Species Preservation: The Northern Spotted Owl," March 1994 *Journal of Environmental Eco-nomics and Management* 26(2):111–128. Also C. A. Montgomery and G. M. Brown, Jr., "Economics of Species Preservation: the Spotted Owl Case," April 1992 *Contemporary Economic Policy Issues* 10(2):1–12.

27. Montgomery (*JEEM*) *op. cit.*

28. Montgomery (*JEEM*), page 125.

29. Estimates of the cost impact on housing of the spotted owl ecosystem protection are re-viewed in Chapter 17 on Macroeconomic Growth, Trade, and the Environment.

30. In their analysis, Montgomery et al. define the supply curve in greater detail, as including opportunity cost from foregone possible future sales. The discussion in the text assumes that the small amount of imported timber and lumber is included within the private mar-ket supply curve.

31. In Montgomery and Brown (*JEEM*, page 125) the present value of the welfare loss in producer and consumer surplus is $46 billion. With the hopeful assumption of long-term success of the program, we use the long-term annual equivalent amount approach from Chapter 4, Montgomery's 10 percent discount rate, and define a levelized cost of $4.6 bil-lion. This is rounded to $5 billion in Table 15.10.

32. The $2 million figure results from dividing $5 billion in annual opportunity cost by 2,500 nesting sites. The Babbitt quotation is from Babbitt *op. cit.*, page 1954.

33. Figure 15.5 is adapted from Stephen Swallow, "Economic Issues in Ecosystem Manage-ment," October 1996 *Agricultural and Resource Economics Review* 25(2):83–100.

34. Swallow, *op. cit.*

35. There is some tension between different species protection tactics. Corridors between core areas provide an enhanced genetic pool for large carnivores. However, they can also open up old-growth areas for predators of the migratory songbirds. Old-growth forest gives considerable defense to such species as the hermit thrush and wood thrush, while multi-use activities may improve access for their predators and parasites, such as cow-birds and raccoons. See Robert A. Askins, "Hostile Landscapes and the Decline of Mi-gratory Songbirds," March 31, 1995 *Science* 267:1956–1957. Swallow (1996, *op. cit.*) fol-lowing Noss and Cooperrider, suggests designing the cores and buffers to avoid this problem. He also proposes multiple linked core-buffer-corridor sets. Also see R. F. Noss and A. Y. Cooperrider, *Saving Nature's Legacy: Protecting and Restoring Biodiversity* (Washington, DC: Island Press, 1994).

36. Personal communication, Una Moneypenny (Cornell University) and Peggy Olwell, National Park Service Endangered and Threatened Species Coordinator, November 8, 1996.

37. Technically, the mammals in the study were lagomorpha, carnivora, and artiodactyla. This is loosely rabbits, carnivores, and large grazing animals. The question of 'returns to scale' for species and area size is complicated by the minimum territorial requirements of large

mammals. Some further reading on this issue is W. B. Newmark, *Mammalian Richness, Colonization, and Extinction in Western North American National Parks*, Ph.D. dissertation, University of Michigan, Ann Arbor, Michigan, 1988 (the 0.1 elasticity noted in the text is from this work); R. H. MacArthur and E. O. Wilson, *The Theory of Island Biogeography* (Princeton, NJ: Princeton University Press, 1967); and R. Leakey and R. Lewin, *The Sixth Extinction: Patterns of Life and the Future of Mankind* (New York: Doubleday, 1995).

38. The previously cited *Global Biodiversity Assessment* UNEP Report (pages 1036–1052 and also pages 893–903) discusses these legal questions in depth. Also, see W. Lesser, *Sustainable Use of Genetic Resources under the Convention on Biological Diversity: Exploring Access and Benefit Sharing Issues* (London: CABI, 1998). Lesser was a member of the UNEP panel.

CHAPTER 16

THE KRUGER NATIONAL PARK
IN A NEW SOUTH AFRICA

Introduction

The Kruger National Park brings into a real, current focus many of the concepts explored previously[1]: biodiversity, positive external environmental value, contingent valuation and the measurement of environmental benefits, equity between different income levels, sustainability, population pressure, resource depletion and pollution, community participation, and the interaction between environment and economic development. This single park brings into one setting most of the issues in environmental economics that concern protected areas in developing countries.[2]

It remains to be seen whether the park can continue its tradition of excellence. In part, as we shall see, the values that led to its 20th Century success created many of the problems that threaten its survival in the 21st Century.

The map (Figure 16.1) shows seven of the 700 protected natural areas in Southern Africa. Five of these (Kruger, Mana Pools and Hwange in Zimbabwe, Okavango and Kalahari in Botswana) are generally recognized as major scientific and tourist areas. Two others, Hluhluwe-Umfolozi and Phinda, are shown because their operations and management are relevant to some of the policy problems concerning the Kruger National Park.

The Positive Ledger: Conservation and Ecosystem Protection

One facet of the Kruger National Park success is evident in Table 16.1. It lists species that are endangered throughout Africa, but living in the park at stable population levels in generally natural ecosystems.

These successfully protected endangered species are part of a larger success story. At the time of the origins of the park in 1902, the smaller reserve then held few people or wildlife. There were no elephants, nor were there any white rhino. These animals as well as zebra, buffalo, and antelope had been hunted out during the Anglo-Boer War, or killed by disease. Careful, on-the-ground tracking in 1903 counted exactly one black rhino, five each of hippo and giraffe, and nine lions.[3]

Now, a century later, effective management of nature and tourism has generated a tremendous success. The 5 million acres of the Kruger National Park (KNP) combine

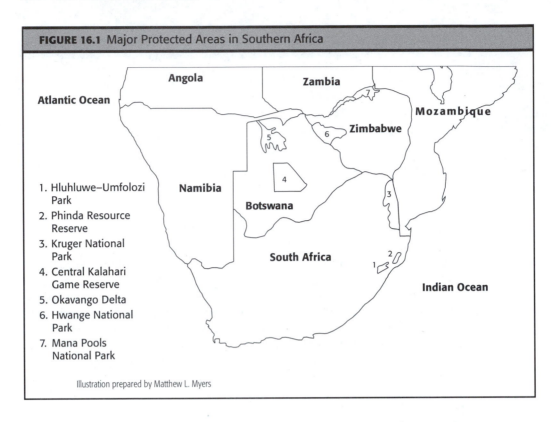

FIGURE 16.1 Major Protected Areas in Southern Africa

1. Hluhluwe–Umfolozi Park
2. Phinda Resource Reserve
3. Kruger National Park
4. Central Kalahari Game Reserve
5. Okavango Delta
6. Hwange National Park
7. Mana Pools National Park

Illustration prepared by Matthew L. Myers

with 525,000 acres in private game reserves, on the unfenced western edge of the park, to create a dramatic picture of wildlife success. Table 16.2 shows the unique nature of KNP's success.

Historically, the park's management achieved its success by a single-minded, disciplined focus on the park itself. It has a significant research program that provides the basis for what is fairly called scientific management. Typically, 150 research projects are underway at any one time. They cover a wide range of topics, including tsetse fly and malaria, cheetah demographics, elephant ecology, and water and air pollution.

Ecology and Management

This emphasis on the integration of science and management reflects the contemporary reality of wilderness conservation. Wilderness protection becomes management. Fences, for example, are necessary to separate animals from people, but, in the process, the fences halt the seasonal and drought cycle migrations of wildebeest and elephant. Animal populations in a wilderness are, in one specific sense, artificial, in that habitat, food, and predation are all influenced, and strongly so, by human actions on both sides of a park's fence. By the late 1990s, the major rivers in

TABLE 16.1 Successfully Protected Endangered Species in the Kruger National Park (selected)[4]

Popular, Common Name of Species	Historic Range	Scientific Names
Cheetah	India, Iran, Middle East, Africa	*Acinonyx jubatus*
Leopard	Asia and Africa	*Panthera pardus*
Elephant	Africa	*Loxodonta africana*
Black rhinoceros	Africa, and separate species in India, Nepal, and Indonesia (endangered)	*Diceronis bicornis*
White rhinoceros	Southern Africa (not endangered) and Central Africa (endangered)	*Ceratotherium simum*
Aardvark (also called antbear)	Sub-Sahara Africa	*Orycteropus afer*
Secretary bird	Sub-Sahara Africa	*Sagittarius serpentarius*
Ostrich	Middle East, Africa	*Struthio camelus*
Nile crocodile	Africa	*Crocodylia niloticus*

Note: The endangered species shown here appear on the IUCN red list, the CITES list, or the USFWS list. Remember that each organization uses different criteria in defining its list. See Chapter 15 for this information.

the park were no longer reliably flowing throughout the year. All ceased normal surface flow at least once in that decade. This is because diversions for agriculture and industry, and perhaps climate change, have periodically eliminated the rivers' flow through the park into Mozambique. Wells and windmill pumps now create ponds and lakes, providing substitute water sources for the absent rivers. The loss of rivers is man-made. Consequently, the *absence* of wells and ponds would also be a significant human intervention.

In the chapter on biodiversity we addressed the complex subject of the definition of biodiversity and the "state of nature."[5] Policy makers for wilderness parks, whether Yellowstone in the United States or KNP in Africa, have difficult judgment calls to make. The relative population sizes of grasses, trees, grazing animals and predators all change in response to the frequent drying-up of rivers. How is a natural environment defined? Would separate zones for cheetahs, wild dogs, and lions be appropriate? If human decisions influence these processes and populations, is inaction in response to outside-the-fence human actions itself a form of intervention?

Consider the trade-off between elephant populations and diversity in the park's ecosystem. A typical adult consumes 400–500 pounds of grass and tree material each day. An elephant can grow to 14 feet in height, with a weight of 7 tons. Apart

TABLE 16.2 Wildlife in the Kruger National Park in 1903 and 1993

	1903	1993
Elephant	0	7,300
Black rhino	1	220
White rhino	"exterminated"	1,400
Hippo	5	2,700
Giraffe	5	5,700
Buffalo	8	28,000
Eland	"exterminated"	850
Roan	"exterminated"	420
Tsessebe	"exterminated"	1,200
Wildebeest	50	13,500
Kudu	35	10,500
Ostrich	"exterminated"	some
Zebra	40	31,000
Impala	9,000	130,000
Lions	9	2,300
Leopard	"numerous"	900
Cheetah	"very scarce"	250
Crocodiles	"swarming"	"several thousand"
Visitors	0	648,000*
Cars	0	200,000
Revenue	0	$26 million

*In 1994.

Source: See Note 3.

from humans, adult elephants have no enemies. Lions, crocodiles, rhinos, and all other animals do not dispute water or grazing with adult elephants.

A large clan may be led by a healthy, mature "grandmother" and can include sisters, daughters, and their young daughters and sons. Adult males have less predictable arrangements. They may travel singly, in twos or threes, or in small groups. An adult male may join a clan to mate with one of the females. The actual arrangements are less precise than this, and families and friendships change in response to rainfall, population growth, culling, and poaching.

A clan may have its own home range of 200-plus square miles. These home ranges will be larger in drier locations, and they expand in dry years. Ian Whyte,[6] the source of these data, believes that clans' ranges may overlap, but each clan avoids the others' core range.

Rainfall averages 20 inches annually. It falls in heavy storms in the 6-month summer rainy season. Conceptually, the interaction between rainfall, soil, grass,

FIGURE 16.2 Rainfall, Soil, and Carrying Capacity

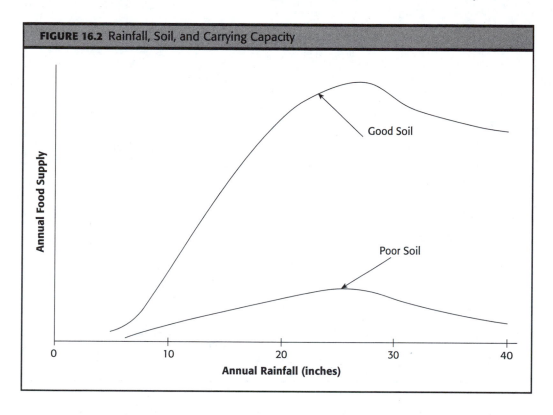

and carrying capacity is represented in Figure 16.2. Higher rainfall means more grass; one study reports a five-fold difference in grass and forage because of rainfall fluctuation.[7] This generally results in higher populations of grazers and predators. But not always: wildebeest and zebra may decline because their short grasses are crowded out in wet years.

The reality represented in the figure raises unpleasant choices. Now consider Figure 16.3. On the horizontal axis, the first curve falls to zero for 10,000 elephants. This means, representationally, that a KNP elephant population of 10,000 would completely exterminate the park's baobab trees.

The baobab is itself unique, reaching 100 feet in circumference and 80 feet in height. An ancient this size will be more than 4,000 years old. In other words, individual trees of this age began growth before the development of classical Rome and Athenian civilization. Because their unique spongy composition holds moisture, they are favorite targets for hungry and thirsty elephants in drought years. With an elephant population considerably above the park's current 7,000 level, dry years would see the destruction of the remaining baobabs.

Figure 16.3 also represents a second curve farther to the right. Elephants usually have a net population increase of 5 percent annually. If climate permitted, elephant numbers might grow from 7,500 to 20,000 in 20 years. A series of severe drought years following several good years, impacting a population of 20,000 elephants in the park, would mean a painful death by starvation of something on the order of

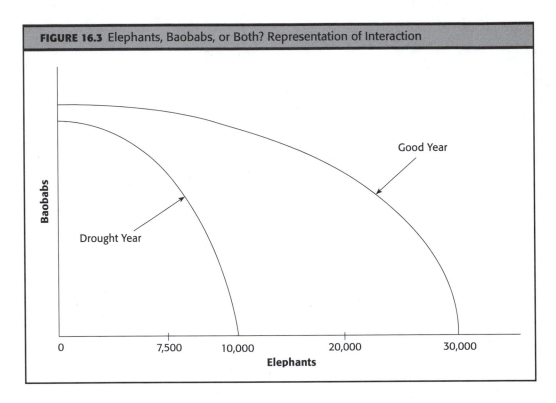

FIGURE 16.3 Elephants, Baobabs, or Both? Representation of Interaction

5,000 to 15,000 elephants. This would parallel the mass deaths of wildlife in Zimbabwe in the drought years in the early 1990s.

This interaction between elephant and baobab numbers in the park is similar to the economic concept of the 'production possibility frontier.' Each curve represents the best possible combination, given the assumption about drought or a good year for rain. For any level of the elephant population, the graph shows the maximum baobab population. And for any level of baobab numbers in the park, the curves show the maximum elephant population which can coexist with this number of baobabs.

We can transfer this concept to ecological relationships and refer to it as a 'coexistence possibility frontier.' The entire frontier shrinks or expands according to rainfall level.[8]

Of course, the numbers are used here illustratively, but, given the present state of the art of ecological knowledge, they are the right order of magnitude. The Kruger National Park management has to make intentional decisions about elephant population levels.

In this discussion, the baobab tree has been used as a type of marker for ecosystem health and biodiversity. The dimensions of the elephant population dilemma are much larger. In Kenya, the Amboseli National Park has been managed to maximize the number of elephants, which attract tourists. As a result, the Amboseli has become less habitable for many of its animal species of 30 years ago. Rhino, giraffe, large antelope, baboons, and monkeys have been lost or greatly reduced in number as Amboseli's growing elephant population destroyed 90 percent of its woodland.[9]

This discussion summarized the scientific basis for birth control, culling, or translocating elephants out of the park, thus keeping both stable elephant population levels as well as the healthy diversity of the park's natural ecosystem.

The argument against culling is philosophical. One well-said observation has been made by an architect of the earlier culling policy:

> *To repose in close proximity of a herd of elephants going quietly about their business is an emotional experience. One does not have to sit for long before their intelligence, playfulness, compassion and tolerance become evident. [This instills] a feeling of empathy which subsequently will not easily tolerate the concept of killing these wonderful animals.*[10]

Economic Problems and Opportunities: Hunting, the Poaching Problem, the Ivory Ban

The KNP and many other parks are threatened by economics as well as by possible loss of endangered species. There is growing concern that poverty in surrounding communities is a long-term hazard to the continuation of the protected areas.

One new program in Zimbabwe created to address this economic problem is CAMPFIRE: Communal Areas Management Programme for Indigenous Resources. It has been supported by the U.S. Agency for International Development, and assisted by the World Wildlife Fund. In Zimbabwe, rural communities are participating in wildlife management to earn income from hunting trophy rights sales.

Consider a hypothetical $10,000 paid by the hunter for a trophy hunting permit and an additional $10,000 paid to the safari operator. (Typically, the hunter is from an OECD or Middle Eastern country.) The local village might, for example, receive $5,000. Part would be spent on projects, such as a corn mill, or perhaps a CAMPFIRE vehicle. The remainder would be distributed on a cash basis to residents. For some rural areas, these payments, on the order of $50 per household annually, equal total cash income from all other sources.[11] The accomplishment is clear: villagers discourage poaching and illegal settlement, promote conservation, develop local projects, and increase their household income.

The major problems are twofold. First, CAMPFIRE is most effective in sparsely populated regions with significant wildlife, especially elephants. One successful location in northern Zimbabwe, for example, has only 20,000 residents living in 1,000 square miles. The second problem relates to economic sustainability. The capital costs, such as fencing, have been paid by USAID and the World Wildlife Fund. If this outside funding ceases, it is unclear whether CAMPFIRE can continue.[12]

It is clear, however, that with 1–2 million people living around the Kruger National Park, hunting trophy income is unlikely to have significant potential on a wide basis. For example, if the 300 or so elephants now removed annually were all removed by trophy hunting permits at $10,000 for each permit, this would provide only $3 per capita annually.

There is another problem with hunting that is not widely known. It is psychological, or more specifically, concerning animal psychology. How do large mammals come to view humans if they have been subjected to hunting? Here, hunting means

TABLE 16.3 Human Deaths Involving Wildlife, 1993

1. Mabalingwe Reserve. Woman tourist killed by hippo. February.
2. Pilanesberg Reserve. Tourist killed after relocated elephant tossed car. April.
3. KNP. Chief anti-poaching ranger gored and trampled. April.
4. Phinda Reserve. Woman at a dinner partially eaten by relocated lion. April.
5. Hoedspruit near KNP. Farm worker eaten after climbing game farm fence. June.
6. Etosha National Park, Namibia. Tourist killed by lions. August.
7. Mabula Game Lodge. Ranger killed by lions while feeding them. August.
8. KNP. Ranger trampled by wounded elephant. Poachers suspected in wounding. September.
9. Lion Park near Johannesburg. Tourists awaken sleeping lions for group photo of lions and tourists. Two tourists are killed; lions "shake the pair by their necks." October.
10. Komati River near KNP. Woman fishing is bitten and trampled by hippo. November.

Source: D. Chapman, memo, December 6, 1993. Ten of the deaths were in South Africa, and one was in nearby Namibia.

for sport, food, poaching, or culling. Park staff assert that, on two occasions, cow elephants with calves have used trees to attack airplanes. In each case, the plane was involved in a culling operation directed against the elephants.[13]

In one year, 1993, eleven persons in game reserves were killed by large animals. These incidents are summarized in Table 16.3. Four occurred in or near the Kruger National Park. One victim was the chief anti-poaching ranger.[14] Several of the incidents may involve animals that were shot or relocated.

One serious obstacle to the introduction of hunting in the Kruger is the interaction between hunting, animal life, and tourism. Today, the Kruger mammals do not associate vehicles with hostile intent. A car, even an open vehicle, can approach a relaxed lion or elephant as close as 30 yards before irritating the animal. Antelope and baboons are equally accustomed to tourists. This accommodation of tourists by animals is possible now because hunting is absent within the park.

Katherine Payne points out that elephants are highly social. The highest impulse that clan leaders have is to protect their relatives. They have long and detailed memories, with great intelligence. Some animals that have been stressed by hunting or culling react with fear, belligerence, or both.[15]

The coexistence of wildlife and tourism could be terminated, however, if hunting were to be initiated. The Kruger animals may be unable to differentiate vehicles, planes, and people on foot, according to whether they are hunters, scientists, or tourists. The smaller hunted animals may learn to avoid all humans, including tourists. The larger animals would probably have a more complex reaction. They could become quick to anger or flee, or might learn to retaliate against humans.

Perhaps future work will clarify this question of the triangular psychological interaction between tourists, large animals, and hunters.

Poaching arises because local incomes are very low, and the profit can be many multiples of annual income. Wholesale, ivory sells for more than $1,000 per pound in Asia.[16] At the ground level, the poacher might receive 10 percent of this, or $100 per pound. For a male elephant with two 20-pound tusks, the poacher may receive $4,000 for a few hours of grisly work with a chainsaw. Rhino horn prices are comparable.

Both elephant and rhino are protected by international agreement; trade in rhino horn is prohibited by the CITES agreements discussed in the previous chapter. The CITES agreements affecting trade in elephant ivory are more complex. From 1989 to 1997, the African elephant was listed in Appendix I, as an endangered species. All trade in ivory was banned globally. However, in 1997, three countries in Southern Africa (Namibia, Botswana, and Zimbabwe) sought and received Appendix II listing. Trade in ivory from these countries is now allowed, commencing in 1999.[17]

In general, the CITES agreements on rhino horn and elephant ivory seem to have had a beneficial effect. The Ivory Ban, in particular, seems to have halted the steep decline in elephant numbers. The total African elephant population is probably around 500,000.[18]

Figure 16.4 shows the economic logic of these international agreements. The situation a decade ago is represented by demand curve D_1. Two different anti-poaching philosophies are also illustrated. MC_H represents high costs to poachers, particularly high risk. It is based upon a high-security approach, which raises the costs to poachers of gaining illegal ivory or horn. In the Kruger National Park, for example, a ranger involved in poaching received a lengthy prison sentence, and many poachers have died.[19] The intersection of MC_H and D_1 define the price P_A and quantity Q_A. The CITES bans shift the demand curve down to the new lower level D_2. Now, the price is a much lower P_B, and poaching has been forced down to Q_B. In fact, retail demand for carved ivory fell 75 percent during the period of the full Ivory Ban.[20]

A different security approach is taken in Central Africa. In spite of dedicated efforts by individual rangers, government officials have been involved in poaching, and funds are limited and declining for security and protection measures. This is represented by the low-security marginal cost curve MC_L. (Remember, this means low cost to poachers.) The pre-ban situation has a very high poaching quantity Q_C, and a low price P_C.

The effect of the ban in low-security areas would be at the D_2 and MC_L intersection. (This intersection is not shown on the graph.) In this case, with minimal park security, the ban has a smaller effect on reducing the equilibrium price for ivory and horn.

However, in general it is economics that underlies the effectiveness of the CITES bans that reduce poaching levels, even in low-security African reserves.

Suppose the ban were to be accompanied by an aggressive advertising campaign attacking the presumed aphrodisiacal and medicinal properties of elephant and rhino parts. The demand curve would be pushed below D_2, further reducing the prices for illegally traded rhino and elephant material. The amount of poaching would also decline further.[21]

FIGURE 16.4 Economics and the CITES Bans

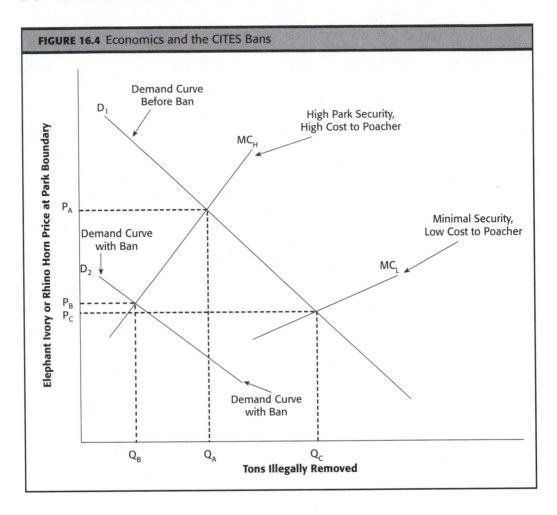

The Kruger National Park has maintained its elephant and rhino populations against poaching by an aggressive policy whereby park rangers often work with the South African army and police. However, another reserve, the Hluhluwe-Umfolozi Park in northern KwaZulu-Natal, is a major part of rhino protection activities. Its 1,600 white rhino and 350 black rhino rank with the Kruger in protecting the largest rhino populations in the world. Although it has only 5 percent the area of the KNP, the KwaZulu-Natal Parks Board has so successfully protected rhinos that this park has been the source of relocated animals throughout the world.

Notwithstanding its much larger size, the Kruger National Park has a comparable 1,800 white rhino and a black rhino population in the neighborhood of 350. Taken together, these two parks protect one-half of the African white rhinos and a fourth of the continent's black rhinos.[22] Because of heavy poaching throughout Africa, the KNP, and the Hluhluwe-Umfolozi Park each year hold a rising fraction of the declining totals. In the mid-1990s, aggressive anti-poaching security measures had stabilized rhino populations in both rhino species in each park. Of course, as noted above, aggressive security has been more effective with the relatively success-ful implementation of the CITES bans on trade in elephant and rhino parts.

As we have noted, the depressed level of rural incomes is one factor influencing motivation for poaching. This introduces a question of much new interest: can the Kruger Park and others provide significant incentives for economic growth?

The Land Question, the Apartheid Legacy, and Livestock

In South Africa, 87 percent of the country's land had been reserved for Whites. Blacks, accounting for more than 80 percent of the country's population, had, in general, been denied access to good agricultural land.[23] With the final dismantle-ment of apartheid in the 1994 elections, the Kruger Park was the subject of propos-als to develop cattle and livestock grazing for the residents of the surrounding poverty-stricken areas. (It should be noted, however, that the area of Kruger Na-tional Park itself was not significantly populated by either Blacks or Whites when the park was formed.)

As background, it is important to recognize the negative attitudes toward parks that developed in response to the nearly exclusive use of them by Whites. Table 16.4 represents three versions of the negative attitude. Many of the people living around the Park had been forcibly relocated there by police actions during the apartheid era. Others were refugees from the civil war in adjacent Mozambique.

As a consequence, the new Minister of Land Affairs in South Africa raised the question of opening the Kruger Park to domestic cattle grazing for Blacks.[24] This

---

TABLE 16.4 Critical Perspectives on Wildlife and Ecosystem Protection[25]

Mamphela Ramphele—"Narrow environmental thinking is also reflected in the willingness of individuals and institutions to donate millions of rands to save endangered species. [Would they] lift a finger to prevent the unnecessary deaths of children from diseases caused by poverty? Black South Africans associate such people with a white-dominated culture which accords greater respect to pets than to blacks."

Jacklyn Cock and Eddie Koch—"Infant mortality rates [do not] have the same fashionable appeal as the conservation of the black rhino. The result is that many South Africans view environmental issues as white middle-class concerns."

Alpheus Zungu—"The people in the community are divided. Many still associate the word 'conservation' with the white man coming to steal their land and give it to the animals. The jobs created by the Hluhluwe-Umfolozi reserve are helping us. But I think we need to see more benefits."

TABLE 16.5 Agricultural Potential in the Kruger National Park[26]

	Extensive Development	Unimproved
A. Yields, per year		
Corn (maize)	32 bushels/acre	8 bushels/acre
Livestock	20 acres per animal	30 acres per animal
B. Land area		
Corn (maize)	62,000 acres	Same
Livestock	5 million acres	Same
C. Total income, per year		
Corn (maize)	$1.8 million annually	$600,000 annually
Livestock	$15.4 million annually	$4.6 million annually
Total	$17.2 million annually	$5.2 million annually
D. Required public investment	$114 million	$4 million

has understandable appeal to impoverished households that seek to improve their economic situation through work. However, the natural ecology of the park is not hospitable to agriculture. The soil and rainfall combine to define an area that has low yields for corn as well as livestock. The agricultural potential is summarized in Table 16.5.

The table for the park shows limited potential. Without improvements, the yields for corn and livestock are low. The 62,000 acres studied for corn were the locations with the greatest potential for crops; the rest of the park has less potential. If almost all of the Kruger were converted to cattle, the annual income with extensive development would be $15.4 million for livestock and $1.8 million for corn.

The income data for traditional unimproved agriculture is less promising. The total estimate is $5.2 million per year. Considering the endemic poverty that is prevalent now in the traditional agricultural areas around the park, and also the very low potential within the park, this policy would condemn the agriculturalists to permanent economic deprivation.

One major economic problem here is opportunity cost, which is expressed in two ways. First, is expansion of low-income agriculture the most productive use of public sector funds? Within the general Kruger National Park region, would investment in education and roads be more productive? Second, how much potential opportunity for economic growth is lost if the park is converted to agriculture? To this point in the discussion, there has been considerable emphasis on the positive nonmarket values arising from the park. However, there is economic potential for community development that arises from the park itself.

Fees and Community Development

In the mid-1990s, the fee for a car's entrance to Kruger National Park was about $18.[27] The fee was the same for one day or one week. Of the 600 to 700 thousand annual visitors, about 12 percent were high-income visitors, from countries beyond Southern Africa. They pay the same fees as South Africans. These figures define apparent fee revenue on the order of $5 to $10 million.

Now suppose that fees are increased tenfold for foreign visitors, and doubled for South Africans. If visitation were to be unchanged, total fee revenue would triple to almost $20 million. Immediately, it should be noted that this value, by itself, far exceeds potential trophy hunting income, and is comparable to possible agricultural income potential.

The question is whether there would be a significant decrease in visitors, which would reduce income. Usually, economists assume that higher price reduces sales, and maximum revenue will have a price between the lowest and highest possible.

However, the KNP has developed a unique rationing system. Something less than 3 percent of the park is developed with gravel and asphalt roads and buildings. The maximum overnight capacity is 3,500.[28] Reservations are often made 6 months to a year in advance, and it is not uncommon for all lodging to be reserved. This implies an economic situation similar to that outlined in Figure 16.5.

FIGURE 16.5 Fees, Revenue, and Ecosystem Rationing

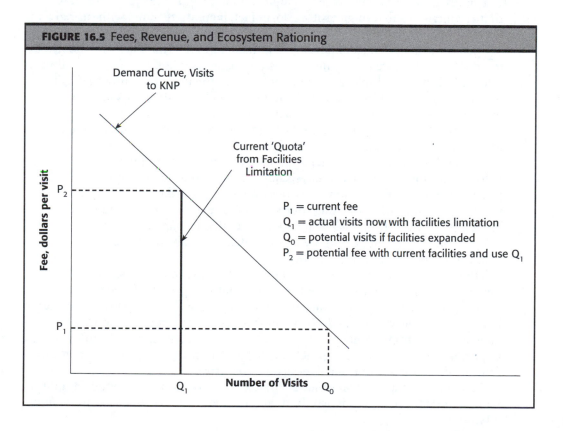

Demand Curve, Visits to KNP

Current 'Quota' from Facilities Limitation

P_1 = current fee
Q_1 = actual visits now with facilities limitation
Q_0 = potential visits if facilities expanded
P_2 = potential fee with current facilities and use Q_1

Fee, dollars per visit

Number of Visits

The dark bar represents the maximum visits at Q_1 with the current level of development. The park has a very low fee, P_1, and if more facilities existed, demand would be a much larger Q_0. However, with the current facilities limit at Q_1, the fee could be raised to P_2. The revenue increase would be considerable.

Should roads and lodging be increased to handle larger numbers of visitors beyond the current 700,000? An important point to consider here is the externality effect of potential crowding. More visitors would negatively impact each other, and the natural ecosystem itself. We might imagine a relationship wherein ecosystem existence value declines sharply if actual ecotourism use increases above the current level. Perhaps the current use is the 'tourist carrying capacity.'

Another explanation for the absence of a decline in foreign visitor attendance when the fee increases relates to overall travel cost. Assume the typical foreign visitors are from Japan or Europe. They may be in South Africa on business, or to visit the Kruger and other protected areas. The visitor may spend $3,000 on airfare, hotels, etc. outside the park. The current park fee is less than one-half of 1 percent of the trip cost. Raising this fee tenfold for foreign visitors would add less than three percent to total trip cost. For foreign visitors, a $90 fee might be less than the cost of one night's lodging and dinner in the visitor's home country. In the context of this illustration, the higher fee for foreign park visitors alone would add on the order of $6 million to annual revenue.[29]

Empirical work on this subject is limited. One recent study by Lisa Chase finds that fee increases to foreign visitors do, in fact, increase revenue without reducing visitation significantly.[30]

'Ecotourism' as a concept developed in the late 1980s. It implies or connotes the travel of OECD citizens to natural areas, and suggests that the economic multiplier effect of foreign tourism can promote economic growth. In the proper perspective, it has a positive contribution to make to growth in living standards in Africa. However, it cannot be assumed to be a magic pill for development. Kenya, for example, holds considerable ecotourism assets. But it has experienced considerable decline in per capita income since 1980.[31]

It would seem that the Kruger National Park has a role to play in economic development in its region. The analysis here suggests that fee revenue has the most potential of any of the economic options available to the park.

The general concept of using tourist and fee revenue for community development has been widely discussed, and parks and private game reserves are viewed as 'engines of development.'[32] CAMPFIRE (discussed above) is perhaps the most widely known program.

However, the practical problems in implementation of this concept are difficult. One successful private firm is the Conservation Corporation. It is active in private sector game reserves, and operates the Phinda Reserve near Hluhluwe-Umfolozi. It is similar in some ways to the KNP: it emphasizes ecosystem protection, and follows an aggressive antipoaching policy. However, its management policy differs in one important respect that is not practical for the Kruger: perhaps more than three-fourths of its visitors are from high-income countries.[33]

In another respect, the private Phinda Reserve and the public Hluhluwe-Umfolozi Park operate similarly: both allow supervised wood-cutting for community use.

More importantly, both reserves have abandoned the traditional international aid practice of transmitting all financial support to community leadership groups. Each reserve has a local project manager who dispenses funds directly to local groups for building stores, schools, water, and sanitation facilities. Their participation is much more proactive and specific than was common in the 1980s and early 1990s.[34]

One basic problem is that the identification of economic efficiency in park management involves at least four types of knowledge. First, the nature of the interaction between tourism levels and park ecosystems is a new area for research. Is there actually a 'tourist carrying capacity' for protected areas? Second, what is the magnitude of the positive external social values? Third, can the park's responsibility for community development be defined? Finally, the fourth subject is perhaps the easiest to quantify with our current methods: the demand curves for park visits by South Africans and foreign visitors.

Contingent Valuation, Conclusion

John Douglas Holland used the contingent valuation method in his economic study of Hluhluwe and three other KwaZulu-Natal reserves.[35] Of the four areas he studied, the greatest nonuse preservation value arose at Hluhluwe. His overall conclusions are relevant to parks throughout Africa.

▲ Continue to use park revenues for park management
▲ Increase user charges because the typical visitor is willing to pay considerably more
▲ Develop a two-tier fee system for domestic and overseas visitors
▲ Implement a user fee for international research
▲ Raise concession fees, and consider room taxes for nearby park-dependent tourist facilities
▲ Consider royalties for park-focused commercial activities such as movies and commercial advertising
▲ Develop revenue from existence values by means of special stamp funds or other mechanisms
▲ Keep wilderness character in wilderness parks

The last two entries raise a new possibility for international environmental policy. The Global Environmental Facility of the World Bank has embarked upon a worldwide program to provide financial support for biodiversity protection in developing countries. It has initiated a white rhino conservation program in Malaysia and Indonesia.[36]

The Kruger National Park is unique in Africa with regard to several of the biodiversity dimensions introduced in Chapter 15. The mature elephants and rhinos live with intact horns and tusks, the plant ecosystem is healthy, there are stable free-roaming populations of grazers and predators, there are stable population levels for endangered species, and the park is accessible to African and international visitors in a semi-wilderness. Given the importance of existence value as a positive external effect, perhaps the Kruger National Park should receive international support to help address its regional problems. In any event, the policy issues arising from protected area management in low-income countries will grow in importance.

Questions for Discussion and Analysis

1. In forestry economics, 'extinction' of old-growth Douglas fir in a local area by clear-cutting is financially more rewarding than sustainable harvesting. (Remember Table 14.5 in Chapter 14.) Analyze this question for a population of 7,000 elephants, assuming 5 percent annual population increase, $4,000 from ivory sales for each male, and a time preference discount rate of 20 percent.

2. Considering Figure 16.4, duplicate the MC_L part of the graph but complete the MC_L intersection with D_2. Discuss the results. Are they applicable to Kenya and Zambia?

3. Analyze the agricultural potential for the Kruger National Park (Table 16.5) with a benefit-cost analysis in two steps. First, assume that the public investment infrastructure lasts 20 years, and use a 15 percent discount rate. (Use either present value or the levelized annual amount approach.) What are the net benefits? Second, assume that the Kruger National Park revenue of $26 million annually is lost if the park is converted to agriculture. Recalculate net benefits.

4. Most environmental economists accept the concept that ecosystem externality values require many protected areas to be managed so that ecotourism visitation is at less than revenue-maximizing levels. However, in the context of protected areas similar to the Kruger National Park, many economists would favor using higher fees rather than facilities quotas to control visitation. Which do you prefer? Is the issue relevant to U.S. parks? Explain your thinking.

5. If you have read Chapter 6, consider the applicability of the theory of sustainability to the question of elephant populations outside protected areas. Some economists argue that community management of elephants and their ecosystems for hunting would lead to economically optimal results, compared to open-access hunting. Show this graphically. Discuss the potential problems with this policy in the Kruger National Park.

Notes to Chapter 16

1. Rick Lomba, before his untimely death, nearly completed an extraordinary video film on African wildlife protection and utilization, on domestic cattle, and on the issues facing food and development aid in Africa. He was killed in 1994 by a tiger while filming rescue efforts in the Luanda Zoo in Angola during the civil war there. The film includes a review of some of the issues facing the Kruger National Park.
2. Most of the topics listed in the text were taken up in earlier chapters. However, Chapter 20 on sustainability and endangered species is relevant.
3. J. Stevenson-Hamilton, "Report on the Sabi Game Reserve for the Year Ending August 1903," originally available in the Kruger National Park Library, Skukuza.

4. Table 16.1 shows some of the difficulties in implementing endangered species concepts. The African elephant, for example, is considered vulnerable by the IUCN, and threatened by the U.S. Fish and Wildlife Service. It is on CITES Appendix 1 list ("endangered"), except in Zimbabwe, Botswana, and Namibia, which are on the Appendix II list. However, the rapid decline in African elephant populations halted in the mid-1990s at a level on the order of 500,000. Further decline is likely, but extinction in reserves is highly improbable unless there is a total breakdown in public and private reserve management in Southern Africa. See the discussion of poaching and the ivory ban later in the chapter, and Chapter 15 on biodiversity.

   The Asian elephant in India and Nepal is at risk, according to every source, but is a different species.

   The white rhinoceros is not formally considered endangered in Southern Africa, but is clearly approaching extinction in Zaire and Central Africa. Heavy poaching pressure (discussed below) carries significant hazards for free-ranging populations.

   While necessarily a matter of judgment, as well as scientific fact, the table of successfully protected endangered species represents one facet of the KNP achievements.

5. Also recall the issue of nonhuman value in Chapters 5 and 15.

6. Ian Whyte estimates the ranges with a typical area of 625 km², with significant variations in size for different clans. Rainfall averages 500 millimeters annually. It is drier in the north of the park and wetter in the south. The African seasons have directly opposite months to the seasons in the Northern Hemisphere. Sources are Ian Whyte, "The Movement Patterns of Elephant in the Kruger National Park in Response to Culling and Environmental Stimuli," 1993 *Pachyderm* 16:72–80; D. Paynter and W. Nussey, *Kruger: Portrait of a National Park* (Halfway House, South Africa: Southern Book Publishers, 1992), pages 81–84; U. De V. Pienaar, "Implications of Progressive Desiccation of the Transvaal Lowveld," 1985 *Koedoe* 28:93–165.

7. This discussion and Figure 16.2 are suggested by "Elephant-Habitat Working Group, Discussion Three," 1993 *Pachyderm* 17:10–18, and R. H. V. Bell, "Carrying Capacity and Off-Take Quotas," in Bell and E. McShane-Caluzi, eds., *Conservation and Wildlife Management in Africa* (Washington, DC: U.S. Peace Corps, 1985). Also, Heywood and Watson (*op. cit.* Chapter 15), page 834.

8. The name 'coexistence possibility frontier' for baobabs and elephants was suggested by John R. Moroney, personal communication.

9. There is an extensive literature on the interaction of high elephant population levels with the surrounding ecosystems. Some of the available publications are: Ian Whyte, "Culling for Survival," November 1994 *Custos*, pages 22–27; R. N. Owen-Smith, *Megaherbivores* (New York: Cambridge University Press, 1988), Chapter 12; P. Van Wyk and N. Fairall, "The Influence of the African Elephant on the Vegetation of the Kruger National Park," 1969 *Koedoe* 12:57–89; R. M. Laws, "Elephants as Agents of Habitat and Landscape Change in East Africa," 1970 *Oikos* 21:1–15. Three less technical publications are L. A. Isbell, "The Vervets' Year of Doom," August 1994 *Natural History*, pages 49–54; R. Bonner, *At the Hand of Man* (New York: Knopf, 1993), especially pages 223–226; and C. Sugal, "Elephants and People on a Crowded Continent: The Costs of Sharing Habitat," May/June 1997 *Worldwatch* 10(3):18–27.

10. The quotation is from Whyte, "Culling," *op. cit.,* page 22.

11. "Elephants Seen in a New Light," *Johannesburg Star Weekly*, August 12–18, 1993, page 13. Russell D. Taylor, "Elephant Management in Nyaminyami District, Zimbabwe," 1993 *Pachyderm* 17:19–29. Kay Muir and Jan Bojö, "Economic Policy, Wildlife, and Land Use in Zimbabwe," World Bank Environment Department Working Paper No. 68, September 1994.

12. Taylor, *op. cit.* A critical view is held by Chris Cole, a rural development worker and Extension Policy Analyst, KwaZulu-Natal: "Considering the vast quantities of financial resources committed to the CAMPFIRE project against the community benefits, I find it difficult to consider CAMPFIRE a success." (Personal communication, March 4, 1996.)

13. Paynter and Nussey, *op. cit.,* page 98.

14. I went to the ranger's office in Skukusa for a meeting with him on the day of his funeral, not being aware of his death.

15. Payne has pioneered work in elephant communications (e.g., K. B. Payne et al., "Infrasonic Calls of the Asian Elephant," 1986 *Behavioral Ecology and Sociology* 18:297–301.) Her *Silent Thunder: In the Presence of Elephants* will be less technical. Thirty-five years ago, U. De V. Pienaar et al. made this same point, pages 69–70 in "An Aerial Census of Elephant and Buffalo in the Kruger National Park, and the Implications Thereof on Intended Management Schemes," 1966 *Koedoe* 9:40–107.

16. "Ivory Haul," Johannesburg *Business Day* May 5, 1993. E. B. Martin, "Rhino Poaching in Namibia from 1980 to 1990 and the Illegal Trade in the Horn," 1993 *Pachyderm* 17:47, and "A Survey of Rhino Products for Retail Sale in Bangkok in Early 1992," 1992 *Pachyderm* 15:53–56.

17. The regulation of trade is very strict. See "African Elephant and the June 1997 CITES Meeting," December 1997 *Rhino and Elephant Journal*, pages 8–12.

18. Greg Overton, using probability concepts analogous to Chapter 9's discussion of oil resources, arrives at 579,000; "Update on the African Elephant Database," December 1997 *Rhino and Elephant Journal*, pages 13–16.

19. Personal communications, 1993.

20. Esmond Bradley Martin, "The Effects of the International Ivory Bans on Zimbabwe's Ivory Industry," November–December 1991 *SWARA* 14(6).

21. J. Khanna and J. Harford emphasize the importance of shifting the demand curve downward in "The Ivory Trade Ban: Is It Effective?" November 1996 *Ecological Economics* 19(2):147–155. Also see Gardner Brown and David Layton, "Saving Rhinos," presented February 27, 1998 in the Schulze-Robinson Seminar Series on Environmental Economics, Cornell University.

22. M. Brooks, "Chairman's Report: African Rhino Specialist Group," 1994 *Pachyderm* 18:16–18; W. Charlton-Perkins and R. de la Harpe, *Hluhluwe Umfolozi Park* (Cape Town: Struik, 1995).

23. Jacklyn Cock and Eddie Koch, eds., *Going Green: People, Politics, and the Environment in South Africa* (Cape Town: Oxford University Press, 1991), page 187.

24. D. Hanekom and L. Liebenberg, "Utilisation of National Parks with Special Reference to the Costs and Benefits of Communities," 1994 *Bulletin of the Grasslands Society of South Africa* 5(2):25–36, especially page 28. Also Durban *Daily News*, April 15, 1993, page 8. Also see "Land Lessons," Johannesburg *Mail and Guardian*, February 6 to 12, 1998, page 59.

25. Sources for Table 16.4: Mamphela Ramphele, ed., *Restoring the Land: Environment and Change in Post-Apartheid South Africa* (London: Panos, 1991), page 6. *Going Green: People, Politics, and the Environment in South Africa, op. cit.,* pages 2 and 6. Alpheus Zungu is quoted in Angus Begg, "A Fine Balance," August/September 1995 *On Track*, pages 30–33. Jane Carruthers makes a similar point in her chapter "The Other Side of the Fence," *The Kruger National Park: A Social and Political History* (Pietermaritzburg: University of Natal Press, 1995).

26. The original article of course uses hectares (2.47 acres), and South African rand (R3.5 per US$ at the time). From W. G. Englebrecht and P. T. van der Walt, "Notes on the Economic Use of the Kruger National Park," 1993 *Koedoe* 36(2):113–119. Assume a 20-year

period for repaying the initial costs of opening up the KNP to agriculture, and use a 10 percent interest rate in the Chapter 4 framework. Deforestation cost (at $4 million) has a levelized cost of $0.5 million, giving a net benefit for traditional agriculture of $4.7 million annually (i.e., $5.2 million less $.5 million per year).

With the more costly extensive development, $114 million initial investment translates into a levelized cost of $13.4 million. The net benefit is a lower $3.8 million (i.e., $17.2 million less $13.4 million per year).

27. Specifically, $6 per adult, and $6 for any car, for a day or a week. The text figure of $18 assumes a representative two adults in a car. This excludes revenue from accommodations, supplies, and other items.

28. From National Parks Board, *Kruger*, 1986. There are 3,000 beds in huts and lodges, and 500 campsites. Vehicles are limited to a maximum of 5,000 on peak days (N. J. Dennis and B. Scholes, *The Kruger National Park*, Cape Town: New Holland, 1995, page 30). Remember the total KNP size is 5 million acres. The average density on the highest peak days is 1,000 acres per vehicle.

29. For this hypothetical case, assume each car with an $18 fee carries two visitors, averaging $9 per visitor. A tenfold increase for 75,000 or so foreign visitors would be $6 million. Remember, this is illustrative.

30. Lisa Chase, "Capturing the Benefits of Ecotourism: The Economics of National Park Entrance Fees in Costa Rica," Cornell University M.S. thesis, January 1996. The locations that Chase studied in Costa Rica had nearby substitutes. With respect to the KNP, the locations mentioned at the beginning of the chapter are substitutes, as are the private reserves on the park's western border. In a U.S. context, variations in National Park Area fees do not appear to significantly affect visitation; memorandum, Njoroge Ngure to Duane Chapman, January 5, 1999, on his econometric analysis of factors influencing visitation rates.

31. World Bank, *World Development Report*, 1995 (page 162) and 1982 (page 110) editions show considerable decline in per capita GNP between 1980 and 1993, in inflation-adjusted exchange rate dollars.

32. From Fourie, page 123. J. Fourie, "Comments on National Parks and Future Relations with Neighboring Communities," 1994 *Koedoe* 37(1):123–136. The most widely read general discussion is Michael Wells and Katrina Brandon, *People and Parks*, World Bank, 1992.

33. The Conservation Corporation also operates the Ngala and Londolozi Game Reserves on the KNP western border. As the map indicates, their Phinda Resource Reserve is considerably to the south of the KNP.

34. A brief, excellent, on-the-ground report is the Angus Begg article cited above. The Palobara Foundation, working with Palobara Mining, follows a similar effective directed policy in community development. (This latter opinion is my judgment based upon personal inspection with John Volmink, then Director of the University of Natal Center for Applied Science and Mathematics Education.)

35. See Holland's Ph.D. dissertation, *A Determination and Analysis of Preservation Values for Protected Areas*, University of Natal-Pietermaritzberg, 1993. The first recommendation in this list is my phrasing; it seems to be implicitly understood in his work. The contingent valuation results are in his Chapter 4: the mean value was $140 (R490) annually.

36. See 1994 *Pachyderm* 18:3–8.

CHAPTER 17

MACROECONOMICS, TRADE, AND ENVIRONMENT

Introduction

Macroeconomics is the study of national and international aggregates of economic output, living standards, income, prices and inflation, business cycles, and economic growth and development. The interaction of environmental protection with these important economic variables, and with trade, are perhaps the most contentious issues in environmental economics. In this chapter, we review empirical work on the subject, and find contrasting conclusions in almost every topic: price impact, income levels, trade and environment, and productivity.

Macroeconomic analysis typically concludes that environmental protection costs have relatively small impact on producer costs and consumer prices. In contrast, engineering studies of individual commodities typically find much higher cost and price impact. It is that contrast that we will examine first.

Consumer Prices and Environmental Protection Costs

In the attainment of pollution control and environmental protection, higher costs of production are necessarily incurred by some economic sectors. Consider the increased costs of buying a new home. There are three obvious components. First, general inflation throughout the economy increases home construction cost. This is easily factored out with the usual deflation methods.[1] Second, as seen in the Forestry Economics chapter, lumber prices are rising in real terms. Finally, the costs of residential building lots are rising for many reasons, particularly because of environmental factors.

The cost of an average new house increased 362 percent in the 20 years to the mid-1990s.[2] However, taking inflation into account, the real housing cost increase was 20 percent. Much of this cost increase arose from environmental protection. For a $200,000 new home in Table 17.1, environmental costs are incurred through wetland mitigation, tree protection, and other items which are mandated by federal, state, or local authorities.

These environmental features of U.S. residential communities are widely supported, and there are clear environmental benefits from good water supply and sewerage: waterborne gastrointestinal illnesses are generally absent in the United

TABLE 17.1 Illustrative New Home Costs[3]	
Labor	$40,000
Lumber, panels, wood products	$15,000
Other materials (windows, doors, electrical, etc.)	$60,000
Marketing, management, profit, interest	$45,000
Land purchase	$20,000
Environmental site costs (wetland mitigation, storm water and erosion control, tree protection, permitting process)	$20,000
Total Cost, Illustration	$200,000

Note: Also see the lumber cost discussion in Note 5.

States. Other local environmental benefits of regulation include reduced soil erosion, the aesthetic gain from underground utility lines, and less tree loss in construction. All of these characteristics benefit both the homeowners and their community, and clearly illustrate the economic concept of positive externality.

The difficulty in pinpointing environmental impact on housing cost is emphasized by Figure 17.1 on lumber prices. As we saw in Chapters 14 and 15, new forestry practices related to selective harvesting and spotted owl ecosystem protection began in the 1990s. At the same time, old-growth Douglas fir is being depleted, and the availability of low-cost lumber is being reduced. As the figure shows in the Reference Case, lumber prices would be increasing even in the absence of the new forest policies. Based upon unpublished data from builders, industry, and Forest Service economists, $2,000 is a best-guess estimate of the magnitude of housing cost increase attributable to national forestry and endangered species protection policy. In other words, overall home purchase price to the homeowner may be about 1 percent higher because of the lumber cost–environmental protection link.

However, environmental policy in other sectors can reduce wood product costs. Note the lower curve below the reference case in the figure. Haynes and Adams believe that if cardboard and paper recycling increase in the United States to the 50 percent levels practiced in Europe and parts of Asia, then lumber prices would be 25 percent lower than would otherwise be the case. As we saw in Chapter 10, achieving this level of paper recycling might or might not be the type of policy where efficiency would be enhanced by a recycling subsidy.

Haynes and Adams also note that current acid rain levels reduce lumber yield per acre by 5 percent to 10 percent. (See Chapter 14.) Perhaps the new acid rain policies described in Chapter 11 may decrease this loss.

Very high environmental cost impact is the main characteristic of the calculations in Figure 17.2. In some ways, these amounts exaggerate the cost of environmental protection. For example, although new car purchase cost is higher, vehicle

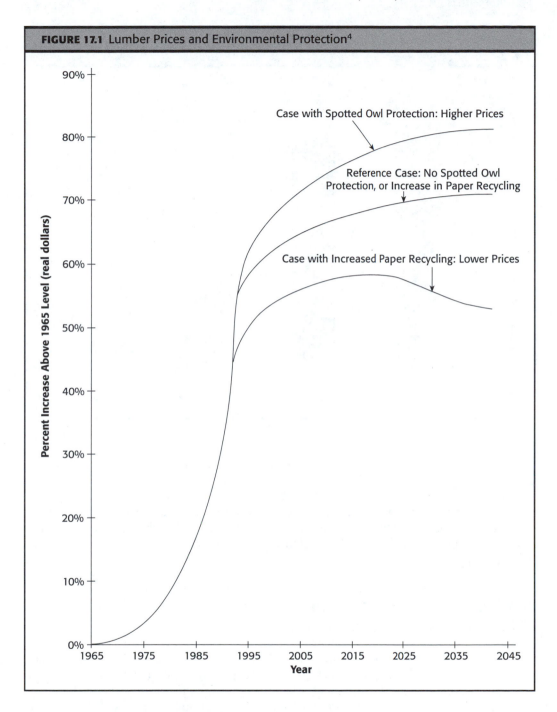

FIGURE 17.1 Lumber Prices and Environmental Protection[4]

Case with Spotted Owl Protection: Higher Prices

Reference Case: No Spotted Owl Protection, or Increase in Paper Recycling

Case with Increased Paper Recycling: Lower Prices

Percent Increase Above 1965 Level (real dollars)

Year

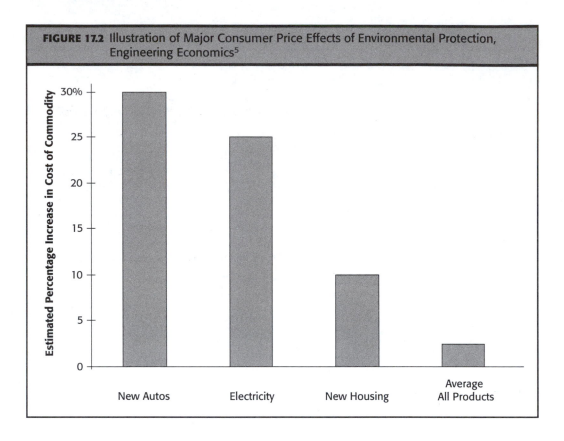

FIGURE 17.2 Illustration of Major Consumer Price Effects of Environmental Protection, Engineering Economics[5]

travel costs per mile remain low because today's vehicles last longer and use inexpensive gasoline. In addition, benefit-cost analyses generally show high net economic benefits resulting from the value of improved health.[6]

The approach used in Figure 17.2 is often termed the 'engineering method' because it analyzes the cost of particular physical items. In contrast, the macroeconomic approach usually finds much lower cost and price impact from environmental policies.

The Macroeconomic Approach to the Impact of Environmental Costs

In the previous section, we examined estimates of cost increases in consumer goods where those estimates are based upon the engineering approach to calculating the costs of the individual components of a product or manufacturing process. Typically, large-scale macroeconomic models of the U.S. economy give very different estimates of the economic impact of environmental protection costs. For the Clean Air Act, Dale Jorgenson and Peter Wilcoxen performed a macroeconomic analysis which is the basis for Table 17.2.[7]

TABLE 17.2 Major Impacts of Clean Air Act, Macroeconomic Approach[8]

Sector	Price Change	Output/ Consumption	Employment
Vehicles	+4.0%	−5.0%	−1.2%
Gasoline	+3.1%	−3.1%	−0.8%
Food	+0.9%	+0.5%	+0.7%
Furniture	+0.8%	+0.6%	+0.8%
Per capita personal consumption	+1.0%	−1.0%	na
GNP	na	−1.0%	na

In their study, the two industries most affected by Clean Air Act costs are motor vehicle manufacturing and gasoline production from petroleum refining. But, notice that the Jorgenson-Wilcoxen price increase for vehicles is far lower than the estimate in Figure 17.2. Again, the difference is typical.[9]

Food and furniture are also shown in Table 17.2. While these two sectors also experienced price increases, their sales and employment have actually increased slightly.

Why is this? The explanation for this macroeconomic finding lies in economic theory. Notice that the price increases for vehicles and gasoline are about four times greater than the price increases for food and furniture. The important point here is that the Clean Air Act changed the relative prices of these sectors, making food and furniture relatively cheaper, compared to vehicles and gasoline. To some extent, households that drive less have more discretionary time and money to use at home, and somewhat greater inclination to increase their expenditures on household food and furniture.

The economic concepts that explain this are generally introduced in courses in microeconomics. (The student without this background should pass over the analysis of Figure 17.3, and take up the discussion of employment impact directly below.)

Consider Figure 17.3. In the initial situation without the Clean Air Act, the consumer has disposable income at the budget level B_1, and reaches the utility indifference curve UI_1. The result is miles traveled at T_1 and food and furniture consumption at F_1. (Of course, other expenditure categories are not shown.)

The Clean Air Act raises costs and prices for both sets of purchases, but the price increase for miles traveled is much greater. This creates a lower budget line B_2. Now, the consumer reaches the lower indifference curve UI_2, with consumption levels T_2 and F_2.

Understandably, because the price increase for miles traveled (vehicles and gasoline) is much higher, the ratio of food and furniture to miles traveled has increased. But, note also that F_2 is actually slightly greater than F_1, even though the Clean Air Act increased somewhat the prices in this home consumption category. Since the figure shows a major change in relative prices, F (food and furniture) increases.

FIGURE 17.3 Change in Consumption Patterns from Clean Air Act Price Increases

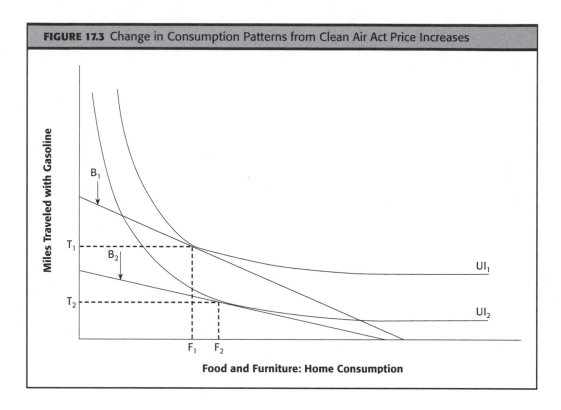

The relationships in Figure 17.3 reflect the same kinds of relationships as in Table 17.2; the Clean Air Act increased prices and costs for some sectors much more than for other sectors. As a result, some sectors with small price increases experienced slight increases in sales and output because of changes in relative prices. Again, remember that overall utility (including the value of environmental protection) has presumably increased for most households.

With respect to employment, the impact of the Clean Air Act parallels the impact on output. Table 17.2 shows small employment gains in food and furniture, and employment loss in vehicles and gasoline.

On a regional basis within the United States, income and employment effects can be more pronounced. For example, in the 1990s, Kane County, Utah, experienced a significant shift away from lumber and mining activity and toward tourism. As a result, employment paying $25 per hour was replaced by work with $5 per hour wages. Even though more people in each family went to work, average household income fell by 25 percent.[10]

A very different regional picture emerges in the work of Jane Hall and her colleagues on regional economic effects of Southern California's air pollution control success.[11] Their basic finding is that pollution levels in the 1960s were so harmful that further economic growth would have been inhibited if air quality had not been improved. In fact, major gains in air quality were accompanied by significant growth in employment, population, and income.

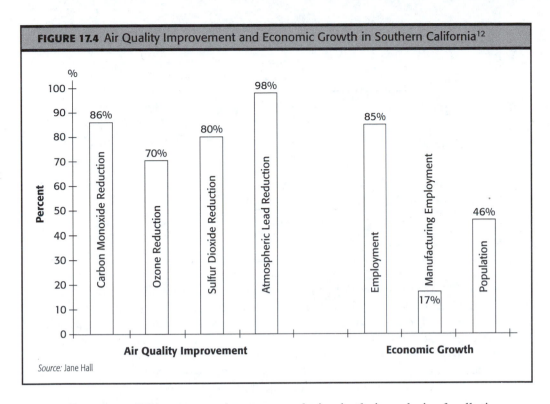

FIGURE 17.4 Air Quality Improvement and Economic Growth in Southern California[12]

Source: Jane Hall

Berman and Biu come to the same conclusion in their analysis of pollution control in Southern California. In fact, they find that employment has been very slightly increased by pollution control policies in the region.[13]

In Figure 17.4, the air pollution gains are impressive. But it should be remembered that Southern California continues to have the highest pollution levels of any urban area in the country.

The economic data in the figure show that growth in Southern California surpassed the U.S. averages in all three categories: employment, manufacturing jobs, and population.[14] One clearly negative aspect of growth in Southern California is the decline in average wages, which fell 29 percent over the period. This decline exceeds the fall in real wages for the United States[15] and has been attributed in part to competition from low-wage manufacturing with minimal pollution control expense. The considerable controversy about the issue of trade, income levels, and the environment is reviewed later in the chapter.

Climate Change Policy and Macroeconomics

As concern about climate change grows, both government and industry have undertaken macroeconomic analyses similar to the Jorgenson-Wilcoxen work on air pollution control. The results are considerably different according to each study.

In the U.S. Council of Economic Advisors' study in 1997, a carbon tax of $100 per ton was estimated to be the level necessary to reduce demand for energy to levels

TABLE 17.3 Carbon in Fuels and the Price Effect of a $100 per Ton Carbon Tax[16]		
Fuel	Carbon Content	Price Impact of $100 per Ton Carbon Tax
Gasoline	5.35 pounds carbon per gallon	27¢ per gallon
Natural gas	31.8 pounds carbon per MBtu	$1.59 per MBtu
Coal-powered electricity	.57 pounds carbon per kWh	2.85¢/kWh

Note: A $100 ton tax is 5¢ per pound of carbon contained in each fuel. On an energy basis, natural gas would have the lowest tax because it has less carbon. (On a dollars per MBtu basis used by the consumer, the figures would be $2.16/MBtu for gasoline and $8.35/MBtu for coal generated electricity.)

where CO_2 (carbon dioxide) emissions would return to 1990 levels. The macroeconomic effects were insignificant: no noticeable change in future GNP, employment, or inflation. (Table 17.3 shows the tax impact on gasoline, natural gas, and electricity.)

In contrast, a U.S. Department of Energy study completed at the same time projected major losses in U.S. production of aluminum, steel, and paper. This study concluded that a carbon tax in the United States alone would drive these industries to relocate much of their production outside the country.[17]

Robert Repetto and Duncan Austin completed an extensive review of 16 macroeconomic models and their forecasts of the responses of the U.S. economy to stabilized, lower CO_2 emissions. They define a 'best case' with several optimistic but plausible assumptions. Consumers install efficient levels of compact fluorescent lighting, for example (remember Chapter 7), and solar and nuclear power are expanded to reduce fossil fuel use (Chapter 8). They also assume that industry in developing countries will adopt the best technologies with help, and that revenues from the sale of marketable CO_2 permits will be used to reduce taxes on employment and investment. Finally, their work calculates the positive impact on GDP from reduced air pollution and climate change.

The result? Future macroeconomic growth is actually increased, by a small one-tenth of a percent annually. When they remove these positive assumptions, the effect of a carbon tax is a small negative one-tenth of a percent annual impact. Their overall conclusion is that "with sensible public policies and international cooperation, carbon dioxide emissions can be reduced with minimal impact on the economy."[18]

Trade, Pollution, and the Environmental Kuznets Curve: The Issues

In the preceding discussion of macroeconomics, we noted the conclusions of the Hall group and Berman and Bui that air pollution control enhanced growth in Southern California. We also discussed a U.S. industry study of a carbon tax inspired by climate change and their finding that considerable energy-intensive manufacturing might relocate outside of the United States. These topics are facets of the trade–environment debate, a dialogue that has exploded in the last 10 years.

In the influential review on this subject by the Jaffee group, more than 100 studies were analyzed. Perhaps the most important finding is best put in their words: "The data reveal that international differences in environmental costs, as a fraction of total production costs, are trivial compared with apparent differences in labor costs and productivity."[19] In this respect Jaffee represents the consensus of economists. In Table 17.4, this perspective is summarized along with two opposing views.

The Optimists, led intellectually by Michael Porter, believe that environmental regulation can stimulate technological innovation that lowers costs and improves competitiveness (more about this later). The Pessimists are clearly in the minority, arguing that differential environmental regulation is stimulating the growth of both industry and pollution in developing countries.

However, before reviewing the perspectives of the Optimists and Pessimists, it is helpful to focus more clearly on the complex, logical components of the economists' consensus on economics, trade, and environment. A broad division of the global market for a pollution-intensive nonferrous metal is shown in Figure 17.5. In Panel A, supply functions represent the two divisions: a high-income group, and a developing-country group. This is roughly representative of world copper markets where copper use in manufacturing is primarily in high-income countries, and production of copper is primarily in developing countries.

TABLE 17.4 The Economic Perspective on the Trade and Environment Issue[20]

1. *The General Consensus:* Pollution control costs are generally small, and have little or no impact on employment or wages in high-income countries. Transboundary pollution is usually minor, and the harmonization of international environmental standards is unnecessary. As the Environmental Kuznets Curve predicts, rising income will lead to lower pollution levels in developing countries. *(Grossman, Jaffee, Kruger, Portnoy, Repetto, Stavins)*

2. *The Optimists:* Environmental regulation in a free-trade environment stimulates innovation, productivity growth, and a strong competitive position. Again, the harmonization of international standards is unnecessary. *(Porter, Goodstein, Hall)*

3. *The Pessimists:* Environmental protection costs are significant in pollution-intensive industries, and encourage industrial growth for export in countries without significant pollution control. In addition, low wages make it impossible for municipalities to finance sewage treatment or waste disposal through local taxes. Transboundary and global pollution is growing, and the harmonization of minimum standards is necessary to prevent a "race to the bottom." *(OTA, Kanbur, Chapman)*

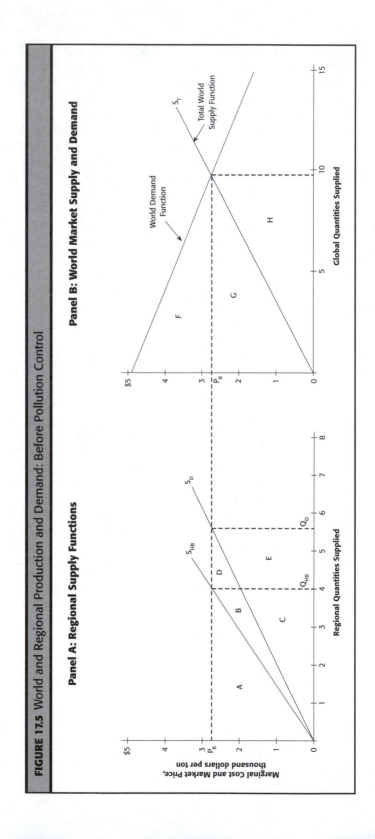

FIGURE 17.5 World and Regional Production and Demand: Before Pollution Control

TABLE 17.5 Consumer and Producer Surplus in Figures 17.5 and 17.7 from Production, Consumption, and Trade

	High Income Consuming Region	*Developing Region*	*Global Totals*
Producer revenue	A + B + C	A + B + C + D + E	G + H
Producer cost	B + C	C + E	H
Producer surplus	A	A + B + D	G
Consumer surplus	Most of F	Part of F	F
Social welfare	A + F − ENV	A + B + D − ENV	F + G − ENV

The supply function S_{HB} represents metal production in high-income countries before environmental protection, and S_D is the developing country supply function. Lower overall labor costs and perhaps resource endowment place S_D to the right of S_{HB}; S_D will supply more metal than S_{HB} at any price level.

Given the world market price P_B, production in each region is defined as Q_{HB} and Q_D. Producers' surplus in the high-income group is 'A' in the figure, and this surplus for the developing region is 'A' + 'B' + 'D.' (Remember these concepts from Chapter 1.) The graphical definitions for this and other economic concepts are in Table 17.5.

The global market is in Panel B. The total world supply function is S_T, and it is the sum of the two separate supply functions. It is the global markets for supply and demand that determine the equilibrium price P_B.

Environmental damage in this pollution-intensive industry is significant without pollution control.[21] It is reflected in Figure 17.6: global damage equals the sum of the amounts in each of the two regions. The "After" case shows significantly less global pollution after the unilateral implementation of pollution control in the high-income region.

To understand this, we must return to economics, this time Figure 17.7. First, observe that the new higher-cost supply curve for S_{HN} is to the left of the S_{HB}, which represented high-income regional supply before environmental protection.[22] Now, at any price, S_{HN} will supply less metal than the old S_{HB}. Panel B shows the new global market equilibrium for price and output.

What are the major changes as reflected in the differences between the two cases and their figures? First, the goal of environmental improvement in the high-income region has been achieved. In addition, although market forces have increased developing-country production and pollution, that increase is far less than the other region's reduction, so total global pollution damage is less.

In the high-income region, there is loss for producers and a very slight fall in consumer surplus from fewer sales at the new and higher price. But keep in mind that the gain in environmental protection surpasses the loss. Obviously, the incidence of loss and gain can vary within the high-income region.

It is of particular interest that the developing region also has a net gain. It makes up more than half of the production cutback in the high-income region, and now

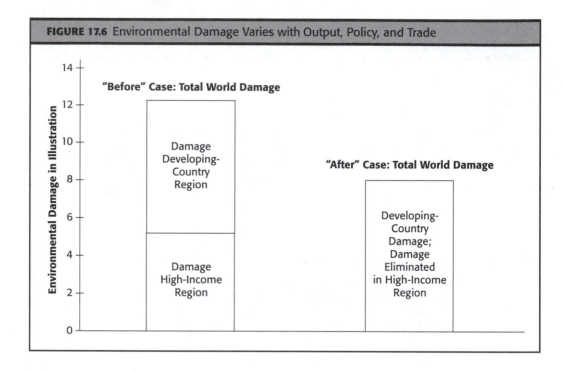

FIGURE 17.6 Environmental Damage Varies with Output, Policy, and Trade

sells more at a higher price. Consequently, the gain in producer surplus in the developing region more than offsets the smaller increase in environmental damage.

The major economic changes from pollution control for a pollution-intensive region are summarized in Table 17.6. Although the subject is difficult in its details, this illustration lays out the logic of the 'Consensus' position. If one country or region raises environmental standards, everyone is a winner. No international standards are necessary because each nation or region acting according to its own value preferences is enhancing national and global welfare.

TABLE 17.6 Major Trade and Environment Changes in Figures 17.5 and 17.7

	High-Income Consuming Region	Developing Region	Global Totals
Producer surplus and production	LARGE DECLINE	LARGE INCREASE	small decline
Consumer surplus	small decline	—	small decline
Environmental damage	LARGE REDUCTION	Increase	LARGE REDUCTION
Social welfare	Increase	Increase	Increase

FIGURE 17.7 New Prices, Production with Pollution Control in the High-Income Region

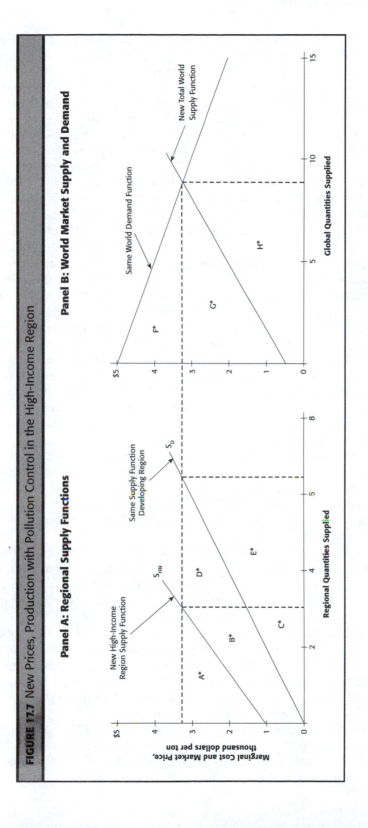

Panel A: Regional Supply Functions

Panel B: World Market Supply and Demand

This Consensus position also rests upon the findings of the Environmental Kuznets Curve (EKC), introduced in Chapter 2. In this perspective, economic growth first increases, then reduces pollution. (See Figure 2.2.) This is further support for the 'no international standards' view. The majority of economists are comfortable with this interpretation of the broad empirical evidence supporting the EKC.[23]

Andreoni and Levinson modify the Consensus position. They believe that the EKC exists because of two basic characteristics of the global economy.[24] First, there are increasing returns to scale from pollution abatement, and second, rising incomes encourage investment in abatement. They take no position on international standards, but support regulation within individual countries.

The Optimist view goes forward and makes an argument it partially shares with industrial ecologists: environmental standards can lead to new technologies that lower costs. This is the Porter Theory, articulated by Michael Porter and others.[25] In Figure 17.7, under this concept, S_{HN} would now be to the right of the old S_{HB}. Consequently, under this theory, producers in the high income region can actually produce more at lower cost. Working out the full details in this case would show lower market price, higher global output and sales, increased consumer surplus and producer surplus in this region, and less environmental damage.

If producers in developing regions chose to adopt the new technologies (and were allowed to do so by patent owners), then similar benefits would accrue in these regions. Obviously, this is an attractive theory, with broad economic as well as environmental benefits. There are some cases where this environmental improvement–cost reduction technology has emerged. Until the 1980s, sulfur emissions from metal ore smelting were a problem for worker health as well as the environment. For many years, the only pollution control technology was tall smokestacks, which dispersed the sulfur oxides rather than controlling them.

However, the 1980s saw the development of three new technologies. First, sulfur is itself captured and burned as a source of energy in the smelting process. Second, the final sulfur releases are captured and converted into sulfuric acid. Finally, this sulfuric acid is reused in chemical and electrical mining processes to produce metal, or is sold commercially. The overall result is both lower cost and near-elimination of acid rain emissions.

Today, metal can be produced with 5 percent or less of the amount of sulfur release than was common 25 years ago. As the Porter Theory suggests, new technology not only solved a serious environmental problem, it also reduced overall production costs.[26] This is a major achievement. As new research is completed, the debate for and against the Porter Theory should be resolved.

The Pessimists' view from Table 17.4 is held by a small minority of economists.[27] This perspective sees transboundary pollution between Mexico and the United States as important. The salinity of the Colorado River as it discharges into Mexico is important for Mexican agriculture. In the same way, air pollution from Mexican mines and factories affects the United States, as does the sewage from the border communities on the Rio Grande and Tijuana rivers.

The Pessimists interpret the apparent Environmental Kuznets Curve as resulting from the growth in trade of pollution-intensive exports manufactured in developing countries for export to consumers from high-income OECD countries.[28]

TABLE 17.7 Productivity, Wages, Environment: International Steel Industry, 1993

Country	Wages $/hr	Productivity tons/employee	Environmental Standards and Practice
U.S.	$30	500	Highest
Japan	$33	450	High
Canada	$22	400	High
W. Europe	$22	375	High
Korea	$10	300	Low
Brazil	$4	250	None?
Russia	$1	150	None?

Source: Jacobsen Steel Consultants, Pittsburgh, PA, 1995, prepared for USAID.

For the Pessimists, the conclusions from Figure 17.7 would be redrawn as follows: the supply curve S_{HN}, because of much higher environmental protection costs, would be shifted much farther left. With this pessimistic high-cost S_{HN}, much lower quantities of metal would be supplied at any price. The new global equilibrium would have a significantly higher price, and developing-country producers would displace most or all of the previous production in the high-income region. As a consequence of this pessimistic assumption, global environmental damage might be increased by the elimination of most production in the high-income region.

Consequently, in some specialized circumstances, the result of unilateral environmental policies can be a net increase in global pollution, and an increase in transboundary pollution affecting the high-income region.[29]

The pessimistic viewpoint is the only perspective whose logic supports the harmonizing of minimum international pollution standards. As the 21st Century grows, these three positions will continue to be debated in making global policy.

A final note on labor and the trade and environment debate. There is some empirical evidence that environmental standards, wages, and productivity are all positively related. Table 17.7 shows international estimates of the steel industry prepared by Jacobsen Steel Consultants. It appears that high labor productivity encourages both effective pollution control and high wages.

Summary

Detailed industrial engineering studies report significant impact on producer costs and consumer prices for pollution control and environmental protection for some commodities. Some examples of goods with high-cost impact, as evaluated with the engineering method, are new vehicles and electricity (from air pollution control) and housing (from timber policy and environmental protection on the home site).

However, these results are generally contradicted by macroeconomic findings which typically report small price impacts. The macro analysis also finds that slightly higher production cost and prices for pollution-intensive goods reduces demand for those commodities, but can increase demand for other items.

In aggregate, GNP per capita may be 1 percent lower than otherwise as a consequence of the Clean Air Act. However, it should be remembered from Chapter 11 that the national benefits of the act appear to significantly exceed its costs. In Southern California, population increase and economic growth have occurred simultaneously with and perhaps because of major reductions in air pollution levels.

The macroeconomic consequences of policies to reduce climate change are especially controversial. A carbon tax sufficiently large to affect energy use and temperature change would be significant. But different studies report opposite results, from minimal impact to major industrial relocation.

In the trade and environment debate, three contending positions have emerged. The Consensus school of thought generally agrees with the Environmental Kuznets Curve hypothesis, believing that trade encourages economic growth in developing countries, and this economic growth will ultimately cause developing countries to reduce pollution levels that are now rising. (This was explained more fully in Chapter 2.)

The Optimists hold a stronger position: environmental protection and regulation stimulate innovation. The Porter theory argues that environment-driven innovation improves the global competitive standing of firms that are leaders in environmental improvement.

Both of these positions (Consensus and Optimists) believe that international harmonization of pollution standards is unnecessary. Market forces left undisturbed create the necessary incentives for global pollution reduction.

The Pessimist perspective is held by a minority of economists. It sees a harmonization of minimum standards as essential to avoid an international "race to the bottom" where countries compete for growth in pollution-intensive industry by offering minimal standards as incentives.

Macroeconomic analysis has not yet been extended to the interaction between income, productivity, and environmental protection. In the global steel industry, however, wages, productivity, and pollution control are closely linked. The old chestnut, "more research is needed," is very appropriate here. The next few years may see the emergence of new research findings that resolve these difficult but important issues.

Questions for Discussion and Analysis

1. This chapter shows that the Clean Air Act has increased gasoline prices, as shown in Table 17.2. But elsewhere in the book (Figure 9.2, for example), gasoline prices are said to have declined to historically low levels at the end of the 20th Century. Explain this apparent contradiction.

2. Suppose the elasticity of gasoline consumption with respect to price is −0.5 and carbon in fuels is taxed on the basis of $100 per ton. If gasoline sells for $1 per gallon

before the tax and the tax is added to the price, what would be the percentage reduction in gasoline consumption?

3. Some economists conclude that taxing carbon to reduce CO_2 emissions would leave GNP unaffected or increase it slightly. Others find that aluminum, steel, and paper production in the United States would experience major losses. Can you reconcile these findings?

4. Summarize in your own words the three basic economic perspectives on trade and environment. Do you favor one of the three? Why?

5. Reexamine the discussion of income levels and clean water in Chapter 12 in the context of the Environmental Kuznets Curve.

Notes to Chapter 17

1. Remember the method for calculating inflation-adjusted real dollars from Chapter 2.
2. The sources for the housing cost data are National Association of Home Builders, Weyerhauser, and U.S. National Forest Service economists, all private communications. Since general inflation in the CPI was 301 percent over the 20-year period (1974–1994), the nominal price increase of 362 percent translates into a real price increase of 20 percent over the period.
3. The house in Table 17.1 is assumed to be 2,000 square feet of finished space, with one floor and a basement, with a covered garage, and includes appliances, carpeting, and three bathrooms. This average new home is built with 17,000 board feet of lumber and 10,000 square feet of plywood and wood panels. (From USEIA, *Renewable Energy Annual* 1996, page 20.) In addition to the gains in environmental externalities discussed in the text, a new home now, compared to a generation ago, has lower heating costs and is more comfortable, as discussed in Chapter 7. Other data sources are the same as in Note 2.
4. Figure 17.1 is a simplified recalculation of the data of Richard Haynes and Darius Adams, "The Timber Situation in the United States," May 1992 *Journal of Forestry*, pages 38–42. Incidentally, a recent study of lumber industry employment concluded that growth in real GNP and in home construction influence lumber industry output and employment much more than National Forest policy; D. M. Burton, "A Structural Analysis of National Forest Policy and Employment," August 1997 *American Journal of Agricultural Economics* 79(3):964–974.
5. In Figure 17.2, because of the uncertainty, the percentages are rounded to the nearest 5 percent, except for the last entry. The environmental cost estimate for a new automobile includes both safety and pollution control, from American Automobile Manufacturers Association, *Motor Vehicle 1996 Facts and Figures*, page 60. Remember (Chapter 11) that a new car has about only 5 percent of the emissions per mile typical of the pre–Clean Air Act vehicles.

   The electricity estimate (25 percent) assumes that environmental costs constitute 50 percent of generating costs, and 10 percent of transmission and distribution costs. See Chapman, *Energy Resources op. cit.,* page 267.

   The new housing figure (10 percent) is partially explained in the text: $2,000 higher lumber costs and $20,000 environmental site costs, totalling 22 percent, rounded to the nearest 5 percent, or 20 percent. (Gregg Easterbrook believes $5,000 has been added to new home costs by spotted-owl-induced policy, in his *A Moment on the Earth* (New York: Viking,

1995), page 227.) The average all products figure (2.5 percent) is from the 1995 estimate for GNP cost from pollution control, by Alan Carlin, discussed by Eban Goodstein, *Economics and the Environment* (Englewood Cliffs, NJ: Prentice-Hall, 1995), pages 109–110.

6. Remember the low current price of gasoline in real dollars; from Chapters 1 and 9. Benefit-cost analysis of air pollution control was examined in Chapter 11.

7. As with the acid rain program, the Clean Air Act is a major subject in the economics of air pollution in Chapter 11. The Jorgenson-Wilcoxen work is described in the following Note 8 to Table 17.2.

8. Table 17.2 is based upon data in USEPA, *The Benefits and Costs of the Clean Air Act, 1970–1995*, 1997, Appendix A, "Cost and Macroeconomic Modelling." This Appendix describes the structure and analysis of the Jorgenson-Wilcoxen model. In that report, data are reported in a format that uses the Act as the reference base case, and estimates percentage differences for the year 1990. Table 17.2, in contrast, uses as a reference the absence of the Act. Aggregate national employment, apparently, is assumed to be fixed in both cases. Since the aggregate personal consumption declines by 1 percent because of the costs of the Act, I assumed for the table that an appropriate defined price index would be 1 percent higher. Incidentally, the full analysis covers 35 sectors.

9. The causes for the difference in estimates between macroeconomic and engineering studies are discussed in U.S. Office of Technology Assessment, *Industry, Technology, and the Environment*, by Peter Blair, 1994; and D. Chapman, "Environmental Standards and International Trade in Automobiles and Copper," Summer 1991 *Natural Resources Journal*, 31(3):449–461.

10. *High Country News*, April 14, 1997, page 8.

11. See Chapter 11's discussion of air pollution in Southern California. The work of Hall and her group is reported in J. Hall, et al., *The Automobile, Air Pollution Regulation and the Economy of Southern California*, Institute for Economic and Environmental Studies, California State University, Fullerton, California, April 1995, and in D. C. Hall and J. V. Hall, eds., *Advances in the Economics of Environmental Resources*, Volume 2, *Air Pollution and Regional Economic Performance* (Greenwich, CT: JAI, 1997). Also South Coast Air Quality Management District, "The Southland's War on Smog," Diamond Bar, CA, 1997.

12. See Note 11 above.

13. E. Berman and L. T. M. Bui, *Cleaning the Air: Implications of Environmental Regulation for the Economy and the Environment; Evidence from the South Coast Air Basin*, Economic Policy Institute, Washington, DC, forthcoming.

14. The national U.S. figures for growth in the same period were 53 percent increase in employment, 4 percent decline in manufacturing jobs, and 24 percent population growth. From Hall, *op. cit.*

15. The data for Southern California wages are from Hall, *op. cit.*, which are deflated by the CPI. U.S. data from U.S. Council of Economic Advisors, *Economic Report of the President*, February 1997: the average real weekly wage for the U.S. was 11 percent lower in 1990 than in 1965. Incidentally, Los Angeles ranked fifth in the U.S. in wage levels.

16. The sources used to calculate the carbon content in Table 17.3 are T. Drennen, *Economic Development and Climate Change*, Ph.D. dissertation, Cornell University, 1993, pages 10 and 34; and June 1997 *Monthly Energy Review*, page 149 and Appendix C. Also, USEIA, *Emissions of Greenhouse Gases in the United States*, 1987–1994, page 76. To estimate home energy emissions of carbon, use the techniques in Chapter 8.

17. The period analyzed in the CEA study is 2000 to 2020. One of the models used in the study projects a small GDP loss for a few years, followed by a positive impact in GDP growth from 2014 to 2020. The three models and their results are discussed in detail in U.S. Council of Economic Advisors, Interagency Analytical Team, "Economic Effects of Cli-

mate Change Policies," memorandum, June 1997. The DOE study projected losses in cement, oil refining, and chemical manufacturing. Taken together, the industries used 70 percent of the energy in U.S. manufacturing. *Environment Reporter*, July 18, 1997, page 554.

18. R. Repetto and D. Austin, "The Costs of Climate Protection," World Resources Institute, Washington, DC, 1997. Also see R. B. Howarth, "Energy Efficiency and Economic Growth," and S. J. DeCanio, "Economic Modelling and the False Tradeoff between Environmental Protection and Economic Growth," both in October 1997 *Contemporary Economic Policy* 15(4):1–9 and 10–27. In addition, John Moroney finds that, for high-income countries, variations in energy use are not associated with variations in income. From his "Output and Energy: An International Analysis," July 1989 *Energy Journal* 10(3):1–18.

19. A. B. Jaffee, S. R. Peterson, P. R. Portnoy, and R. N. Stavins, "Environmental Regulation and the Competitiveness of U.S. Manufacturing: What Does the Evidence Tell Us?" March 1995 *Journal of Economic Literature* 33:132–163.

20. Table 17.4 summarizes the literature reviews and analysis in Jaffee, Peterson, Portnoy, and Stavins, *op. cit.;* G. Grossman and A. Krueger, "Economic Growth and the Environment," 1995 *Quarterly Journal of Economics* 110(2):352–377; P. Krugman, "What Should Trade Negotiators Negotiate About?" March 1997 *Journal of Economic Literature* 35(1):113–182; R. Repetto, *Jobs, Competitiveness, and Environmental Regulation* (Baltimore, MD: Resources for the Future, 1995). The Environmental Kuznets Curve appeared in Chapters 2 and 12. Also M. E. Porter and C. Linde, "Toward a New Conception of the Environment-Competitiveness Relationship," Fall 1995 *Economic Perspectives* 9(4):97–118; E. Goodstein, *op. cit.,* Chapter 7; J. Hall and A. Puri, *Performance of the Southern California Economy*, in D. Hall and J. Hall, eds., *Air Pollution and Regional Economic Performance, op. cit.*

    In addition, U.S. Office of Technology Assessment (OTA), *Industry, Technology, and the Environment: Competitive Challenges and Business Opportunities*, OTA-ITE-586, 1994; D. Chapman, "Environmental Standards and International Trade in Automobiles and Copper: The Case for a Social Tariff," Winter 1991 *Natural Resources Journal* 31:449–461; and D. Chapman, J. Agras, and V. Suri, "International Law, Industrial Location, and Pollution," Fall 1995 *Indiana Journal of Global Legal Studies* 3(1):5–33. Ravi Kanbur, "An Assessment of the Environmental Case for International Collective Action," Robinson-Schulze Seminar, Cornell University, March 25, 1998. Also R. Kanbur, M. Keen, S. V. Wijnbergen, "Industrial Competitiveness, Environmental Regulation and Direct Foreign Investment," in I. Goldin and L. A. Winters, eds., *The Economics of Sustainable Development* (Cambridge, Great Britain: Cambridge University Press, 1995).

21. This example assumes the same damage per ton of emissions regardless of the location of source or deposition. Recall our previous analysis of health and environmental valuation in high income and developing countries in Chapter 3. Also see Table 18.7, and the discussion of benefits transfer in Chapter 3.

22. Based upon my field experience with metals smelting with and without environmental protection, a value assuming that all environmental protection costs represent one-third of total cost is appropriate. Also, see the preceding Note 20, and Chapman (*Natural Resources Journal, op. cit.*). The following text mention of nearly complete pollution control is based upon new actual facilities using modern technology in New Mexico. The numerical values and equations used in the illustration in Figures 17.5, 17.6, and 17.7 are available from the author.

23. For extensive bibliographies of work done on the EKC, see "Special Issue: The Environmental Kuznets Curve," May 1998 *Ecological Economics*, 25(2).

24. J. Andreoni and A. Levinson, "The Simple Analytics of the Environmental Kuznets Curve," NBER Working Paper No. 6739, 1998.

25. See Porter and Linde *op. cit.,* and M. E. Porter, "America's Green Strategy," April 1991 *Scientific American*, page 168; M. E. Porter, *The Competitive Advantage of Nations* (New York: Macmillan, 1990) pages 647, 648. Porter uses chemicals and plastics to demonstrate the theory.

26. A. Barbera and V. McConnell report that copper and related nonferrous metals experienced an increase in total factor productivity between 1960 and 1980. Paper, chemicals, and iron/steel experienced productivity declines. See their "Environmental Regulation and Industry Productivity," January 1990 *Journal of Environmental Economics and Management* 18(1):50–65. The simultaneous occurrence of lower total cost and high environmental cost exists because the new technology is a major advancement from older smelter technology.

    In the case where there are no commercial markets for byproduct sulfuric acid, the new technology can save considerable producer cost by venting unneeded sulfur oxides into the atmosphere. This is being done in one country bordering the United States.

27. See Chapman and Office of Technology Assessment, Note 20. It is hoped that my consignment of my view to such a lesser status will be seen as a modest attempt to represent the profession's general views in an unbiased and correct form.

28. Vivek Suri and D. Chapman find that with manufactured imports and exports included in the analysis for energy, the turning point for the EKC rises to $144,000 GDP per capita. In other words, income levels would have to reach nearly $150,000 for the positive part of the EKC curve to "kick in." Agras and Chapman do not support Suri-Chapman, finding that fluctuations in oil prices replace trade as an important factor. I must point to the partially opposing views expressed in Suri-Chapman and Agras-Chapman. See V. Suri and D. Chapman, "Economic Growth, Trade, and Energy: Implications for the Environmental Kuznets Curve," Special Issue *Ecological Economics op. cit.* Also, J. Agras and D. Chapman, "A Dynamic Approach to the Environmental Kuznets Curve," February 1999 *Ecological Economics* 28 (2): 267–277.

29. B. R. Copeland and M. S. Taylor, "Trade and Transboundary Pollution," September 1995 *American Economic Review* 85(4):716–737. Also, Chapman, Agras, Suri, *op. cit.* Interesting cases involve the Carbon I and II power plants and the Nacozari copper smelter in Mexico. Each facility is producing an intermediate good which is used in the production of commodities for export to the United States. With limited or no sulfur oxide controls, each facility has become a major source of acid rain deposition in the United States. Here, the United States benefits from lower consumer prices and also is affected by the negative externality of air pollution impacting the Big Bend National Park in Texas and the Grand Canyon National Park in Arizona. See "Diplomatic Haze Pervades Air Pollution Dispute at Big Bend National Park," *New York Times* June 7, 1996, Also W. C. Malm, "Atmospheric Haze: Its Sources and Effects on Visibility in Rural Areas of the Continental United States," 1989 *Environmental Monitoring* 12:203–225, especially the analysis of Mexican pollution and its impact on the Big Bend and Grand Canyon Parks.

CHAPTER 18

CLIMATE CHANGE:
ECONOMICS AND POLICY

Introduction: Economics, Science, and Uncertainty

At the beginning of Chapter 1, we raised the question as to whether industrial resources such as petroleum and metal ores should be considered environmental resources. Traditionally, for most of the history of the field, the study of these resources was considered to be independent of environmental topics. But here, in reviewing the state of knowledge of the economics of climate change, it becomes clear that the effective limitation on coal and total energy use is not resource depletion. It is the nature of the interaction of energy use with the global atmosphere and the earth's environment that may ultimately limit our use of energy.

The basic economic questions are these: (1) How does economics influence the growth in atmospheric gases that lead to global warming? (2) What are the economic consequences of climate change? (3) Are there cost-effective technologies to avoid significant climate change? (4) Can we use public policies that are both efficient and equitable, and that will lead to significant benefits compared to costs?

With this complex topic, the basic questions could be stated differently. Many others might be appropriate, but these four questions can serve as an introduction to the economic dimensions of the problem. As with many of our subjects, there will be continued change in the nature of the problem and in our understanding of it. Before turning to economics, however, it is helpful to introduce the basic science that gives us our knowledge about climate change.

Table 18.1 shows the latest thinking about the warming impact of different anthropogenic gases. ('Anthropogenic' and some other terms are defined in Table 18.2.) One focus in climate change research is on the interactive growth in global temperature and these greenhouse gases. Figure 18.1 shows the measured change in the temperature at the earth's surface. There was no clear growth in greenhouse gases in the atmosphere until petroleum use accelerated in the early part of the 20th Century. From that point, average temperature has risen by 0.6 degrees C, equivalent to 1.1 degrees F. The average global temperature is now about 15 degrees C, or 59 degrees F.[1]

There are also negative factors that reduce the earth's temperature. Mount Pinatubo's eruption in the Philippines had a dramatic effect. Its effect on shielding

330 The Global Environment

TABLE 18.1 Major Sources of Growth and Reduction in Global Temperature, 1990s[2]

A. Factors Increasing the Greenhouse Effect

Greenhouse Gas Factor	Sources	Proportional Ratio to CO_2 Effect Index = 100
Carbon dioxide (CO_2) growth: 4% per decade	Energy use	100%
Methane (CH_4) growth: 6% per decade	Oil and gas production, agriculture, wetlands	30%
Ozone (O_3)	Energy use	19%
Chlorofluorocarbons (CFCs)	Air conditioning, refrigeration, solvents	15%
Nitrous oxide (N_2O) growth: 2.5% per decade	Fertilizer, acid manufacture	9%
Soot from fuels	Energy use	7%
Greater solar radiation	Sun	19%

B. Factors Reducing the Greenhouse Effect

Aerosol-cloud interaction	Energy, agriculture, deforestation	−49%
Sulfate aerosols	Coal, energy; metal smelting	−25%
Biomass soot	Wood, biomass burning	−12%
Volcanic emissions	Mount Pinatubo, an example	*

*Comments: The negative impact of the Mt. Pinatubo eruption was, for a short time, larger than all of the positive factors combined. On a different point, the magnitude of total anthropogenic impact on global temperature is 10 times that of natural solar radiation. Aerosol and anthropogenic are defined in Table 18.2. See the Appendix. Estimates are for changes from pre-industrial 1850 to the 1990s.

TABLE 18.2 Climate Change Definitions

Anthropogenic: factors affecting climate that originate in human activity.

Aerosol: very small liquid or solid particles in a gas. For example, very small soot particles, sulfur emissions, and ozone in an air pollution smog.

Greenhouse Gases: a general term referring to the positive and negative factors outlined in Table 18.1. Since the net effect works to retain heat, it is analogous to a greenhouse.

GCM: general circulation model of the earth's atmosphere and climate.

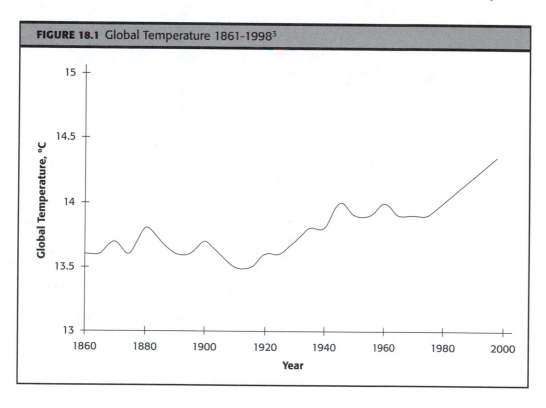

FIGURE 18.1 Global Temperature 1861-1998[3]

the earth from its normal solar radiation for a few years was actually great enough to reduce the average temperature. Sulfur emission aerosols also reduce the earth's temperature.

In the upper section of Table 18.1, note that the sun burned a little brighter at the end of the 20th Century than it did in 1850, and this has contributed somewhat to the temperature increase.

Scientists are working to integrate all of these factors into the analysis of the earth's climate. They use a type of computer model termed 'GCM,' a general circulation model of the earth's climate and atmosphere. By taking into account both the anthropogenic and natural factors in Table 18.1, the modern GCM can reproduce the observed curve of global temperature in Figure 18.1.

Considering that the annual temperature increase to date averages only one-hundredth of a degree Fahrenheit, it may be surprising to note that there is clear evidence of the consequences of warming in two aspects of the earth's surface: sea-level rise, and glacial melting. In the past 100 years, a typical glacier has retreated more than a kilometer.[4] In the same time interval, tidal changes show that sea level has risen about 17.5 cm (7 inches).[5]

Very roughly stated, a continuation of existing trends in economic growth and energy use would lead to an overall doubling of GHG factors in the early part of the 22nd Century. (GHG means greenhouse gases; see Table 18.2.) The best scientific guesses, midway in the range of plausible projections, are that this would cause an approximate 2.5 degrees C (4.5 degrees F) global temperature increase, and a sea-level rise of about 50 cm (20 inches).[6]

There is considerable scientific speculation arising from empirical analysis of weather statistics in the United States. The last several years have seen warmer nights (on average), cloudier days, and more intensive rainstorms.[7] The scientific record, unfortunately, is not yet sufficiently developed to enable us to make any judgment with confidence about the permanency of these possible regional trends or their relationships to greenhouse gases.

The examination of factors affecting global warming in Table 18.1 leads to a clear emphasis on carbon dioxide and energy use as the main factors determining the future path of the greenhouse effect. Figure 18.2 emphasizes the importance of the interaction between carbon dioxide and global temperature.[8]

The table on scientific data (Table 18.3) has important economic implications because it shows the importance of anthropogenic sources in burning carbon and the emissions released into the atmosphere. Notice that the atmosphere has been absorbing about 3.5 billion tons of anthropogenic carbon emissions each year; this is just under one-half of the human releases. Consequently, the world's growing use of energy is rapidly translated into greater concentration of CO_2 as a greenhouse gas.

In the disposition section of the table, the new growth of forests on abandoned farmland and early logging areas is absorbing a significant amount of CO_2 from the atmosphere. (Remember the discussion of this in Chapter 14 on forestry economics.)

'Fertilization' in the table refers to an apparent acceleration in worldwide photosynthesis. The very small increases in CO_2 concentration and global temperature seem to be increasing the rate at which trees and plants are removing CO_2 from the atmosphere as part of their growth processes.

A final note on interpretation. Scientists refer to CO_2 sources and concentration, but actually measure this in terms of carbon (C) rather than carbon dioxide (CO_2). Therefore, while the table lists 8 billion tons of anthropogenic carbon, this is actually contained in 29 billion tons of carbon dioxide.

Is it possible that we will use up and exhaust our fossil fuels in a way that will limit the impact on the atmosphere? Remember Table 9.1 in Chapter 9 on the economically accessible coal resources. They are sufficient, without new technologies, for a few thousand years. If conventional petroleum and natural gas become scarce at some future date, sufficient coal remains to continue to expand conventional energy use. At the end of this chapter, we will note again the current status of renewable energy economics, in the context of the complex challenge that global climate change poses for renewable energy development.

Obviously, there are considerable differences in the certainty of the different kinds of knowledge. Table 18.4 is organized on the basis of the degree of confidence of these different categories.[9]

The Nordhaus Geoeconomic Analysis

In the early 1980s, as part of the first National Academy of Science review of climate change, William Nordhaus at Yale University began to publish his first work that integrated the analytical techniques of economics and the physical sciences. In

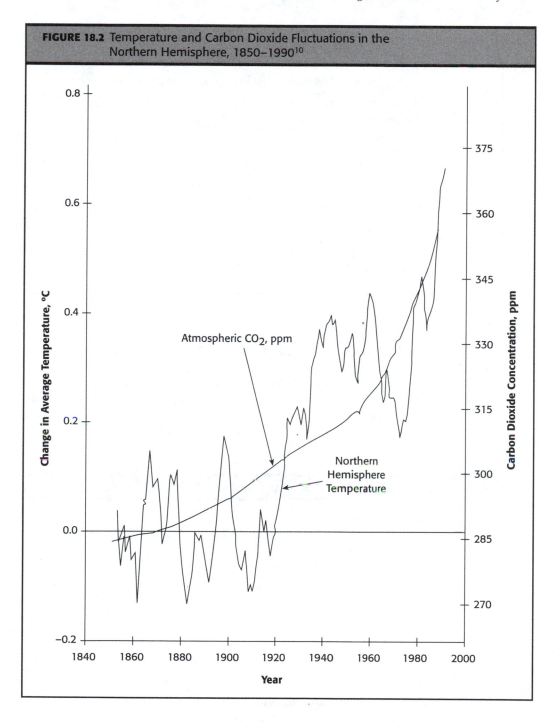

FIGURE 18.2 Temperature and Carbon Dioxide Fluctuations in the Northern Hemisphere, 1850–1990[10]

TABLE 18.3 The World Carbon Budget,[11] measured in U.S. tons of carbon, annual average for 1980s, rounded	
Anthropogenic Sources of Carbon Dioxide (billion tons)	
A. Energy use emissions	6.0
B. Deforestation in the tropics	2.0
C. Total, both sources	8.0
Disposition of Anthropogenic Carbon (billion tons)	
A. Atmosphere	3.5
B. Ocean absorption	2.0
C. New forest growth, northern hemisphere	0.5
D. 'Fertilization,' other factors	2.0
E. Total, all categories	8.0

later work throughout the 1990s, Nordhaus and other analysts have created an impressive body of literature that defines much of the current policy perspective on climate change.[12]

The most significant conclusion from the Nordhaus work is the finding that the climate change problem is apparently not important in economic terms. A century from now, by the year 2100, the apparent economic gain from the best policy is $350 billion, which is only a small fraction of the world's economy at that time, a gain of two-tenths

TABLE 18.4 Confidence and Certainty in Climate Change Knowledge

A.   Almost Certain
    1. Energy use, CO_2 emissions, and CO_2 in the atmosphere are each increasing.
    2. Average global temperature is growing very slowly.
    3. Mountain glaciers are shrinking.
    4. Sea level is rising very slowly.
 	
B.   Probable
    1. The carbon budget.
    2. Remaining energy resources.
 	
C.   Uncertain
    1. Change in temperature, precipitation in any location.
    2. Impact on African desertification.
    3. Positive and negative impact on particular areas.
    4. Rate of change in energy use, carbon budget, climate.

of one percent. The size of the world economy is projected to be about $200 trillion then, regardless of climate control policies. Nordhaus and Yang summarize their conclusions: "These results indicate that the stakes in controlling global warming are modest in the context of overall economic activity over the next century."[13]

The apparent lack of severity of the problem in their work arises from several economic assumptions, especially the assumptions related to discounting, energy use, and future damage.

The discounting question links numerical values to serious philosophical questions. Simply stated, how do we value future damage incurred by the generations of later centuries? Suppose, for illustration, we consider a single catastrophic year in 2100 with an economic damage of $500 billion. If we discount this at a 3 percent rate, it is reduced to a present value of $26 billion.[14]

Now suppose today's generation could avert this hypothetical calamity with the expenditure of $50 billion. Costs would exceed benefits under these economic assumptions. But, if we avoid discounting, or (as discussed in Chapter 4) assume a 0 percent rate for environmental discounting, then it is a clear decision to spend the $50 billion now to avoid the $500 billion disaster a century later. Remember that this is hypothetical: actual future damages, as discussed in Table 18.4 above, remain uncertain at this time. Before turning to the state of economic knowledge about potential future damage, we should note how Nordhaus handles this discounting issue with sensitivity analysis. When the discount rate in the model is set at 1 percent rather than 3 percent, then the best policy becomes a reduction in energy use of 16 percent rather than 9 percent.[15] The explanation for this change in policy results is to be found in the structure of geoeconomic models. As we noted, the lower discount rate (1 percent here) makes future damage more important to today's generation; consequently, it seems logical to make a greater reduction in energy use and CO_2 emissions.

There is an extensive literature on this debate. The consensus is clearly that some small value on the order of 3 percent should be used. However, there continue to be advocates of the other approaches.[16] Richard Norgaard and Robert Howarth in particular argue that inter-generational equity requires a zero discounting approach for future damage. And, recall from Chapter 4 that the Cropper and Portnoy contingent valuation survey implies that environmental discounting is very different from commercial and financial discounting, and that century-long environmental discount rates may be zero.[17]

Economic damage in the geoeconomic models is based upon the mathematical representation of selected studies, and the expert opinions of physical scientists and economists. The general view is that, for the 21st Century, the economic impact will be minimal on the United States and other high-income countries. It may be higher on lower-income countries. One study by the R. S. J. Tol group concludes that the United States and Canada might experience a loss of 1.5 percent of GDP, but the damage in Africa would be 9 percent of GDP.[18]

The net effect of climate change appears to be negative, even if small, for the next few decades. However, some aspects could be positive. There may be significant adaptation that reduces or eliminates losses. In agriculture, for example, the profitable corn-soybean belt may expand northward. In timber production, fast-growing Southern loblolly pine plantations and forest ecosystems would displace

TABLE 18.5 Very Low Probability Climate Related Catastrophe[19]

1. Hurricane Andrew, 1992, Florida; economic damage of $30 billion
2. Chicago, Illinois, 1995 summer heat wave; 1,000 deaths
3. Bangladesh cyclone, 1985; 100,000 deaths
4. Peruvian el niño cholera pandemic, 1991; 300,000 cases
5. California flood, 1997; 125,000 people evacuated
6. China floods, 1998; 14 million people evacuated

existing Northern forests.[20] As another example, very cold regions may become warmer, requiring less heating energy and lower winter heating bills. In reviewing the impact of climate change on Russia and Eastern Europe, the Tol study concluded that the net economic impact would be positive.

There remains the problem of low probability–high damage events, illustrated in Table 18.5. Again, it must be emphasized that these kinds of tragic events have not been proven to be caused by global climate change. While scientists continue to analyze the data for possible linkage, the consensus favors a low-impact perspective on the 21st Century.

Notwithstanding this near-term consensus perspective of one century, it should also be noted that much higher average global temperature increases in the range of 10 to 15 degrees Fahrenheit would have an unpredictable but much greater impact.[21]

The third and final subject to review under the geoeconomic modelling approach is the relationship between CO_2 emissions, energy use, and income levels. In economic terminology, this is defined as 'carbon intensity,' the ratio of tons of carbon released into the atmosphere to each thousand dollars of Gross Domestic Product.[22] Nordhaus and Yang project that this carbon intensity ratio will decline significantly, and other geoeconomic modelers assume similar declines in carbon intensity.[23]

The significance of this assumption is that world economic living standards can rise without proportional increases in global CO_2 emissions. However, the empirical data are mixed, offering support for this assumption, as well as support for its rejection. While the United States, Japan, and Western Europe have all reduced carbon intensity since 1970, in developing countries the opposite has happened; carbon intensity is higher. On a global basis, the average is unchanged over a quarter of a century.[24]

The dramatic importance of modelling assumptions for carbon intensity is apparent in Figure 18.3. The two highest carbon emission projections both reflect a continuation of the recent experience of stable overall carbon intensity. The two lowest projections use the common assumption of a global decline in carbon intensity.

The Global Division: Income and Energy Use

One of the major dividing lines in global climate policy is between today's high-income, high energy use economies, and those countries with lower income that are increasing both their income levels and energy use at rapid rates. On a per capita basis, energy use is now seven times higher in the high-income countries.[25]

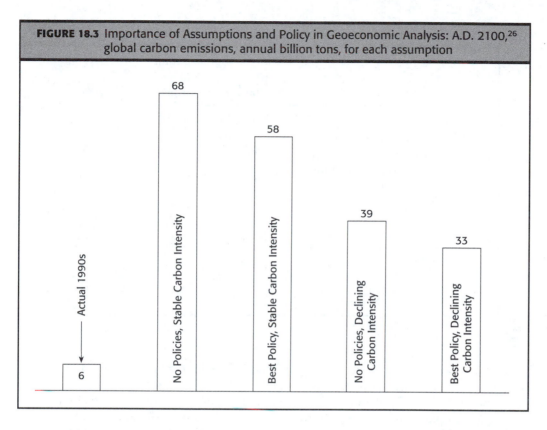

FIGURE 18.3 Importance of Assumptions and Policy in Geoeconomic Analysis: A.D. 2100,[26] global carbon emissions, annual billion tons, for each assumption

Although Japan, North America, and Western Europe taken together have held carbon emissions nearly constant, the countries of Asia, Africa, and Latin America have increased carbon releases by more than 4 percent annually. The countries in economic transition in the former Soviet Union and Eastern Europe have, because of their economic decline in the 1990s, reduced their carbon emissions by 34 percent. (Table 18.6 shows these data.) If these former Communist countries begin to show economic growth, their carbon emissions as well as the global total will increase rapidly.

The dilemma, then, is whether to focus climate change policy on countries with the highest incomes and emissions (e.g., the United States), or the highest growth rates in incomes and emissions (e.g., China).[27]

The problem is particularly vexing because transnational externalities are highly significant on a regional world basis. If one country reduces carbon emissions on a unilateral basis, the benefits of reduced climate change damage are broadly received by other countries.

The value of life and mortality in high-income and developing countries presents another set of serious methodological and ethical issues for economists addressing climate change. Consider the data in Table 18.7. The assumption of 100,000 potential deaths in the United States and India is hypothetical, and taken from the Intergovernmental Panel on Climate Change (IPCC).[28] However, the different values for life and for discount rates arise from the discussion of these points in the earlier Chapters 3 and 4.

TABLE 18.6 Carbon Emissions from Energy, billion metric tons of carbon per year

	1990	Annual Rate of Growth	1996
Japan	0.3	0%	0.3
Asia,* Africa, Latin America, and Middle East	1.7	4.5%	2.3
Russia, Ukraine, economies in transition	1.3	−7.0%	0.8
Western Europe	1.0	0%	1.0
North America	1.5	+1.5%	1.6
Totals	5.8	+1.0%	6.0

*Excludes Japan.

Source: U.S. EIA, *International Energy Annual 1996* Table H1. Amounts to nearest tenth of a billion. Growth rates are calculated from original data and rounded to nearest half percent. Australia and New Zealand are not shown separately; their total grew from 0.082 billion tons to 0.089.

Using normal procedures, the potential future damage is discounted to present values. The results show that 100,000 potential deaths would be valued at $309 billion for U.S. residents, but at nine-thousandths of one percent of this for India.

By implication, a tightly narrow view of economic efficiency would require global climate change mortality mitigation to be focused on the United States, and not India. Further, if we assume that energy use reduction is less costly in India than in the United States, then a narrow view of efficiency would lead to energy reduction in India to protect residents of the United States.

We need not accept these implications to realize that this is an ethical problem with global political implications. A wholly opposite perspective would arise from the Polluter Pays Principle, introduced in Chapter 5. From this perspective, the United States, as a major energy user and producer of greenhouse gases, should reduce energy use to help protect India.

TABLE 18.7 The Value of Life: India and the United States

Country	Year	Number Killed	Value of a Statistical Life	Discount Rate	Present Value of Future Deaths
United States	2050	100,000	$3.5 million	2.5%	$309 billion
India	2050	100,000	$120,000	13%	$27 million

Source: See text. Assume 50-year discounting for present value.

It is not clear if one or the other perspective is correct, but we know that this problem in economic analysis will be reflected in international policy.

Economic Policies

One way to approach the economic dimension of policy is to restate the basic demand curve concepts in the context of carbon emissions:

$$C = f * E \qquad (18\text{-}1)$$

$$E = TECH * N^{\alpha} * P^{\beta} * Y^{\gamma}, \alpha \text{ and } \gamma > 0, \beta < 0 \qquad (18\text{-}2)$$

The first relationship recognizes the carbon emission factor "f" as the link between energy consumption "E" and carbon emissions "C." In the 1990s, the global f is about 18 million tons carbon for each "Q" of global energy use. (A "Q" is one quadrillion Btus[29].) There are very significant differences here by fuel type. Petroleum is near the average with 23 tons of carbon emissions per Q. Natural gas is much lower, and coal is higher.[30] There are no net carbon releases from nuclear power, solar power, hydro or wind power, and sustainable fuelwood.

The second equation shows a complex relationship. Technology ("TECH") reflects the variability in energy use which was partially reviewed in earlier chapters on household energy and renewable energy. As we saw in those chapters, cost-effective energy conservation often faces economic obstacles to rapid implementation. In Table 18.8, some of the better-known technologies are listed, with some of the problems slowing implementation.

TABLE 18.8 Potential Technological Gains in Reducing Global Carbon Emissions[31]

Technology	Economic Obstacles
Better lighting	Quality of light; high capital cost
Efficient insulation	High capital cost
Smaller, lighter vehicles	Quality, comfort
Shift to rail, bus	Time, availability
Denser communities	Aesthetics; psychology
Industrial recycling	Cost
More natural gas, less coal	Regional availability
Increase solar, renewable energy	High cost; regional availability
Greater use of wood products, fuelwood	Air pollution, cost
Nuclear power generation	Nuclear fuel waste, safety, cost

Global energy use is increasing at about 2 percent annually. In order to reduce the growth in emissions, there must be workable economic policies that reduce future energy use.

It is certain that one factor in Equation (18-2) will continue to grow: world population (N). It is less certain but widely believed that world income Y will continue to rise. Therefore, in economic terms, the negative impact of higher energy prices P must be great enough to overcome the positive impact on energy demand of rising world population and income.

In Equation (18-2), the parameters α, β, γ represent the 'elasticities' of the impact of population, income, and energy price on greenhouse gas emissions. In other words, for emissions to decline, the importance of energy price increases and price elasticity must be greater than population and income increases and their elasticities.[32]

However, the magnitude of tax-linked price increases necessary to reduce growth in carbon emissions is very significant: on the order of $1.50 per gallon of gas. Given the differences in carbon content for each type of energy, an overall global carbon tax rising from $5 per ton in 2000 to $30 per ton in 2100 would give the right economic incentives for choosing energy types with no carbon, or less carbon. This might reduce the growth in emissions by 15 percent.[33]

Referring to the possibility of marketable permits examined in depth in Chapters 11 and 12, this policy tool would theoretically achieve the same efficient results as a carbon tax. The use of marketable permits has become a significant new part of global policy-making since the Kyoto Treaty.

The Kyoto Protocol

The Kyoto Protocol is more widely known as the Kyoto Climate Treaty.[34] It will be a benchmark in the global response to the evolving climate change issue. With 160 countries and 10,000 participants, it defines a general goal for Europe, Russia, Japan, and North America. They agreed to reduce their aggregate greenhouse gas emissions 5 percent below their 1990 level by the year 2010.[35]

Developing countries make no commitments.

The basic elements of the treaty are described in Table 18.9. The commitments are important to compare to the actual data in Table 18.6. The United States, Japan, and Western Europe have stayed nearly constant in emissions since 1990, and in Kyoto they agreed to reductions of 6 percent to 8 percent.

Russia and the Ukraine, however, were more than 30 percent lower in 1996 than in 1990. Their commitment to stabilize at the 1990 level provides opportunity for them to participate in the trading mechanism by selling credits.

Finally, note that developing countries are showing major growth in actual CO_2 emissions in Table 18.6, but made no commitments in the Kyoto Treaty.

The treaty defined sources of greenhouse gases to include five other gases in addition to CO_2, and each country's calculations may include reductions in atmospheric CO_2 from forest regrowth.

TABLE 18.9 The Kyoto Climate Change Treaty, 1997[36]

A. The Commitments to Lower CO_2 Emissions Below 1990 Levels by 2000:

Developing countries	No commitments
European Union	-8 percent
Japan	-6 percent
Russia and Ukraine	0 percent
United States	-7 percent

B. Greenhouse Gas Sources: Energy use, agricultural, forestry.

C. Economic Incentives: Remove subsidies to energy use.

D. Joint Implementation: Financial subsidies to developing countries earn shelter credits for OECD countries.

E. Marketable Permits: OECD countries can purchase permits from Russia, Ukraine, perhaps developing countries.

Economic subsidies which promote the production of commodities that release greenhouse gases should be subject to "reduction or phasing out" according to the agreement.[37] However, there is no numerical goal or administrative mechanism to monitor this goal.

The "Joint Implementation" program in the treaty is intended to encourage companies or governments to provide assistance to developing countries. As an example, a U.S. utility might have a computer technology which reduces coal requirements for power generation. If it offers this technology to a group of electric utilities in developing countries, it could use the 'credit' for reduced developing country emissions to increase its own releases. This program is also know as "The Clean Development Mechanism."[38]

Finally, the marketable permits part of the treaty was included in response to proposals from the United States, Canada, and Australia.[39] The program would basically follow the outline described in Chapter 11 for acid rain sulfur emission permits.[40] Given that the commitment level for Russia and the Ukraine (Table 18.9) is considerably above actual emissions, one avenue for trading in CO_2 emission permits would be the purchase of permits by the United States, Canada, and Western Europe from Russia and the Ukraine.

Overall, this is a major global agreement. However, by itself as defined in 1997, the Kyoto Treaty will not noticeably affect either the growth in emissions or the accumulation of CO_2 in the atmosphere. Simply put, the treaty limits growth in emissions in countries where emissions are not growing, and does not affect the countries where emissions are growing rapidly. But future revisions will use the framework of the Kyoto Treaty to implement substantive goals and economic incentives.

Conclusion

The four questions which began the chapter cannot yet be fully answered. At this point, we are best able to answer the first question. Economic influences are important and perhaps primary in influencing fossil energy use, which is the source of CO_2, the major greenhouse gas. Major price increases in energy would be necessary to stabilize or reduce global energy use.

Estimates of the economic consequences of climate change are uncertain. As Table 18.4 emphasized, the considerable uncertainty of predicting regional and local impact makes current estimates of economic damage premature.

Are there cost-effective technologies to avoid significant climate change? This is perhaps the most controversial issue. It brings into play other major issues: on price and income impact (from Chapter 17, Macroeconomics), the issue of cost-effective but underutilized conservation technologies (Chapter 7), and the competitiveness of renewable energy in the marketplace (Chapter 8). In the context of climate change economics, there is considerable debate about the magnitude of potential CO_2 reductions which also reduce costs of the services and goods associated with CO_2. The IPCC report reviewed eleven studies that analyzed technologies and policies that would reduce emissions at no cost, or with cost reductions.[41]

Surprisingly, the fourth question on economics and public policy can be stated simply. In the abstract, the tools of optimization, environmental valuation, and marginal analysis of costs and benefits would seem the appropriate approach to decision-making. Individual consumers and businesses will do their own benefit-cost analyses, and if global policy uses taxation or marketable permits correctly, the right decisions will be made.

The individual actions that produce greenhouse gases are mundane: an average car releases one pound of CO_2 per mile traveled, and a normal 100-Watt bulb used for a week releases more than 2 pounds of CO_2.[42] In the end, it is individual actions that are the object of policy.

The broad objective is to determine the national and international policies that will lead business and consumers to make choices that result in lesser greenhouse gas emissions in a world with growing population and income. Figure 18.4 represents policy scenarios. The high emissions curve in Panel A represents a continuation of present global economic trends, but with slowly declining carbon intensity per dollar of world economic output. Panel B shows how the emissions in Panel A accumulate in the atmosphere as concentration levels of CO_2. The high emissions curve from Panel A has become a high concentration curve in the lower panel. Temperature change, whether Fahrenheit or centigrade, is significant.

The lower dashed emissions curve in Panel A, which peaks and declines, represents major economic shifts, requiring actual reductions in CO_2 emissions below current levels. These reductions imply considerable emphasis on the policies in Table 18.8 as well as much higher prices for carbon-based energy, through taxation or marketable permits.

For the dashed curve, global emissions in 2200 are no higher than in 2000. But, notice that this reduction in emissions still results in the atmospheric concentration level rising to stabilize at twice current levels,[43] and at a higher temperature level.

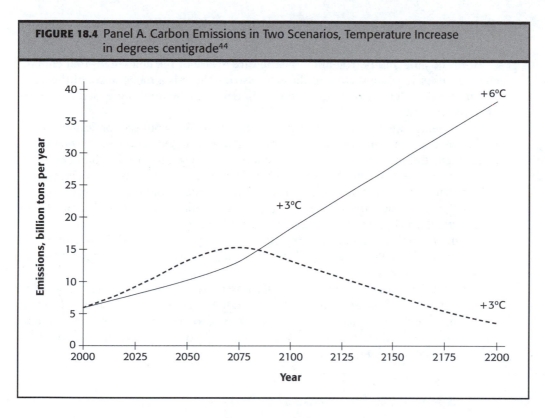

FIGURE 18.4 Panel A. Carbon Emissions in Two Scenarios, Temperature Increase in degrees centigrade[44]

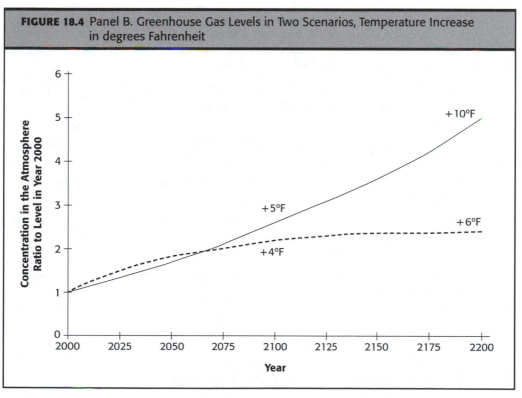

FIGURE 18.4 Panel B. Greenhouse Gas Levels in Two Scenarios, Temperature Increase in degrees Fahrenheit

Both the auto and petroleum industries are aware of the challenges that climate change raises. In some sectors of these industries, there is a recognition of the need for higher petroleum prices, more fuel-efficient vehicles, and increased use of renewable energy.[45]

Future generations have many responsibilities in working out economic approaches to the climate change problem. First, they must verify or correct the scientific knowledge and its uncertainties that were introduced at the beginning of the chapter.

Second, as the geoeconomic work by Nordhaus and others indicates, goals must be defined within the context of current and future macroeconomic and energy policies.

Third, the division between high-income, high energy use societies and those with low but accelerating energy use must be reconciled.

It is not possible to define the correct policies today; but it is possible to see that the definition and framing of the global climate change question is closely linked to economics.

The specific agreements in the 1997 Kyoto Treaty will, by themselves, have little impact on emissions, as explained in the preceding section. But it is correct to see it as a "framework" in which the evolving state of knowledge of economics, science, and technology will be used to define and frame both the global and national responses to climate change.

Questions for Discussion and Analysis

1. Consider the questions of cost-effective energy conservation (Chapter 7), renewable energy cost (Chapter 8), and the macroeconomics of higher energy prices (Chapter 17). Which side do you favor on the issue of the potential for reducing energy and CO_2 emissions while increasing global living standards?

2. Turn to Figure 18.4, and assume that annual carbon emissions are 300 percent higher at the end of the 21st Century. What would be the projected average temperature change?

3. Can you make a similar estimate, using the 68 billion tons carbon emissions per year number from Figure 18.3?

4. Should energy use be reduced in low-income countries if that is more cost effective? Does the Coase Theorem have implications for this?

5. The three leading candidates for utilization in global climate change policy are (1) marketable permits, (2) carbon and energy taxation, and (3) regulation. Which do you support, if any? Why?

6. You are given these assumptions for current global carbon demand and supply, with Q being billion tons of carbon.

   a. $MC = \$25$

   b. $P = \$37 - 2 * Q$

   c. $P = MC$

   What are the current values for price and quantity?

7. Now, in projecting future global carbon emissions, assume that 100 years from now, marginal cost rises slightly, but the demand curve rises significantly because of growing world population and income. The projected market relations are:

   d. $MC_{100} = \$30$

   e. $P_{100} = \$74 - 2 * Q_{100}$

   f. $P_{100} = MC_{100} + TAX$

There are two questions. First, what would carbon price and emissions be with no tax or other policy? Second, what tax (or equivalent marketable permit policy) would keep carbon use at a 6 billion tons per year level?

Appendix: Understanding Solar Insolation and Climate Change

One of the basic terms is a concept used in Chapter 7 on household energy, the Watt. Remember that a 100-Watt bulb used for 10 hours is equivalent to a kilowatt hour. To convey the relative sizes of natural and human factors, we begin with defining natural solar radiation as averaging nearly one kilowatt hour of energy yearly per average square inch of the earth's surface.

This is a serious simplification. Scientists do not use the term "kWh/square inch/year." Their standard unit is Watts per square meter, abbreviated Wm^{-2}. In this framework, average annual incoming solar radiation, after allowing for day-night and seasonal variations, is 342 Wm^{-2} reaching the atmosphere. An average of 168 Wm^{-2} is absorbed at the earth's surface. On an annual basis, it is equivalent to .95 kWh/year/square inch, and has been rounded to one in the preceding paragraph. Another term is 'forcing,' or 'radiative forcing.' This is the change in solar or terrestrial radiation affecting the earth's atmosphere. See the IPCC volumes in Note 1 for a complete discussion.

Notes to Chapter 18

1. The basic work of the Intergovernmental Panel on Climate Change is Volume I, *Climate Change 1995: The Science of Climate Change* (Cambridge, UK: Cambridge University Press, 1996), and the other volumes, Volume II, *Climate Change 1995: Impacts, Adaptations and Mitigation*, and Volume III, *Climate Change 1995: Economic and Social Dimensions*. These reports are usually abbreviated as IPCC. Figures 18.1 and 18.2 represent the average temperatures over both land and sea, but exclude Antarctica. Alaskan and Siberian average temperature has risen 5 degrees F since 1970; *New York Times*, August 18, 1998.
2. IPCC Volume 1, pages 20–21 and Chapter 2.
3. *Ibid.,* page 26, and *New York Times*, June 8, 1998.
4. More precisely, 1.23 km (.74 miles) in 94 years. Johannes Oerlemans, "Quantifying Global Warming from the Retreat of Glaciers," April 8, 1994 *Science* 264:243–244. The author estimates each degree C increase shortens the typical glacier by 2 km.

5. IPCC, Volume I, pages 29–30. Their exact figures are a sea-level rise of 10 to 25 cm. The text figure (17.5 cm) is the median value of this range.

6. IPCC, Volume I, pages 40, 41. For the last 20 years, an assumption that GHG doubling leads to a greater 4.5 degree C (8 degree F) change appears more accurate. *Ibid.,* page 37.

7. IPCC Volume I, pages 4 and 28–30.

8. The other greenhouse gases (methane, lower atmosphere ozone, and CFCs) have also been increasing exponentially. Figure 18.1 is smoothed by showing temperature as averages in rolling five-year periods; Figure 18.2 shows annual variation. The impact of CFC emissions and substitutes is particularly complex. The immediate, direct warming impact of the CFC aerosols themselves is positive. However, through their effect upon upper-level ozone depletion in the stratosphere, they also cause a cooling effect. Because of the effectiveness of the Montreal Protocol as amended, CFC concentrations will decline. See IPCC Volume I.

9. Table 18.4 is an interpretation and simplification of complex issues. Other authors may have different categories.

10. Sources for Figure 18.2 are Richard A. Kerr, "Sun's Role in Warming Is Discounted," April 1995 *Science,* 268:28–29; David J. Thomson, "The Seasons, Global Temperature, and Precession," *ibid.,* pages 59–67; and J. T. Houghton, G. J. Jenkins, and J. J. Ephraums, eds., *Climate Change: The IPCC Scientific Assessment* (Cambridge, UK: Cambridge University Press, 1990), page 9. Also, R. C. Wilson, "Total Solar Irradiance Trend," September 1997 *Science,* 277:1963–1965.

11. IPCC Volume 1, page 79. Numbers are rounded to the nearest half-billion. Original data is in metric tons. Carbon dioxide has 3.67 times the weight of carbon. The first source listed (energy use) also includes emissions from cement manufacture. In the U.S., cement and other industrial manufacturing contribute about 1 percent of the total CO_2 emissions. From USEIA, *Emissions of Greenhouse Gases in the United States 1987–1994* (Washington, DC: USGPO, 1995).

12. W. D. Nordhaus and G. Yohe, "Future Carbon Dioxide Emissions from Fossil Fuels," in *Changing Climate* (Washington, DC: National Research Council, 1983). There is an extensive literature which has built upon the Nordhaus work, including (1) A. S. Manne and R. G. Richels, *Buying Greenhouse Insurance: The Economic Costs of CO_2 Emissions Limits* (Cambridge, MA: MIT Press, 1993); (2) W. R. Cline, *The Economics of Global Warming* (Washington, DC: Institute for International Economics, 1992); (3) D. Chapman, V. Suri, and S. G. Hall, "Rolling Dice for the Future of the Planet," July 1995 *Contemporary Economic Policy* 13(3):1–9; (4) W. D. Nordhaus and Z. Yang, "A Regional Dynamic General Equilibrium Model of Alternative Climate Change Strategies," September 1996 *American Economic Review* 86(4):741–765; (5) P. A. Schultz and J. F. Kasting, "Optimal Reductions in CO_2 Emissions," *Energy Policy,* in press; (6) E. J. Barron, D. Chapman, J. F. Kasting, N. Khanna, A. Z. Rose, P. A. Schultz, *Penn State–Cornell Integrated Assessment Model,* Earth Systems Science Center, Pennsylvania State University, November 1996, and Cornell University Working Paper ARME 96-19; (7) R. B. Howarth, "Climate Change and Overlapping Generations," October 1996 *Contemporary Economic Policy* 14(4):100–111. Although I disagree with some of the substantive assumptions and policy conclusions, I am pleased to acknowledge the debt we owe to the intellectual originality and value of Nordhaus's approach.

13. These figures are all in 1990 dollars, and from Nordhaus and Yang, *op. cit.* With no global policies, a temperature increase of 3 degrees centigrade (5.4 degrees Fahrenheit) is projected by 2100.

14. As in Chapter 4, NPV = $500 billion $\div (1.03)^{100}$ = $26 billion. With a zero discount rate, the answer is very different: NPV = $500 billion $\div (1.0)^{100}$ = $500 billion.

15. Nordhaus and Yang, pages 754 and 760. The figures in the text here apply to the United States, in 2000. The economic literature defines a percentage reduction in energy use as a 'control rate.'

16. Kenneth Arrow (a Nobel laureate) and five other leading economists contributed Chapter 4 on discounting to IPCC Volume II. They generally endorse the Nordhaus position.

17. See the discussion of the Cropper-Portnoy work in Chapter 4. Howarth analyses the early Nordhaus work in R. B. Howarth, "Climate Change and Overlapping Generations," *op. cit.* Note 12.

18. The work of the Tol group as well as that of several other studies is summarized in IPCC, Volume III, Chapter 6. W. R. Cline takes issue with R. Mendelsohn and Nordhaus in their debate "The Impact of Global Warming on Agriculture: Comment and Reply," December 1996 *American Economic Review* 86(5):1309–1315.

19. The sources for Table 18.5 are IPCC, Volume II, Chapter 6; R. R. Colwell, "Global Climate and Infectious Disease: The Cholera Paradigm," December 20, 1996 *Science* 274:2025–2031. Also, U.S. National Weather Service, *July 1995 Heat Wave* (Washington, DC: U.S. Department of Commerce, National Oceanic and Atmospheric Administration, and National Weather Service, 1995), page iii for Chicago and the Midwest, and the *New York Times* January 16, 1997 on flooding and evacuations in Idaho and Nevada as well as California. *New York Times* August 22, 1998 on flooding in China. Also, L. S. Kalkstein and G. Tan analyze the relationship between global warming and mortality in "Human Health," Chapter 5 in *As Climate Changes*, K. M. Strzepek and J. B. Smith, eds. (Cambridge, UK: Cambridge University Press, 1995).

20. See B. Sohngen and R. Mendelsohn, "Valuing the Impact of Large-Scale Ecological Change in a Market: The Effect of Climate Change on U.S. Timber," September 1998 *American Economic Review*, 88(4):686–710. Also, R. Mendelsohn, W. D. Nordhaus, and D. Shaw, "The Impact of Global Warming on Agriculture: A Ricardian Analysis," September 1994 *American Economic Review* 84(4):753–771.

21. IPCC Volume II, page 208.

22. Arithmetically, carbon tons per $1,000 GDP is the same as billion tons per trillion dollars of GDP. Remember that the difference between GDP and GNP is explained in the first section in Chapter 2.

23. In A. S. Manne and R. G. Richels, *Buying Greenhouse Insurance: The Economic Costs of CO_2 Emission Limits* (Cambridge, MA: MIT Press, 1993), page 157, the authors assume a reduction of one-half of one percent annually in carbon intensity.

24. Based upon data in USEIA, *International Energy Annual 1993*, and World Bank, *World Development Report 1996*. Also Nordhaus 1994 *op. cit.,* page 67.

25. Based on data in the World Development Report 1996, and the USEIA, *op. cit.*

26. The two low projections in Figure 18.3 are the cooperative and market solutions in Nordhaus and Yang, page 751. The two high projections in the figure assume no decline in carbon intensity, and are 75 percent higher than the low projections. The actual value for the 1990s is from Table 18.3 in this chapter.

27. The Nordhaus and Yang analysis projects GDP growth at about 3 percent in the developing world and China, and 1 percent in the U.S. and Europe.

28. IPCC Volume III, pages 132 and 196–197. We used a similar illustration for Bangladesh and the United States in N. Khanna and D. Chapman, "Time Preference, Abatement Costs, and International Climate Policy," April 1996 *Contemporary Economic Policy*, 14(2):56–66.

29. The "Q," an American unit, represents one quadrillion Btus. Internationally, the exaJoule (EJ) is widely used. They are broadly equivalent: one EJ = .948 Q. In international units, the aggregate global "f" factor was .0156 GT of carbon per EJ.

30. In international metric units, natural gas releases 14 million metric tons of carbon per exaJoule, while the respective figures are 20 for oil and 25 for coal. Multiply these numbers by 1.16 to get U.S. units. See IPCC Volume II, page 14.

31. These technologies are discussed in detail in IPCC Volume II, *op. cit.,* and the Special Issue on the IPCC: Impacts, Adaptations, and Mitigations, 1996 *Energy Policy* 24(10/11).

32. Mathematically, for emissions to decline where technology is neutral, $|\beta\dot{P}| > \alpha\dot{N} + \gamma\dot{Y}$; $\dot{P}$ represents the growth rate in energy prices, and $\dot{N}$ and $\dot{Y}$ are population and per capita income growth rates. See D. Chapman and T. Drennen, "Equity and Effectiveness of Possible CO_2 Treaty Proposals," July 1990 *Contemporary Policy Issues*, 8(3):16–28.

33. Nordhaus and Yang; N. Khanna and D. Chapman, "Climate Policy and Petroleum Depletion," Cornell University ARME Working Paper 97-01, January 1997. Using a very different cost-based approach instead of the demand approach, Manne and Richels (page 59) conclude that a carbon tax of $200 per ton (four times the cost of coal) would be necessary to make noncarbon renewable technologies competitive.

34. Its formal name: Kyoto Protocol to the United Nations Framework Convention on Climate Change, United Nations, December 10, 1997.

35. There are 39 countries listed in Annex I with specific commitments. In addition to the 39 countries in the regions named here in the text, the list also includes Australia, Iceland, and New Zealand. There are variations in both base year and target year for some countries and for some GHGs.

36. Table 18.9 is based upon the 1997 Protocol (*op. cit.*). Also see S. Dunn, "After Kyoto," March/April 1998 *Worldwatch* 11(2):33–35; and R. J. Kopp, R. D. Morgenstern, and M. A. Toman, "Climate Change Policy after Kyoto," Winter 1998 *Resources*, pages 4–6.

37. Protocol, page 3, Article 2.

38. Protocol, page 13, Article 12.

39. Protocol, page 8, Article 6.

40. In the preceding chapter, the section on Climate Change Policy and Macroeconomics reviews current thinking about the impact of the treaty on energy-intensive industries and on income growth.

41. IPCC Volume III, pages 309–312.

42. According to T. Drennen, *Economic Development and Climate Change*, Ph.D. dissertation, Cornell University, 1993, page 10. In Chapter 7, Table 7.11, we see that heating a normal home in the Northern United States with natural gas produces 9 tons of CO_2 each winter. The amount of CO_2 released from heating the same home with electric panels is twice this amount.

43. As noted in the text, a net doubling of greenhouse gas factors translates roughly into a 4.5 degrees F (2.5 degrees C) average temperature increase. This commonly used 'rule of thumb' is ΔT degrees C = 3.607 ln (ratio of future concentration to current concentration).

44. Sources for Figure 18.4 are (1) for the lower scenario, the S1000 case in IPCC Volume I, page 25; and (2) for the higher scenario, the market solution case in Nordhaus and Yang.

45. Toyota Motor Corporation, "The World Is Ready for Greener Cars," November 1997. American Petroleum Institute, "Climate Change Commitments," December 1977; see especially the discussion on taxation. In an interview, a General Motors executive supported "a modest increase in American taxes on gasoline and other fossil fuels to make high-mileage vehicles more popular;" *New York Times*, January 5, 1998. Also, see the study on renewable energy and conservation by the oil company Shell International, discussed in Chapter 8.

PART VI

ECOLOGICAL ECONOMICS, SUSTAINABILITY, AND ENVIRONMENT

CHAPTER 19

ECOLOGICAL ECONOMICS: AN EMERGING ALTERNATIVE TO ENVIRONMENTAL ECONOMICS

BY JON ERICKSON

Given the generally traditional focus of this text on environmental economics, it is useful to examine the foundation of economic theory and its application to the environment. The chapter begins by contrasting neoclassical economic analysis of the environment with the synthesis of philosophy, ecology, and economics that is evolving under the umbrella of ecological economics. We then examine climate change to illustrate the growing dissatisfaction with a neoclassical approach to analyzing environmental problems; the discussion emphasizes the usefulness of communicating across disciplines. Next follows an introduction to alternative paradigms to economic growth, including limits, sustainable development, and coevolution. The chapter concludes with a historical perspective on the transition between economic paradigms.

The Environment and the Economic Tradition

Adam Smith's *The Wealth of Nations* in 1776 marked the dawn of modern economic thought;[1] his work was founded on two fundamental tenets of self-interest and natural liberty. In criticizing the mercantilist economy of his time, Smith argued for a reduction in the role of government intervention.[2] The market economy was seen as just and amenable to the individual self-interested pursuit of happiness. The aggregate of these self-interested pursuits, in turn, would maximize social welfare and thus the wealth of nations.

There was some dissent about what came to be known as classical economics. Jeremy Bentham, John Stuart Mill, David Ricardo, and Thomas Malthus questioned the selfishly rational tone of economics during its formative years, demanding that economics address issues of the common good. The social utilitarians, typified by Mill's *Principles of Political Economy*,[3] wanted to move economics beyond its growing focus on personal utility and markets and toward social concerns.

Nevertheless, the closing of the 19th Century marked the beginning of the neoclassical era in economics, and the mainstream emphasis in economics continued to follow the tradition of self-interest. Economics quickly became grounded in marginal analysis, descriptive rather than prescriptive, and scientific in nature. Faith in markets was preeminent, and only isolated cases of market failure justified government intervention or any social tinkering. A. C. Pigou in his *Economics of Welfare* briefly brought environmental considerations into the arena of welfare analysis.[4] His work developed the concepts of negative and positive externalities arising from economic activity. However, accounting for externalities was still within the realm of self-interested rationality.

The Keynesian period of economics emerging from the Great Depression of the 1930s established economics as the policy tool for promoting economic growth through government intervention.[5] Social concerns such as unemployment and inflation came into focus under Keynes, but environmental considerations continued to be excluded. After World War II, the negative externalities of economic growth began to show significant impact on water, air, and land resources. Yet even as the environmental movement became rooted in the U.S. collective conscious, neoclassical economics paid little attention. As noted in Chapter 4, the American Economic Association's 1969 *Readings in Welfare Economics* by Kenneth Arrow and Tibor Scitovsky made no reference to the environment. The notable exceptions to this exclusion were developments in the area of natural resource economics. In particular, Ciracy-Wantrup's *Resource Conservation: Economics and Policies* helped define the field of resource economics,[6] evolving from turn-of-the century resource conservation movements. His advocacy of safe minimum standards predated by two decades this concept's use in environmental policy.

Environmental economics didn't come into focus as a discipline until the early 1970s. Its development was primarily a reaction to significant environmental policy initiatives in the United States, including the Air Quality Act of 1967, the National Environmental Policy Act of 1969, the Clean Water Act of 1972, and the Endangered Species Act of 1973. At the same time, environmentalism as a social movement was typified by the first Earth Day on April 22, 1970. Both government policy and social concerns stemmed from Malthusian predictions of environmental catastrophes and an environmental movement finding popularity among the general public.

Environmental economics eventually became a full-fledged academic concern with the establishment of the Association for Environmental and Resource Economists in 1978. Environmental considerations quickly found their place in the tradition of benefit-cost analysis. External social costs and values were also logical extensions of the neoclassical tradition. As has been described in Chapters 2–6, the scope and breadth of topics involving environmental economics also called for modifications in discounting theory, value of life and risk estimates, and methodological developments to value nonmarket goods.

Environmental Economics: Running on Faith

While environmental variables were necessary and useful modifications to neoclassical theory, environmental economics continues to depend on the basic assumptions and priorities of market and welfare theory as reviewed in Chapters 1 and 6. These foundations emphasize the concepts of allocation and optimization, and the neoclassical assumption of continuous growth in material living standards. In environmental economics, if a numerical human benefit can be assigned to an environmental amenity, then it too can be allocated and optimized as with any other market good. The field of environmental economics has from the start both followed and questioned this neoclassical faith.

Environmental amenities, however, are also basic security goods. For instance, the supply and allocation of dependable food, clean water, diversity of species, and protection from the harmful effects of climate change are 'goods' that will determine the course of humanity in the 21st Century and beyond. To this extent, environmental economics is important in its scope. Placing a value on these nonmarket goods attempts to represent positive environmental values alongside traditional market goods in resource allocation decisions.

However, even with adjustments to economic optimization and corrections for environmental market failures, the assurance of these goods for current and future generations is largely left to the fate of Adam Smith's 'invisible hand.' Over two hundred years after *The Wealth of Nations*, self-interest and natural liberty remain central to the study of neoclassical economics. We maximize profits and minimize costs. Individual liberties and the right to consume dominate economic theory.

The basic security goods, however, may not be guaranteed in a "winner takes all" individualistic society. What will remain for future generations is that which isn't utilized by current consumption. Many contemporary students of economics are interested in alternatives to anthropocentric science, economy, and society. As did the generation of classical economists before them, today's students search for moral truths in economics.

This chapter accepts the importance of environmental economics but questions its neoclassical foundation. Should environmental questions be viewed in terms of absolute constraints or as incidental outcomes of cost-benefit analysis? What roles do ethics and religion play? Should the physical laws of thermodynamics be considered with the social laws of economics? And ultimately, how are we to view ourselves—as endpoint of a deterministic evolution, or just a beat in the metronome of geological time? Similar questions first challenged the classical economists and have recently found a home in the new discipline of ecological economics.

The Evolution of Ecological Economics

Perhaps most central to the study of economics is a long-standing preoccupation with the human condition. John Kenneth Galbraith, in his historical analysis of economic thought, traces its beginnings as far back as the writings of Aristotle, more than two millennia ago. A central theme in Galbraith's reconstruction is that "economic ideas are always and intimately a product of their own time and place; they cannot be seen apart from the world they interpret."[7]

In Richard Norgaard's analysis, the 20th-Century pursuit of human advancement rested unconditionally on a faith in science and technology—a belief in progress through modernity.[8] This belief holds that as problems—externalities—arise, they can ultimately be solved through human ingenuity and technological innovation. In essence: we can always produce more and more with less and less; we can replace what's exploited through substitution; we can sidestep inconvenient transition and conservation through adaptation.

Dispelling the faith in modernity is perhaps the outstanding feature of the new assault on the neoclassical tradition. Ecological economics reflects what Norgaard summarizes as prudence, pluralism, and process.[9] Prudence shuns the strong optimism of the technological 'fix.' Pluralism calls for the use of many disciplinary perspectives in formulating ideas, a realization that there is always more than one approach to problem-solving. Process draws attention away from the endpoint (i.e., an optimal solution) and places it on the path to pluralistic solutions. In this light, ecological economics cannot be defined as a traditional discipline. It incorporates methodological pluralism and an ever-changing social process.

The actual discipline of ecological economics wasn't officially recognized until the establishment of the International Society for Ecological Economics (ISEE) in 1988. The work of economists such as Nicholas Georgescu-Roegen, Kenneth Boulding, Herman Daly, and Richard Norgaard, together with ecologists such as Robert Costanza, Robert Goodland, Howard Odum, and Paul and Ann Ehrlich, laid the foundation for a disciplinarily inclusive society. Some of its premises were an awareness of biophysical principles that limit economic activities and of the interactive evolution of natural and social systems through time, and an abandonment of absolute faith in progress through growth.

The incorporation of biophysics into economics is attributed to Georgescu-Roegen. Essentially, he argues, the economic problem is one of entropy, from the second law of thermodynamics. Only a finite amount of low-entropy energy can exist in a finite system, and low-entropy energy "continuously and irrevocably dwindles away."[10] Also, from the first law of thermodynamics, matter or energy can neither be created nor destroyed. In terms of the economic process, matter and energy enter as low-entropy inputs and exit as high-entropy waste. These concepts, generally omitted from traditional flow and stock diagrams in economic theory, have contributed to a better understanding of relative versus absolute scarcity, the importance of scale, and the limits to a fossil-fueled economy.

Again, echoes of classical economists such as Malthus[11] can be found in these warnings of absolute constraints to economic growth. Neoclassical economics, in contrast, has been more concerned with relative scarcity. Oil, minerals, and other geologically scarce low-entropy resources are not economically scarce as long as supply meets demand through equilibrium price mechanisms. In fact, as Chapter 9 emphasizes, real oil prices have recently been at the lowest level in history. So how, the neoclassical economist argues, can oil be scarce? Shouldn't scarcity be reflected through increasing demand followed by increases in equilibrium prices over time?

The ecological economics perspective, however, recognizes the importance of absolute scarcity, or limits on production over time.[12] In terms of intertemporal production possibility frontiers and intergenerational equity, absolute scarcity of natural resources and environmental systems ultimately defines economic well-being. David Ricardo, the classical economist, also spoke of long-run limits to economic growth and the finality of a stationary state in which natural resources and technological fixes are exhausted.[13]

Scale also matters. However, the aggregate size of global consumption and production is not of interest in the neoclassical formulation. The ecological economic perspective, in contrast, views human economies as a subsystem of their larger ecosystems. Healthy ecosystems breed healthy economies, and the appropriate scale of economic activity is considered essential to maintaining ecosystem health. An optimal scale requires that an economy's throughput—the flow from raw materials, to commodities, to waste—remain within the ecosystem's regenerative and absorptive capacity.[14]

Working through these complications and interconnections between economy and environment requires a certain degree of "systems thinking." Again, this is in contrast to a neoclassical reductionist methodology where explanation of economic phenomena calls for a Newtonian mechanization[15] and simplification of parts. Most notable in promoting a systems approach is the lifetime work of Kenneth Boulding. The most often-cited work of Boulding is his seminal article, "The Economics of the Coming Spaceship Earth," first published for Resources for the Future in 1966.[16] In this work and elsewhere[17] Boulding laid the groundwork for viewing economics in terms of 'open' and 'closed' systems. Boulding emphasized the laws of thermodynamics and warned against what he termed the "cowboy" doctrine of limitless growth.[18] In contrast, he considered:

> *The closed economy of the future might similarly be called the "spaceman" economy, in which the earth has become a single spaceship, without unlimited resources of anything, either for extraction or for pollution. . . .*[19]

Studying systems dynamics also requires an evolutionary framework of long-term, interdependent changes. Boulding and others created what has come to be called evolutionary economics, a precursor to much of the work in ecological economics today. (This subject is taken up separately later in the chapter.)

Herman Daly is another visionary in the development of ecological economics. While not quite as pessimistic as Georgescu-Roegen, Daly has most significantly argued the merits of a 'steady-state' economy and rejected the ideology of continuing growth. To Daly, a steady-state economy exists where throughput is held constant, and allocation among competing uses is allowed to vary in response to market forces. This approach is quite different from the classical 'stationary state,' which postulates that an absence of growth could only be the result of resource exhaustion or a technological freeze. In the steady-state economy, growth is capped before complete exploitation. Attention is drawn away from quantitative growth and placed on qualitative improvement, what Daly calls 'sustainable development.'[20] During his tenure at the World Bank, he advocated lending and restructuring policies based not on quantitative growth but on this view of sustainable development.

For instance, he recommended qualitative change through population control, redistribution of wealth and income, technical improvements in resource productivity, and a realization of the interconnectedness of the global community.

This global community includes both human and nonhuman species, which necessarily adds a component of spiritual and religious thinking beyond the usual constraints of economics. Daly has written with John Cobb (a theologian) on the need to move away from an anthropocentric society and toward biospheric thinking.[21] They argue that the human species is morally obligated to protect all species.

At one extreme on this philosophical spectrum is the Gaia hypothesis. First championed by James Lovelock in 1979, this theory transforms the discussion of social purpose into global spiritualism, arguing that Planet Earth functions as one organism. Human activity, in our anthropocentric pursuit of utility, will necessarily affect the planet. But earth's global systems will ultimately maintain balance. The social movement spawned by such hypotheses, often called 'deep ecology,' takes the position that "we humans have no special rights, only obligations to the community of Gaia."[22]

Clearly, ecological economics covers a wide range of ideas. It has mainly grown out of the economics community, from economists with a classical rather than neoclassical orientation. Of course, many contributions to this new discipline have been made by such ecologists as Paul and Ann Ehrlich, Garrett Hardin, and Robert Costanza (the first president of the International Society for Ecological Economics), as well as physicists, chaos theorists, environmentalists, and experts from other disciplines worldwide. In addition to Daly, today's most influential ideas in ecological economics include Costanza's work in defining and promoting the organizational aspects of ecological economics; Norgaard and Gowdy's development of a coevolutionary approach to the economy-environment interface; the work of Cleveland et al., which tightens the debate on biophysical limits to growth; and the new international emphasis on sustainability, developing each country's perspective on growth and intragenerational (i.e., within a generation) equity.[23]

The teaching of ecological economics is beginning to make some inroads. The first textbook on ecological economics has been published,[24] and the first Ph.D. degree program in Ecological Economics was established at Rensselaer Polytechnic Institute in Troy, New York.

Other reviews of ecological economics are of interest. Krishnan et al. completed a comprehensive survey of the field's literature. Sahu and Nayak prepared a comparison of ecological economics with neoclassical environmental economics, contrasting the primary differences in paradigm, scarcity perception, problem-solving orientation, and range of integration. Turner et al. have also helped define the ecological economics perspective.[25] To clarify these distinctions, the next section invokes the example of the economics of climate change.

Climate Change

The global externalities of climate change, mainly due to anthropogenic emissions of greenhouse gases (GHG) from fossil fuel use and land conversion, may become one of the most significant environmental challenges of our time. The impacts of a rapid climate change have been discussed by physical, biological, and social scientists for over two decades.

The purpose here is to review the popular neoclassical approach to policy regarding climate change, and to compare this with the alternative interdisciplinary perspective of ecological economics outlined in the last section.

The neoclassical approach involves framing the climate change problem in a benefit-cost analysis, similar to traditional, local analysis of air or water pollution. The questions posed include: Should economies invest now in the hopes of averting future damage from such potential problems as increased storm severity, higher sea levels, and intercontinental drought? Or do we wait, adapt as necessary, and hope for the best? Further complicating matters is the fact that, as Chapter 18 explains, a warmer climate could be a boon rather than a problem in some areas. For example, some agricultural regions may benefit from longer growing periods. It is also possible that increased concentration of carbon dioxide in the atmosphere could benefit plant growth through improved photosynthesis and water use efficiency—a "CO_2 fertilization effect."[26] From the economist's standpoint, the challenge is to categorize both the cost of limiting current emissions and the benefits of reducing the future climatic impact.

The previous chapter recognized William Nordhaus's significant contribution to this daunting task. His analysis of the economics of climate change asks us to count all the benefits and costs before we irrationally pursue growth-limiting prescriptions. A sense of the economic rationality of his work is evident in a sampling of titles: "To Slow or Not to Slow: The Economics of the Greenhouse Effect," "An Optimal Transition Path for Controlling Greenhouse Gases," and *Managing the Global Commons: The Economics of Climate Change.*[27] The central questions to this body of literature are: Can society rationalize averting global climate change at the expense of economic growth? Must an either-or decision be made?

A critique of the mechanics and sensitivity of the Nordhaus model has been taken up by others.[28] The focus here is on the philosophical foundation of the analysis—questioning the rationality of *Homo economicus*.[29] To do this, one need only focus on the first equation in the Nordhaus model: the utility maximization specification. The problem, represented in Equation (19-1), is to choose the optimal level of investment $[I_t]$ and control rate $[CR_t]$ in GHG abatement over time in order to maximize U, global utility. Utility is assumed to depend on world population $[N_t]$, the natural logarithm of per capita consumption $[c(t)]$, and a social discount rate $[\rho]$.[30]

$$\underset{\{I_t, CR_t\}}{\text{Max U}} = \sum_{t=1}^{H} \frac{N_t * [\ln c(t)]}{(1 + \rho)^t} \qquad (19\text{-}1)$$

The variable of per capita consumption $[c(t)]$ seems intuitively appealing—if each person in the global economy is able to consume more in each time period, then we're all better off. There is a flaw, however, in this intuition. Per capita consumption is merely an average, and an average can be boosted by increasing consumption of a below *or* above average person. In other words, the distribution of consumption has no value. If the average is boosted by increasing consumption of the top 5 percent income class, then global utility is improved, but perhaps at the expense of global welfare.

The vast difference between rich and poor, or between rich and working class, is apparent between countries and within them. In writing about the United States, Michael Yates notes that as working class Americans struggle to make ends meet, the rich are wealthier now than at any time since World War II.[31] Yates cites Kloby in reporting that between 1963 and 1983, wealth rose by 9.7 percent for the richest 0.5 percent of all families, while the poorest 90 percent experienced a 6.7 percent decline.[32] In *The State of Working America*,[33] Mishel and Bernstein found that the difference between rich and poor is increasingly dramatic. Between 1977 and 1990, average real family income fell for the poorest 60 percent of all families, while it increased by 33 percent for the richest 20 percent, and increased by over 95 percent for the wealthiest 1 percent. The decline in income of the lower percentiles of the wealth distribution is just recently starting to pull the average family income down, while the purchasing power of U.S. weekly earnings is currently no higher than it was in 1967.[34]

Certainly there is much dissatisfaction with the rich getting richer and the poor getting poorer. Is this an appropriate model of global utility? Superficially, perhaps a better model would be maximizing the minimum, as proposed by John Rawls in *A Theory of Justice*.[35] (See Chapter 5.) This means increasing global utility by improving the living standards of poorer groups. For instance, one of three children is born every day into absolute poverty. Absolute poverty is defined by the income level below which a minimum nutritionally adequate diet (plus essential nonfood requirements) is not affordable.[36] To improve the well-being of those in absolute poverty without altering the quantitative scale of the macroeconomy would require a redistribution of resources.

For example, UNICEF estimates that an investment of $25 billion per year over a decade could control the major childhood diseases, halve child malnutrition, reduce child deaths by 4 million a year, bring safe water and sanitation to all communities, provide basic education for all children, and make family planning universally available. In comparison, as Figure 19.1 demonstrates, the United States spends over $30 billion per year on beer. Of the $40 billion a year spent by Western industrialized nations on bilateral aid, a mere 10 percent is earmarked for meeting these most basic human needs.[37]

Comparing a pack of cigarettes or a can of beer with a polio vaccination introduces a second fundamental problem in modeling global utility on per capita consumption: no distinction is made between welfare and specific goods. In the global maximization problem, a $100 pair of sneakers has the same value as $100 worth of rice. In welfare terms, however, rice should be much more valuable than the latest athletic shoes. If the global economy had only one hundred more dollars to spend, which good would provide more global welfare? This has long been recognized as the "diamond and water paradox."

In a narrow sense, the concepts of consumers' surplus and consumers' value from Chapter 1 resolve the paradox by measuring economic welfare as the monetary value of the area under the demand curves. Nevertheless, the fundamental problem is the measurement of utility in monetary terms.

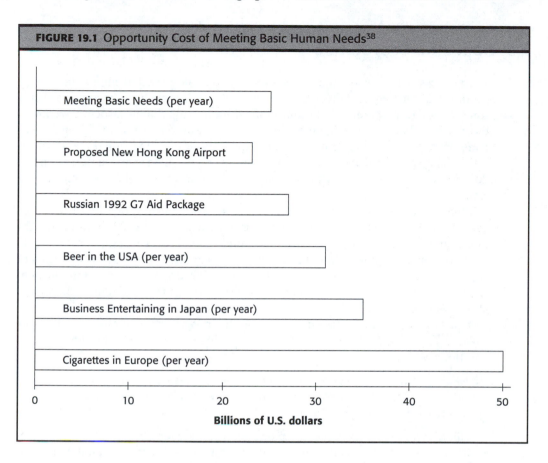

FIGURE 19.1 Opportunity Cost of Meeting Basic Human Needs[38]

Meeting Basic Needs (per year)

Proposed New Hong Kong Airport

Russian 1992 G7 Aid Package

Beer in the USA (per year)

Business Entertaining in Japan (per year)

Cigarettes in Europe (per year)

0   10   20   30   40   50

Billions of U.S. dollars

So, in contrast, a more prudent model of climate change economics would not choose a GHG control rate that resulted in the inundation of a poor Bangladesh while a rich Manhattan adapts and remains unscathed behind a sea wall. Rather, a prudent model might start with a decision to protect the people of Bangladesh, to realize this future cost and compare it with the current cost of abatement. Focusing on a safe minimum standard shifts emphasis away from an optimal solution and concerns itself with the process of achieving risk- and welfare-oriented goals.

The science of climate change also provides an ideal case study of the benefits of interdisciplinary work and a focus on *process* rather than optimal *outcomes*. Working to understand the social, economic, and biophysical dimensions of climate change has been a dynamic social process, not a charted optimal path. As Norgaard explains, "When astro-physicists, dealing in microns and microseconds, come together with evolutionary biologists, dealing on continental scales over millennia, there must be some softening of traditional disciplinary mortar."[39] These multidisciplinary efforts have been the breeding ground for ecological economics and its evolution.

A New Paradigm: Limits, Sustainable Development, Coevolution

There is a growing sense among economists and ecologists that human consumption of world physical resources has grown too large. Yet we have become so accustomed to equating increased consumption with progress that as a society we know no other way. Two U.S. presidential elections were won on very strong growth platforms, despite a vice president who had written about our "Dysfunctional Civilization" and "disharmony in our relationship to the earth, which stems in part from our addiction to a pattern of consuming ever-larger quantities of the resources of the earth. . . ."[40]

Table 19.1 offers examples of per capita waste and consumption by the average U.S. citizen. An average 150-pound person is annually creating 287 times his weight in carbon dioxide emissions, 13 times his weight in solid waste, and consuming 48 times his weight in coal. At these rates, and with a growing population, our current and future ecological impact looks significant. The dogma of economic growth raises an unavoidable question: can the earth support a society of tens of billions of U.S. consumers?

Most striking is our impact on global biodiversity. Richard Leakey and Roger Lewin in *The Sixth Extinction* argue that we are living in a tragically unique time in evolutionary history:

> *Dominant as no other species has been in the history of life on Earth,* Homo Sapiens *is in the throes of causing a major biological crisis, a mass extinction, the sixth such event to have occurred in the past half billion years.*[41]

Only five times before has mass extinction run its course over such a brief geological instant.[42] The current rate of species extinction is controversial, with estimates ranging from 17,000 to 100,000 species lost per year. However, an extinction

TABLE 19.1 A Sample of the U.S. Per Capita "Waste" Line[43]

	Annual per Capita	*Units*
Waste		
CO_2 emissions	43,064	pounds
SO_2 emissions	181	pounds
Solid waste	2,000	pounds
Consumption		
Motor gasoline	460	gallons
Coal	7,219	pounds
Vehicle miles traveled	9,006	miles
Replacement		
Fertility rate	2.1	children/woman

rate of 30,000 a year is 120,000 times above what is considered normal: one species lost every four years.[44]

Limits to Growth

The major cause of such mass extinction has been our quantitative growth, or economic scale, and our resulting consumption of ecosystem space. Global deforestation is most alarming. Leakey and Lewin reviewed two independent studies by the World Resources Institute and the United Nations Food and Agriculture Organization, each reporting deforestation rates in the range of 80,000 square miles per year. At this rate, tropical forests may be reduced to 10 percent of their original cover early in the 21st Century.[45]

Contemporary arguments for an absolute limit to this unprecedented human growth began with the report of The Club of Rome's Project on the Predicament of Mankind. As explained in Chapter 10, the Meadows group constructed a computer model of exponential growth in population, industrial capital, food production, non-renewable resource consumption, and pollution, within geologically and geographically defined physical and social limits. Assuming the then-current rates of exponential growth, they found "the limits to growth on this planet will be reached sometime within the next one hundred years" and that the "most probable result will be a rather sudden and uncontrollable decline in both population and industrial capacity."[46]

The Meadows work highlighted physical, environmental, and social limits to growing material consumption as the causes of projected societal collapse. Unfortunately, the physical limits hypothesis (i.e., limits in energy and mineral resources, fresh water, and arable land) became the most popular forecast of their larger body of work. Under their exponential index scenario, the world's reserves of copper, lead, mercury, natural gas, petroleum, tin, and zinc were all predicted to be depleted within the seven-year period 1985–1992.[47] However, through changes in demand, increased recycling, substitution possibilities, and discovered geological reserves, limits to 20th Century growth imposed by absolute scarcity were largely avoided. For this reason, the "Limits to Growth" hypothesis has more often than not been rejected by mainstream economists.

However, this rejection ignores the other half of their story: limits to our environmental and social resources. In 1972, the Meadows group warned that, if resources proved sufficient for continued economic expansion, economic collapse would follow environmental catastrophe. As evidence, consider that the waste-assimilating capacity of our atmosphere and oceans cannot absorb the CO_2 emissions from 600 million automobiles and other energy uses, increasing the probability of dramatic global climate change.

On the social front, demand for education, health services, and political stability continues to be greater than our ability to provide it to much of the global citizenry. The 1993 *Human Development Report* found for all developing countries (about 77 percent of the world's population) a 40 percent secondary school enrollment ratio, and 72 percent, 68 percent, and 55 percent of the population with access to health services, safe water, and sanitation, respectively.[48]

Twenty years later, Meadows et al.[49] produced a sequel to the original report, correctly emphasizing indications that global pollution, social instability, and absolute scarcity would ultimately limit our energy and materials use. While the first report alluded to the possibility of altering exponential growth rates and obtaining ecological and economic sustainability, the 1992 work concluded that society would now have to contract, particularly in materialistic consumption, in order to come back within sustainable limits. Table 19.2 illustrates worldwide growth in selected activities between the publication of the reports.

The Limits to Growth argument stems from the ecologists' concept of carrying capacity: a finite boundary to economic expansion, resource extraction, and social stability. Clearly, if there is any truth to the ecologist's vision of limits to the human "waste" line, then the traditional economic paradigm of growth must be discarded.

Joel Cohen (as discussed in Chapter 10) has thoroughly reviewed the debate over limits to population growth in his book *How Many People Can the Earth Support?*[50] While the answers to this question range from less than 1 billion to more than 100 billion, he finds that more than half fall between 4 and 16 billion. With a

TABLE 19.2 Worldwide Growth in Selected Human Activities and Products[51]

	1970	1990
Human population	3.6 billion	5.3 billion
Registered automobiles	250 million	560 million
Km driven/year (OECD only)		
by passenger cars	2,584 billion	4,489 billion
by trucks	666 billion	1,536 million
Oil consumption/year	17 billion bls	24 billion bls
Natural gas consumption/year	31 trillion cu ft	70 trillion cu ft
Coal consumption/year	2.3 billion tons	5.2 billion tons
Electric generating capacity	1.1 billion kW	2.6 billion kW
Electricity generation/year, by		
nuclear power plants	79 tWh	1,884 tWh
U.S. soft drink consumption/year	150 million bls	364 million bls
U.S. beer consumption/year	125 million bls	187 million bls
U.S. aluminum consumed/year for		
beer and soft drink containers	72,700 tonnes	1,251,900 tonnes
Municipal waste generated/year		
(OECD countries only)	302 million tonnes	420 million tonnes

Abbreviations:

km = kilometer(s)
OECD = Organization for Economic Cooperation and Development
cu ft = cubic feet
kW = kilowatt
tWh = terawatt-hours
bls = barrels
tonne = one metric ton (2,205 pounds or 1,000 kilograms)

current global population of over 6 billion and growth of nearly 100 million per year, we are entering an era of tremendous population demands on our planet's finite carrying capacity.

Optimal social scale does not enter into the calculus of economic growth. More "stuff" in the long run is always preferred. In fact, environmental worries are addressed, in the neoclassical tradition, through improvements in efficiency. Environmental impact, in the most general sense, equals population times per capita consumption times efficiency of consumption. As Bill McKibben notes:

> We have tended to focus on the efficiency issues (in this equation)—new technologies, better cars, recycling, and so on—because they are politically and emotionally the most palatable: they allow us to avoid the question of our place on the planet, they offer us the possibility of extending our current patterns of use for at least another generation or two.[52]

In contrast, the Limits to Growth literature offers a paradigm of absolute constraint, the possibility of a society sustained within a supportive ecosystem, but likely at the expense of political and emotional palatability.

Sustainable Development

Sustainable development has also been considered a defining paradigm from ecological economics for a post-consumerism global economy. (This is the subject of the next chapter, by Richard Bishop and Richard Woodward. The theory of sustainable use was introduced in Chapter 6 and applied to agriculture and forestry in Chapters 13 and 14.) Sustainable development means many things to many different people. Its present popularity in government, business, academic literature, and the popular press, however, has done more to dilute the concept than support it.

Table 19.3 illustrates a range of perspectives on sustainable development. The interdisciplinary approach comes closest to matching the Limits to Growth paradigm. The Nobel Laureate Robert Solow perhaps best summarizes the neoclassical perspective on sustainable development; he calls it a matter of intergenerational equity—providing to our children and grandchildren ad infinitum opportunities similar to those our generation enjoyed. Equity is the ability to maintain current levels of material consumption into the future. Given human and natural capital depreciation, as well as nonrenewable resource depletion, this version of sustainable development requires each generation to invest in capital stock and environmental resources, i.e., growth.

Contrasted with the limits to growth paradigm, 'sustainable' and 'growth' uttered in the same phrase seem contradictory. Substitution of new products or improvements in efficiency may allow continued economic growth in the near term, but the jury is still out on the environmental and social limits to this growth. Because of these conflicting goals and the political unwillingness to recognize limits, sustainable development has not yet become a real guiding principle.

From an institutional perspective, Howarth and Norgaard conclude: "If development is not sustainable, it is because the institutions through which the present provides for the future have not evolved in consonance with changes in social and economic structures, technology, and population pressure."[53] This perspective

TABLE 19.3 Perspectives on Sustainable Development[54]

Perspective	Sustainable Development As:	Key Concepts	Source
Academic-interdisciplinary	"... sustainable scale of economic activity within the ecological life-support system."	Carrying capacity, sustain welfare, environmental quality	Arrow et al., 1995 (page 521)
Academic-neoclassical economics	"... [endowing future generations] with whatever it takes to achieve a standard of living at least as good as our own and to look after their next generation similarly."	Intergenerational equity, capital investment	Solow, 1992 (page 15)
Business	"... integrat[ing] environmental considerations into our operations and into our long-range planning...."	Sustainable growth	Kennedy, 1992 (page 2)
Development agency	"... a new era of economic growth, one that must be based on policies that sustain and expand the environmental resource base."	Sustainable technological progress, no absolute limits, intragenerational equity	World Commission, 1987 (The Bruntland Report) (page 1)
Government	"... policies that encourage economic growth, job creation, and effective use of our natural and cultural resources."	Good economic policy protects the environment and good environmental policy strengthens the economy	White House, 1993

places demands on intergenerational equity while recognizing a social evolutionary process, the subject of the next possible paradigm.

Lessons from Coevolution

The father of modern theories of evolution is Charles Darwin.[55] Jones suggests "classical economics as the scaffolding for evolutionary biology" with the writings of Thomas Malthus, Adam Smith, and others influencing Darwin.[56] (This is ironic given the current tendency to apply paradigms from evolutionary biology to the problems of economics.)

In studying social evolution, a particularly useful subsection of evolutionary biology is coevolution. It is a process of "evolutionary change of two closely interacting species where the fitness of the genetic traits within each species is largely governed by the dominant genetic traits of the other."[57] Coevolution accounts for change through selection, trial, error, and the survival of what proves fit. In a social context, it envisions social and biological systems evolving together along a random, but deterministic, time line within physical environmental constraints—"random" because what changes will occur are unknown; "deterministic" because change will certainly occur.

Under this paradigm there are no universal truths. In fact, coevolution promotes the virtues of diversity as a proving ground for functionality. In turn, "what works" is itself always changing.

Figure 19.2 describes some of the critical interactions of a coevolutionary social system. In direct contrast to modernity, there is no directionality in a coevolutionary model. The 20th Century version of progress starts with a problem, introduces science and the virtues of technological development, and unconditionally expects a solution. Under a science-knows-best paradigm, the solution to unsustainable development is simply to accelerate technological change—not dissimilar to the business, development agency, and government perspectives on sustainable development from Table 19.3.

Coevolution, however, cannot predict or be operationalized as conveniently as a utility maximization problem. This is perhaps not very satisfying. But coevolution sheds light on the complexity of the social-natural-physical system, which in turn provides insight into how to behave as individuals and how to structure our societies. It focuses less on finding the optimal solution than on asking the right questions. How should we take advantage of a coevolutionary process we cannot control? What are the catalysts to coevolutionary processes?

Norgaard explores U.S. pesticide policy as an example of the coevolutionary process. He also examines agricultural development in the Amazon for lessons from a coevolutionary perspective.[58] In the Amazon case, Norgaard argues that the application of Western agriculture and global market theory to a tropical ecosystem and culture has failed completely. On the other hand, traditional knowledge and cultures, which coevolved with this specific ecosystem, have repeatedly proven more reliable. John Gowdy explores hunting and gathering societies, and concludes that they represent perhaps "the most successful lifestyle humans have yet devised."[59] Success is considered in terms of their compatibility with the long-run sustainability of the ecosystem and exemplary egalitarian societal structure. He, too,

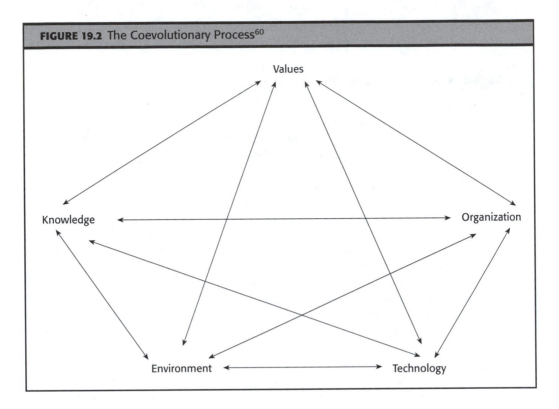

FIGURE 19.2 The Coevolutionary Process[60]

argues against the universal applicability of modern market economies, demonstrating that the 'economic man' most often characterized in utility maximization problems is misleading. He believes that humans have not historically exhibited unlimited wants or purely egocentric behavior without altruism or concern for environmental externalities.

By its nature, a paradigm of coevolution cannot be applied to all problems. Norgaard argues, however, that recognizing an underlying coevolutionary process between social and natural systems can be helpful in formulating lessons to help guide social processes. Some lessons include:[61]

1. Experiment on a small scale and monitor the evolutionary chain of events. This is particularly useful in avoiding past mistakes regarding the unforeseen consequences of technology transfer.
2. Experiments with long-term commitments should be avoided. The perfect example here is the set of problems caused by a policy of irretrievable nuclear-waste burial.
3. Diversity in coevolving systems is inherently good; without it, stagnation is likely. Diversity in cultures, ecosystems, and species provides greater opportunity for natural selection to determine what is fit.
4. Emphasize evolutionary processes rather than mechanical fixes. For instance, encourage diversity instead of relying on monotypical technical fixes. This allows great flexibility in responding to new challenges.

5.   Cultures first evolved around ecosystems, then around hydrocarbons. Will the next focal point of social evolution be sustainability?

Concluding Remarks: Choices and Change

The very first lesson students of economics learn is that economics is the study of choices.[62] This is perhaps something all economists can agree on, whether they call themselves neoclassical, environmental, or ecological. Traditionally the choices have been framed in terms of how best to employ scarce resources to produce commodities and distribute them for consumption. Within this realm, economics has been very amenable to marginal analysis and the mathematics of optimization, and during the neoclassical age it has become more a science of choice than the instrument of social change originally envisioned by the classical economists.

Choices, however, are increasingly difficult to make. The environmental consequences of our individually rational choices include the prospect of dramatically changing the global climate as well as damaging biodiversity—in essence, resetting the evolutionary clock. The social consequences include a widening of global income disparity, the institutionalization of poverty, and the failure to support an exploding human population. The discipline of environmental economics addresses these consequences, but has been somewhat limited due to a dependence on the consumption-oriented, individualistic growth paradigm of neoclassical economics.

This chapter addresses the broader choice of paradigms. The relatively new discipline of ecological economics was presented as an alternative to environmental economics. More specifically, the paradigms of limits, sustainable development, and coevolution were discussed as alternatives to a market-driven model of economic growth.

The transition to a new paradigm has been discussed for decades, but is slow in coming. John Livingston in *Rogue Primate* concedes that:

> . . . *no one knows how a new paradigm or a new metaphysic, no matter how cogently drafted, is to be gotten into the human bloodstream. You don't legislate things of this kind. You evolve into them, and out of them.*[63]

As evidence of this social evolution, consider the last large-scale shift in paradigm from the mercantilist to the free-market era. Galbraith notes that the mercantilist era that preceded industrialization and competition evolved over a half-century of change. Before the industrial revolution, the wealthy merchant class discouraged competition for fear of bringing prices too low. The success of the state in this era was measured by the success of its merchant class's pursuit of wealth. The welfare of individuals or households was irrelevant.[64]

Even before the shift in paradigm from merchant to individual, the emphasis on profit-seeking behavior was itself a gradual evolution. In premercantilist economic history, wealth was largely viewed with suspicion and its pursuit was felt to be immoral. In fact, early Christian doctrine condemned the use of interest on loans.[65]

Economic thought continues to evolve. In neoclassical economics, the pursuit of wealth gained gradual acceptance. Might the next defining economic concept be the pursuit of sustainability?

Questions for Discussion and Analysis

1. What is ecological economics?

2. List what you believe to be the three most important concepts in ecological economics. Compare your list to that of another student. Do they agree?

3. Do you consider yourself to be either a neoclassical or an ecological economist? Explain.

4. How does the Erickson perspective on climate change in this chapter compare to the Nordhaus perspective in the previous chapter?

5. Consider Chapter 10's review of economic aspects of population growth and resource depletion. Do you think resource exhaustion or pollution will prove to be a more important question? How do you think the author of this chapter would answer the same question?

6. Compare the several definitions of sustainability in Table 19.3.

7. Discuss the major components of the coevolution concept.

8. This textbook includes 18 or 19 chapters that would generally be considered mainstream environmental economics. Do you think that this chapter by Erickson successfully makes the case that ecological economics is an alternative to environmental economics?

9. Assume you wish to join a professional society in economics that publishes research on environmental subjects, but you can only afford to join one of the three! Would it be the American Economic Association, the Association of Environmental and Resource Economists, or the International Society for Ecological Economics?

Notes to Chapter 19

1. Adam Smith, *The Wealth of Nations* (London: Dent, 1910). First printed in London, 1776.
2. Smith, however, was more concerned with the moral implications of self-interested behavior than he has been given credit for. In his work on the *Theory of Moral Sentiments* (1759), which preceded *The Wealth of Nations*, Smith argues that our conscience (what he calls "the impartial spectator") will also play a role in guiding our decisions. See Robert Heilbroner, *Teachings from the Worldly Philosophy* (New York: Norton, 1996).
3. John Stuart Mill, *Principles of Political Economy*, Seventh Edition (London: Oxford University Press, 1994). First published in 1848.
4. A. C. Pigou, *The Economics of Welfare*, Fourth Edition (London: MacMillan, 1952). First published in 1920.
5. John Maynard Keynes, *The General Theory of Employment, Interest, and Money* (New York: Harcourt, Brace, 1964). First published in 1936.
6. S. V. Ciriacy-Wantrup, *Resource Conservation: Economics and Policies* (California: University of California Division of Agricultural Sciences, 1963). First edition published by the University of California Press in 1952.
7. John K. Galbraith, *Economics in Perspective: A Critical History* (Boston, MA: Houghton Mifflin, 1987).

8. Richard B. Norgaard, *Development Betrayed: The End of Progress and a Coevolutionary Revisioning of the Future* (London/New York: Routledge, 1994). See also John M. Gowdy, "Progress and Environmental Sustainability," Spring 1994 *Environmental Ethics* 16:41–55.

9. These categories were suggested by Richard Norgaard in a seminar at Cornell University.

10. Nicholas Georgescu-Roegen, "Energy and Economic Myths," January 1975 *Southern Economic Journal* 41(3):347–381, page 359.

11. Thomas Malthus, an ordained clergyman, is known for his writing on absolute limits to population growth. He argued that a fixed amount of land accompanied by an increasing population would lead to diminishing returns and a declining per capita food supply. In turn, standards of living would decline to a level where population would cease to grow. See Thomas Robert Malthus, *An Essay on the Principle of Population*, Philip Appleman, ed. (New York: Norton, 1976). First published anonymously in 1798.

12. See John Gowdy, *Coevolutionary Economics: The Economy, Society and the Environment*, (Boston, MA: Kluwer, 1994), page 8; and John Gowdy and Sabine O'Hara, *Economic Theory for Environmentalists* (Delray Beach, FL: St. Lucie, 1995), pages 48–51.

13. David Ricardo, *Principles of Political Economy and Taxation* (London: Everyman, 1926). First published in 1817.

14. Herman E. Daly, *Beyond Growth: The Economics of Sustainable Development* (Boston, MA: Beacon, 1996), page 27.

15. 'Newtonian' refers to the scientific tradition of explaining phenomena or processes by reducing them to parts and universal rules.

16. Kenneth E. Boulding, "The Economics of the Coming Spaceship Earth," pages 3–14 in H. Jarrett, ed., *Environmental Quality in a Growing Economy* (Baltimore: Johns Hopkins, 1966).

17. See Kenneth E. Boulding, *The World as a Total System* (Beverly Hills, CA: Sage Publications, 1985); and Kenneth E. Boulding, *Towards a New Economics* (England: Elgar, 1992).

18. Boulding used the phrase "cowboy economy" to describe an economy where resources are thought to be limitless, as they perhaps seemed during the European settlement of the western United States. Modern-day cowboys or ranchers, however, are well aware of the limits to resources on a daily basis.

19. Boulding, "Spaceship Earth," *op. cit.* (see Note 16).

20. Daly *op. cit.* (see Note 14), page 31.

21. See Herman E. Daly and John B. Cobb, Jr., *For the Common Good: Redirecting the Economy Toward Community, the Environment, and a Sustainable Future* (Boston, MA: Beacon, 1989). Recall the discussion of 'natural rights' and 'nonhuman value' in Chapters 5 and 15.

22. James Lovelock, *Gaia: A New Look at Life on Earth* (London: Oxford University Press, 1995), page viii. First published in 1979.

23. Robert Costanza, editor, *Ecological Economics: The Science and Management of Sustainability* (New York: Columbia University Press, 1991); Norgaard *op. cit.* (see Note 8); John Gowdy, *Coevolutionary Economics: The Economy, Society and the Environment* (Boston, MA: Kluwer, 1994); Cutler J. Cleveland, Robert Costanza, Charles A. S. Hall, and Robert Kaufmann, "Energy and the U.S. Economy: a Biophysical Perspective," August 1984 *Science* 225:890–897.

24. Robert Costanza, John Cumberland, Herman Daly, Robert Goodland, and Richard Norgaard, *An Introduction to Ecological Economics* (Boca Raton, FL: St. Lucie, 1997). This is a good resource for the book's detailed discussions of "The Historical Development of Economics and Ecology" (pages 19–75) and "Problems and Principles of Ecological Economics" (pages 77–167).

25. Rajaram Krishnan, Jonathan M. Harris, and Neva R. Goodwin, eds., *A Survey of Ecological Economics* (Washington, DC: Island, 1995); Nirmal C. Sahu and Bibhudatta Nayak, "Niche Diversification in Environmental/Ecological Economics," 1994 *Ecological Economics* 11:9–19; Kerry Turner, Charles Perrings, and Carl Folke, "Ecological Economics: Paradigm or Perspective," pages 25–49 in Jeroen C. J. M. van den Bergh and Jan van der Straaten, eds., *Economy and Ecosystems in Change: Analytical and Historical Approaches* (Cheltenham, UK: Elgar, 1997).

26. For a critique, in the spirit of ecological economics, of CO_2 fertilization claims, see Jon D. Erickson, "From Ecology to Economics: The Case Against CO_2 Fertilization," 1993 *Ecological Economics* 8:157–175; and David H. Wolfe and Jon D. Erickson, "Carbon Dioxide Effects on Plants: Uncertainties and Implications for Modeling Crop Response to Climate Change," pages 153–178 in Harry Kaiser and Thomas Drennen, eds., *Agricultural Dimensions of Global Climate Change* (Delray Beach, FL: St. Lucie, 1993).

27. William D. Nordhaus, "To Slow or Not to Slow: The Economics of the Greenhouse Effect," July 1991 *The Economic Journal* 101:920–937; William D. Nordhaus, "An Optimal Transition Path for Controlling Greenhouse Gases," November 1992 *Science* 258:1315–1319; William D. Nordhaus, *Managing the Global Commons: The Economics of Climate Change* (Cambridge, MA: MIT Press, 1995).

28. For instance: Duane Chapman, Vivek Suri, and Steven G. Hall, "Rolling DICE for the Future of the Planet," July 1995 *Contemporary Economic Policy* 13:1–9; Donna Lee and James Roumasset, "Optimizing Global Warming: An Intermediate Approach," presented at the 84th Annual Meeting of the American Agricultural Economics Association, San Antonio, TX, July 28–31, 1996; Neha Khanna and Duane Chapman, "Climate Policy and Petroleum Depletion in an Optimal Growth Framework," Cornell ARME Staff Paper 97-7, November 1997; Robert K. Kaufmann, "The Economic Impact of Global Climate Change: Making Sure the 'DICE' Model isn't Loaded," *Climatic Change*, in press.

29. Literally meaning "economic man," the stereotypical decision-maker in the self-interest model. This nomenclature was first used by Max Lerner in an introduction to Adam Smith's *The Wealth of Nations*, First Modern Library Edition (New York: Random House, 1937).

30. Nordhaus *op. cit.* (see Note 27, 1992).

31. Michael D. Yates, *Longer Hours, Fewer Jobs: Employment & Unemployment in the United States* (New York: Monthly Review Press, 1994), page 11.

32. Jerry Kloby, "The Growing Divide: Class Polarization in the 1980s," September 1987 *Monthly Review* 39(4).

33. Lawrence Mishel and Jared Bernstein, *The State of Working America* (Armonk, NY: M. E. Sharpe, Inc., 1993).

34. Yates *op. cit.,* pages 10 and 11.

35. Rawls proposes a classic thought experiment in which a "veil of ignorance" is placed over each participant, effectively blinding any socioeconomic identity they may have. In setting up an initial situation that is fair, he argues that principles of justice will be chosen that require (1) equal rights to basic liberties, and (2) social and economic inequalities arranged for the greatest benefit of the least advantaged (the difference principle). See John Rawls, *A Theory of Justice* (Cambridge, MA: Harvard University Press, 1971).

36. Calculated from Table 10 (Regional Summaries), pages 98–99 in UNICEF, *The State of the World's Children 1996* (New York: Oxford University Press, 1996).

37. UNICEF, *The State of the World's Children 1993* (New York: Oxford University Press, 1993), Figure 1, page 2.

38. *Ibid.*

39. Norgaard *op. cit.* (see Note 8).

40. Al Gore, *Earth in the Balance: Ecology and the Human Spirit* (Boston, MA: Houghton Mifflin Co., 1992), page 223.

41. Richard Leakey and Roger Lewin, *The Sixth Extinction: Patterns of Life and the Future of Humankind* (New York: Doubleday, 1995), page 245.

42. Defined when at least 65 percent of marine animal species became extinct. Extreme changes in life's history are most readily inferred from the marine fossil record as these organisms are more likely to become fossilized and thus have provided a more complete fossil record. The Big Five, however, are also evident in the terrestrial record. *Ibid.,* pages 44–45.

43. Notes to Table 19.1:
    a. World Resources Institute, *World Resources 1994–95* (New York: Oxford University Press, 1994). CO_2 in 1991 emissions from Table 23.1, page 363. SO_2 in 1991 emissions from Table 23.5, page 367.
    b. P. William Reidhead, *Environmental Costs and Optimal Unit Pricing for Municipal Solid Waste Services,* M.S. thesis (Ithaca, NY: Cornell University, 1996), page 1. Includes both residential and commercial solid waste for 1989.
    c. U.S. Energy Information Administration, *Monthly Energy Review,* DOE/EIA-0035 (96/05), U.S. Department of Energy, Washington, DC, May 1996. Gas statistics from 1995, Table 3.4, page 57. Coal statistics from 1995, Table 6.1, page 87. Per capita calculation assumes a U.S. population of 260.6 million.
    d. U.S. Environmental Protection Agency, *National Air Quality and Emissions Trend Report 1994,* EPA 454/R-95-014, U.S. EPA, Office of Air Quality Planning and Standards, Research Triangle Park, NC, October 1995, Figure 1.3, page 1–4. 1994 data.
    e. UNICEF *op. cit.* (see Note 37), Table 5, page 88. 1994 data.
    f. Also see Table 10.2 in Chapter 10 on per capita recycling and waste.

44. Leakey and Lewin *op.cit.,* page 241.

45. *Ibid.,* page 237.

46. Donnella H. Meadows, Dennis L. Meadows, Jorgen Randers and William W. Behrens III, *The Limits to Growth* (New York: Universe Books, 1972), page 23.

47. This scenario calculated the number of years known global reserves would last assuming consumption growing exponentially at the average annual rate of growth. *Ibid.,* Table 4, pages 56–60.

48. United Nations Development Program, *Human Development Report 1993* (New York: Oxford University Press, 1993).

49. Donnella H. Meadows, Dennis L. Meadows, and J. Randers, *Beyond the Limits: Confronting Global Collapse, Envisioning a Sustainable Future* (Post Mills, VT: Chelsea Green Publishing Co., 1992).

50. Joel E. Cohen, *How Many People Can the Earth Support?* (New York: Norton, 1995).

51. Meadows *op. cit.* (see Note 49).

52. Bill McKibben, *The Comforting Whirlwind: God, Job, and the Scale of Creation* (Grand Rapids, MI: Eerdmans, 1994), page 43.

53. Richard B. Howarth and Richard B. Norgaard, "Environmental Valuation under Sustainable Development," May 1992 *American Economic Review* 82(2):473–477, page 473.

54. K. Arrow, B. Bolin, R. Costanza, P. Dasgupta, C. Folke, C. S. Holling, B. Jansson, S. Levin, K. Maler, C. Perrings, and D. Pimental, "Economic Growth, Carrying Capacity, and the Environment," April 1995 *Science* 268, page 521; Robert Solow, "An Almost Practical Step Toward Sustainability," an Invited Lecture on the Occasion of the Fortieth Anniversary of Resources for the Future, Washington, DC, October 8, 1992, page 15; Robert D. Kennedy (CEO, Union Carbide Corp.), "Sustainable Development: The Hinge of History," Industry Forum on Environment and Development, Rio de Janeiro, May 28, 1992, page 2; World Commission on Environment and Development, *Our Common Future*

(New York: Oxford University Press, 1987); White House, Office of the Press Secretary, "On Earth Summit Anniversary President Creates Council on Sustainable Development," Press Release, June 14, 1993.

55. Charles Darwin, *On the Origin of Species—A Facsimile of the First Edition* (Cambridge, MA: Harvard University Press, 1964). *Origin* was first published in 1859. Although Darwin is most often credited as the father of evolution, Alfred R. Wallace is recognized as a codiscoverer of natural selection. See Stephen Jay Gould, *Ever Since Darwin: Reflections in Natural History* (New York: Norton, 1977), page 25.

56. Lamar Jones, "The Institutionalists and *On the Origin of Species*: A Case of Mistaken Identity," 1986 *Southern Economic Journal* 52(4):1043–1055, page 1043.

57. Norgaard *op. cit.* (see Note 8), page 26.

58. *Ibid.,* page 121. See also Richard B. Norgaard, "Sociosystem and Ecosystem Coevolution in the Amazon," 1981 *Journal of Environmental Economics and Management* 8:238–254.

59. Gowdy *op. cit.* (see Note 12), page 27. See also, John M. Gowdy, *Limited Wants, Unlimited Means: A Reader on Hunter-Gatherer Economics and the Environment* (Washington, DC: Island, 1997).

60. Figure 19.2 is from Norgaard (Note 8), page 27.

61. Norgaard *op. cit.* (see Note 8).

62. For example: Paul A. Samuelson and William D. Nordhaus, *Economics*, Twelfth Edition (New York: McGraw-Hill, 1985), page 4; J. R. Clark and Michael Veseth, *Microeconomics: Cost and Choice* (San Diego, CA: Harcourt Brace Jovanovich, 1987), page 4; Robert H. Frank, *Microeconomics and Behavior*, Second Edition (New York: McGraw-Hill, 1994), page 3.

63. John A. Livingston, *Rogue Primate: an Exploration of Human Domestication* (Toronto, Canada: Roberts Rinehart Publishers, 1994), page viii.

64. Galbraith *op. cit.* (see Note 7), page 38.

65. *Ibid.,* page 22.

CHAPTER 20

SUSTAINABILITY, ECONOMY, AND ENVIRONMENT

BY RICHARD C. BISHOP AND RICHARD T. WOODWARD

The most often cited definition of sustainability is that proposed by the World Commission on Environment and Development:

Sustainable development is development that meets the needs of the present without compromising the ability of future generations to meet their needs.[1]

This chapter takes the World Commission's definition as a point of departure to explore the economic principles that can be applied when sustainability is a social goal.

The World Commission's definition is subject to many interpretations. Here, we will define an economy as sustainable if later generations will have economic opportunities on a per capita basis that are at least as large as the economic opportunities enjoyed by earlier generations. The first section elaborates on this idea in a very simple "Hardtack World."[2] In such a world, there are only two generations and one nonrenewable resource, a fixed quantity of 'hardtack.' Hardtack is a hard biscuit or bread made from flour and water that does not deteriorate in quantity or quality over time. We shall assume that occupants of that world have only a fixed supply of hardtack to satisfy the wants of both generations. Hardtack will thus serve as a crude representation of the finiteness of the earth. Though very simple, the Hardtack World will allow us to focus attention on the essentials of sustainability without all the complexity that makes our world so difficult to deal with. We shall see, for example, that sustainability issues are, to the economist, issues of intergenerational fairness and that there are no inherent conflicts between economic efficiency and sustainability.

With such principles gleaned from the Hardtack World, we will next turn to the real world. It will not take long to learn that addressing sustainability issues in the real world is a difficult task. The sustainability of real-world economies depends in complex ways on the existence of and substitutability between many renewable and nonrenewable resources, on the availability and quality of labor and capital as well as natural resources, on technological progress, and on other social forces. Moreover, sustainability in the real world will require coming to grips with uncertainty.

Despite the many contrasts between the Hardtack World and the real world, some basic conclusions carry over: (1) A sustainable economy is achieved when the economic opportunities of each succeeding generation are at least as large as those enjoyed by earlier generations. (2) It is possible, at least in principle, for an economy to be both efficient and sustainable. We need not think of efficiency and sustainability as inherently conflicting goals. (3) Achieving an efficient, sustainable economy may require what we shall term *sustainability constraints*. In a Hardtack World with only two generations, the sustainability constraint is simple: Allow the first generation to eat no more than half the hardtack. This will leave the future generation enough hardtack to be at least as well off as the current generation was. Likewise, in the real world, achieving sustainability may require that constraints be imposed on the economic activities of earlier generations in order to enhance the economic opportunities of later generations.

The final two sections of this chapter will show how the idea of sustainability constraints might be applied to two policy issues explored in earlier chapters, global warming and endangered species. Both sets of issues are central to sustainability in the minds of many. Both illustrate the problems of extreme uncertainty that surround decision-making about sustainability.

Sustainability in a Hardtack World

The Hardtack World will be assumed to be inhabited by entities that are similar to, but in some ways quite different from, the human inhabitants of our world. They are like real people in that they get hungry and achieve more satisfaction the more food they eat (at least up to a point), but they only gain enjoyment ('utility') from eating hardtack. They also differ from us in that their generations do not overlap. One generation lives for the prescribed period and then dies, to be succeeded by the next generation. For simplicity, we will assume that the Hardtack World will have two and only two generations. That is, the first or 'current generation' lives for a length of time prescribed by its creator, to be replaced at its death by the 'future generation.' When the future generation has lived for the prescribed period, it dies and their planet will no longer be inhabited. Furthermore, these creatures have no capacity for population growth or decline. The current generation reproduces itself exactly in terms of numbers in the future generation. Finally, at its genesis, the current generation receives from its creator an 'endowment' of hardtack, and this is all the hardtack that will ever be available to satisfy the hunger of the current and the future generation. The 'endowment' of the second generation is simply the hardtack that the current generation did not eat.

The economic choices confronting the Hardtack World can be portrayed graphically. Begin with Figure 20.1. Here we show the economic well-being or 'utility' of either the current generation, U_c, or the future generation, U_f, on the vertical axis. The curve in Figure 20.1 will be referred to as the 'utility curve.' Since only hardtack is enjoyable to eat, utility depends only on the amount of hardtack consumed dur-

FIGURE 20.1 Utility as a Function of Hardtrack Consumption

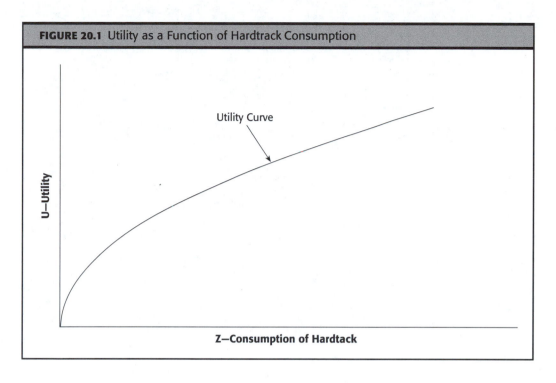

ing each generation's lifespan. Consumption is Z_c for the current generation and Z_f for the future generation. We assume that members of the two generations enjoy hardtack equally, so the same utility curve applies to both. Also, the utility curve is shaped the way it is to reflect the assumption of 'diminishing marginal utility.' A small amount of hardtack eaten will add a lot to well-being, but the effect diminishes as more and more is eaten and the generation in question comes closer and closer to being 'full.' To make the problem interesting, we will assume that hardtack is 'scarce.' That is, there is not enough hardtack so that all the people of both generations can have as much hardtack as they might like.

Possible ways to divide the fixed, limited amount of hardtack between the two generations during their respective lifespans are portrayed in Figure 20.2. This graph shows the amount of hardtack eaten by the future generation (Z_f) on the horizontal axis and the amount eaten by the current generation (Z_c) on the vertical axis. The total endowment of hardtack issued to the current generation at creation will equal L, as shown on the vertical axis. The two generations can divide the box of hardtack at any point along 'consumption possibilities line' as shown in this graph. For example, as one extreme, the current generation could eat all the hardtack ($Z_c = L$). Then there would be no hardtack left for the future generation ($Z_f = 0$). This is represented by point $Z_c = L$ on the consumption possibilities line. We will assume that subsistence is not a problem. Perhaps the Hardtack World has abundant supplies of mud which can be eaten for survival, but which the inhabitants gain no utility from eating. As we move down along the vertical axis of Figure 20.2, the current generation will consume less and less, leaving more and more hardtack for

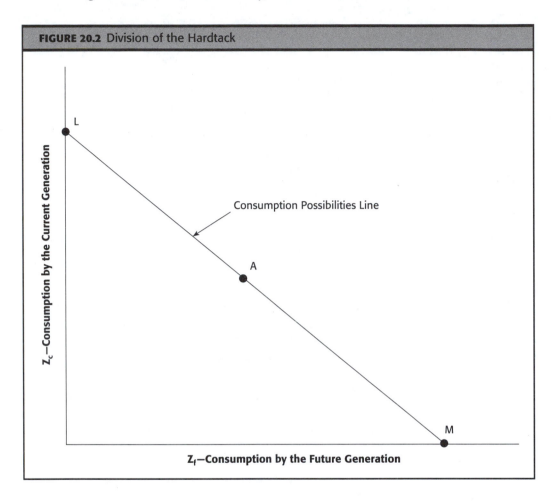

FIGURE 20.2 Division of the Hardtack

the future. If all the hardtack is left for the future generation, then $Z_c = 0$ and the future generation would consume the entire initial endowment of hardtack. This is point $Z_f = M$ in the graph. Of course, since hardtack doesn't deteriorate, the amount L initially available can become M, if $Z_c = 0$. In between these extremes are various possible divisions of the box of hardtack between the two generations. For example, point A would imply an equal division of the box of hardtack between the two generations. Moving to the right of point A would involve more consumption by the future generation than the current generation consumes.

We combine the parts of this simple economy in Figure 20.3. There, positive amounts are measured in all directions from the origin. Above the origin, we measure the utility of the future generation. To the right of the origin is the utility of the current generation. Below the origin is the hardtack consumption of the current generation, and to the left is consumption for the future generation. The consumption possibility line now appears in the southwest (lower left-hand) quadrant. To place it there, we simply rotated Figure 20.2 by 180°. The northwest (upper left-hand) quadrant is like Figure 20.1, except that it has been flipped over. Think of it

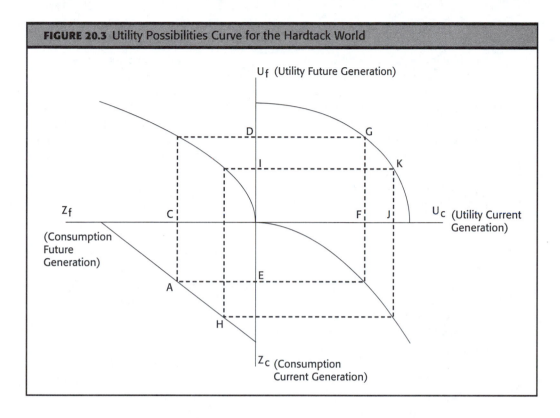

FIGURE 20.3 Utility Possibilities Curve for the Hardtack World

as a mirror image of Figure 20.1 if that helps. In the northwest quadrant we show how the future generation's utility depends on how much hardtack it consumes. The southeast (lower right-hand) quadrant portrays the relationship between the utility of the current generation and its hardtack consumption and was constructed by rotating Figure 20.1 by 90° to the right.

The purpose of Figure 20.3 is to construct the curve in the northeast quadrant, the so-called 'utility possibilities curve' (UPC). The UPC combines what we know about the utility of the two generations depending on their hardtack consumption with the overall limit on hardtack availability. Pick any point on the consumption possibilities line, say point A. See what it implies for the utility of the future generation by finding out how much hardtack it will consume, at point C. Then, read off the utility that this will provide for the future generation, at point D. Likewise, the distribution A will lead to hardtack consumption of E for the current generation, which yields it a utility of F. Utility for the current generation of F and for the future generation of D combine to form point G on the UPC.

Now choose another point on the consumption possibilities line, say point H. This would provide the future generation with a smaller utility of I and the current generation with utility of J, so that the corresponding point on the UPC is K. Do this for all points on the consumption possibilities line and you can trace out the complete UPC. Thus, the UPC shows all possible combinations of utility for the two generations that can be achieved with the initial endowment of hardtack.

The UPC is important because any point on it is economically efficient for the Hardtack World. This result may not be transparent at first. As a general rule, economic efficiency is achieved when all choices within an economy have been made so that it is impossible to make one person better off without leaving someone else worse off. In our Hardtack World, the economic choice is very simple: how much hardtack will the current generations consume? At any point on the UPC, the future generation can be made better off only by receiving more hardtack and this can be accomplished only if the current generation is made worse off by having its hardtack consumption reduced. The reverse also holds. Moving from left to right along the UPC means that the current generation is made better off, but only by reducing hardtack in the endowment of the future generation. Once this economy has its generations consuming at any point on the UPC, it is impossible to make one generation better off without making the other worse off. That means that all points on the UPC are equally economically efficient.

Now we are ready to consider sustainability in the Hardtack World. The current generation must decide how large an endowment will be left for the future generation. Assume that the current generation has the goal of leaving enough hardtack so that the future generation can achieve at least as high a level of utility as the current generation enjoyed. We would take this to mean that the current generation has taken "sustainability" as one of its goals. In other words, *sustainability is achieved when each generation leaves its successor an endowment sufficient to allow the next generation to achieve a level of per capita well-being at least equal to the level of well-being enjoyed by the earlier generation.* This goal can be achieved if the current generation imposes on itself what we will call a 'sustainability constraint.' For the hardtack economy, the sustainability constraint requires that the current generation eat no more than half the initial endowment. In Figure 20.3, this means that the current generation's consumption can be no larger than point E. If the current generation chooses to respect the sustainability constraint, then there will be enough hardtack in the endowment of the future generation to allow it to achieve at least a utility level of D. If the future generation is left an endowment that is less than that required by the sustainability constraint, then its utility will be forced down and to the right along the UPC, to levels of utility below the level that was possible for its predecessor. This would be the case, for example, if point K on the UPC were chosen.

Though simple, we believe that the Hardtack World can be used to identify some principles that will be relevant when we consider sustainability in the real world.

▲   *From an economic perspective, the goal of achieving sustainability has to do with whether intergenerational endowments are fair or equitable to future generations.* The current generation has to decide how much hardtack will be in the future generation's endowment. This is a choice about intergenerational economic fairness or equity. As we have seen, one way to address whether sustainability has been achieved is to ask whether the current generation will leave an endowment that will be sufficiently large to allow the future generation to be at least as well off on a per capita basis as the current generation was.

▲   *There is no inherent conflict between efficiency and sustainability.* The sustainability constraint simply placed limits on deciding which of the efficient points on the UPC might ultimately be chosen. Any point on the UPC that is above and to the left of point G is both efficient and sustainable. To be sure, the current generation may have to make sacrifices to meet the sustainability constraint by not consuming as much hardtack as it might otherwise prefer. However, this should be viewed as an intergenerational transfer of wealth and not as a reduction in the efficiency of the current generation's economy.

▲ *Most economists will be reluctant to endorse sustainability as a social goal.* Many economists advocate efficiency as a goal. However, they are reluctant to take stands on issues of fairness, feeling that doing so would involve moral and ethical judgments that economics does not equip them to make. Thus, they view fairness issues as better left to others like politicians and philosophers. Because sustainability issues are issues of intergenerational fairness, most economists will feel that they do not have a scientific basis for advocating sustainability as a societal goal. Of course, the same principle works in reverse: economists also lack the scientific basis for objecting to sustainability as a goal. Refusing to take a stand on sustainability limits the role of economics in policy debates over sustainability, but not as much as one might think at first glance. If, based on arguments from outside of economics, sustainability is *assumed* to be a social goal, then economic analysis can provide insights into the implications of the goal and how it might be implemented efficiently. That is basically what we attempt to do in this chapter.

▲ *One way to think about implementing a sustainability goal would be to set sustainability constraints on the economic activities of the current generation in order to assure that future generations will have endowments sufficient to realize the goal.* If sustainability is a goal in the Hardtack World, this goal could be implemented by constraining the current generation to eat no more than half the hardtack. This is a primitive example of a sustainability constraint. The idea is that members of the current generation would constrain their economic activities in order to enhance the economic opportunities of future generations.

As we have repeatedly pointed out, the Hardtack World, though it provides some interesting insights, is a great oversimplification of reality. It is considerably different from the traditional concepts of sustainable harvesting and resource depletion introduced in earlier chapters. Thus, let us consider how sustainability might work in the real world.

Sustainability in the Real World

No one can deny that we are using many of earth's nonrenewable resources at a rapid rate. Nor would anyone deny that we are substantially degrading many of earth's renewable resources. Many of those who raise concerns about sustainability worry that we are adversely affecting the ability of future generations to enjoy levels of living comparable to what we in the developed world are now enjoying. They would argue that our world has a lot in common with the Hardtack World and that we of the current generation are in a sense eating too much of the hardtack. As they see it, today's economies must be redirected toward more sustainable development paths. In our terms, this can be interpreted as advocating sustainability constraints. Advocates of sustainability envision restrictions on current economic activities to enhance the endowments of future generations. As we begin to consider how such restrictions might work in practice, it is important to recognize several ways in which our real world differs from the Hardtack World.

First, in the Hardtack World there was only one nonrenewable resource, hardtack. The real world has a diverse array of such resources ranging from oil, uranium, and coal to various metallic ores such as those containing iron, aluminum, and copper. Furthermore, at least within limits, nonrenewables are often substitutable for each other. Coal is substitutable for oil or vice versa. Glass (from silica) or plastics (from oil) may be substitutable for metals. Just as the supply of hardtack for the later generation depended on how much the earlier generation ate, so, in the real world, will future generations inherit more or fewer of these nonrenewables depending on how many are used by earlier generations. Even so, the variety and abundance of nonrenewables and their potential substitutability mean that it is hard to say when use of nonrenewables violates the goal of sustainability.

Second, real-world endowments include renewable resources as well as nonrenewables. We earth dwellers have forests, soils, fish populations, and many other resources that are capable of satisfying many of our wants and those of our successors on the planet indefinitely if they are managed appropriately. Furthermore, if those living in the Hardtack World run out of hardtack, they have no alternatives. In the real world, renewable resources are substitutable for nonrenewables, at least up to a point. When some nonrenewables become more scarce over time due to cumulative use, potential substitutes may include not only other nonrenewables, but renewable resources as well. Within limits, wood or paper products might be substituted for scarce metals, for example, or gasohol and solar energy for dwindling fossil fuels.

Third, real-world endowments are not limited to natural resources. Future endowments will include factories, machines, and tools of nearly infinite variety. They will also include infrastructure such as skyscrapers, housing, schools, commercial and other buildings, transportation networks, bridges, and the like. Moreover, just as we of the current generation have inherited the architecture, sculpture, paintings, literature, and music of the past, so will we add to the artistic endowment of our descendants. Human capital in the form of educational levels and accumulated knowledge about which institutions work and which are likely to fail are also part of the bargain. The endowments of the Hardtack World were limited to a single item. As these examples illustrate, a full list of the items in the endowments that real world economies provide to succeeding generations would be long indeed.

Fourth, it is also clear that natural and nonnatural resources are substitutable for each other, at least up to a point. This is important because it means that whether and how sustainability will be achieved in the real world will not depend on natural resources alone. In maintaining and enhancing the output of goods, services, and environmental amenities, capital and labor may constitute substitutes (again within limits) for natural resources that have become increasingly scarce over the years. For example, if some type of agricultural land becomes scarce, output may still increase through more intensive cultivation of remaining productive land using additional capital and labor. As limits on the ability of air and water to absorb wastes are reached, capital in the form of pollution control equipment may be able to convert the wastes to other less environmentally harmful forms. SO_2 scrubbers currently being installed on power plants are an example. No such opportunities for substitution were available in our Hardtack World.

Fifth, many economists believe that technological progress will do much to help resolve increasing scarcity of natural resources in the future. Technological progress simply involves learning new ways to do things. Technological progress was (by assumption) nonexistent in the Hardtack Economy. In the real world, new technologies aid in resource discovery. For example, aerial photography has greatly enhanced our ability to find new minerals. As described in Chapter 10, new technologies can also increase our efficiency in resource recovery. Ores that would not have been considered economic to mine only a decade or two ago because of low concentration of desired minerals can now be exploited using modern technologies. Groundwater that could not previously be economically used in agriculture can now be pumped at acceptable costs. Furthermore, alternative techniques often involve substitution of capital, labor, and energy for natural resources. For example, new recycling technologies are reducing dependence on virgin raw materials in many sectors of modern economies. Historically, techniques to saw logs into boards involved large amounts of sawdust and other waste. More sophisticated modern saws greatly increase the quantity of boards yielded by logs and useful products can now be produced from the remaining sawdust and other waste. In the context of sustainability, progress in technology—and ultimately in the physical and biological sciences—has to be a major determinant of the economic prospects of future generations.

Economists also believe that market mechanisms will help address diminishing availability of some high-quality natural resources. The idea here is that as specific natural resources become more and more scarce, they will command higher and higher prices. These increasing prices will provide powerful incentives to search for more abundant natural resources to use as substitutes. They will also increase incentives to substitute capital and labor for the increasingly scarce, increasingly costly natural resources. Higher prices will also stimulate the search for new technologies to find cheaper substitutes. An interesting example is occurring in the western United States where increasingly scarce water has motivated the lining of canals to prevent seepage. In economic terms, this is a substitution of capital for an increasingly scarce water supply. To the extent that substitution does not resolve problems of growing natural resource scarcity, increasing costs of natural resource inputs will be reflected in higher prices for consumer goods. As consumers see higher prices for the resource-intensive products, they will have incentives to switch to less resource-intensive products. Dwellers in our Hardtack World had no access to such processes as they tried to cope with their limited endowment of hardtack.

For a variety of reasons, many environmental and other natural resources are not traded on markets. For such resources, market incentives are likely to be ineffective in counterbalancing resource depletion and degradation. Where market incentives are not present, government action may be needed to provide needed incentives to substitute and innovate. Here, too, present-day societies seem to be progressing. Through actions of government and private groups, new pollution control techniques have come on line. We are also probably getting better at rigging up social mechanisms to protect environmental resources from pollution and overexploitation. For example, progress is being made in protecting commercially important fish stocks from overexploitation.

Although we do not live in a Hardtack World, sustainability can be defined in the same way: *A real-world economy is fully sustainable if each succeeding generation has economic opportunities at least as large as the economic opportunities enjoyed by its predecessor.* The economic opportunities of each generation are determined by the full endowment of renewable, nonrenewable, and nonnatural resources it receives and by the possibilities for substitution among resources in that endowment. Substitutability depends on past and current rates of technological progress and on existing institutions such as markets and governmental institutions to manage nonmarket resources.

In the Hardtack Economy, the sustainability debate was very simple. How much hardtack should the current generation eat? In the real world, the sustainability debate is much more complex and tends to center on the potential limits of substitution and technological change. It is as if humankind were involved in a "Great Race" between two opposing sets of forces. On the one side are depletion of nonrenewable resources and degradation or outright destruction of renewable resources. These forces tend to reduce the economic opportunities that future generations will enjoy. On the other side of the Great Race are a set of forces we might call collectively "social progress." Here are progress in science and technology, cumulative stocks of physical and human capital, accumulated arts, and progress in constructing social institutions. Social progress tends to enhance the endowments of succeeding generations, increasing their economic opportunities.

Most people would agree that, so far, humankind is winning the Great Race. Social progress has more than outpaced resource depletion and degradation. Nevertheless, how long this can continue is the subject of great disagreement. Some people, including many economists, are optimistic that social progress will continue to win into the indefinite future. In essence, they are arguing that sustainability constraints are not needed now and will not be needed in the foreseeable future. According to this group, the stage is already set for expanding economic opportunities into the indefinite future. Others are not so sanguine. They fear that limits on earth's resources combined with limits on substitutability, technological change, and other contributors to social progress will soon lead to declining economic opportunities for succeeding generations and perhaps even for the current generations.

The debate over how long we can hope to win the Great Race is very old in economics, going back at least two centuries to Malthus. It will not be settled soon. Honest, intelligent, well-meaning people will continue to disagree. This is important because to some extent it changes the debate to one over how to deal with uncertainty. Perhaps the fears of those who worry about sustainability will prove unfounded. On the other hand, perhaps humankind's current course will lead to declining economic opportunities for many people within the next century. The choices we make must explicitly consider the fact that no one knows. In economic jargon, decision-making about sustainability is 'decision-making under uncertainty.' The daunting extent of this uncertainty will become clearer as we turn next to global warming and potential extinction of species. Those concerned about sustainability argue that, in the face of this uncertainty, we should be taking steps now to enhance the endowments of future generations by slowing the rate of global warming and preserving endangered species (and biodiversity more broadly defined), among other things. Those who are more optimistic fear that the sustainability constraints being advocated will involve great sacrifices in order to benefit future generations that will already be richer than we were. The pessimists in turn worry about what will happen if the optimists are wrong about future prospects for economic growth.

Global Warming

As we saw in Chapter 18, there is a growing consensus among scientists that earth is getting warmer. This is coming about primarily because of our extensive use of fossil fuels. As we burn coal, oil, natural gas, and wood and engage in other economic activities, we are releasing greenhouse gases, mostly CO_2, into the atmosphere. What, if any, measures should be taken now and in the near future to slow the rate of global warming is a question being hotly debated by scientists, environmentalists, economists, the business community, and citizens at large.

The prospect of significant adverse economic effects from global warming makes an ideal setting for considering how a goal of sustainability might affect the choices we make today. To summarize part of Chapter 18, recall the work of William Nordhaus, an economist at Yale University. He and his colleagues developed an integrated computer simulation that weds a model of climate change with a model of the world economy.[3] He calls this model the DICE model, where DICE stands for the Dynamic Integrated Climate Economy. This model can be used to explore alternative policies that would change greenhouse gas emissions and thus affect the rate of global warming. In particular, Nordhaus treats greenhouse gas emissions as an externality. He takes as his baseline for analysis the rate of global warming that would occur without controls and compares this with a control policy that would promote economic efficiency by maximizing the present value of the world economy.

We propose the following thought experiment, which we call the 'expert panel problem.' This problem was explored in much more detail by Woodward and Bishop.[4] We will *assume* that the Nordhaus model is correct about all aspects of global warming and climate change. This is quite a stretch. Like any device of this kind, the DICE model makes assumptions at many points where experts would disagree. That's why we call this section a thought experiment. "What if" the DICE model is correct about global warming and climate change? We will allow uncertainty to creep in at only one point. Suppose, once earth's climates have changed in the ways predicted within the DICE model, there is uncertainty about how serious the economic damages will be. In other words, a 'panel of experts' disagrees about how damaging climate change will be to the world economy.

There is evidence that experts are indeed uncertain about the economic effects of climate change. Nordhaus himself conducted a survey of experts dealing with the topic.[5] Those surveyed were chosen by their peers as individuals with an in-depth understanding of the likely economic effects of global warming. Some were from the scientific community and others were economists. Among other things, the survey asked the experts what they thought would be the damages to Gross World

Product (GWP) from a 3°C warming of the planet by the year 2090. The answers varied from no economic loss to a loss of 20 percent of GWP per year.

So, the expert panel problem is posed this way. Suppose that a public decision-maker is charged with determining what to do about greenhouse gas emissions. We will assume that our decision-maker wants to do what is economically efficient, but that she also is concerned that the policy chosen is fair to future generations. That is, she accepts both efficiency and sustainability as social goals. She has a panel of experts to advise her. All these experts are equally qualified, and they are assumed to fall into two and only two camps. One camp holds the opinion that the effects of global warming will be relatively modest. This group of experts will be assumed to have adopted what we will term the 'modest impact prediction.' This is the view upon which most of Nordhaus's results are built. Under the modest impact prediction, a 3°C temperature rise only results in a 1.3 percent reduction in GWP. The other camp will be assumed to be quite pessimistic. They believe that what Nordhaus has called the 'catastrophic case' is the correct view. Under this 'catastrophic prediction,' a 2.5°C increase in temperature is predicted to cause damages of about 2.7 percent of GWP, while a 3°C increase will lead to a 24 percent reduction in GWP. Nordhaus states that the catastrophic prediction would be appropriate if "as the temperature increase passes 3°C, an irreversible set of geophysical reactions takes place that wreck human civilizations."[6] Finally, we assume that our decision-maker is unable to judge the likelihood that one or the other group of experts is correct.

Before continuing, one other aspect may need some clarification. Many readers may be surprised by the relatively innocuous effects of global warming under the modest impact prediction. Actually, this view is held by many economists. They argue that modern economies are not very dependent on climate. To be sure, there are exceptions like agriculture and forestry, but these are relatively small components of modern economies, particularly in the developed world. Right now agriculture accounts for only 1.5 percent of the U.S. economy as measured by Gross Domestic Product and forestry constitutes less than 1 percent. Furthermore, the history of humankind is replete with examples of how adaptable people are to the many existing climates on earth, from the arctic to the deserts and tropics. Hence, many economists are rather sanguine about global warming, although the debate continues. Of particular concern are the developing economies with their heavy dependence on agriculture and countries with large areas near sea level. Sea level is expected to rise with rising average global temperatures.

Now, return to our decision-maker. Let us suppose that while she cannot say with any confidence which group is most likely to be right, she believes that one group or the other will ultimately be proven correct. At least as a starting point for arriving at her decision, she wishes to consider two alternatives, one that will be ideal if those who predict modest impacts are correct and another that will be ideal if the catastrophic prediction is correct. In considering these alternatives, she believes that future generations will be able to observe what happens to the economy over the period between now and toward the end of the next century and determine which of the 20th-Century experts were right. Presumably, future decision-makers can then make appropriate choices in light of the true, known effects of global warming on the world economy. In particular, they may find that our decision-maker was wrong. She may

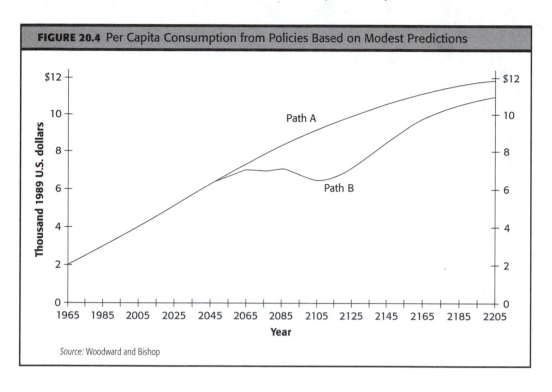

FIGURE 20.4 Per Capita Consumption from Policies Based on Modest Predictions

Source: Woodward and Bishop

have chosen to plan based on the assumptions of modest impacts when the cata-strophic prediction was correct or vice versa. If so, they can make corrections.

Figures 20.4 and 20.5 depict what will happen to per capita consumption as calculated using the DICE model, depending on which alternative the current decision-maker chooses and which set of experts turns out to be correct. Figure 20.4 assumes she decides to plan based on modest impacts. To implement this choice she would make relatively moderate reductions in worldwide greenhouse gas emissions of around 10 percent in order to correct the global warming exter-nality. If those predicting modest impacts turn out to be correct, then per capita consumption grows along Path A, reaching somewhat more than $8,000 by the year 2085. Since our decision-maker guessed right about which experts would be correct, there would be no reason to change policies when this has been verified. On the other hand, if future decision-makers find out that the catastrophic pre-diction is correct, then they will have to push the "panic button." DICE predicts that the efficient thing to do at that point is to immediately reduce greenhouse gas emissions by 99 percent! The catastrophic effects of global warming will man-ifest themselves in stable or declining world consumption and this trend will be exacerbated by the extreme policies needed to reduce emissions, yielding Path B.

Figure 20.5 shows what happens if our decision-maker sets emissions controls based on the catastrophic prediction. DICE indicates that under this assumption much more stringent emissions controls would be called for, beginning now at 20 percent reductions compared to 1985 levels and going to well over 50 percent

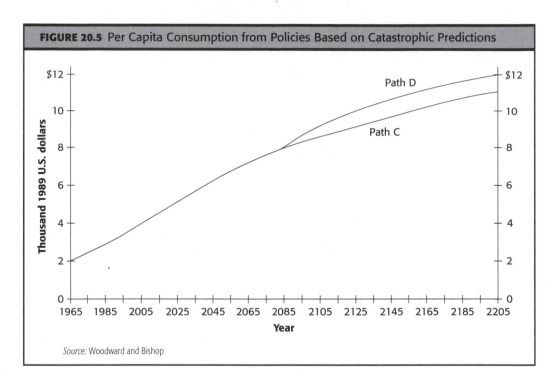

FIGURE 20.5 Per Capita Consumption from Policies Based on Catastrophic Predictions

Source: Woodward and Bishop

reductions by the middle of the next century. If this group of experts turns out to be correct, then catastrophe is avoided and per capita consumption follows Path C in Figure 20.5. On the other hand, if it is eventually learned that the modest impact prediction was true, emissions controls are relaxed and per capita consumption moves up quickly along Path D.

How might our decision-maker view these paths? First, note that all the paths satisfy her goal of economic efficiency. If she only knew which experts were correct, she would know exactly what to do, choosing either Path A or C. And, even if she is wrong in choosing which set of experts to believe, she knows what would need to be done to make an *efficient* correction once the truth comes out (Path B or D), although it will turn out with benefit of hindsight that her choice was less than efficient over the years between the time she made her decision and the point in time when the truth comes out.

Second, Paths A, C, and D satisfy her goal of sustainability. Future generations will not just be equally well-off relative to their predecessors, they will be better-off. This is not true of Path B, where per capita consumption and hence per capita well-being take a serious dip that lasts for several decades as a result of the global warming catastrophe. If it were safe to assume that the burden of the losses would be equally distributed across the global population at that time, there might be a lot of comfort in the fact that, even though per capita consumption dips, it always remains at levels well above those enjoyed only a few decades earlier. However, it is more plausible that the losses would be centered in particular regions of the world where the weather would have huge adverse impacts on regional economies. Truly catastrophic levels of suffering might well occur in some regions, while other regions emerged relatively unscathed. Remember Nordhaus's "irreversible set of geophysical reactions . . . that wreck human civilizations."

Being interested in efficiency, the decision-maker will likely want to know the present value of economic output[7] along the various paths. DICE uses a discount rate of 3 percent. Interestingly, the present value of output comes out very close, regardless of which path turns out to be the true one.[8] Even catastrophe has little effect on the present value because, with a discount rate of 3 percent, it occurs far enough in the future that it carries little weight.

It seems plausible, therefore, that our decision-maker will give very serious consideration to choosing emissions based on the advice of those experts who predict the catastrophic outcome. This alternative does not look bad from an efficiency perspective and, in keeping with her sustainability goal, it will avoid imposing on future generations the risk of catastrophic global warming.

At this point, we leave our decision-maker to further ponder her alternatives. She still has a lot to think about. For example, she may want to consider further the equity of the choice that will ultimately lead down Path C or Path D. If she chooses this alternative, she will have to find a way to immediately begin to make major reductions in greenhouse gas emissions. One often-mentioned way of reducing them would be a stiff tax on emissions of carbon dioxide and other greenhouse gases. But the people paying these taxes would be doing so from incomes of half what the experts predict incomes to be when catastrophe strikes. (The graphs show that per capita consumption now is less than $4,000, while it will be in the neighborhood of $7,000 when the catastrophe comes.) She might wonder whether the generations with higher per capita incomes would be better able to help those who might suffer from the eventual effects of global warming. On the other hand, if she hires more experts, she may find some who will suggest that the DICE model is overly optimistic about the prospects for economic growth in the next century. Also, she may not be happy with the alternatives she has considered so far. Other alternatives exist that are more stringent than would be called for under the modest impact prediction but less drastic than would be called for by assuming that catastrophe is definitely coming.

What have we learned about sustainability and global warming? Much more would need to be said before the alternatives under consideration by today's real world decision-makers could be evaluated. Still, some conclusions can be summarized.

▲ *Even if efficiency were the sole goal, the problem should not be ignored. Emissions of greenhouse gases may impose significant external costs on future generations.* Efficiency alone would dictate that corrective actions be taken.

▲ *If sustainability is also a goal, alternatives other than those based on "middle of the road" economic assumptions need to be considered.* For example, in the expert panel problem, limiting the analysis to alternatives designed to address the modest impact prediction could place future generations at considerable risk. The potential repercussions of being wrong need to be explicitly analyzed. We are dealing here with basic determinants of worldwide weather. We can argue about its relative economic importance, but that worldwide weather carries considerable importance cannot be overlooked. Any list of the necessities of life would include food, for example, and food production does, and will likely continue to, depend on weather. In the face of all the uncertainty that we of the current generation face about how fundamental physical and biological processes work, the potential implications of making mistakes must be central to the consideration of what it means to be sustainable.

▲ *Sustainability constraints may be implemented in different ways depending on circumstances.* In the Hardtack World, the sustainability constraint was a limit on total hardtack to be consumed by all members of the current generation combined. Measures to implement this constraint might well have taken the form of a legal dictum. For example, recall the initial endowment is L pounds of hardtack, so that the sustainability constraint allows the current generation to consume no more than L/2 pounds. If the current generation consists of n persons, then this would mean that there are (L/2)/n pounds per person. The sustainability constraint might then be implemented through a legal dictum: Members of the current generation shall not eat more than (L/2)/n pounds of hardtack. In dealing with global warming in our world, the sustainability constraint, if one is to be implemented, would be a set of limits on emissions of carbon and other greenhouse gases over time.

Implementation could take several forms. If, as suggested above, the decision-maker ultimately decides on a tax on greenhouse gas emissions, the sustainability constraint will have been implemented in a way that allows some discretion on the part of individual firms and consumers. They can choose whether to reduce greenhouse gas emissions and pay fewer greenhouse gas taxes or emit more and see their total greenhouse gas taxes rise. The idea is that such a tax will create incentives for those who can reduce emissions most cheaply to do so. This will tend to achieve the sustainability-constrained level of emissions at minimum social costs.

▲ *Recalling the children's story of "Chicken Little" is not helpful here.* It might be argued that we will do serious harm to ourselves if we allow economic policy to be dictated by alarmists, the Chicken Littles of the world. Obviously, good sense must be exercised in determining which Chicken Littles we listen to. Suppose a scientific Chicken Little says the sky is falling. If he is on the fringe of his discipline and his results and predictions are viewed by peers as being highly speculative, he will need to be ignored. However, in the children's story, Chicken Little is not a member of the National Academy of Sciences. If this scientific Chicken Little is well respected by large numbers of peers who believe that his results are supported empirically and his predictions are scientifically plausible, then the possibility that the sky will actually fall is relevant to public decision-making.

Endangered Species

Chapter 15 highlighted the economic issues associated with loss of biodiversity. From viruses to insects and plants to mammals, there are thought to be approximately 14 million species on earth. Only a handful of these species are directly useful to humans. Consider food, for example. Out of the some 50,000 vertebrate species, only 30 to 40 are used in agriculture. Ninety percent of food from plants comes from only 103 species. Furthermore, some species of viruses, bacteria, and insects are downright harmful. It is tempting to conclude that most of earth's species are either worthless or harmful. Why all the fuss about loss of species and biological diversity more generally?

In this chapter we will deal explicitly with loss of species. We are limiting ourselves, therefore, to only one of the levels of biodiversity. Diversity at the genetic level and diversity of plant and animal communities and ecosystems are considered by most biologists to be important as well. One would infer that intergenerational endowments will be affected by biodiversity at all levels. Still, dealing only with species diversity will make this section much easier.

Is the potential extinction of species a trivial issue because, at any point in time, nearly all species are either harmful or worthless? Several points need to be raised against writing off the problem of extinction as an economically trivial one. First, historical perspective mediates against complacency. Over the millennia of human existence, living things have been economically important in innumerable ways. Not only are they a source of food, but also building materials, aesthetic enjoyment, energy, paper products, pharmaceuticals, transportation, recreation, and other desired commodities and services. We should think of the biosphere as a vast reservoir of potential resources. Any one generation may be directly dependent on only a small subset of living things, but over time, different generations meet their needs using different subsets. Loss of species narrows the reservoir of potential resources from which future generations can pick and choose to meet their wants and needs.

Second, *direct* usefulness only tells part of the story. We do not normally appreciate the fact that those species upon which we depend directly are only the tip of the dependency iceberg. Few of us stop to realize, for example, the indirect but essential role that microbes in the soil play in our food supply. In a broader sense, many ecologists now suspect that biodiversity plays an important role in the stability of ecosystems. Organisms may seem trivial to us yet contribute to the stability of ecosystems we would consider essential. At some level, biodiversity contributes to the life-support functions of the earth.

Third, uncertainty appears once again. It is not hard to find examples of plants and animals that are now useful, but were previously considered useless. Chapter 15 told about the potentially very important new drug for fighting cancer, taxol, which was discovered in the bark of the Pacific yew, a native of the old-growth forests of the Pacific Northwest. It was thought to be worthless only a few years ago. It is impossible to predict which items from the reservoir of potential resources can be discarded with impunity and which will prove to be important new resources in the future. Stated from a different angle, extinction creates the risk that the lost species would have proven to be an economically important resource in the future. Uncertainty is magnified when we turn to the broader life-support functions of earth's living things. Most species have yet to even be discovered. We are a long way from understanding how each fits into the web of relationships that supports life on earth.

Fourth, so far as we know, extinction is irreversible. Some people look to progress in genetic engineering and cloning as reasons to be less concerned about loss of species. Interestingly, however, biologists, including those working in genetics, are among the most vocal groups in raising the alarm about loss of biodiversity. We do not yet know the limits of new technologies in genetics. It is also hard to figure out the extent to which it will be feasible to recreate lost species without having a copy of the original to use as a 'blueprint.' Finally, progress in genetics and cloning technology will depend for the foreseeable future on genes collected in nature.

From the perspective taken in this chapter, then, the earth's stock of species appears to be an important part of the endowment that future generations will receive. One way to enhance that endowment would be to avoid extinction of species. This harkens back to a fairly old argument: the safe minimum standard. S. V. Ciriacy-Wantrup was one of the founding fathers of environmental and resource economics. He argued for making a 'safe minimum standard of conservation' an objective of public policy.[9] The safe minimum standard would be achieved for an endangered species when sufficient numbers and habitat are maintained to assure, with high probability, the long-term survival of the species. The safe minimum standard may be interpreted as a sustainability constraint.

When Ciriacy-Wantrup said that the safe minimum standard should be one objective of policy, he did so to recognize that society has many objectives and that those objectives will often compete for scarce resources. He reasoned that ordinarily it should not cost very much to maintain minimal numbers and habitat. However, by raising the issue, he was at least implicitly allowing for the possibility that, in some exceptional cases, costs could be large enough to warrant a choice in favor of extinction. Bishop was more explicit. He argued that a safe minimum standard should be maintained for all species, except in special cases where the social costs were unacceptably large.[10] Under this recommendation, the safe minimum standard is a sustainability constraint that would be maintained, except in those cases where an explicit decision is made to relax it due to unacceptably high social costs.

So, let's call on our decision-maker again. Suppose she has resolved global warming policy and is now assigned to determine endangered-species policy. Her sustainability goal would be enhanced by making a safe minimum standard the *ordinary* rule for dealing with individual endangered species. As the economy grinds along from day to day and year to year, steps would more or less automatically be taken to maintain species' numbers and habitats in order to avoid most extinctions. This policy would enhance sustainability by increasing the number of living species in the endowments of succeeding generations, thus enhancing their reservoir of potential resources and helping to avoid possible harm to the earth's life-support system. Where costs are potentially large, an *extraordinary* decision process[11] would kick in, where the social costs of maintaining the safe minimum standard in that specific case would be carefully measured. At the culmination of the extraordinary decision process, the decision-maker would judge explicitly whether the costs are unacceptably large in that one case.

Economists can contribute to the extraordinary decision process by estimating the social costs of the safe minimum standard as accurately as possible. Out-of-pocket costs, such as those incurred for research and for activities to protect and manage needed habitats, should be counted among these costs. So should opportunity costs such as those associated with maintaining habitats. For example, to maintain a habitat, it may be necessary to forego the benefits of developing some of the natural resources found there. If so, then the value of those resources becomes part of the opportunity costs of preserving the species. In addition, in some cases, the species maintained may impose externalities that should be counted as well. An example here would be predation of wolves on livestock. Against these costs must be weighed the known, measurable benefits of preserving the species and necessary parts of its habitat. The social costs of the safe minimum standard will then be the sum of out-of-pocket costs, opportunity costs, and any other costs (like predation by wolves) minus the off-setting benefits of preservation.

In some cases, preservation benefits will exceed the costs. In such cases, the social costs of the safe minimum standard will, in effect, be negative. In Chapter 15, a case where this is likely to be true was considered. This is the case of the northern spotted owl, a resident of the old-growth forests in the Pacific Northwest. Though the opportunity costs and other costs of maintaining the spotted owl are large, available evidence indicates that the benefits of maintaining the species and the old-growth forests it depends upon, when properly accounted for, are likely to be even larger. In such cases, preservation will enhance the economic well-being of both present and future generations.

The problem will be more thorny in cases where the net social costs of the safe minimum standard are positive and large. Here, the decision-maker will have to judge whether the costs are still within acceptable limits. Economists will be of less help to her at this point, because an issue of economic fairness lies at the crux of the problem. Our decision-maker must ask whether the sacrifice to current and near-term generations in terms of social costs of the safe minimum standard is too much to bear in order to enhance the species endowment that future generations will inherit in the long run. As we have noted above, most economists believe that they lack a scientific basis for making recommendations regarding what is and is not fair. Instead, such decisions must be made by society as a whole, presumably by the people who are democratically elected and those whom elected officials appoint to make such choices.

Lest this way of approaching endangered species choices be judged prematurely to be farfetched, we would add that actual decision-making under the current version of the U.S. Endangered Species Act parallels what we have described in interesting ways. This law specifically forbids agencies of the federal government to take any steps that will contribute to the extinction of a species of plant or animal and mandates that steps be taken to avoid extinction of species where possible. However, it also establishes a committee of high-level government officials empowered to grant exceptions to the law. This committee is sometimes referred to informally as the "God Squad," because it has the power to decide against preservation of a species if it judges that the sacrifices associated with preservation are excessive.

What then can be said about biodiversity and sustainability from an economic perspective?

▲ *Potential extinction of species raises an issue of economic efficiency.* Because the benefits of preserving species are largely outside the market system, economists will need to use nonmarket valuation techniques to assess benefits. Limiting the economic analysis to market impacts will neglect potentially significant public benefits of species preservation. Once assessed, such benefits may exceed preservation costs, indicating that preservation is efficient. The northern spotted owl may be a case in point.

▲ *Where benefits exceed costs, preservation would also help satisfy a sustainability goal.* The warnings about the hazards of biodiversity loss being voiced by natural scientists would lead us to conclude that species diversity is an important ingredient in the endowment that future generations will inherit. Where the benefits of species preservation exceed the cost, preservation will promote both efficiency and equity.

▲ *Where estimated costs of preserving species exceed estimates of benefits, the difference can be viewed as the net social costs of a safe minimum standard.* This captures the burden that current and near-term generations would bear if preservation is chosen in order to enhance the endowment that future generations will receive. If sustainability is a goal, then "business as usual" should involve the preservation of endangered species, unless the net social costs are potentially large.

▲ *Where the net social costs of the safe minimum standard for a given species are potentially large, an extraordinary decision-making process is needed to consider whether an exception to normal practice should be made.* Economists should carefully assess as many social costs and benefits of preservation as can reasonably be measured; the results should be handed off to those empowered by society to make hard choices about what is fair. Social decision-makers will then decide whether the burden on current and near-term generations of the safe minimum standard is unacceptably large. In essence, they need to ask whether maintaining the safe minimum standard in that particular case is so costly that it is unfair to ask current and near-term future generations to bear the burden in order to enhance the endowments of future generations.

▲ *Though it predates the sustainability debate, the safe minimum standard can be interpreted as a sustainability constraint.* Like other such constraints, the safe minimum standard seeks to circumscribe day-to-day economic activities in order to maintain and enhance the endowments of future generations. While the safe minimum standard for global temperatures might be implemented through a tax, here it might take the form of legal dicta like those in the U.S. Endangered Species Act.

▲ *Real-world choices of this kind are likely to involve considerations beyond those mentioned so far.* For example, we have yet to mention intragenerational equity, equity within generations. Real-world decision-makers are likely to judge the burden implied by the social costs of the safe minimum standard differently, depending on whether those who will actually bear those costs are rich or poor. While we have spoken in terms of monetary costs, the concept of social cost will likely need to be broadened in real-world applications.

▲ *All that we have said about species diversity and the safe minimum standard probably applies to biodiversity more generally.* Biological diversity at all levels may contribute to intergenerational endowments.

Sustainability and Economics: Final Thoughts

Lest the reader get the wrong impression, there is much that we have said in this chapter that many economists would question. As we have repeatedly stressed, sustainability has to do with intergenerational fairness. As such, many economists do not feel comfortable with it. This is partly because of their aversion to making any judgments about equity, but it goes deeper than that. Addressing sustainability means dealing with time spans and levels of uncertainty that are much greater than economists are used to dealing with. Rather than the months, years, and decades that most economic analyses consider, sustainability is about decades, centuries, and millennia. Over such long time spans, uncertainty takes center stage.

It tells us a lot about the perspective that many economists bring to sustainability to note that much of what is taught in economic theory courses simply assumes that time and uncertainty do not exist. Time and uncertainty are brought in as complicating factors only after students have mastered the basics.[12] Once time and uncertainty are assumed away or greatly simplified, economic theory can focus on tradeoffs at the margin. Long spans of time and uncertainty may limit the usefulness of concepts that involve minute fine-tuning of economic processes at the margin. For example, marginal analysis would seem to mediate against a strategy like the safe minimum standard for endangered species. Instead, the training of conventional economists would point them toward somehow trading off endangered species against each other and against other goods, services, and amenities at the margin. For this reason, economists find that sustainability puts them on a foreign and vaguely threatening playing field.

Finally, as we have noted, sustainability takes economists back to a very old debate within their discipline. Starting with Malthus, possible limits to economic growth have been a recurring theme in economics. The old economists earned the title of the "dismal scientists" because of their pessimism about long-term prospects. Modern economists have turned 180° in this regard. Many economists are now among the most optimistic of scholars when future prospects are discussed. When considering whether they ought to be concerned about ever-increasing exhaustion and degradation of resources, most would probably argue that substitution and technological progress are very much under-appreciated by other disciplines and the lay public. This view of the future, where there are no obvious limits to what we have termed social progress, makes economists inherently dubious about the need to even consider sustainability. If each generation will be richer than its predecessor, why worry?

Still, for those who are not so optimistic, this chapter has shown that economics provides some useful concepts. The fundamental distinction that economists maintain between equity and efficiency leads to an economic definition of sustainability and clarifies its relationship to economic efficiency. Furthermore, we believe that it is useful to think of measures that promote sustainability as sustainability constraints. Such constraints would restrict current economic activities in ways that would arguably enhance the endowments of future generations, thus improving their economic opportunities.

Our case studies of global warming and species diversity help to illustrate what sorts of policy tools might be used to implement such constraints. A tax on emissions of carbon dioxide and other greenhouse gases might be used to constrain the rate of global warming. On the other hand, taking the Endangered Species Act as a model, more direct prohibitions on actions that will adversely impact endangered species may make sense in that context. Measures to implement sustainability constraints will have to be tailored to particular resources and circumstances.

Modern societies have many goals: high levels of employment; low inflation; widely available, cost-effective medical care; national security in a sometimes hostile world; etc. If sustainability becomes well entrenched as part of these goals, economics can help implement it. It can help clarify the issues and it can help, within limits, to evaluate policy alternatives for goal implementation.

Questions for Discussion and Analysis

1. Is any point on the utility possibilities curve in Figure 20.3 Pareto Optimal? Explain.

2. Bishop and Woodward argue that economists may refuse to advocate sustainability but may accept it as a goal held by the larger society. Do you agree? Why?

3. How does the concept of sustainability in this chapter compare to the theories of sustainable harvesting and resource depletion in Chapter 6?

4. What significant differences do the authors note between the Hardtack World and the real-world economy?

5. Explain your perspective as to whether humankind is winning the 'Great Race.'

6. Define the 'safe minimum standard' and apply it to the discussion of uncertainty and climate change policy.

7. Do you agree that nonmarket externality values should be incorporated into the economic analysis of endangered species protection?

Notes to Chapter 20

1. WCED (World Commission on Environment and Development), *Our Common Future* (Oxford: Oxford University Press, 1987).
2. The hardtack economy was, to our knowledge, first explored by Talbot Page in *Conservation and Economic Efficiency* (Baltimore and London: Johns Hopkins Press for Resources for the Future, 1977).
3. William D. Nordhaus, *Managing the Global Commons: The Economics of Climate Change.* (Cambridge, MA: MIT Press, 1994).

4. Richard T. Woodward and Richard C. Bishop, "How to Decide When Experts Disagree: Uncertainty-Based Choice Rules in Environmental Policy," 1997 *Land Economics* 73(4):492–507.

5. William D. Nordhaus, "Expert Opinion on Climatic Change," January–February, 1994 *American Scientist* 82:45-52.

6. Nordhaus *op. cit., Managing the Global Commons,* page 115.

7. The DICE model calculates the present value of utility rather than a monetary present value. This, of course, raises a host of issues that we will not attempt to take the time and space to deal with.

8. Woodward and Bishop *op. cit.,* page 504.

9. S. V. Ciriacy-Wantrup, *Resource Conservation: Economics and Policies* (Berkeley: University of California Press, 1952).

10. Richard C. Bishop, "Endangered Species and Uncertainty: The Economics of a Safe Minimum Standard." February 1978 *American Journal of Agricultural Economics* 60:10–18.

11. Thinking about enforcing the safe minimum standard as a constraint on day-to-day economic activities and subjecting possible exceptions to an extraordinary decision process is due to Alan Randall and Michael C. Farmer, "Benefits, Costs, and the Safe Minimum Standard of Conservation" in *Handbook of Environmental Economics,* Daniel W. Bromley, ed. (Cambridge, MA: Blackwell, 1995).

12. We also followed this route in the current chapter by beginning with the Hardtack World. There was no uncertainty in that world and only two periods.

AN ECONOMIC PERSPECTIVE ON THE EVOLUTION OF ENVIRONMENTAL LEGISLATION AND POLICY

BY ANDREA KREINER

This textbook has explored the theory and practice of environmental economics relating to environmental protection and resource management and utilization. To understand environmental economics, it is important to understand the context in which these concepts and theories were developed. That context is the historical development of environmental legislation and policy. This appendix presents a historical overview of the development of U.S. environmental legislation and policy, with particular focus on the link between the laws and economic issues and concepts. The development of environmental legislation and policy in the United States can be pictured as a scale, balancing protection of scarce environmental resources on one side and utilization of these resources for economic gain on the other.

Environmental resources encompass what are traditionally termed 'natural resources' (e.g., forests, wilderness areas, flora and fauna, etc.) as well as what are termed 'environmental media' (e.g., air, water, etc.). Natural resources are typically measured in quantity terms, such as acres of forestland (Chapter 14). The environmental media are typically measured in quality terms, such as whether the water in a lake is fishable or swimmable (Chapter 12). However, qualitative factors are also considered for natural resources, for example, the pristine nature of wilderness; and quantitative factors are used for environmental media, for example, the amount of groundwater resources available for drinking water.

The two types of resources can be defined as environmental resources. They are often public goods, and they all have externality values. Both concepts were introduced in Chapter 1. It is important to remember that an externality is a value not reflected in the workings of normal markets. It is the cost or benefit to society that results from the use or quality of the resource.

When legislation and policy are developed, the scale is tipped to one side or the other by the significance society places on the quantity or quality of the resource.

Here we use the term 'societal value' to denote the significance society is placing on the resource. This is a simpler version of the concept of 'social value,' which has a specific economic meaning (and was discussed in Chapters 1, 6, and 15). When the public perceives a resource as scarce, the societal value of the resource is increased. If the resource's societal value becomes high enough, society determines that protection is warranted; resource protection is the primary focus of legislation and policy.

When society does not view a resource as scarce, the resource is available for utilization. Coal, for example, is a resource that society does not view as scarce. Global coal supplies are extensive (Chapter 9) and available from a variety of locations. Thus, coal is available for mining without any quantity restrictions.

Societal perception of scarcity and the physical reality of scarcity are at times unrelated. (This has been especially true for oil, as explained in Chapters 9 and 10.) However, for policy development, it is the perception of scarcity that creates the public will for protection. Until a resource is perceived to be scarce or once the resource has been initially protected and the immediate threat to it has been eliminated, the opportunity costs incurred from resource protection take on greater significance in policy development and implementation.

As an example, let's look at the resource 'air.' In the past, air was considered nearly inexhaustible, the belief being that it could handle whatever pollutants were released into it. In economics, it was seen as a public good. Over time, as more was learned about the health and environmental effects of pollutants in air (e.g., the link of particulates to asthma irritation, acid rain deposition problems, the potential link of toxic chemicals to cancers, the reduction in the upper ozone layer leading to increased skin cancer incidence), society gained an appreciation of 'clean air.' What was once thought inexhaustible came to be valued as a resource that was becoming increasingly scarce as a result of increasing pollutant emissions. The air's capacity to absorb pollutants did not change; society's perception of an acceptable standard of clean air became articulated as air quality deteriorated.

The past 40 years have seen the scale shift back and forth cyclically, striving to achieve a sustainable balance between resource protection and utilization. This pattern occurred throughout all aspects of resource management—from forest resources, to endangered species, to clean air and water.

The country's growing sense of scarcity in environmental resources has been the impetus for each of the landmark environmental statutes. It is the historical development of environmental legislation and policy that defines the framework for environmental economics. The benchmark environmental legislation table presents the environmental statutes with their relevant chapters in this text.

Before the Civil War, forested land was abundant and thus held little societal value. In the latter half of the 19th Century, railroads opened up the interior of the United States for development. As Americans settled much of the country, forests were cleared for lumber and for agriculture. Forest areas were considerably reduced, and in 1891 Congress enacted the Forest Preservation Act.[1] This act empowered the president to set aside public lands as "reservations" and to establish restrictions on the use of these lands, without the need to consult with the Congress.[2]

In the late 1800s and into the early 1900s, most of the legislation addressed the growing scarcity of land and of scenic, unique geologic resources. (In the words of the day, these scenic and unusual geological features were termed "natural wonders.") Forestland was protected by the setting aside of areas and making them unavailable for homesteading or logging; scenic resources were to be similarly protected in reserves. Public concern over commercialization and destruction of national scenic resources led first to the establishment of national parks and then to the creation of the National Park Service in 1916. High societal value and concern about the risk of degradation of these resources is evidenced in the purpose of the act, "... to conserve the scenery and the natural and historic objects and the wildlife therein and to provide for the enjoyment of the same in such manner and by such means as will leave them unimpaired for the enjoyment of future generations."[3]

Public perception of resource scarcity reached a historically high level in the 1970s. The growing environmental movement brought about widespread public awareness of the negative environmental impacts of industrial society. Legislation was enacted to address the real and perceived threats to clean water and air, endangered species, and wilderness.[4] The public was demanding immediate results; thus these laws relied mainly on prohibitive policies to prevent further resource loss.

The Clean Water Act of 1972 set goals of zero discharge of pollutants and established a system of permitting for facilities that released pollutants into the environment. Costly control systems were required to reduce the amount of pollutants discharged into waterways.

Clean air was not viewed as being as scarce a resource as clean water, which is reflected in the slower development of proscriptive clean air acts. The Clean Air Act of 1970 set ambient air quality standards and required each state to develop a plan for attaining the standards through controls on stationary point sources of pollution, such as industrial operations and power plants. The Act focused on the cleanup of areas with deteriorated air quality. It also established the basis for automobile pollution emissions standards. By 1977, it became evident that air quality was not improving quickly enough. The Clean Air Act Amendments of 1977 added minimum control requirements to be applied throughout the country[5] and required

TABLE A Benchmark Environmental Legislation	
Act and Year	*Major Relevant Chapter in Book*
Forest Preservation Act (1891)	
Forest Management Act (1897, 1976)	Chapter 14
Wilderness Act (1964, 1975, 1978)	Chapters 14, 15
Clean Air Act (1970, 1977, 1990)	Chapter 11
Clean Water Act (1972, 1977)	Chapter 12
Endangered Species Act (1973, 1978)	Chapter 15
Resource Conservation and Recovery Act (1976, 1984)	Chapter 10
Pollution Prevention Act (1990)	Chapter 10

states to set incremental progress goals toward attaining the air quality standards. The 1977 amendments recognized clean air areas as a scarce resource that warranted protection, introducing the Prevention of Significant Deterioration (PSD) program, which places additional control requirements to prevent the deterioration of areas attaining the air quality standards.[6]

The Endangered Species Act of 1973 focused on biological resources and created a comprehensive program to protect rare species of plants and animals. Although viewed as the landmark legislation, this was not the first endangered species statute. The Endangered Species Preservation Act of 1966[7] had been an uncontroversial statute that prohibited the taking of endangered species in federal wildlife refuges.

Each of these laws was based on the concept of protecting scarce environmental resources through prohibitive policies: a company is prohibited from releasing more than X tons of a pollutant, people are prohibited from "taking" an endangered species.[8]

Hazardous and solid wastes and leaking underground storage tanks were contaminating groundwater, another resource whose scarcity became highlighted in the 1970s. A different approach was taken in the law covering these wastes, the Resource Conservation and Recovery Act (RCRA). Rather than legislating a prohibitive policy, the law established an extensive regulatory program to manage the handling and disposal of these wastes. During this period, the use of command and control regulation as a policy tool was greatly increasing under laws such as RCRA, the Clean Air Act, and the Clean Water Act. Economic analysis was playing only a minor role in environmental policy development and implementation; perceived environmental resource scarcity was the main driving factor.

The approaches established in these initial laws created inefficiencies since, for the most part, they did not allow for balancing the benefits from protecting the scarce resources and reaching the desired goals with the costs of complying with the laws and regulations. The implementation of these laws resulted in significant environmental benefits, but also in high costs to those impacted by the laws and ensuing regulations.

Amendments to the laws addressed problems in the initial acts or were developed in response to issues, mainly costs, created by those acts. The Wilderness Act of 1964 was followed by the Eastern Wilderness Act of 1975,[9] which addressed management issues and redefined wilderness to enable wilderness areas to be established in nonpristine regions of the country.[10]

The Endangered Species Act was reauthorized in 1978.[11] The initial law had delayed and stopped a number of federal development projects (see Chapter 4) and as a result came under political pressure. The 1978 amendments added an "escape valve" and proposals for designation of critical habitat would be required to submit an economic impact statement.

By the 1980s, other problems in addition to cost were becoming evident with this system of legislation. Pollution was not always eliminated, but sometimes simply transformed. For example, the release of sulfur emissions into the air from the burning of coal in power plants is prevented through use of scrubbers. Scrubbers produce a sulfuric acid wastewater that needs to be treated before being discharged. Treatment of this wastewater results in a sludge, which is itself a hazardous waste.

The 1980s brought a more conservative approach in Congress toward environmental protection, with compliance costs and economic development playing a more prominent role in environmental policy making. The balance of the scale tipped away from resource protection and toward resource utilization. Few new requirements were instituted during this period, and enforcement of existing regulations was of diminished concern to the administration of the U.S. Environmental Protection Agency (EPA).

The 1984 Hazardous and Solid Waste Amendments recognized the importance of reducing the amount of waste generated but added no requirements for waste prevention actions. During the 1980s, states and the EPA began to establish voluntary programs, providing assistance and incentives to businesses to reduce their waste and pollutant generation. These efforts culminated in the Pollution Prevention Act of 1990.[12] The Pollution Prevention Act established source reduction as the first priority in waste management, followed by recycling, treatment, and disposal. Again, though, no requirements for preventive actions were included in the law.

A similar "tipping of the scales" regarding the Forest Preservation Act had occurred a century earlier. In response to the president's use of his broad, sweeping authority to protect forestland, Congress repealed the 1891 Act. The Forest Management Act of 1897 established a functional office in the Department of the Interior with the purpose of managing the forest reserves.[13] This change from restricting uses to managing the resource was supported by timber interests but opposed by irrigation interests who wanted watershed protection.[14]

The National Forest Management Act of 1976[15] included an overhaul of the Forest Service's statutory authority. The use of clear-cutting as a management approach in the national forests had created a public crisis over perceived impending forest scarcity. This new act expanded the required forest preservation and planning activities.[16]

The Endangered American Wilderness Act of 1978 addressed concerns regarding the potential loss of high-quality, undeveloped, and seriously threatened national forests and brought them under protection as de facto wilderness areas.[17] The rising scarcity of public wildlands close to population centers also led to the act being used to create new nonpristine wilderness areas near cities.

Just as the initial prohibitive policies resulted in high costs and inefficiencies, the revisions to the laws and reduced enforcement of regulations created new issues and concerns. The public once again began to perceive environmental quality as a scarce resource that needed stronger protection; the scales tipped back to resource protection, but not quite as far as occurred under the initial statutes.

The backlash from the lack of continued air quality improvement in the 1980s coalesced in 1990 with the enactment of the Clean Air Act Amendments of 1990 (CAAA).[18] Generally a very proscriptive piece of legislation, the CAAA increased requirements for new sources in nonattainment areas, established a detailed facility permitting program, and phased out ozone-depleting chemicals. However, this legislation was also the first to incorporate significant economic and market approaches to achieving environmental improvement, including emissions trading and banking, 'bubbling' of facilities under single permits, and emissions fees.

In the late 1990s, concerns were raised again regarding costs, efficiency, and effectiveness of existing legislation and regulatory approaches. Innovative regulatory and resource management approaches based on the theoretical economic and market models developed by economists in the 1970 and 1980s were tested.

As we enter the 21st Century, new environmental problems and issues are emerging on both a national and international level. Climate change, biodiversity, and global economic growth issues are moving to the forefront of public debate and policy making. How each is handled will depend upon the value placed on each of these issues by society. Environmental economics in this textbook reflects society's continuing search in analysis, policy, and law for the right balance between sustainability, environmental resource use, environmental protection, and material living standards.

Notes to Appendix

1. CH. 561, 26 Stat. 1095, 16 U.S.C. 471 (repealed).
2. Wellman, J. Douglas, *Wildland Recreation Policy* (New York: John Wiley & Sons, 1987), pages 2–3.
3. Pub. L. 235; 39 Stat. 535; 16 U.S.C. et. seq.
4. The major acts passed in this period included the Federal Water Pollution Control Act of 1972 (Pub. L. 92-500, Oct. 18, 1972, 86 Stat. 816) as amended by the Clean Water Act of 1977 (Pub. L. 92-500) (the combination is commonly referred to as the Clean Water Act); Clean Air Act of 1970 (Pub. L. 91-604, Dec. 31, 1970, 84 Stat. 1705) and Clean Air Act Amendments of 1977 (Pub. L. 95-095, 91 Stat. 688); Endangered Species Act of 1973 (Pub. L. 93-205, Dec. 28, 1973, 87 Stat. 884); Wilderness Act of 1964 (Pub. L. 88-577, Sept. 3, 1964, 78 Stat. 890); and Resource Conservation and Recovery Act of 1976 and the Hazardous and Solid Waste Amendments of 1984, 42 U.S.C. 6901 et. seq.
5. These minimum controls are referred to as reasonably achievable control technologies (RACTS). RACTS do not take economics into account; they are based solely on emissions reductions.
6. Personal communications with Daryl Tyler, Administrator, Air Resources Section, Delaware Department of Natural Resources and Environmental Control, July 1998.
7. Pub. L. 89-669, Oct. 15, 1966, 80 Stat. 926.
8. Yaffee, Steven Lewis, *Prohibitive Policy* (Cambridge, MA: MIT Press, 1982), page 13.
9. Pub. L. 93-622.
10. Wellman, page 187.
11. Pub. L. 95-632, Nov. 10, 1978; 92 Stat. 375.
12. Pub. L. 101-508, Title 6, 104 Stat. 1388. The Pollution Prevention Act defines 'source reduction' as any practice that reduces the generation of any hazardous substance, pollutant, or contaminant.
13. Ch. 2, 30 Stat. 11, 16 U.S.C. 473-475.
14. Wellman, page 75 and Nash, Roderick, *Wilderness and the American Mind* (New Haven, CT: Yale University Press, 1967), page 137.
15. Pub. L. 94-588, Oct. 22, 1976, 90 Stat. 2949, 16 U.S.C. 1600-1614. Historical note: In 1905, to consolidate forestry responsibilities, the responsibility for managing the forest reserves was transferred from the Department of the Interior to the Department of Agriculture, and the Bureau of Forestry was changed into the U.S. Forest Service.
16. Wellman, pages 188–190.
17. *Ibid.* These areas were moved from being managed as national forests to being protected as national wildernesses. 16 U.S.C. 1132.
18. Pub. L. 101-549, 104 Stat. 2399.